Critical Essays on

KATE CHOPIN

CRITICAL ESSAYS
ON
AMERICAN LITERATURE

James Nagel, General Editor
University of Georgia, Athens

Critical Essays on
KATE CHOPIN

edited by

ALICE HALL PETRY

G. K. Hall & Co.
An Imprint of Simon & Schuster Macmillan
New York

Prentice Hall International
London   Mexico City   New Delhi   Singapore   Sydney   Toronto

G. K. Hall & Co.
An Imprint of Simon & Schuster Macmillan
1633 Broadway
New York, NY 10019

Library of Congress Cataloging-in-Publication Data

Critical essays on Kate Chopin/edited by Alice Hall Petry.
    p. cm.—(Critical essays on American literature)
  Includes bibliographical references and index.
  ISBN 0-7838-0032-0
  1. Chopin, Kate, 1851-1904—Criticism and interpretation.
  2. Women and literature—Louisiana—History—19th century.
  3. Louisiana—In literature. I. Petry, Alice Hall, 1951-
  II. Series.
  PS1294.C63C75 1996
  813'.4—dc20   95-47583
                                                CIP

The paper used in this publication meets the minimum requirements of
American National Standard for Information Sciences—Permanence of Paper
for Printed Library Materials. ANSI Z3948-1984. ∞™
10 9 8 7 6 5 4 3 2 1

Printed in the United States of America

for
Jim and Linda Hall

Contents

ORIGINAL ESSAYS

General Editor's Note

♦

This series seeks to anthologize the most important criticism on a wide variety of topics and writers in American literature. Our readers will find in various volumes not only a generous selection of reprinted articles and reviews but original essays, bibliographies, manuscript sections, and other materials brought to public attention for the first time. This volume, *Critical Essays on Kate Chopin,* is the most comprehensive collection of essays ever published on one of the most important writers in the United States. It contains both a sizable gathering of early reviews and a broad selection of more modern scholarship as well. Among the authors of reprinted articles and reviews are Joseph J. Reilly, Kenneth Eble, Peggy Skaggs, Joyce Dyer, Robert D. Arner, Ruth Sullivan, and Stewart Smith. Furthermore, in addition to a substantial introduction by Alice Hall Petry are six original essays commissioned specifically for publication in this volume, by Margaret D. Bauer on "Désirée's Baby," Lawrence I. Berkove on the romances in "At the 'Cadian Ball" and "The Storm," Linda Wagner-Martin on the young men in Chopin's works, Heather Kirk Thomas on "Athénaïse," Nancy A. Walker on the woman of letters in Chopin's fiction, Kathryn Lee Seidel on painting in *The Awakening,* and Priscilla Leder on that novel in historical context. We are confident that this book will make a permanent and significant contribution to the study of American literature.

James Nagel
University of Georgia, Athens

Publisher's Note

◆

Producing a volume that contains both newly commissioned and reprinted material presents the publisher with the challenge of balancing the desire to achieve stylistic consistency with the need to preserve the integrity of works first published elsewhere. In the Critical Essays series, essays commissioned especially for a particular volume are edited to be consistent with G. K. Hall's house style; reprinted essays appear in the style in which they were first published, with only typographical errors corrected. Consequently, shifts in style from one essay to another are the result of our efforts to be faithful to each text as it was originally published.

Introduction

◆

ALICE HALL PETRY

The career of Kate Chopin (1850–1904) is one of the more remarkable success stories of American literary history. She did not begin writing seriously until early middle age, when the death of her husband left her with six small children to support. But she went on to produce nearly a hundred short stories, three novels, and one play, as well as numerous poems, essays, reviews, and musical compositions—all within the span of only a dozen years. A consummate artist, she also tried to be a consummate businesswoman; early on, she sought to expand her literary market beyond her native St. Louis and adopted home of Louisiana, and she soon became a fixture of such nationally known journals as *Vogue* and the *Atlantic Monthly*. Her two story collections, *Bayou Folk* (1894) and *A Night in Acadie* (1897), confirmed her sterling reputation as a writer—a reputation that would be shaken only with the release of her controversial novel, *The Awakening,* in 1899. Chopin produced little after its publication and died just five years later. Largely forgotten for the first half of the 20th century, her work began to attract serious attention in 1932, with the release of Daniel S. Rankin's appreciative but flawed critical biography, *Kate Chopin and Her Creole Stories.* For nearly forty more years, critics in the United States and Europe occasionally would cite her as a writer who deserved to be better known, but it was not until 1969, when Norwegian scholar Per Seyersted published his two landmark volumes—*Kate Chopin: A Critical Biography* and *The Complete Works of Kate Chopin*—that her life and achievements were finally brought to the attention of the critical community. Since then, it has come to be almost de rigueur to include at least one Kate Chopin story in anthologies devoted to American literature, the short story, Southern fiction, or women's literature; moreover, *The Awakening,* often accompanied by several of her stories, has been available virtually continuously in a series of paperback editions. Now at the end of the 20th century, Chopin, like her contemporary Emily Dickinson, seems clearly destined to enjoy continued serious scholarly attention and widespread popular acclaim.

Although much of Chopin's astonishing success can be attributed to the feminist movement that began in the late 1960s, as well as to the revisionist impulse in literary history that has led to the rediscovery of so many writers (especially female) of the 19th century, Chopin's work has significance beyond the political. Her beautifully crafted, ironic tales reflect the brilliance of a woman drawing upon her own life, as well as upon her era's interest in realism, naturalism, and issues of selfhood, to probe timeless questions about identity and morality in the human sphere.

KATE CHOPIN'S LIFE AND CAREER

Unlike for some 19th-century American authors, the details of Kate Chopin's life are fairly well documented, thanks to the research of Daniel S. Rankin, Per Seyersted, and most recently, Emily Toth, whose reliable *Kate Chopin* provided the biographical information used in the following pages.[1]

Kate Chopin, née Catherine O'Flaherty, was born in St. Louis, Missouri, on 8 February 1850 (not 1851, as most sources report). Her mother, Eliza Faris O'Flaherty, came from an old French family of considerable local prominence but middling resources. Apparently for her family's financial security, in 1844 at the age of sixteen, Eliza married the successful Irish-born businessman Thomas O'Flaherty, a thirty-nine–year–old widower with a young son. Thus Kate was born into privilege. In his business ventures, her father dealt in real estate and supplied both pioneers and the U.S. Army, his wealth enabling his family to live in a mansion with four slaves. Because of his prominence in St. Louis, he was aboard the first train to cross the newly opened Gasconade Bridge, which collapsed during a ceremony on 1 November 1855, killing him and numerous other city dignitaries. He left his estate to Eliza, who never remarried.

Upon the death of her father, when she was just five, Kate became a member of what was, but for her half-brother, George, and older brother, Thomas, a distaff household. Kate lived with a younger sister, Jane (who died in infancy), her mother, and her great-grandmother, Victoire Verdon Charleville (ca. 1780–1863). Mme. Charleville took responsibility for Kate's early education, teaching her French and piano and instilling in her pride for the women of the Charleville family—including Mme. Charleville's own mother, "La Verdon" (ca. 1745–96), who owned a fleet of vessels trading between St. Louis and New Orleans, who legally separated from her husband, and who evidently had at least one child out of wedlock. Her example was not lost on young Kate, who understood that women could be as tough-minded and self-reliant as men, that gender roles had more to do with economic power than with biology, and that social institutions, such as marriage, often were at cross-purposes with natural impulses, including sexual passion.

Although these elements would be prominent in the adult Chopin's writings, they seem to have had surprisingly little impact on her as a schoolgirl. Altogether she spent some thirteen years at the church-affiliated Academy of the Sacred Heart in St. Louis. Like many future writers, she was not a particularly distinguished student, but she apparently had no problems with the Academy's strictures and evidently got along well with the Sacred Heart nuns who taught her. At the Academy, she met her best friend for life, Kitty Garesché, who herself joined the Sisters of the Sacred Heart in 1870. However, even the very young Chopin seemed to have few close friends and a marked preference for solitary pursuits. In addition to practicing piano (a naturally talented musician, she could play "by ear"), Chopin apparently spent her time reading alone in the family's attic. According to Emily Toth, Chopin as a young girl read the works of Charles Dickens and Sir Walter Scott, as well as popular novels by English, French, and American women, including Susan Warner (*The Wide Wide World*), Grace Aguilar (*Days of Bruce*), and Catherine Thérèse Woillez (*Orphans of Moscow; or, the Young Governess*). For the most part, however, these writers should not be counted as direct influences on Chopin. If anything, she rejected the 19th century's peculiar brand of literary sentimentality, which posited all orphan girls as plucky, all governesses as resourceful, all marriages as made in heaven, and all endings as happy. As Toth notes dryly, her early readings taught the young Kate Chopin an important lesson: "not to believe everything she read."[2]

Her readings seem only to have nurtured an unsentimental attitude forged under personal duress. As noted, her father died violently when she was just five, and at least one sibling died in infancy. The Civil War years compounded her losses. Less than a month after the death of her great-grandmother in January 1863, her beloved half-brother, George, a Confederate soldier, died of typhoid fever at age twenty-three. The family of her best friend, the Gareschés, was forced to leave St. Louis owing to war-time politics. Young Kate, ardently pro-Confederate, nearly became a war casualty herself when she tore down the American flag that had been hung from her porch by Union authorities; she narrowly avoided being arrested for a crime punishable by death. In such a world, so devoid of sentimentality, that her own courtship would be unemotional is not surprising. However, it is quite surprising that she would marry a man who had avoided serving the Confederate cause.

When exactly she met Oscar Chopin of New Orleans is unknown, although the introduction seems to have come when she was presented to St. Louis society after her graduation from the Academy in 1868. She disliked the role of debutante (" 'I am invited to a ball and I go.—I dance with people I despise; [and] amuse myself with men whose only talent lies in their feet' "[3]), so perhaps she preferred the role of wife—even though, as the son of a French-born physician, Oscar Chopin had spent the Civil War years in France rather than serve in the Confederate Army. But the handsome, French-speaking Oscar was pursuing the career of cotton factor (i.e., the middleman between cotton growers and buyers), and it was a potentially lucrative trade, especially with the high-interest loans factors often made to growers. The couple married in St. Louis on 9 June 1870, honeymooned all summer in Europe, and settled in New Orleans that fall. Their five sons and one daughter were born between 1871 and 1879, and the Chopins lived well in New Orleans, generally vacationing at Grand Isle, the setting for much of *The Awakening.* However, a yellow fever epidemic and poor cotton crops in 1878 and 1879 essentially ruined the cotton industry—and Oscar Chopin's business. To save money, the Chopins moved to French-speaking Cloutierville in Natchitoches Parish, in the Cane River area of north central Louisiana, where Oscar had family and land holdings.

In Cloutierville, Oscar ran a general store, where his wife often waited on customers. She frequently rode horses (astride rather than side-saddle) and studied the local residents, many of whom eventually would appear, thinly veiled, in her stories. Although both Chopins worked hard, Oscar often extended credit to his customers; by the time he died suddenly of malaria in December 1882, the family was in debt. Left with six children to support, Kate Chopin initially remained in Cloutierville, efficiently running the general store and alleviating her loneliness by consorting with a handsome, but hot-tempered and married, local farmer, Albert Sampite—reportedly the prototype for Alcée Arobin of *The Awakening* and for the more sensitive Alcée Laballière of "At the 'Cadian Ball" and "The Storm." In mid-1884, Chopin moved back to St. Louis to live with her mother, but Eliza died within the year and Kate began to write. Her "Polka for Piano," named in honor of her young daughter Lélia, was published in 1888, whereas her first literary publication, a poem entitled "If It Might Be," appeared in January 1889. Soon, however, she channeled her energies into fiction, composing the short story "Wiser Than a God" in June 1889. It was published that December in the *Philadelphia Musical Journal.* Another short story, "A Point at Issue!," composed in August 1889, appeared in the *St. Louis Post-Dispatch* on 27 October 1889. Thus Kate Chopin's writing career was launched.

Then, as now, novels carried more prestige than short stories and had greater potential as sources of income. These facts were not lost on the business-minded Chopin, who began her novel *At Fault* on 5 July 1889. Unable to interest a commercial press in the story, she published it at her own expense in September 1890. (Another novel written in 1890, *Young Dr. Gosse,* was destroyed.) Meanwhile, Chopin continued to write, attempting to widen her potential market by working in a variety of genres but, as Phyllis Vanlandingham observes, never quite fathoming the relationship between author and editor (or publisher). It was a difficulty that probably cost her a fortune in royalties—but that safeguarded her artistic freedom to write *The Awakening.*[4] In October 1891, she wrote a play entitled *An Embarrassing Position,* which appeared in the St. Louis *Mirror.* On 8 March 1891, the *St. Louis Post-Dispatch* published her essay entitled "Revival of Wrestling," one of her many translations. Chopin was especially taken by the ironic tales of French author Guy de Maupassant ("I read his stories and marvelled at them. Here was life, not fiction"[5]); her translations of his stories, including "It?," "Solitude,"

"Night," and "For Sale," appeared periodically in St. Louis publications in the 1890s. (For the texts, see Thomas H. Bonner, Jr., *The Kate Chopin Companion, with Chopin's Translations from French Fiction* [Westport, Conn.: The Greenwood Press, 1988].) Her own stories tended to be either comparably ironic, adult-oriented tales for *Vogue, Century,* and the *Atlantic Monthly,* or more readily marketable, sentimentalized children's stories for *Youth's Companion* or *Harper's Young People.* Chopin's best adult fiction was gathered in two collections: *Bayou Folk,* published in 1894 by the noted Boston publisher of Houghton, Mifflin, and Company, and *A Night in Acadie,* released by a Chicago house, Way & Williams, in 1897. A third story collection, *A Vocation and a Voice,* was accepted for publication by Herbert S. Stone & Company of Chicago, but in February 1900, the acceptance was withdrawn as the firm cut back its list. Chopin may well have interpreted the withdrawal as a negative response to the controversy surrounding her novel *The Awakening.* Originally titled *A Solitary Soul,* it was apparently begun in June 1897 and completed the following January, being published more than a year later, in April 1899. Contrary to popular belief, *The Awakening* was neither banned from local libraries nor uniformly condemned by the press. True, many reviews were harsh, but Chopin evidently had anticipated the response and in fact continued to write poems and stories, including such excellent tales as "Elizabeth Stock's One Story" (March 1898), "Charlie" (April 1900), and "The White Eagle" (May 1900). As Heather Kirk Thomas argues persuasively, the curtailment of Chopin's work after the release of *The Awakening* seems to have resulted primarily from problems with her health, especially her vision, rather than from bitterness over bad press or a loss of faith in her writing ability.[6] Indeed, Chopin's ill health took its toll, and the end came quickly. After spending a long, unusually hot day at the St. Louis World's Fair, Chopin complained of a severe headache and suddenly died of a massive cerebral hemorrhage on 22 August 1904. She had just turned fifty-four.

At the time of her death, Chopin was well-known in a variety of personae. To her acquaintances in Cloutierville, she was the city woman who smoked Cuban cigarettes, wore a short black wig, and dallied with a married farmer. In St. Louis, she was respected both for her salons and for her writings, her reputation as a nationally known author remaining surprisingly intact despite the criticism of *The Awakening.* In the country as a whole, she was acknowledged as a gifted and prolific writer, who well deserved inclusion in the first edition of *Who's Who in America* in 1900. At the time of her death, Chopin was regarded as a bright light on the national literary scene, admired for her unsentimentalized renderings of the South; for her unblinking recognition of the complexities of race, gender, and economics; for her willingness to challenge the idea of the "well-made story" in the interests of probing the nuances of human psychology; for her technical and stylistic skills; and for her keen sensitivity to the plight of women in the 19th century. The subsequent rapid loss of her reputation is no reflection on her or her achievement. It may be attributed to the tendency of literary historians to categorize her too simplistically as part of the "local color" movement, which by the turn of the century was rapidly losing respectability, and by the marginalization of female authors during the canonization of male writers at approximately the same historical moment. Neither factor can gainsay that Kate Chopin was an exceptional writer who richly deserves the acclaim she has enjoyed since the late 1960s.

CRITICAL RESPONSE

The critical response to Chopin's writings comprises mostly contemporary reviews (the publication of which roughly corresponds to the dozen years of her career) and the evaluations of the academic community dating from the publication of Per Seyersted's biography of Chopin and *The Complete Works* in 1969; she received scant attention in the years between her death in 1904 and the Seyersted revival. The following pages are not intended to offer an exhaustive account of either the contemporary or the modern responses to Chopin; rather, they present an overview of an enormous and growing record of published criticism.

The Contemporary Response

As noted, Chopin became a productive, successful author relatively quickly, as confirmed by the meticulous records she kept. True, writing did not make her financially independent, as it did her contemporary, Mary E. Wilkins Freeman, and in fact Chopin's primary support continued to be rental income from inherited property. However, early on she began placing good stories in the best-known periodicals of her era, doing so without a long apprenticeship such as Nathaniel Hawthorne had. The first criticism of her work thus came at the dawn of her career from the editors and readers of those magazines she regarded as her potential market.

This mother of six was a keen appraiser of the lucrative field of children's literature, and she placed "For Marse Chouchoute" in the popular *Youth's Companion* in March 1891, a scant three years after the private printing in St. Louis of her musical composition "Polka for Piano." She seemed particularly interested, however, in writing for magazines with mature audiences, and the desire led her to *Vogue* magazine, noted in the 1890s for its receptivity to unconventional, nonmoralizing literature. The first Chopin story to appear in *Vogue* was "Dr. Chevalier's Lie," written in September 1891 and published 5 October 1893. The pathetic but nonjudgmental tale of a country girl forced into prostitution to survive in the city, it was one of a series of *Vogue* stories (including "Désirée's Baby" and "La Belle Zoraïde") in which Chopin explored such unsavory topics as miscegenation, suicide, illegitimacy, and madness. Sophisticated *Vogue* editors and readers evidently took no offense to either the subject matter or Chopin's nonmoralistic stance; other magazines were less understanding. Chopin, like most American authors of the late 19th century, was eager to place her work in the widely read *Atlantic Monthly*. She had courted the approval of its editor, William Dean Howells, sending him a copy of her privately published novel *At Fault* and modeling her play on his own efforts at drama. But Howells had committed himself to endorsing in literature only " 'the more smiling aspects of life, which are the more American' " and to censoring " 'certain facts of life which are not usually talked of before young people, and especially young ladies.' "[7] The *Atlantic* did accept some of Chopin's work, such as the story "Athénaïse," in which a rather dull-witted young woman, disenchanted with marriage, returns happily to her husband when she learns she is pregnant; however, Chopin rarely modified her writing to suit an editor. Her best work appeared in *Vogue* and *Century*. (She did revise "A No-Account Creole" at the suggestion of *Century* editor Richard Watson Gilder, and the story was published January 1894.)

A novel, far more than stories written for the magazine trade, could deal directly with unsettling topics. There would be no skittish editors concerned about distributing "filth" to the households of unsuspecting (female) subscribers; and, if published at the author's expense, there would be no publisher pandering to popular taste in the interest of sales. *At Fault,* written between July 1889 and April 1890, was published for Chopin by the Nixon-Jones Printing Company of St. Louis in September 1890. One of the earliest fictional treatments of divorce, *At Fault* traces the triangular relationship between Thérèse Lafirme, a business-minded widow in Natchitoches; David Hosmer, a St. Louis lumber merchant interested in the forests she owns; and Fanny Hosmer, the alcoholic wife he had divorced two years before. At Thérèse's insistence, David aborts their romance to remarry Fanny, who eventually drowns in the river, while in pursuit of whiskey, thus conveniently enabling Thérèse and David to wed. Despite the creaky plotting, *At Fault* raises disturbing questions about the wisdom of doing the "right" thing (such as honoring marriage vows); about the capacity of the American woman (the "angel in the house") to engage in substance abuse; about the blurry distinctions between sexual chemistry, romance, and conjugal love; and about the impact of environment on moral growth. Chopin herself distributed the review copies, which garnered mixed responses; the most positive reviews, not surprisingly, were local. In a piece entitled "A St. Louis Novelist," the anonymous reviewer for the *St. Louis Post-Dispatch* praised Chopin for the novel's lack of didacticism and abundance of moral issues, as well as for its artistry. However, another St. Louis newspaper, the conservative *Republic,* berated Fanny for drinking to excess and Chopin for using inappropriate language ("I cannot recall an instance, in or out of fiction, in which an American 'country store' has been alluded to as a 'shop,' unless by some unregenerate Englishman"). Outside of St. Louis, the *New Orleans Daily Picayune* noted that "the life of a handsome Creole widow of 30 is charmingly related in the book," while *The Nation,* though praising Chopin for her skills in recording dialect and characterization, added the author and publisher to the list of those who might be "at fault" for this relentlessly over-plotted tale of woe.[8] Overall, the critical response was not the harbinger of a brilliant novelistic career, but it was certainly positive enough to encourage Chopin to continue producing books. Hence in accordance with the practice of her era, she sought to collect in book form the best and/or most commercially appealing of the stories that she had so far placed in periodicals.

Twenty-three of her adult tales, sketches, and children's stories were collected in her second book, *Bayou Folk* (1894). That its publisher was Houghton, Mifflin of Boston enhanced her national reputation while guaranteeing strong distribution and marketing. Most of the stories in the volume were set in the Cane River country around Cloutierville, enabling Chopin to use her musician's ear to record the distinctive French Louisiana dialect of that area and to draw upon her keen understanding of human psychology in an isolated rural environment; unfortunately the setting also led some commentators to classify Chopin as a "local colorist," a term already pejorative in the mid-1890s. As one might expect, most reviewers resorted to quaint pronouncements routinely used to describe local color writers. The reviewer for *The Critic* gushed over Chopin's exotic setting, the Louisiana bayous—"They are the abodes of humidity, shadiness, shy sylvan life, the terrifying alligator, the cane-brake, the melodious mosquito"—and praised her "fine eye for picturesque situations." Closer to home, the *New Orleans Daily Picayune* predicted that stories this "charming" and "delightful" would make Chopin "popular throughout the state." Lacking any regional nepotism, the reviewer for the *Hartford Daily Courant,* clearly entertained by this glimpse of "unsophisticate [*sic*] forms of life," noted that Chopin's tales would "be in time of value as historic documents."[9]

But Chopin's concerns in these stories were far from those of most local colorists. Eschewing their trademark sentimentality and refusing to poke fun at the "bayou folk" for the amusement of non-Southern readers, Chopin delved into such verboten topics as domestic violence ("In Sabine"), sexual passion ("At the 'Cadian Ball"), and marital breakdown ("Mme. Célestin's Divorce"). Some reviewers did recognize the importance of these matters and their relationship to European fictional models. The commentator for the *Review of Reviews,* for example, observed astutely that *Bayou Folk* "might remind some readers of certain of finished bits of Maupassant and other French 'short story' masters." And whether or not they recognized Chopin's French connection, several reviewers singled out for praise a quality of Chopin's writing that is noted too rarely in current criticism; that is, her technical and stylistic mastery. The commentator for *Public Opinion,* for example, noted how tightly Chopin had "woven" the "threads" of her stories, and how "pleasing and artistic" was her mingling of disparate emotions. The reviewer for the *St. Louis Post-Dispatch* praised Chopin's "delicacy of touch" and that "almost austere adherence to art," especially her "moderation and economy of expression." Perhaps this well-justified emphasis on the beauty of her writing was in part a means of not dealing with Chopin's often unsettling subject matter. Whatever the case, *Bayou Folk* garnered much stronger reviews than *At Fault* and confirmed Chopin's growing national reputation. Soon after the story collection was released, her St. Louis friend William Schuyler penned "Kate Chopin." One of the earliest and most appreciative accounts of her life and work, it appeared in the August 1894 issue of the popular Boston-based magazine, *The Writer*.[10]

Chopin's second collection of short stories, *A Night in Acadie*, was published in November 1897 by a less well-known press, Way & Williams of Chicago. It contains material that predates her first collection and is noteworthy for several finely wrought and thematically daring tales. "Regret," for example, explores a self-sufficient, seemingly happy woman's sudden remorse over never having had children. "A Sentimental Soul" probes the allure of illicit love, the power of sexual fantasy, and the capacity of a social role—even a self-imposed, meaningless one—to lend purpose to life. And "Athénaïse" explores the similarities between marriage and slavery and how the prospect of impending motherhood can render those similarities palatable to a particular kind of woman. As expected, most St. Louis newspapers responded warmly to the collection. Noted the *Post-Dispatch,* in reading Chopin's tales "one feels that one is in the hands of an artist and that all is well." Even the reviewer for *The Nation*, a generally staid publication, was dazzled, although a bit condescending: "enough there is of artistic in the best sense to hold the reader from cover to cover, transported for the time to a region of fierce passions, medieval chivalry, combined with rags and bad grammar, a soft, sliding Creole accent, and the tragedies and comedies that loom with special meaning in a sparsely settled country." But Jeannette L. Gilder, writing for *The Critic,* questioned Chopin's predilection for focusing on the daily lives of ordinary people: "She is never very exciting or dramatic; there is even a slight feeling after reading about six of the stories, that one has read something very like the seventh before." She also criticized Chopin's inclusion of "slight and unnecessary coarseness." Even so, Gilder recommended the collection.[11] However, dismay over Chopin's "coarseness" would be even more prevalent in the critical response to the book already underway when *A Night in Acadie* was published. Completed in January 1898 and published in April 1899 by Herbert S. Stone & Company of Chicago, *The Awakening* was destined to be Chopin's most controversial book.

Most of Chopin's contemporaries seemed taken aback by *The Awakening,* though perhaps not to the degree widely believed today. Much of the venom in the negative reviews was directed at Edna Pontellier (primarily for selfishly refusing to subscribe to the cult of "true womanhood"[12]) or at Chopin herself (for failing to continue writing her light-hearted, charming tales, which in fact had much darker edges than the reviewers' cheery adjectives would suggest). Frances Porcher, herself a mother, chastised Edna in the St. Louis *Mirror* for turning her back on her family when that "ugly, cruel, loathsome monster Passion" came to life. The whole sordid tale, concluded Porcher, "leaves one sick of human nature." The error-riddled review in the *St. Louis Republic* likewise lamented the selfishness of the antiheroine: "so the woman who did not want anything but her own way drowned herself."[13] The reviewer for *The Nation* concurred, noting that *The Awakening* is "the sad story of a Southern lady who wanted to do what she wanted to. From wanting to, she did, with disastrous consequences." Had she "flirted less and looked after her children more," continues the reviewer, "we need not have been put to the unpleasantness of reading about her and the temptations she trumped up for herself." But where the reviewer for *The Nation* was able to infer a lesson from the tale (whether or not it was a lesson intended by the author), other reviewers were appalled at the novel's utter lack of a didactic strain. The *St. Louis Daily Globe-Democrat,* the only publication consistently hostile to Chopin in her hometown, lamented that *The Awakening* "is not a healthy book; if it points [to] any particular moral or teaches any lesson, the fact is not apparent." The reviewer for the *Providence Sunday Journal* seemed even more aghast. Noting that "the purport of the story can hardly be described in language fit for publication," he theorized desperately that "Miss Chopin did not herself realise [*sic*] what she was doing when she wrote it." Even more regrettable than the plot, he purported, was its potential impact on impressionable readers: "The worst of such stories is that they will come into the hands of youth, leading them to dwell on things that only matured persons can understand, and promoting unholy imaginations and unclean desires." The Cult of Howells was alive and well.[14]

Nevertheless, a surprisingly large number of Chopin's contemporaries had positive responses to *The Awakening.* The novel's first review, written by Lucy Monroe for *Book News,* lauded Chopin's treatment of female psychology: "in reading it you have the impression of being in the very heart of things, you feel the throb of the machinery, you see and understand the slight transitions of thought, the momentary impulses, the quick sensations of the hardness of life, which govern so much of our action." Likewise enthusiastic was Chopin's St. Louis friend Charles L. Deyo. Writing for the *Post-Dispatch,* Deyo cited the "flawless art" of the book: "in delicious English, quick with life, never a word too much, simple and pure, the story proceeds with classic severity through a labyrinth of doubt and temptation and dumb despair." But beyond artistry, he praised the brilliance of Chopin's portrait of Edna. Acknowledging freely that *The Awakening* would not be appropriate for younger readers ("it is for seasoned souls, for those who have lived, who have ripened under the gracious or ungracious sun of experience"), Deyo concluded that "It is sad and mad and bad, but it is all consummate art." The

Boston Beacon, meanwhile, tended to exonerate Edna, blaming the "villain" for the "breaking down [of Edna's] reserve so that her judgment is baffled." Her tragic story is further explained not by the exigencies of female sexuality but by "the immorality of a marriage of convenience." And the *New York Times Saturday Review* likewise defended both Edna and her creator: "Would it have been better had Mrs. Kate Chopin's heroine slept on forever and never had an awakening? . . . The author has a clever way of managing a difficult subject, and wisely tempers the emotional elements found in the situation. Such is the cleverness in the handling of the story that you feel pity for the most unfortunate of her sex." These are not discouraging words.[15]

In sum, the contemporary critical response to *The Awakening* was, at worst, mixed rather than negative.[16] The long held, but incorrect perception that the response was overwhelmingly negative may be attributed to three factors. First, some commentators seem to have taken too seriously Chopin's tongue-in-cheek appraisal of her own novel in *Book News* (July 1899): "I never dreamed of Mrs. Pontellier making such a mess of things and working out her own damnation as she did. If I had had the slightest intimation of such a thing[,] I would have excluded her from the company. But when I found out what she was up to, the play was half over and it was then too late."[17] It is possible that some took these words as a statement of regret. Next, Chopin did dramatically reduce her literary output after publishing *The Awakening;* however, as noted, ill health seems more responsible for the decline than ill feelings. The cause-and-effect theory is convenient, but unjust; moreover, this explanation must be tempered by the observation that Chopin did continue to write after *The Awakening*'s publication. According to Toth's primary bibliography, Chopin produced approximately twenty stories, poems, and essays between the release of the novel in April 1899 and her death in 1904. Finally, the canard that Chopin bitterly ceased writing in reaction to criticism of her final novel was voiced most dramatically by the earliest 20th-century commentators. This opinion has lasted so long because of those voices and to be frank, because the story is such a good one. The very scenario—a hard-working, widowed mother of six, crushed by the unjust criticism leveled at her finest novel, vows never to write again, dying shortly thereafter—is so compelling that it is as difficult to challenge as George Washington's chopping down a cherry tree. But where Washington had his Parson Weems to spread the (distorted) word, Chopin has had a small army of biographers and scholars to do the deed. The scenario has constituted a subtext of virtually the entire posthumous critical response to Chopin's life and work.

The Modern Response

As noted, most of the modern criticism of Kate Chopin dates from 1969. However, she was never entirely forgotten by critics and literary historians, and the academy's rediscovery of Chopin began earlier (albeit haltingly) than generally realized.

In 1909, a scant five years after Chopin's death, Percival Pollard in *Their Day in Court* offered a lengthy attack on Chopin, in particular on the amorality (read "female sexuality") of *The Awakening,* that clearly echoes the most negative of the contemporary reviews. It is a novel, snips Pollard, that "asked us to believe that a young woman who had been several years married, and had borne children, had never, in all that time, been properly 'awake.' It would be an arresting question for students of sleep-walking." He has no patience with Edna, whom he clearly regards as a strumpet: "We were asked to believe that *Edna* was devoid of coquetry; that she did not know the cheap delights of promiscuous conquests; though sometimes on the street glances from strange eyes lingered in her memory, disturbing her. Well, then those are the women to look out for." And he is especially annoyed by Chopin, who having "already distinguished [herself] for charming *contes* of Creole life," lowered herself in a "deliberate case of pandering" to the most prurient literary tastes of her day.[18]

Subsequent early commentators (all male) were somewhat less cynical, though some undercut their appreciative remarks by confining Chopin to the modest realm of regional writers. In 1915, the influential Fred Lewis Pattee seemed unsure whether to praise Chopin for her narrative "genius" or for the extemporaneous artlessness supposedly underlying it ("she wrote story after story almost without effort and wholly without study of narrative art"). Despite her purported status as a narrational *idiot savant,* Chopin did create in "Désirée's Baby" what Pattee regarded as a "well-nigh perfect" story.[19] In 1932, Father Daniel S. Rankin in his doctoral dissertation, *Kate Chopin and Her Creole Stories,* drew upon his interviews with Chopin's descendants, acquaintances, and friends (including the long-lived Kitty Garesché) to create a flesh-and-blood Chopin. Despite occasionally dubious scholarship and some discomfort with Chopin's frank portrayals of sexuality, Rankin reveals himself as an appreciative and enthusiastic reader of Chopin.

Rankin's positivism, however, was not felt immediately in the academy. In 1936, Arthur Hobson Quinn had nothing supportive to say about Chopin or Edna Pontellier ("the basic fault lies in Edna's utter selfishness . . . and the novel belongs rather among studies of morbid psychology than local color"), but the following year, Joseph J. Reilly, writing for *The Commonweal,* declared Chopin "incomparably the greatest American short story writer of her sex"— a gender-qualified compliment, but a compliment nonetheless.[20] But the real support for Chopin at this juncture came from overseas. In 1946, French critic Cyrille Arnavon discussed Chopin within the context of American literary realism in an essay appearing in Henri Kerst's *Romanciers Américains Contemporains;* he then published a French translation of *The Awakening* under the title *Edna* in Paris in 1953. Not only was the novel available once again, but it was accompanied by Arnavon's sensible introduction, in which he compared *The Awakening* to *Madame Bovary,* pondered the psychoanalytical ramifications of Edna's suicide, and praised Chopin as a sensitive woman with timeless insights.[21]

Alleged amorality was not an issue for Arnavon, nor did it concern the American Chopin commentators of the 1950s. Van Wyck Brooks, in his influential *The Confident Years* (1952), termed *The Awakening* "one small perfect book that mattered more than the whole life-work of many a prolific writer" and a "beautiful novel" that "should have been remembered." Robert Cantwell, writing for the "Old Books" section of *The Georgia Review* in 1956, helped shape the future response to Chopin by perpetuating the story that the negative reaction to *The Awakening* effectively ended her career ("Mrs. Chopin was disgusted, and, apart from a few short stories, wrote nothing more"), while lamenting her supposed lack of technical proficiency ("Mrs. Chopin had an extraordinary distaste for the elementary mechanics of fiction—getting people into and out of rooms, the *he saids* and *she saids* of romance"). But Cantwell did feel that Chopin had one exceptional gift, "a heightened sensuous awareness, awake and alive." Kenneth Eble, writing for the *Western Humanities Review* the same year, was even more blunt: "Quite frankly, the book is about sex. Not only is it about sex, but the very texture of the writing is sensuous, if not sensual, from the first to the last." Of course, Edna's awakening involved far more than hormones, but Eble's willingness to accept sexuality as an integral part of the ecology of the novel was a healthy corrective to the judgmental posture assumed by Pollard and the other early critics. Eble's final exhortation to the academy to restore *The Awakening* to its rightful place "among novels worthy of preservation" would not, however, be acted upon for several more years. The turning point came in the 1960s.[22]

In 1962, Edmund Wilson argued in *Patriotic Gore* that *The Awakening* does not qualify as a " 'problem novel.' No case for free love or women's rights or the injustice of marriage is argued." (A "problem novel" explored some social problem, usually involving the poor or the disenfranchised.) Wilson seemed unsure of how he felt about the "serene amoralism" exhibited by Chopin, but he was quite certain that Robert Lebrun confirmed himself "an all too honorable young fellow" by declining to sleep with Edna. Presumably this rendered Edna a not very honorable young woman. But four years later, Larzer Ziff in *The American 1890s* presented less-qualified praise for Chopin, thanks largely to her Gallic sensibilities. The "masterful economy of setting and character and the precision of style" in *The Awakening* are, according to Ziff, directly attributable to the example of Flaubert; furthermore, Chopin's use of Creole (read "French") settings made her stories more acceptable to magazine publishers, who would risk losing readership by printing similar stories set in more typical American locales. More importantly, Ziff articulated what would be the touchstone of much Chopin criticism thereafter: *The Awakening* "did not attack the institution of the family, but it rejected the family as the automatic equivalent of feminine self-fulfillment, and on the very eve of the twentieth century it raised the question of what woman was to do with the freedom she struggled toward."[23]

Although Ziff wrote so eloquently on behalf of Chopin in 1966, the still-largely male academy remained ambivalent about her, as witnessed by the appearance the following year of George Arms's important but essentially patriarchal evaluation of Chopin in Clarence Gohdes's *Essays on American Literature in Honor of Jay B. Hubbell.* But even as students of American literature read the words of Ziff and Arms, Per Seyersted, a Norwegian student of Cyrille Arnavon at Harvard University, was completing his solid critical biography of Chopin and editing her *Complete Works.* Both books appeared in 1969, just when the newly emerging feminist movement was actively encouraging the rediscovery of writings by American women marginalized by the male-dominated academy. The time was ripe for the resurrection of Kate Chopin.

The release of paperback editions of her work made Chopin readily available in the classroom (a vital first step in generating scholarly interest in a writer) and to the general public for the first time in decades. Probably the most important of these editions was *"The Awakening" and Other Stories* (1970). In his excellent introduction, Lewis Leary singled out for the first time the central concerns of Chopin scholars. He was sensitive to Chopin's place in American letters, astutely recognizing connections between *The Awakening* and Walt Whitman's *Song of Myself* and detecting the influences of George Washington Cable and Sarah Orne Jewett on the body of Chopin's work. He recognized Chopin's technical and stylistic virtuosity, arguing that only Jewett and Henry James among her contemporaries "had produced fiction more artfully designed." He embraced the ambiguous ending of *The Awakening,* which "seems inevitably to invite questions" rather than provide easy answers. And he made the startlingly feminist observation that Chopin's women characters "struggle against submitting" to the expectations of a "man-managed society." Overtly or otherwise, most Chopin critics since 1970 have owed an intellectual debt to one or more of Lewis Leary's points.[24]

A new (or rediscovered) writer has "arrived" when scholars make efforts to articulate his or her place in literature. Comparisons to predecessors and contemporaries, and/or theories regarding impact on later writers, can serve to legitimatize an author or, more perversely, to challenge originality. Chopin scholarship has involved all the above. She was unusually well-read, having knowledge of Continental (especially French), contemporary American, and Russian literature. Her alleged indebtedness to other writers is variously identified as stylistic, technical, or thematic, although some commentators stress parallel independent development rather than influence per se.

The writer whose name is linked most often with Chopin's is Gustave Flaubert. Willa Cather, in an 1899 newspaper review of *The Awakening,* had termed it a "Creole *Bovary,*" and various subsequent commentators, including Arnavon and Eble, have noted the Flaubertian parallels. Perhaps predictably, this position, which seems too readily to compromise Chopin's originality, has engendered some backlash. For example, Lawrence Thornton in *"The Awakening: A Political Romance"* (reprinted in this volume) points out that, whereas both Emma Bovary and Edna Pontellier are susceptible to "romantic codes" in literature and society, Edna's susceptibility gives way to at least a partial understanding of the lie that animates her fantasies. That understanding, suggests Thornton, leads to far more psychic pain for her than is suffered by Emma.[25] Charles W. Mayer in "Isabel Archer, Edna Pontellier, and the Romantic Self" takes a different tack, arguing that Edna's brand of individualism is so insistently American that she really has little in common with her less independent Gallic counterpart. And Thomas Bonner, Jr., notes that, unlike Flaubert, Chopin is quite empathetic toward the awakening of a woman's sexual desire—a fundamental difference that leads to qualitatively different texts.[26]

Other Continental and American writers have also been linked to Chopin, with a few subjected to similar efforts to qualify those linkages. Rosemary F. Franklin, for example, argues that the original title of *The Awakening, A Solitary Soul*, may well point to the direct influence of Edgar Allan Poe, whose poems on sleeping, dreaming, and waking include "The Lake." But Franklin also notes that "Chopin's aesthetic was . . . the opposite of Poe's": thus Chopin "pays Poe an ironic compliment" by showing how "powerfully seductive" was Poe's impact on Edna. Antony H. Harrison, noting that English author A. C. Swinburne is "the only contemporary writer quoted in *The Awakening*," writes that "Chopin's work, like so many of Swinburne's poems, presents a critique of capitalist social values, repressive patriarchal mores, and the social as well as the religious institutions that perpetuate both. The impetus for this critique with Chopin, as with Swinburne, is the obstacled quest for total fulfillment of romantic 'Desire' (in all its sexual, emotional, psychological, and spiritual manifestations)." Even so, Chopin emerges as the more insightful of the two: the "subtextual dialogue" of her novel "insists that, for all his radicalism, Swinburne—like Edna Pontellier—has been a dupe of romantic illusions he has perpetuated throughout his career."[27]

Meanwhile, Thomas Bonner, the most astute chronicler of Chopin's literary connections, points out that she is known to have read Emile Zola, Guy de Maupassant, Leo Tolstoy, Ivan Turgenev, and Thomas Hardy (whose *Jude the Obscure* she despised: "The book is detestably bad; it is unpardonably dull; and immoral, chiefly because it is not true"). Though he questions the theory of direct Flaubertian influence, Bonner does argue that Chopin's trademark twist endings are "Maupassant-like," a position lent credence by Chopin's many translations of Maupassant's stories. More subtly, Cynthia Griffin Wolff observes that, like Maupassant, Chopin responds to "the ominous and insistent presence of the margin: the inescapable fact that even our most vital moments must be experienced on the boundary—always threatening to slip away from us into something else, into some dark, undefined contingency."

Eliane Jasenas, however, feels that Chopin worked in diametric opposition to Maupassant, for whom " 'to awaken' means to give up." Indeed, Jasenas goes so far as to maintain that the ostensible French influence on Chopin "is a case of *influence critique,* i.e., an aggressiveness against the authors used, [with] the narrative turning against them or commenting upon them." According to this reading, *The Awakening* "can be seen as a process of liberation from French culture in general."[28]

However extreme Jasenas's position may appear, it does put into clearer perspective the tenuousness of any attempt to connect Chopin with other writers, especially since her reading and general knowledge of culture was so rich and varied. For example, in her "The Second Coming of Aphrodite," Sandra M. Gilbert remarks on the parallels between Chopin and writers as divers as George Eliot, Emily Brontë, Emily Dickinson, and Walt Whitman. Moreover, she argues that Chopin's characteristic "mode of mingled naturalism and symbolism," her "artful combination of surface and symbol," owed much to Turgenev, Maupassant, Honoré de Balzac, and Anton Chekhov. Of course, that same blending of "surface and symbol" could be attributed to the Impressionist movement in painting, which, as Michael T. Gilmore reminds us, gives "priority to the sensations of the artist" while it "actively disfigures or decomposes the external world."[29] However, Dieter Schulz points out that the same qualities also may be attributed to "turn-of-the-century mood poetry and *art nouveau,*" which would help explain the synaesthesia of the final scene of *The Awakening* as well as the insistence on the "natural affinity between woman and water." And Chopin's style also may owe something to the example of Nathaniel Hawthorne, whose *Scarlet Letter* was published the year Chopin was born. Robert Arner makes an interesting case that both Edna Pontellier and Hester Prynne suffer from "uneasiness in the presence of [the] newly awakened sensual self." Furthermore, they share a keen sense of guilt that seems "to originate in a thoroughly Presbyterian social conscience," but Ivy Schweitzer makes an equally compelling case that the differences between Edna and Hester are considerable, residing in the two women's disparate attitudes toward maternity.[30] Chopin's Hawthorne connection thus remains problematic at best.

The same divergence of opinion can be seen regarding Ralph Waldo Emerson. Donald Ringe sees *The Awakening* as the record of Edna's reaction to "what she perceives as [the Emersonian] not-herself—the physical world and the other people in it." Charles W. Mayer argues that both Edna and Isabel Archer strive for "Emersonian idealism," but Virginia Kouidis points out that Edna fails to grasp Emerson entirely and thus literally falls asleep while reading his essays.[31]

The only author who seems universally regarded as a strong, direct influence on Chopin is one who owes much to Emerson: Walt Whitman. Whitman's interest in the individual at odds with society, as well as his lust for life, open sexuality, sensitivity to natural rhythms, and passion for literary experimentation, are clearly evident in Chopin, so much that Harold Bloom bluntly declares *The Awakening* "a Whitmanian book, profoundly so," in which "Edna, like Walt, falls in love with her own body." Perhaps, but as Kenneth M. Price notes in *Whitman and Tradition*, even while embracing Whitman, Chopin seems to have been testing his ideas "against the hard truths of [women's] experience." A woman living in accordance with "Whitman's ideal of comradeship" (i.e., active sexuality) would, after all, probably become pregnant. This testing of Whitmanian ideas owed much to the impact of Darwin, a point made by Bert Bender in two important companion studies, "Kate Chopin's Quarrel with Darwin Before *The Awakening*" and "The Teeth of Desire: *The Awakening* and *The Descent of Man*" (both appearing in this volume). Examining Chopin's novels *At Fault* and *The Awakening,* as well as several of her short stories, Bender argues that initially "Chopin saw the new natural history [as articulated by Darwin] as a resounding defense of Walt Whitman's songs of the 'body electric' or 'the procreant urge of the world.' " But, he continues, Chopin quickly came to feel that "the female plays a far more active and passionate role in the 'sexual struggle' than Darwin had suggested" and that "love" played a dubious role in human courtship. For Bender, Chopin's later female characters (such as Edna Pontellier) were despondent precisely because "there is no song of the self like that which Whitman had sung for 'Modern Man'—no song especially 'of physiology' or of the 'Female equally with the Male' in 'Life Immense . . . under the laws divine' ('One's-Self I Sing')." Bender's essays are vital contributions to the growing body of studies probing the complexities of Chopin's connection to Whitman and her responses to other writers of the 19th century.[32]

Chopin's presumable impact on subsequent writers is of less interest to the academy, although it seems a potentially intriguing field of inquiry. Most commentators couch their remarks to sidestep arguments of direct Chopinesque influence. Dorys Crow Grover, for example, observes that "descendants of [Chopin's] fiction are recognizable today in the work of Tennessee Williams, Erskine Caldwell, Robert Penn Warren and William Faulkner," while Winfried Fluck argues that Chopin's minimalist style "foreshadow[ed] the modernism of Sherwood Anderson and Ernest Hemingway."[33] Although Fluck's observation may be true, it does not necessarily denote direct influence: minimalism also was a trademark of Chopin's contemporary Stephen Crane, whose writings would have been more available to Hemingway than the out-of-print works of Chopin. Katherine Joslin argues that Willa Cather, "although she never acknowledged it as such, gave a literary response" to *The Awakening* when she wrote *The Professor's House* in 1925. And in an interesting twist to the influence issue, Per Seyersted notes that two of Chopin's contemporaries, Theodore Dreiser and Ellen Glasgow, appear *not* to have known of her.[34]

The interest in Chopin's minimalism points to another important aspect of Chopin studies published after 1969, that is, her technical and stylistic achievement. These analyses have been devoted to her short fiction, to her novel *At Fault,* and, above all, to *The Awakening.*

Rather surprising for a writer who produced approximately a hundred short stories, virtually all of which are handily available and widely taught in American colleges, very little work has focused on the artistry of Chopin's stories. The few explications of individual stories have yielded mixed results. Martin Simpson's "Chopin's 'A Shameful Affair,' " for example, is a standard reading of limited usefulness. More rewarding are the analyses by Peggy Skaggs, whose reading of "A Vocation and a Voice" confirms Chopin's interest in issues of male identity (and appears in this volume); by Robert D. Arner, who probes Chopin's handling of sexuality and guilt in the companion pieces "At the 'Cadian Ball" and "The Storm"; and by Susan Wolstenholme, whose efforts to confirm Chopin's indebtedness to Henrik Ibsen and Richard Wagner in "Mrs. Mobry's Reason" shed considerable light on both the story and Chopin's ability to transmute her sources to accommodate her own artistic vision.[35] Also worth noting is Elaine Gardiner's essay on "Ripe Figs," which makes the useful observations that Chopin tends to build her stories around a series of contrasts, that she relies heavily on natural images, and that she structures narrative around cyclical patterns. In addition, Joyce Coyne Dyer offers a series of valuable readings of individual Chopin stories, including "The White Eagle," "A Shameful Affair," and "Fedora" (the last of which is reprinted in this volume).[36]

Arguably the most important explications of individual Chopin stories are those devoted to the widely anthologized "Désirée's Baby." Robert D. Arner, in his essay "Pride and Prejudice" (reprinted in this volume), draws useful connections between the story and that earlier tale of innocence wronged, Samuel Richardson's *Clarissa* (1747–48), while arguing that the underpinning of the story is the perpetual struggle between superego and id. A quite different approach is assumed by Cynthia Griffin Wolff, who points to the story's leitmotif of real and imagined boundaries, and the willing or unwilling breaching of those boundaries, as Chopin's means of exploring personal and psychic space. Less convincing is Ellen Peel's "Semiotic Subversion in 'Désirée's Baby.' " Though it does appear true that Désirée functions essentially as a mirror reflecting the needs of those around her, it seems strained to point out that Chopin "never actually says she dies. Just as it is possible that [Désirée] is partly black, so it is possible that she (with the baby) is alive."[37] It's a neat academic twist, but one wonders what Chopin herself would have thought of it.

Finally, studies that attempt to comment upon more than one Chopin story have proved unevenly rewarding. Bert Bender's "Kate Chopin's Lyrical Short Stories," for example, does little to illuminate the "lyricism" of her work. More worthwhile are Nancy S. Ellis's "Insistent Refrains and Self-Discovery," which traces how music triggers various kinds of "awakenings" in "After the Winter," "At Chênière Caminada," and "A Vocation and a Voice," and three aptly titled essays by Joyce Coyne Dyer: "Techniques of Distancing in the Fiction of Kate Chopin," "Night Images in the Work of Kate Chopin," and "Epiphanies Through Nature in the Stories of Kate Chopin."[38]

A few commentators have drawn interesting connections between Chopin's stories and her novels. Patricia Hopkins Lattin in "Kate Chopin's Repeating Characters," for example, argues insightfully that Chopin (like Faulkner and the metafictionists of current times) often used the same characters in different texts (e.g., the Santien clan of "A No-Account Creole," "Ma'ame Pélagie," "In Sabine," and *At Fault*) so as to generate "a full and rich social reality." Indeed, Lattin notes that it is much easier to understand the newspaperman Gouvernail in "Athénaïse" if one has already read "A Respectable Woman," and Joyce Coyne Dyer would add that this previous experience with Gouvernail guides the reader's reaction to the brief mention of him as a guest at Edna's dinner party in *The Awakening*. Other stories reveal him as a sharp observer of human nature; hence his recitation of lines from "A Cameo" is meant to confirm his belief that Edna's awakening passions will lead only to pain and destruction.[39]

Although the record of scholarship devoted to Chopin's stories is brief, it is even shorter for *At Fault*. Then again, the book is artistically weak. Both Donald A. Ringe in "Cane River World" and Bernard J. Koloski in "The Structure of Kate Chopin's *At Fault*" make the valid point that the novel is intended to probe disparate individuals' responses to a world of rapid (especially technological) change in the post-Reconstruction era. As the machine of the railroad ruptures their garden of a Louisiana forest, everyone in the novel is forced to reconsider his or her values regarding economics, social class, race, gender, and even marriage. The theme is potentially fruitful, but as Lewis Leary notes in "Kate Chopin's Other Novel," this early Chopin effort is marred by weak character development, a contrived plot, superfluous minor characters, and unclear motivation. Unfortunately, his criticisms, which echo those of the novel's contemporary reviewers, are just. One of the few positive commentaries on *At Fault* comes from Joyce Coyne Dyer, who argues that the "bright hued Feathers and Japanese jars" of that novel paved the way for the rich symbolism of the sea in *The Awakening*.[40]

Whereas *At Fault* seems almost to embarrass Chopin scholars, they clearly feel that *The Awakening* is a masterpiece. So numerous are the studies devoted to the artistic excellence of this novel that the discussion here must be limited to just a sampling.

Whether attributed to the influence of Mallarmé, Hawthorne, the Impressionist painters, or anyone else, the symbolism and imagery used so heavily by Chopin in all her fiction appears to reach a high watermark in *The Awakening*. Martha Fodaski Black, for example, explores Chopin's brilliant use of bird imagery in that novel to suggest that *The Awakening* "gives . . . fictional form" to George Bernard Shaw's lament that the women of his era had been reduced to caged birds. Various commentators have remarked on

Chopin's use of water imagery in *The Awakening,* including Sandra M. Gilbert, who reads the entire novel as Chopin's presentation of the Aphrodite/Venus myth as an alternative to the masculinist myth of Jesus Christ; Ivy Schweitzer, for whom the maternal image of the sea is likewise liberating; and Marilyn Hoder-Salmon, whose three-act screenplay of the novel is replete with water imagery.[41] Also intriguing are studies of Chopin's use of symbolic space. Robert White in "Inner and Outer Space in *The Awakening*" draws upon the ideas of Erik Erikson to argue that Edna sought to reject the peaceful inner space of female domesticity—a rejection symbolized most dramatically by her final swim outward to a region without boundaries. Less abstractly, Suzanne W. Jones notes the novel's implicit contrast between New Orleans (confinement) and the Gulf Islands (freedom). To move toward freedom enables one to regain a childlike sense of wholeness and wonder (positive), but the price one pays is exposure to potential destruction. And Anne Rowe argues that Chopin further used the city of New Orleans as metaphor: "As Edna Pontellier's knowledge of New Orleans grows beyond her home and her fixed daily routine, so does her knowledge of herself."[42]

More compelling (if not always more convincing) are studies that focus on two interrelated aspects of artistry in *The Awakening:* language and narration. Many critics are impressed by Chopin's command of these elements; others are unsure whether to blame the creator (Chopin) or the created (Edna) for real or imagined infelicities in the text. In the first group, Paula A. Treichler argues that "*The Awakening* charts Edna Pontellier's growing mastery of the first-person singular, and that when this 'I' has been created, the book has successfully completed its mission and comes to an end." Emily Toth notes how Edna's increasing sense of self is reflected in the shift of her own charactonym from "Mrs. Pontellier" to "Edna Pontellier" to "Edna." Also, Patricia S. Yaeger feels the novel depicts "a frightening antagonism between a feminine subject and the objectifying world of discourse she inhabits," and Jean Wyatt in *Reconstructing Desire* likewise argues that for Edna to step "outside patriarchal territory" to locate her own sexuality and "the female unconscious," she must reject "the discourse [language] of Western culture." This critique sounds quite positive, as does Wyatt's thesis that Chopin uses onomatopoeia (the "rhythmic repetition" of words) to appeal to the reader's own body to empathize with Edna's.[43] Two other scholars would seem to agree: Joseph R. Urgo in "Prologue to Rebellion" theorizes that what awakens in Edna is "the art of telling" and that she kills herself rather than "edit her tale"; and Kenneth M. Price argues that Edna, "unable to constitute a new social order," must resort to "antilanguage."[44] In contrast, Peter Conn in *The Divided Mind* avers that Edna dies precisely because she cannot articulate what she is seeking. It is a position apparently shared by Sam B. Girgus, who feels that the "overall theme" of the novel is "Edna's incoherence and inarticulateness," and by Ruth Sullivan and Stewart Smith, who argue that "Edna does not think; she is driven" (see essay reprinted in this volume). Indeed, on the night of her death, according to Sullivan and Smith, Edna's "thinking produced little self-insight and no rational plan of action. It can hardly be called thinking at all."[45]

Whether one perceives Edna as antilanguage (positive), incoherent (negative), or inarticulate (positive or negative, depending upon whether one sees her as a victim of exclusionary patriarchal discourse), the fact remains that Chopin's use of language is connected intimately with her handling—or mishandling—of narration. Sullivan and Smith challenge the prevailing opinion that Chopin is objective in *The Awakening*, arguing that the point of view is "omniscient and judicial" [i.e., judgmental]. Pat Shaw takes a more technical approach, noting that Edna first appears as a secondary character "in the background of narrative action" and that the reader does not even go inside Edna's psyche until the end of the story. Dorothy Goldman notes further that the narrator disappears in the suicide scene, thereby confirming Edna's being totally alone at the end. The whole issue of whether Chopin was in command of her narrative is approached creatively by Elaine Showalter, who argues that the novel's narration resembles musical impromptu: the style "seems spontaneous and improvised, but it is in fact carefully designed and executed."[46]

Such discussions of language and narration should not be dismissed as academic pother, for they point to the central issue of *The Awakening:* the meaning—or meaninglessness—of Edna's final swim. How one responds to that swim essentially determines how one responds to the novel as a whole and, by extension, to Chopin's achievement as a writer.

Dorothy Goldman fingers part of the problem by noting the textual ambiguity of the novel. She feels that the frequent use of "perhaps" signals that the narrator (or is it Chopin herself?) is just as confused about the awakening as Edna is. (Italian scholar Cristina Giorcelli makes a similar point about Chopin's heavy reliance on " 'as if' [or 'as though'].") Goldman also believes that Edna's offhand remark about Léonce as a husband at the end of Chapter 3—" 'she knew of none better' "—could be seen as high praise, or an insult. Then again, muses Goldman, if it is meant to be ironic, is it Edna's irony? the narrator's? Chopin's?[47]

No wonder reactions to Edna's death range so widely, although many are quite negative. Sullivan and Smith see Edna's demise in unflattering terms: unable to appreciate "her considerate husband," burning with a need to compensate for her own motherlessness, and distressed over Robert's abandonment of her, this clinically depressed woman drowns herself without giving the matter much thought. Peter Conn likewise implicitly condemns Edna and her suicide: having been "treated rather gently in the struggle for existence," the ungrateful Edna kills herself because she can locate no roles to replace the ones (wife of loving rich man; mother of two adorable little boys) she has so foolishly rejected. Her suicide, intended as a rebirth, is thus "regressive." A bit more sympathetic, Winfried Fluck notes that this "movement toward regression reflects the complexity of the situation"; this stance is presumably shared by Paula S. Berggren, who in " 'A Lost Soul': Work Without Hope in *The Awakening*" argues that Edna's death results from her inability to find meaningful "work" in her 19th-century Creole world. The fault is hardly hers, and in fact the plight is shared by Robert. But Sam B. Girgus speaks for many (mostly male) critics in terming Edna "narcissistic," a word that nicely conveys both the novel's water imagery and Edna's ostensible self-absorption.[48]

Not surprisingly, Edna's ostensible confusion over sex and the rhetoric of romance, and/or her confusion over the discrepancy between the language of sex and its actuality, looms large in those critiques that posit her final swim in a negative light, even if the commentators themselves occasionally feel a modicum of sympathy for Edna. Lawrence Thornton sees her suicide as "the logical culmination of despair" borne of her realization that she can be neither married nor alone. More precisely, the "romantic codes" of her world effectively prevent her from assuming a psychologically healthy role beyond those already defined linguistically in her milieu. Other critics are less kind. George M. Spangler in "Kate Chopin's *The Awakening:* A Partial Dissent" argues that Edna kills herself because "she is unable to endure Robert's tender note of rejection," and Nancy Walker, lamenting Edna's inability to appreciate the "concerned and gentle" Léonce, argues that the "suddenness and power" of her "sexual awakening" renders Edna "not really in control of herself." In fact, she hadn't even planned on committing suicide: bear in mind that she had been talking about dinner with Victor Lebrun just before her final walk to the beach. "In effect, Edna drifts into death because she does nothing to stop it."[49]

Other commentators are less quick to attribute Edna's demise to acute depression, confusion over romantic rhetoric, impetuousness, or lethargy; many regard it as a positive assertion of self, an active rather than a reactive (or mindlessly passive) gesture. Anne Goodwyn Jones, for example, believes that by swimming "into the sensuous sea," Edna is "acting in the best way she has discovered to feel power without harming others." Penelope A. LeFew makes a compelling case that Edna's death can be perceived as an affirmative act if set against the ideas of Arthur Schopenhauer, whose philosophy of pessimism centered on the determination of the human will "to strive, search, and desire." Read in these terms, Edna's suicide is positive:

> In Schopenhauer's view, Edna's life force is stronger at her moment of death than at any other time; through willing her own death, she has once more willed her essential self into another state of willing—that which we know as death. "Death is like the setting sun," Schopenhauer observed, "which is only apparently engulfed by night, but actually, itself the source of all light, burns without intermission, brings new days to new worlds. . . ."[50]

Mylène Dressler in "Edna Under the Sun" assumes a more theoretical approach, arguing that with Edna "viewed as a subject engaged fundamentally with the problems and realities of the gaze," her death "refers not to transcendence, or defeat, or even to a hopeless ambiguity, but rather to limitation and possibility as they exist within a construct of Lacanian illumination."[51]

Beth Ann Bassein in *Women and Death* opts for more of a reader-response analysis. While criticizing Chopin for being unable to resist her readers' expectation that "marriage or death [are] the only excusable alternatives subsequent to heterosexual love," Bassein nonetheless pardons Edna for killing herself: "one cannot state categorically that she failed at emancipation." Robert S. Levine in "Circadian Rhythms and Rebellion in Kate Chopin's *The Awakening*" argues that Adèle's childbirth scene had "awakened [Edna] to a vision of the tyranny and horror of the procreative imperative placed on women"; her suicide, then, was an essentially affirmative attempt to "submerge[] herself in dreams beyond contamination." Using a slightly different approach, Joseph R. Urgo in "A Prologue to Rebellion" argues that "Edna's tragedy in *The Awakening* is that she finds that what her story says is unacceptable in her culture, and that in order to live in society she must silence herself. This she rejects." The alternative, according to Urgo, is the "quite logical and perhaps even reasonable choice of death." And Sandra M. Gilbert, in her admittedly "hyperbolic" essay "The Second Coming of Aphrodite," points out that at the end of the novel, Edna "is still swimming. *And how, after all, do we know that she ever dies?*" Edna Pontellier, "Chopin's resurrected Venus[,] is returning to Cyprus or Cythera."[52]

Of course, putting a positive spin on self-destruction is difficult; even those commentators who applaud Edna's motives often seem disconcerted by their own applause. (Bassein, for example, disapproves of a course of action that might "mold the outlook of susceptible readers"—shades of Howells once again.) Perhaps in response to this concern, many critics resist the urge to detect (or impose) closure; unlike Gilbert, they admit freely that Edna dies at the end, but they leave open the implications of that act, opting to argue that the meaning of the ending of *The Awakening* is—indeed was designed to be—ambiguous. As noted, Lewis Leary early on praised the (non)conclusion precisely because it invited questions (and, presumably, thought). Kenneth M. Rosen likewise praises Chopin's "Ambiguity as Art," as does Joseph L. Candela, Jr., who avers that Chopin "carefully preserved the moral ambiguity" regarding Edna's fate. Katherine Kearns would probably concur, as she notes how Chopin "allows one to find one's own place relative to the text. In this, of course, she merely shows one the door that opens onto the labyrinth." Whether this lack of closure is intentional or fortuitous, enhancing or detracting, the fact remains that it leads to widely divergent reactions. And as Andrew Delbanco notes in regard to teaching *The Awakening*, "it can be read with assent by readers of quite opposite positions on issues of sexual politics."[53]

Sexual politics is indeed a subtext of virtually everything written about *The Awakening*. As the preceding pages have suggested, Chopin criticism since 1969 has tended to be affected, one way or another, by the feminist movement with which the rediscovery of Chopin coincided. One may even argue that Kate Chopin would have continued to be forgotten if not for this movement, which posits Edna (and, through her, Chopin herself) as an important prototypical feminist—whether or not either deserves this label. Some critics chafe at this state of affairs. For example, Hugh J. Dawson, appalled by Chopin's "over-cute" descriptions and by that "lifelong adolescent," Edna Pontellier, hopes that *The Awakening,* like St. Christopher, will be "decanonized." Other commentators have more patience with Chopin's purple prose and her depiction of Edna but still question the novel's "canonization" by modern-day feminists. Harold Bloom, while acknowledging that the book "enjoys an eminent status among feminist critics," maintains "that many of them weakly misread the book, which is anything but feminist in its stance." Nancy Walker would seem to agree, remarking that it features "no stance about women's liberation or equality; indeed, the other married women in the novel are presented as happy in their condition." Thus, avers Walker, feminist critics responding to what they wish to see in *The Awakening* "have hastened to find feminism where it did not exist." Phrased elsewhere, what passes for feminist impulses are basically the sexual urges of a confused woman; it is a sterling example, as Quinn would have it, of "morbid psychology." Failing to see Edna's burgeoning sexuality within the gestalt of a much larger psychological phenomenon—"a bit as if, treating *Moby-Dick,* [these critics] called it a book about the whaling industry" (as stated by Priscilla Allen)—they perceive only raging hormones and condemn Edna (and condemn or deny her feminism) in the process.[54]

If nothing else, the feminist movement has so raised consciousness about female psychology that easy diagnoses of "morbidity" have, thankfully, become passé. In their place are feminist-tinged studies that examine, for example, the generally unsatisfactory roles available to most women in Chopin's era, issues involving the nexus of gender and race, or the Creole weltanschauung vis-à-vis women. That Edna is trapped within an Ibsenesque "maternal bondage," a status that confines women even as it ostensibly protects them, is discussed by Dorothy H. Jacobs in "*The Awakening:* A Recognition of Confinement." Granted, some women do seem to thrive in such a state. Paula S. Berggren argues that *The Awakening*'s resident Earth Mother, Adèle Ratignolle, is happy precisely because she so relishes the meaningful roles of wife and mother. But such happiness comes with a price of which Adèle may not even be aware: her selfhood. As Michael T. Gilmore points out, "the model Creole wife is a kind of verbal plagiarist, striving to be as alike in speech as she is in her emotions. Adèle literally parrots her husband at the dinner table, drinking in everything he says, 'laying down her fork the better to listen, chiming in, taking the words out of his mouth.' "[55]

Donald A. Ringe would likely concur, noting that Adèle illustrates a "willing surrender of self to another" and adding that this sacrifice is every bit as dubious as Mlle. Reisz's chronic "self-absorption." Ultimately, opines Kathleen Margaret Lant, Edna comes to realize she can never emulate either Adèle (who lacks a strong sense of self) or Mlle. Reisz (who lacks Edna's passion and who also, surmises Kathryn Lee Seidel, may be yet another 19th-century female artist afflicted with "inversion," i.e., lesbian tendencies). Without a viable alternative female role, Edna comes to behave in a manner that one usually associates with men, and indeed Andrew Delbanco reads *The Awakening* as a "cautionary tale," a de facto "novel of 'passing,' " with Edna seeking to "pass" as a man. It doesn't work. Ultimately Edna is, according to Rosemary F. Franklin, no better off than the unfortunate Psyche: beautiful, dynamic—and enslaved. "The paradigm of Psyche reveals Edna's exploit as heroic, but it also shows where she fails to finish her task and is dragged down by fear of a long and lonely period of change."[56]

The image of the enslaved Psyche points to another important aspect of modern Chopin scholarship: investigations into the nexus of gender and race. Quite justly, most observers note that the pro-Confederate Chopin evinced little direct concern for the status of Blacks in 19th-century America. In part, this noninterest reflects Chopin's ideological orientation. Observes Helen Taylor in her excellent *Gender, Race, and Region,* Chopin "did not identify herself as a southern cheerleader. Though using southern themes and characters, her texts work in opposition to, or dialogue with, European writers who shared her concern with questions of sexuality, bourgeois marriage, and woman's role—primarily in relation to women of Chopin's own race and class." Chopin's lack of direct interest in race also reflected, in part, the zeitgeist: as Bender notes, Charles Darwin's influential *The Descent of Man* "was mistakenly thought to justify much of the most overt racism that raged far into the twentieth century." In effect, there would be little purpose to concerning oneself with conditions that reflected the natural order of things— whether or not that order were God-sanctioned. Even so, Chopin did not ignore Blacks totally in her fiction, and often she handled them in interesting ways. As Eunice Manders observes, in such tales as "The Bênitous' Slave," "Odalie Misses Mass," "Tante Cat'rinette," and "Nég Créol," Chopin did veer away from the stereotypical renderings of Blacks found in stories by such contemporaries as Grace King and Ruth McEnery Stuart; Chopin deliberately undercut the "wretched freeman" character.[57]

Certainly there is surprisingly little sentiment in her rendering of Madame Sylvie, the proud, tough-minded businesswoman of "Athénaïse." But Chopin seemed less interested in Blacks as such than in white women treated as de facto Blacks by virtue of their loss of personal freedom and/or their lack of financial independence. Noting that Edna equates maternity with slavery, for example, Michele A. Birnbaum argues that Edna actually identifies with "the marginalized"; indeed, "Edna first discovers the erotic frontiers of the self by exploiting the less visible constructions of sexual difference associated with the blacks, quadroons, and Acadians in the novel." In

Women on the Color Line, Anna Shannon Elfenbein points out that Edna lives in a New Orleans mansion filled with discreetly invisible dark women who attend to the more menial household tasks. Their existence enables her to live a life of comparative leisure, but "the parameters of [Edna's] privilege are as rigidly defined as those of the menials . . . she fails to see."[58] See them or not, Edna does chafe at her financial dependence on her husband as well as at the fact that he regards her as, in effect, his property. For all intents and purposes, Edna—an attractive woman, but one without marketable talents—is enslaved by her economically powerful husband. This chilling scenario is explored at length by John Carlos Rowe in his superb Marxist reading of *The Awakening* entitled "The Economics of the Body," as well as in fine essays by Doris Davis and Margit Stange.[59]

Interestingly, some commentators (feminist or otherwise) have explored this issue of a woman's nonfreedom by examining the intersection of gender and culture in *The Awakening;* in particular, they see Edna's "feminism" (real or imagined) as complicated by her immediate environment. One such environmental issue is religion. Edna is a Presbyterian from Kentucky who "awakens" in the Roman Catholic world of Creole Louisiana. Nancy Walker argues that Edna is "hypnotized by the sensuous Creoles," whose overt passion for the physical side of life counters the widespread critical assumption that Edna behaves "in a shocking, inexplicable manner"; that is, for a woman in the Creole world, she is behaving quite normally. Sam B. Girgus would seem to agree, arguing how "the story suggests that the openness and freedom of Creole society ultimately undermine Edna's search for freedom because she lacks the maturity and internal stolidity to deal with such an explosion of new experiences and opportunities."[60] Sounds great—but Lawrence Thornton makes a good case that the heightened sexuality and freedom of women in Creole society was an illusion:

> That women could smoke cigarettes, listen to men tell risqué stories, and read French novels soon appears as only a veneer covering a solidly conventional society that titillated itself with flourishes of libertinism. For despite the[ir] apparent standing within the Creole world (a standing, it should be noted, gained solely through marriage), women are presented as an oppressed class.[61]

If anything, Edna's situation is made only more grievous by her misunderstanding of the Creole social and verbal codes that undermine this outsider's "awakening" even while they nurture it. As Adèle warned Robert Lebrun about his flirtation with Edna, " 'She is not one of us; she is not like us. She might make the unfortunate blunder of taking you seriously.' "[62] She does.

A final dimension of feminist-tinged criticism is a counter-sensitivity to the status of male characters in the Chopin canon. Neither Ward Cleaver nor Snidely Whiplash, Léonce Pontellier is seen by Peter Conn as an "obtusely ordinary" fellow, and according to Cynthia Griffin Wolff, he is "a slender vehicle to carry the weight of society's repression of women." It makes no sense to pity him for having an unappreciative wife or to excoriate him for driving that poor woman to suicide. More subtly, Joyce Coyne Dyer argues in "Kate Chopin's Sleeping Bruties" that many of Chopin's *male* characters undergo their own "awakenings," a point echoed by Gina M. Burchard. Perhaps, in the final analysis, Chopin critics, feminist or not, are coming to realize the wisdom of Wolff's observation about Edna: the reader responds to her because she is human, not because she is female. No one can say for sure whether Edna—or Chopin—was a feminist, a nonfeminist, an antifeminist, a closet feminist, a Marxist feminist, or a semi- or unconscious feminist. Perhaps, indeed, Kate Chopin, like Edna, was essentially a figure in-between: a "pontellier"—"one who bridges."[63]

Included in this collection are seven original essays, written by both young and established scholars of Southern literature. Intentionally, and perhaps contrary to reader expectations, they do not all focus on *The Awakening*, though that novel does figure in most of them. These original essays vary widely in subject matter and approach and seem destined to generate further dialogue and scholarly inquiry vis-à-vis Chopin and her writings.

In a reading likely to unsettle some admirers of "Désirée's Baby," Margaret D. Bauer draws upon her substantial knowledge of 19th-century Southern law and history to argue that Armand Aubigny had in fact known all his life that he had Black blood, and that his marriage to the unsuspecting Désirée was part of an elaborate plan to ensure that he, and his progeny, could "pass" successfully. Another potentially controversial essay is by Lawrence I. Berkove. Far from celebrating "free love," argues Berkove, the companion stories "At the 'Cadian Ball" and "The Storm" constitute "a courageous defense of morality" by a woman who in fact disapproved of adulterous liaisons and attacked them vigorously through irony. Morality also concerns Linda Wagner-Martin, who looks at *At Fault* and several early stories to explore how Chopin consistently created young males (and "somewhat androgynous" young women) to show not only the power of sexual passion, but also the power of the moral impulse to thrive despite difficult circumstances. These admirable, attractive young males, argues Wagner-Martin, "possibly kept [Chopin] from being seen as the first man-bashing feminist writer of this century."

Other essays deal more directly with power and female selfhood. Heather Kirk Thomas challenges the widely held belief that Chopin created few Black characters worthy of note by showing how Madame Sylvie of "Athénaïse" is a woman of true power, with confidence, wisdom, and business sense. No "stage darky," she is an impressive foil—indeed, a positive role model—to the naive and impractical Athénaïse. Power also resides in the word, and Nancy A. Walker looks at several Chopin stories, including "Athénaïse," "Miss Witherwell's Mistake," and "Elizabeth Stock's One Story," to show how the acts of reading and writing enabled Chopin to probe issues of women's selfhood while refusing "to privilege a masculine-identified discourse of intellectual analysis." Women's selfhood also concerns Kathryn Lee Seidel. She draws upon her knowledge of women's creativity and turn-of-the-century art to argue that the growth of Edna's selfhood in *The Awakening* is mirrored by the three stages of her own artwork: "her early mimetic work that reinforces the paternalistic values of her culture; her rebellious portraits; and her daring, original drawings that she creates after moving into her own house."

Finally, Priscilla Leder demonstrates how Chopin's most famous novel "incorporates elements of the major literary and intellectual movements of her century while consistently demonstrating their limitations. In doing so, she creates a work that is very much of the end of the century—at once part of it and looking beyond." Janus-faced, *The Awakening,* like Kate Chopin herself, is very much of the 19th century, and of today.

Notes

1.   Daniel S. Rankin, *Kate Chopin and Her Creole Stories* (Philadelphia: University of Pennsylvania Press, 1932). Per Seyersted, *Kate Chopin: A Critical Biography* (Baton Rouge: Louisiana State University Press, 1969). Emily Toth, *Kate Chopin* (New York: William Morrow, 1990). Toth's study was released in paperback (Austin: University of Texas Press) in 1993. Two other brief biocritical studies of Chopin are those of Barbara C. Ewell, *Kate Chopin* (New York: Ungar, 1986), and Peggy Skaggs, *Kate Chopin* (Boston: Twayne, 1985).

2.   Toth, *Kate Chopin,* 53.

3.   Quoted in Toth, *Kate Chopin,* 91.

4.   See Phyllis Vandlandingham, "Kate Chopin and Editors, 'A Singular Class of Men,' " in *Perspectives on Kate Chopin: Proceedings from the Kate Chopin International Conference* [April 6–8, 1989], ed. Grady Ballenger, Karen Cole, Katherine Kearns, and Tom Samet (Natchitoches, La.: Northwestern State University Press, 1992), 159–67.

5.   Kate Chopin, "Confidences," in *The Complete Works of Kate Chopin,* ed. Per Seyersted, foreword by Edmund Wilson, 2 vols. (Baton Rouge: Louisiana State University Press, 1969; one-volume hardcover edition, 1993), 700.

6.   Heather Kirk Thomas, " 'What Are the Prospects for the Book?': Rewriting a Woman's Life," in *Kate Chopin Reconsidered: Beyond the Bayou,* ed. Lynda S. Boren and Sara deSaussure Davis (Baton Rouge: Louisiana State University Press, 1992), 36–57. Thomas notes that Chopin's essay "Development of the Literary West," published in the *Sunday Magazine* book section of the *St. Louis Republic* on 9 December 1900, features a "watercolor portrait [of] a bespectacled, white-haired Chopin, painted by her artist son, Oscar. As this portrait represents the only known image of Chopin wearing eyeglasses, it may furnish another circumstantial clue that her eyesight was affected by her 1899 illness" (53). The text of this essay is reprinted in Thomas's " 'Development of the Literary West': An Undiscovered Kate Chopin Essay," *American Literary Realism, 1870–1910* 22(Winter 1990):69–75. The watercolor portrait is reproduced in Toth, *Kate Chopin,* facing page 273.

7.   Quoted in Toth, *Kate Chopin,* 278.

8.   "A St. Louis Novelist," *St. Louis Post-Dispatch,* October 5, 1890, 31. "Literary News," *St. Louis Republic,* 18 October 1890, 10; quoted in Toth, *Kate Chopin,* 191. "Recent

Publications," *New Orleans Daily Picayune,* 12 October 1890, 15; quoted in Toth, *Kate Chopin,* 192. "Recent Fiction," *The Nation* 53(1 October 1891):264.

9. "Bayou Folk," *The Critic,* 5 May 1894, 299–300. "The New Books," *New Orleans Daily Picayune,* 15 April 1894, 14. "Literary Notices. Recent Fiction," *Hartford Daily Courant,* 19 April 1894, 10.

10. "The New Books," *Review of Reviews* 9(May 1894):625. "Book Reviews," *Public Opinion* 17(12 April 1894):35. "The Book Table," *St. Louis Post-Dispatch,* 8 April 1894, 32; quoted in Toth, *Kate Chopin,* 228. William Schuyler, "Kate Chopin," *The Writer* 7(August 1894):115–17.

11. "Among the New Books," *St. Louis Post-Dispatch,* 11 December 1897, 4. "More Novels," *The Nation* 66(9 June 1898):447. "J. L. G." [Jeannette L. Gilder], "Mrs. Chopin's 'Night in Acadie,' " *The Critic* 29(16 April 1898):266.

12. "The vehemence of the critics' reactions to *The Awakening* and the subsequent near silencing of Chopin attest to the threatening power of Chopin's challenge to the cultural ideology. For each of the four attributes of true womanhood—piety, purity, submissiveness, and domesticity—Chopin created a subversive corollary through the character of Edna Pontellier and raised an alternative discourse on female identity and roles." See Cheryl L. Rose Jacobsen, "Dr. Mandelet's Real Life Counterparts and Their Advice Books: Setting a Context for Edna's Revolt," in *Perspectives on Kate Chopin,* 101–25; the quoted passage is from page 104. In a similar vein, Otis B. Wheeler argues that Edna "outraged most contemporary reviewers not because she committed adultery and subsequently destroyed herself . . . but rather because she so totally rejected the pervasive Victorian notion that sexual love is, or should be, a variety of religious experience. . . ." See "The Five Awakenings of Edna Pontellier," *The Southern Review* 11(January 1975):118–28. The quoted passage is from page 118.

13. Frances Porcher, "Kate Chopin's Novel," *The Mirror* 9(4 May 1899):6; reprinted in Kate Chopin, *The Awakening* ["A Norton Critical Edition"], 2d ed., ed. Margo Culley (New York: W. W. Norton, 1994), 162–63. "Mrs. Chopin's New Book Is the Story of a Lady Most Foolish," *St. Louis Republic,* 30 April 1899, Part IV (magazine), 11; quoted in Toth, *Kate Chopin,* 337.

14. "Recent Novels," *The Nation* 69(3 August 1899):96. "Notes from Bookland," *St. Louis Daily Globe-Democrat,* 13 May 1899, 5; reprinted in Culley, "Norton Critical Edition," 163. "Books of the Week," *Providence Sunday Journal,* 4 June 1899, 15.

15. Lucy Monroe, "Chicago's New Books," *Book News* 17(March 1899):387; reprinted in Toth, *Kate Chopin,* 491; excerpted in Culley, "Norton Critical Edition," 161. C[harles] L. Deyo, "The Newest Books," *St. Louis Post-Dispatch,* 20 May 1899, 4. "Books and Authors," *Boston Beacon,* 24 June 1899, 4; quoted in Toth, *Kate Chopin,* 348. "100 Books for Summer," *New York Times Saturday Review of Books and Art,* 24 June 1899, 408.

16. For a good sampling of contemporary reviews of *The Awakening,* see Culley, "Norton Critical Edition," 161–73.

17. "Aims and Autographs of Authors," *Book News* 17(July 1899):612. The statement is dated 28 May 1899. The text is reprinted in Toth, *Kate Chopin,* 344, and (with a facsimile of Chopin's autograph) in Culley, "Norton Critical Edition," 178.

18. Percival Pollard, *Their Day in Court* (New York: Neale Publishing, 1909; New York: Johnson Reprint, 1969), 41, 42, 45.

19. Fred Lewis Pattee, *A History of American Literature Since 1870* (New York: The Century, 1915), 364, 365.

20. Arthur Hobson Quinn, *American Fiction: An Historical and Critical Survey* (New York: D. Appleton-Century, 1936), 357. Joseph J. Reilly, "Stories by Kate Chopin," *The Commonweal* 25(26 March 1937):607. Interestingly, Reilly dropped the reference to gender when he edited this essay for inclusion in his *Of Books and Men* (New York: Julian Messner, 1942). The section on Chopin concludes, "From Kate Chopin's two volumes of short stories a modest book could be made containing half a dozen tales which her only American superiors in that

field would not disdain to own, a volume which those most proud of American literature would gladly proclaim an addition to its masterpieces" (136). Perhaps the book's publication during World War II, when women enjoyed higher status in society, would account for the shift in tone.

21. Cyrille Arnavon, "Les Débuts du roman réaliste américain et l'influence française," in *Romanciers Américains Contemporains,* ed. Henri Kerst (Paris: Didier, 1946); "Introduction," *Edna* (Paris: Le Club bibliophile de France, 1953); trans. Bjørn Braaten and Emily Toth, in *The Kate Chopin Miscellany,* ed. Per Seyersted and Emily Toth (Natchitoches, Louisiana: Northwestern State University Press, 1979), 168–88.

22. Van Wyck Brooks, *The Confident Years: 1885–1915* (New York: E. P. Dutton, 1952), 341. Robert Cantwell, *"The Awakening* by Kate Chopin," *The Georgia Review* 10(Winter 1956):494, 491, 491. Kenneth Eble, "A Forgotten Novel: Kate Chopin's *The Awakening,"* *Western Humanities Review* 10(Summer 1956):263, 269.

23. Edmund Wilson, *Patriotic Gore: Studies in the Literature of the American Civil War* (New York: Oxford University Press, 1962; reprint, New York: Farrar, Straus & Giroux, 1977), 591, 592, 590. Larzer Ziff, *The American 1890s: Life and Times of a Lost Generation* (New York: Viking, 1966), 300, 304.

24. Lewis Leary, "Introduction," *"The Awakening" and Other Stories by Kate Chopin* (New York: Holt, Rinehart and Winston, 1970), xv, xvii, x–xi.

25. Willa Cather ["Sibert"], "Books and Magazines," *Pittsburgh Leader,* 8 July 1899, 6; reprinted in Culley, "Norton Critical Edition," 170–72. Lawrence Thornton, *"The Awakening:* A Political Romance," *American Literature* 52(March 1980):51.

26. Charles W. Mayer, "Isabel Archer, Edna Pontellier, and the Romantic Self," *Research Studies* [Washington State University] 47(June 1979):88–97. Thomas Bonner, Jr., "Kate Chopin: Tradition and the Moment," in *Southern Literature in Transition: Heritage and Promise,* ed. Philip Castille and William Osborne (Memphis, Tenn.: Memphis State University Press, 1983), 143.

27. Rosemary F. Franklin, "Poe and *The Awakening,"* *Mississippi Quarterly* 47(Winter 1993–94):57. Antony H. Harrison, "Swinburne and the Critique of Ideology in *The Awakening,"* in *Gender and Discourse in Victorian Literature and Art,* ed. Antony H. Harrison and Beverly Taylor (DeKalb, Ill.: Northern Illinois University Press, 1992), 187, 186, 200.

28. Thomas Bonner, Jr., "Kate Chopin's European Consciousness," *American Literary Realism, 1870–1910* 8(Summer 1975):282. Kate Chopin, "As You Like It," *Collected Works,* 714. Cynthia Griffin Wolff, "Kate Chopin and the Fiction of Limits: 'Désirée's Baby,' " *Southern Literary Journal* 10(Spring 1978):126. Eliane Jasenas, "The French Influence in Kate Chopin's *The Awakening,"* *Nineteenth-Century French Studies* 4(Spring 1976):314, 313, 320.

29. Sandra M. Gilbert, "The Second Coming of Aphrodite: Kate Chopin's Fantasy of Desire," *Kenyon Review* N. S. 5(Summer 1983):46. Michael T. Gilmore, "Revolt Against Nature: the Problematic Modernism of *The Awakening,"* in *New Essays on "The Awakening,"* ed. Wendy Martin (New York: Cambridge University Press, 1988), 64.

30. Dieter Schulz, "Notes Toward a *fin-de-siècle* Reading of Kate Chopin's *The Awakening,"* *American Literary Realism, 1870–1910* 25(Spring 1993):70, 74. Robert D. Arner, "Kate Chopin's Realism: 'At the 'Cadian Ball' and 'The Storm,' " *The Markham Review* 2(February 1970):[3]. Ivy Schweitzer, "Maternal Discourse and the Romance of Self-Possession in Kate Chopin's *The Awakening,"* *boundary 2* 17(Spring 1990):158–86.

31. Donald A. Ringe, "Romantic Imagery in Kate Chopin's *The Awakening,"* *American Literature* 43(January 1972):582. Mayer, "Isabel Archer," 90. Virginia M. Kouidis, "Prison into Prism: Emerson's 'Many-Colored Lenses' and the Woman Writer of Early Modernism," in *The Green American Tradition: Essays and Poems for Sherman Paul,* ed. H. Daniel Peck (Baton Rouge: Louisiana State University Press, 1989), 115–34.

32. Harold Bloom, "Introduction," *Kate Chopin* ["Modern Critical Views"], ed. Harold Bloom (New York: Chelsea House, 1987), 1, 2. Kenneth M. Price, *Whitman and Tradition: The*

Poet in His Century (New Haven: Yale University Press, 1990), 114, 100. Bert Bender, "Kate Chopin's Quarrel with Darwin Before *The Awakening*," *Journal of American Studies* 26(August 1992):185–204; quoted passages are from pages 187, 188. Bert Bender, "The Teeth of Desire: *The Awakening* and *The Descent of Man*," *American Literature* 63(September 1991):459–73. Other essays examining the Chopin-Whitman connection include Lewis Leary, "Kate Chopin and Walt Whitman," *Walt Whitman Review* 16(December 1970):120–21; Gregory L. Candela, "Walt Whitman and Kate Chopin: A Further Connection," *Walt Whitman Review* 24(December 1978):163–65; and Elizabeth Balkman House, "*The Awakening*: Kate Chopin's 'Endlessly Rocking' Cycle," *Ball State University Forum* 20(Spring 1979):53–58.

33.   Dorys Crow Grover, "Kate Chopin and the Bayou Country," *Journal of the American Studies Association of Texas* 15(1984):34. Winfried Fluck, "Tentative Transgressions: Kate Chopin's Fiction as a Mode of Symbolic Action," *Studies in American Fiction* 10(Autumn 1982):157.

34.   Katherine Joslin, "Finding the Self at Home: Chopin's *The Awakening* and Cather's *The Professor's House*," in Boren and Davis, *Kate Chopin Reconsidered*, 167. Seyersted, *Kate Chopin*, 196.

35.   Martin Simpson, "Chopin's 'A Shameful Affair,'" *The Explicator* 45(Fall 1986): 59–60. Peggy Skaggs, "The Boy's Quest in Kate Chopin's 'A Vocation and a Voice,'" *American Literature* 51(May 1979):270–76. Arner, "Kate Chopin's Realism." Susan Wolstenholme, "Kate Chopin's Sources for 'Mrs. Mobry's Reason,'" *American Literature* 51(January 1980):540–43.

36.   Elaine Gardiner, "'Ripe Figs': Kate Chopin in Miniature," *Modern Fiction Studies* 28(Autumn 1982):379–82. Joyce Coyne Dyer, "A Note on Kate Chopin's 'The White Eagle,'" *Arizona Quarterly* 40(Summer 1984):189–92; "Symbolic Setting in Kate Chopin's 'A Shameful Affair,'" *Southern Studies* 20(Winter 1981):447–52; "The Restive Brute: The Symbolic Presentation of Repression and Sublimation in Kate Chopin's 'Fedora,'" *Studies in Short Fiction* 18(Summer 1981):261–65.

37.   Robert D. Arner, "Pride and Prejudice: Kate Chopin's 'Désirée's Baby,'" *Mississippi Quarterly* 25(Spring 1972):131–40. Wolff, "Kate Chopin and the Fiction of Limits." Ellen Peel, "Semiotic Subversion in 'Désirée's Baby,'" *American Literature* 62(June 1990):233.

38.   Bert Bender, "Kate Chopin's Lyrical Short Stories," *Studies in Short Fiction* 11(Spring 1974):257–66. Nancy S. Ellis, "Insistent Refrains and Self-Discovery: Accompanied Awakenings in Three Stories by Kate Chopin," in Boren and Davis, *Kate Chopin Reconsidered*, 216–29. Joyce Coyne Dyer, "Techniques of Distancing in the Fiction of Kate Chopin," *Southern Studies* 24(Spring 1985):69–81; "Night Images in the Work of Kate Chopin," *American Literary Realism, 1870–1910* 14(Autumn 1981):216–30; "Epiphanies Through Nature in the Stories of Kate Chopin," *University of Dayton Review* 16(Winter 1983–84):75–81.

39.   Patricia Hopkins Lattin, "Kate Chopin's Repeating Characters," *Mississippi Quarterly* 33(1979–80):21. Joyce Coyne Dyer, "Gouvernail, Kate Chopin's Sensitive Bachelor," *Southern Literary Journal* 14(1981):46–55.

40.   Donald A. Ringe, "Cane River World: Kate Chopin's *At Fault* and Related Stories," *Studies in American Fiction* 3(Autumn 1975):157–66. Bernard J. Koloski, "The Structure of Kate Chopin's *At Fault*," *Studies in American Fiction* 3(Spring 1975):89–95. Lewis Leary, "Kate Chopin's Other Novel," *Southern Literary Journal* 1(December 1968):60–74. Joyce Coyne Dyer, "Bright Hued Feathers and Japanese Jars: Objectification of Character in Kate Chopin's *At Fault*," *Revue de Louisiane / Louisiana Review* 9(Summer 1980):27–35.

41.   Martha Fodaski Black, "The Quintessence of Chopinism," in Boren and Davis, *Kate Chopin Reconsidered*, 113. Gilbert, "The Second Coming of Aphrodite." Schweitzer, "Maternal Discourse." Marilyn Hoder-Salmon, *Kate Chopin's "The Awakening": Screenplay as Interpretation* (Gainesville: University Press of Florida, 1992), esp. 129.

42.   Robert White, "Inner and Outer Space in *The Awakening*," *Mosaic* 17(Winter 1984):97–109. Suzanne W. Jones, "Place, Perception and Identity in *The Awakening*," *Southern*

Quarterly 25(Winter 1987):108–19. Anne Rowe, "New Orleans as Metaphor: Kate Chopin," in *Literary New Orleans: Essays and Meditations,* ed. Richard S. Kennedy (Baton Rouge: Louisiana State University Press, 1992), 36–37.

43. Paula A. Treichler, "The Construction of Ambiguity in *The Awakening:* A Linguistic Analysis," in *Kate Chopin: "The Awakening."* Case Studies in Contemporary Criticism, ed. Nancy A. Walker (Boston: Bedford Books of St. Martin's Press, 1993), 308. Emily Toth, "The Independent Woman and 'Free' Love," *Massachusetts Review* 16(Autumn 1975):659. Patricia S. Yaeger, " 'A Language Which Nobody Understood': Emancipatory Strategies in *The Awakening,*" *Novel* 20(Spring 1987):211. Jean Wyatt, *Reconstructing Desire: The Role of the Unconscious in Women's Reading and Writing* (Chapel Hill: University of North Carolina Press, 1990), 65, 64, 72.

44. Joseph R. Urgo, "A Prologue to Rebellion: *The Awakening* and the Habit of Self-Expression," *Southern Literary Journal* 20(Fall 1987):22–23. Price, *Whitman and Tradition,* 118.

45. Peter Conn, *The Divided Mind: Ideology and Imagination in America, 1898–1917* (New York: Cambridge University Press, 1983). Conn states that "Edna defines neither the illusions from which she recoils nor the conception of herself that is to follow her release from them. She does not define these things because she cannot; and the rest of the novel in a sense merely tracks the fatal consequences of that inability" (166). Sam B. Girgus, *Desire and the Political Unconscious in American Literature: Eros and Ideology* (New York: St. Martin's Press, 1990), 143. Ruth Sullivan and Stewart Smith, "Narrative Stance in Kate Chopin's *The Awakening,*" *Studies in American Fiction* 1(Spring 1973):65, 67.

46. Sullivan and Smith, "Narrative Stance," 63. Pat Shaw, "Putting Audience in Its Place: Psychosexuality and Perspective Shifts in *The Awakening,*" *American Literary Realism, 1870–1910* 23(Fall 1990):62–63. Dorothy Goldman, "Kate Chopin's *The Awakening:* 'Casting Aside that Fictitious Self,' " in *The Modern American Novella,* ed. A. Robert Lee (New York: St. Martin's Press, 1989), 62. Elaine Showalter, "Tradition and the Female Talent: *The Awakening* as a Solitary Book," in Martin, *New Essays,* 47.

47. Goldman, " 'Casting Aside,' " 56. Cristina Giorcelli, "Edna's Wisdom: A Transitional and Numinous Merging," in Martin, *New Essays,* 120. Goldman, " 'Casting Aside,' " 56.

48. Sullivan and Smith, "Narrative Stance," 73. Conn, *The Divided Mind,* 163–64. Fluck, "Tentative Transgressions," 169. Paula S. Berggren, " 'A Lost Soul': Work without Hope in *The Awakening,*" *Regionalism and the Female Imagination* 3(Spring 1977):1–7. Girgus, *Desire,* 140.

49. Thornton, "Political Romance," 62, 51. George M. Spangler, "Kate Chopin's *The Awakening:* A Partial Dissent," *Novel* 3(Spring 1970):254. Nancy Walker, "Feminist or Naturalist: The Social Context of Kate Chopin's *The Awakening,*" *Southern Quarterly* 17(Winter 1979):100, 101, 103.

50. Anne Goodwyn Jones, *Tomorrow Is Another Day: The Woman Writer in the South, 1859–1936* (Baton Rouge: Louisiana State University Press, 1981), 182. Penelope A. LeFew, "Edna Pontellier's Art and Will: The Aesthetics of Schopenhauer in Kate Chopin's *The Awakening,*" in Ballenger et al., *Perspectives on Kate Chopin,* 76, 82.

51. Mylène Dressler, "Edna Under the Sun: Throwing Light on the Subject of *The Awakening,*" *Arizona Quarterly* 48(Autumn 1992):60.

52. Beth Ann Bassein, *Women and Death: Linkages in Western Thought and Literature* (Westport, Conn.: The Greenwood Press, 1984), 114, 115. Robert S. Levine, "Circadian Rhythms and Rebellion in Kate Chopin's *The Awakening,*" *Studies in American Fiction* 10(Spring 1982):78, 79. Urgo, "Prologue," 23. Gilbert, "The Second Coming of Aphrodite," 58 (Gilbert's italics).

53. Bassein, *Women and Death,* 115. Kenneth M. Rosen, "Kate Chopin's *The Awakening:* Ambiguity as Art," *Journal of American Studies* 5(August 1971):197–99. Joseph L. Candela, Jr., "The Domestic Orientation of American Novels, 1893–1913," *American Literary Realism, 1870–1910* 13(Spring 1980):7. Katherine Kearns, "The Nullification of Edna Pontellier,"

American Literature 63(March 1991):88. Andrew Delbanco, "The Half-Life of Edna Pontellier," in Martin, *New Essays,* 91–92.

54.　Hugh J. Dawson, "Kate Chopin's *The Awakening:* A Dissenting Opinion," *American Literary Realism, 1870–1910* 26(Winter 1994):2, 7, 17. Bloom, "Introduction," 1. Walker, "Feminist or Naturalist," 103, 95. Priscilla Allen, "Old Critics and New: The Treatment of Chopin's *The Awakening,*" in *The Authority of Experience: Essays in Feminist Criticism,* ed. Arlyn Diamond and Lee R. Edwards (Amherst: University of Massachusetts Press, 1977), 238.

55.　Dorothy H. Jacobs, "*The Awakening:* A Recognition of Confinement," in Boren and Davis, *Kate Chopin Reconsidered,* 93. Berggren, " 'A Lost Soul.' " Gilmore, "Revolt Against Nature," 67.

56.　Ringe, "Romantic Imagery," 584. Kathleen Margaret Lant, "The Siren of Grand Isle: Adèle's Role in *The Awakening,*" *Southern Studies* 23(Summer 1984):167–75. Kathryn Lee Seidel, "Art is an Unnatural Act: Homoeroticism, Art, and Mademoiselle Reisz in *The Awakening,*" in Ballenger et al., *Perspectives on Kate Chopin,* 85–100; a revised version of this essay appears in *Mississippi Quarterly* 46(Spring 1993):199–214. Delbanco, "The Half-Life," 106, 104. Rosemary F. Franklin, "*The Awakening* and the Failure of Psyche," *American Literature* 56(December 1984):526.

57.　Helen Taylor, *Gender, Race, and Region in the Writings of Grace King, Ruth McEnery Stuart, and Kate Chopin* (Baton Rouge: Louisiana State University Press, 1989), 157. Bender, "Kate Chopin's Quarrel with Darwin," 190. Eunice Manders, "Kate Chopin's 'Wretched Freeman,' " in *Perspectives on Kate Chopin,* 37–45.

58.　Michele A. Birnbaum, " 'Alien Hands': Kate Chopin and the Colonization of Race," *American Literature* 66(June 1994):304, 303. Anna Shannon Elfenbein, *Women on the Color Line: Evolving Stereotypes and the Writings of George Washington Cable, Grace King, Kate Chopin* (Charlottesville: University Press of Virginia, 1989), 150.

59.　John Carlos Rowe, "The Economics of the Body in Kate Chopin's *The Awakening,*" in Boren and Davis, *Kate Chopin Reconsidered,* 117–42; a revised version of this essay appears in Ballenger et al., *Perspectives on Kate Chopin,* 1–24. Doris Davis, "*The Awakening:* The Economics of Tension," in Boren and Davis, *Kate Chopin Reconsidered,*" 143–53; a revised version of this essay appears in Ballenger et al., *Perspectives on Kate Chopin,* 127–37. Margit Stange, "Personal Property: Exchange Value and the Female Self in *The Awakening,*" in Walker, "Case Studies," 201–17.

60.　Walker, "Feminist or Naturalist," 101, 99. Girgus, *Desire,* 146.

61.　Thornton, "A Political Romance," 51–52.

62.　Chopin, *The Awakening, Collected Works,* 900.

63.　Conn, *The Divided Mind,* 163. Cynthia Griffin Wolff, "Thanatos and Eros: Kate Chopin's *The Awakening,*" *American Quarterly* 25(October 1973):454. Joyce Coyne Dyer, "Kate Chopin's Sleeping Bruties," *The Markham Review* 10(Fall/Winter 1980–81):10–15. Gina M. Burchard, "Kate Chopin's Problematical Womanliness: The Frontier of American Feminism," *Journal of the American Studies Association of Texas* 15(1984):35–45. Wolff, "Thanatos and Eros," 450. As Wendy Martin notes, Edna "is not a 'mother-woman,' nor is she a woman warrior. Instead, as her name suggests, she is 'one who bridges'—Pontellier—the traditional affiliative, instrumental, feminine mode and the aggressive, autonomous ideals of the new woman" ("Introduction," *New Essays,* 25).

CONTEMPORARY REVIEWS

◆

At Fault

A St. Louis Novelist.
At Fault, Mrs. Kate Chopin's New Novel.

—

Part of the Scenes Are in St. Louis
and the Characters St. Louisans . . .

—

The most recent plunge into fiction by a local writer is that of Mrs. Kate Chopin, several of whose short stories have been published in the SUNDAY POST-DISPATCH. Her initial effort as a novelist is entitled, "At Fault," and a great deal of the domestic drama set forth in it has St. Louis as its stage setting. Many of its allusions are local, and several of the principal characters are St. Louisans, so that the story is essentially a local one, and will thus prove of unusual interest to residents of the city. The action of "At Fault" turns upon a mistaken idea. David Hosmer, who hails from St. Louis, is a rugged and strong-willed but high-strung and nervous man, who has made an unfortunate marriage, lured thereto by a bundle of feminine weaknesses which by so many strong men are mistaken for indications of womanly character. After several years of wedded misery, during which his wife took to drink, he was forced, or thought he was forced, to separate from her. When she sued for a divorce he interposed no obstacle, and doubled the alimony which was granted her. He plunges into business, which absorbs his whole attention. In furtherance of one of his projects he goes South, where he meets Mrs. Therese Lafirme, a widow of five years—a woman in every respect the opposite of his former wife, highly bred, cultivated, with a knowledge of the world and of affairs seldom possessed by woman, tempered withal by womanly dignity and refinement of character—all uniting to attract a man of Hosmer's stamp in the maturity of his character, and to whom he was a figure of unusual interest. He declares his love and tells his story, but loving him as only such a woman can love, she bids him go back to his wife and reclaim her. He rejects her arguments, but does her bidding, because to obey her is the dearest privilege of his life. He remarries his wife and takes her to the Louisiana planta-

Reprinted from the *St. Louis Post-Dispatch*, 5 October 1890, 31.

tion, where Therese befriends her. But she cannot be reclaimed. Weak, vulgar, commonplace, she resents the friendship of the better woman and soon falls into her old ways. Hosmer's life is more miserable than ever, and Therese's is not less so [o]n seeing the misery she has wrought by her injudicious efforts at duty doing. But Fanny's life is brought to a sudden close, her death being the direct consequence of her thirst for liquor.

Mrs. Chopin has shown in this, her first venture as a novelist, that she has the qualities of a successful fictionist. She has avoided the temptations which beset the path even of experienced writers, and has made herself a place in the literature of the West. Setting out to write a novel, she has written it with no other purpose apparently than to tell the story well. The story suggests its own moral. Mrs. Chopin exhibits more than usual consideration for the reader in keeping her own opinions in the background and letting the situation depend upon its own eloquence for its moral effect. She does not always succeed, but her opinions must be sought in the dialogue, not in the narrative. It is not apparent that she is animated by anything but a deep interest in a deeply interesting situation. It does not appear that she wants to point a moral or indicate a "tendency," but she has cleverly succeeded in displaying a human group charged with suggestion and meaning. And she is equally happy in the management of the plot. It works itself out by the force of its own vitality. With true artistic instinct Mrs. Chopin has kept her hands off the sequence. The procession of events is the natural and necessary outcome of circumstance and character. Even in compassing Fanny's death—the point where under a less clever hand, nature might have been supplanted by mechanism, there is nothing artificial. Indeed, this episode in its preparation and accomplishment is the cleverest exhibition of

ARTISTIC SKILL

in the whole book.

In the fortunes of Gregoire and the whims of Melicent are found materials for a parallel thread, which is woven skillfully into the thread of the main story. These two characters, one a nephew of Mrs. Lafirme, the other Hosmer's sister, are charming in the unaffected naturalness. And there are delightful gleams of plantation life. Happily there is not much dialect, but there is enough to give a relish to the story. Only an instructive and unconscious observer could portray the negro characteristics so faithfully and vividly. Full of humor are the conversations of the darky servants who serve Therese so devotedly—a humor not always perceptible, broad as it is, to the ordinary Northern observer. And the burning of the mill, with its attendant accessories of superstition and death, is a good example of realistic and dramatic power.

The author of "At Fault" does not believe in making people over, sadly in need though they may be of a regenerating process. Indeed, her matter of fact way of taking things and people as they are is sometimes exasperating to a reader who has got into the habit of dreaming of things as he would like to have them. One shudders at hearing Hosmer tell his wife to "shut up," and we protest against Melicent's five engagements. If she really was engaged five times it ought not to be mentioned. We have no objection to realism when applied to Belle Worthington and Lou Dawson, but in the name of an effete prejudice we object to a man like Hosmer saying "shut up."

Altogether Mrs. Chopin has produced a novel which St. Louis can be proud of. The faults of detail which now and then crop out, are not owing to lack of natural skill, but to a want of cunning of hand, which comes with practice, and even these faults are trivial. The story is interesting for itself. To those who like to moralize there is a pretty question of morality put in the remarriage of a divorced couple under the influence of a mistaken sense of duty. Therese acknowledged that her judgment was at fault and before the end comes[,] sees clearly enough that duty cannot be so well-defined by a procrustean code as by individual intelligence applied to individual needs, that moral conditions do not result from good intentions unless the good intentions are rationalized by a good intelligence. In this feature Mrs. Chopin has offered her readers food for speculation—perhaps without intending it. But with whatever mind the book is read it cannot fail to interest, and St. Louis people may be congratulated on having one among them who promises to rival the fame of Miss [Mary Noailles] Murfree.

[From "Recent Fiction"]

It is not quite clear who is cast for the title-rôle in "At Fault," since all the characters have valid pretensions to the part. There is the lady who drinks and the gentleman who gets a divorce from her, the widow who loves and is beloved by him, but who persuades him to remarry his divorced partner and bring her to the Louisiana plantation, where she (the widow) may have a fostering care of the two and help them do their duty to each other. There is also the young lady of many engagements, the negro who commits arson, the young gentleman who shoots him, the Colonel who shoots the young gentleman, the St. Louis lady who goes to matinées and runs off with the matinée-going gentleman. It may not be amiss, in deciding who is "At Fault," to consider as well the claims of the author, the publisher, and the reader. The reverse side to all this is a graphic description of life on a cotton plantation, an aptitude for seizing dialects of whites and blacks alike, no little skill in perceiving and defining character, and a touch which shows that the array of disagreeables was born rather of literary crudity than of want of refinement.

Reprinted from *The Nation* 53 (1 October 1891): 264.

Bayou Folk

BAYOU FOLK

The bayous of Louisiana are among the most characteristic features of its watery landscape—deep gullies or miniature canyons through which a stream, now sluggish, now abundant, now almost invisible, flows beneath huge overhanging trees draped in funereal *barbe espagnole,* the Spanish moss of the tropics. They are the abodes of humidity, shadiness, shy sylvan life, the terrifying alligator, the cane-brake, the melodious mosquito. Along these Acherontian streams used to wander the Chacta Indians, and villages of them may still be seen here and there, while the silent *pirogue* or the 'Cadjen *bâteau* steals over the sombre waters and occasionally scares up a dazzling heron, a whirring *poule d'eau* or a flashing "parrokeet."

It is the folk that inhabit these taciturn wildernesses that Miss (?) Chopin introduces to us in her unpretentious, unheralded little book. She is evidently familiar at first hand with the illiterate Creoles, the old broken-down plantations, the queer *patois* people, the bayou landscapes to which she leads us in these simple tales, whose very simplicity increases their verisimilitude and makes in some cases a powerful impression on the imagination. She takes Middle-Upper Louisiana, as distinct from 'Cadjen country and New Orleans, as the scene of her little dramas, and reproduces for us, often very realistically and pathetically, the oddities in life and character which she has observed there. In her sheaf of twenty-three sketches some are like rude cartoons whose very rudeness brings out a more vivid effect, as in "Beyond the Bayou," "The Return of Alcibiade," "A Rude Awakening" and "For Marse Chouchoute." These are admirable little bits, as effective as a frontispiece by Castaigne. Others are flooded with more color, as "Désirée's Baby" and "Love on the Bon-Dieu." If we are not mistaken, Louisiana has another remarkable observer in this "unannounced" lady, whose keen eyes see even through the green glooms of her prairies and cane-brakes, and see things well worth bringing into the light. Personal familiarity with much of this unique region tells us that Miss Chopin's work is true to nature and often singularly dramatic in substance. There is not the languorous grace of Miss [Grace] King, or the subtlety of [George Washington] Cable, or the delicious humor of Ruth McEnery Stuart, but there is photographic realism, shrewdness of observation and a fine eye for picturesque situations: which is only saying that Miss Chopin is herself, and nobody else.

Reprinted from *The Critic* 21 (5 May 1894): 299–300.

[From "The New Books"]

This charming work contains some twenty-three little sketches, delightful pictures, every one of Creole life and character. It is something that the author is evidently familiar with, the life of the native of Louisiana, especially in the country, and she knows the country well and describes it charmingly, but the great charm of the book, besides its fluent, easy style, is the tender appreciation of the people of whom it treats. Their little prejudices[,] their inherited traits, their insular manners and customs, are all brought out, and in a delicate, appreciative way, that will make the author popular throughout the state. It is a book well worth reading, and very pleasant to read. The tales are delightful in themselves, [even] if they had no meaning but what they carry on their face.

Reprinted from the *New Orleans Daily Picayune*, 15 April 1894, 14.

[From "Literary Notices. Recent Fiction."]

In Kate Chopin's ["]Bayou Folk," we get another of those collections of short tales which are fast enriching American literature by furnishing faithful, artistic transcripts of picturesque local life. These Louisiana sketches with their intimate knowledge of Creole, darkey and Southern white, their quaint dialogue and romance among unsophisticate [*sic*] forms of life, are very charming in themselves and will be in time of value as historic documents, just as the work of [Grace] King, [Thomas Nelson] Page, [Joel Chandler] Harris and [Ruth McEnery] Stuart will be. The volume contains over twenty sketches and its special value lies in the fact that it deals successfully with that 'Cadian country which is comparatively terra incognita to the fictionist.

Reprinted from the *Hartford Daily Courant*, 19 April 1894, 10.

[From "The New Books"]

This is decidedly one of the best volumes of short stories which has appeared for some time. It deals in a very realistic way and with intimate knowledge of various aspects of creole and negro life in Louisiana, mainly in the Natchitoches region near the central part of the State. The narrative is largely in dialect and of sufficient variety of sentiment to make interesting reading throughout. The length of the pieces is all the way from a two-page episode to the opening story, "A No-Account Creole," which occupies some fifty pages. The chapters are exceedingly direct and written simply, without comment. They might remind some readers of certain of finished bits of Maupassant and other French "short story" masters.

Reprinted from *Review of Reviews* 9 (May 1894): 625.

[FROM "BOOK REVIEWS"]
BAYOU FOLK

Kate Chopin has given us in this volume more than twenty delightful short stories, full of the flavor of quaint and picturesque life among the creole folk of the Louisiana bayous. The author is thoroughly at home in this field and thoroughly familiar with creole character, and she has a fresh and lively style of delineating it. Romance, pathos, humor, nobility and meanness, weakness and strength, are so mingled and shaded as to produce most pleasing and artistic effects. And best of all, the threads are so woven in that the close of the story leaves an agreeable impression—things come out right. This volume will but sharpen the appetite of the reader for more of the same kind.

Reprinted from *Public Opinion* 17 (12 April 1894): 35.

A Night in Acadie

"A great truth that is fast slipping away from us," says Agnes Repplier, in one of her charming essays, "is the absolute independence of art—art nourished by imagination and revealing beauty. This is the hand that gilds the grayness of the world; this is the voice that sings in flute tones through the silence of the ages."

Fortunately for all those who echo Miss Repplier's plaint, there are a few choice spirits still to be found in the world of literature who keep fast their hold upon this beautiful escaping art—who have no problems to unfold, no theories to expound, no fatal habit of imparting opinions—and among them must be ranked Kate Chopin. That simplicity is a chief characteristic of the highest art is a truth that has been proclaimed from Plato to Emerson and accepted by the sincerest literary workers from Montaigne to Maupassant, and simplicity is the quality that strikes the understanding reader most forcibly in reading each and all of Mrs. Chopin's delightful short stories. This simplicity and directness of treatment combined with an invariable verity of motive is borne in upon the consciousness of the reader from the very beginning of the story and produces a feeling of confidence similar to that felt at the beginning of a difficult aria by a singer of tried and assured powers. One feels that one is in the hands of an artist and that all is well. As the story proceeds[,] one smiles in indulgent sympathy with the simple loves and hopes of her lowly, single-hearted Creole folk; one trembles between laughter and tears over the mingled humor and pathos of their brief histories. As you pass from one story to another, each so different from the other in the conditions of life surrounding the actors, and yet all alike in their strict adherence to the finished literary method of the author, one is more and more moved to an enthusiasm of intellectual gratification over the assured touch, the perfect balance of values—to speak in painter language—the flashes of insight and the keen artistic sense that holds back the word too much.

In the many reviews of Mrs. Chopin's stories that have appeared[,] the merits most often dwelt upon have been her admirable handling of the patois of the Louisiana bayou country and her truthful delineation of the life of the Creoles and 'Cadians of that region. These are undoubted merits and Mrs. Chopin is happy in having chosen so interesting and picturesque a back-

Reprinted from the *St. Louis Post-Dispatch,* 11 December 1897, 4.

ground for her stories, but she has gifts as a writer that go deeper than mere patois and local description and to which any background would be but an incidental. Psychological truth can be found in everything she writes. She knows the characteristics of the black race through and through and strikes an elemental note now and then to prove it. I know of nothing that Joel Chandler Harris has written that so graphically expresses the mythical connection between the pure Congo African and the animate world of nature, as some of the passages from Mrs. Chopin's story "Tante Cat'rinette."

The whole story is most beautiful[,] both in its motive of self-sacrifice and in its artistic telling. And here I am moved to say a word about this motive of self-sacrifice and devotion that occurs in so many of Mrs. Chopin's stories. It is such simple, sincere and unconscious goodness in these delightful story-people, so unlike the snug [sic] complaisance of the Pharisee, or the sickly sentimentality of the organized charity worker, that one's faith in the better side of human nature is strengthened and renewed after each reading.

Take that humorously pathetic little story, "Ozeme's Holiday," where Ozeme starts out in holiday attire for a few days' pleasure and is constrained by the pure goodness of his heart to spend it in picking a poor negro woman's crop of cotton, which otherwise would be lost, and then the continual protest of his other self against his action and his quaint concealment of it. It is all very touching and entirely charming and human.

Then, there is Cavanelle! How one loves Cavanelle in his simple, unconscious devotion to the poor, delicate sister with her weak, pipe-like voice—and what a character study he is—a gem, a bit of literary art before the exquisite perfection of which one is ineffably content.

Perhaps only one other story in the collection of her last volume will match with this one in the delicacy and finish of its execution and the fine spiritual quality of self-sacrifice, which, as I have said before, enters so much into Mrs. Chopin's stories, and that is "Neg Creol." There is not space to quote from this exquisite vignette from the French market of New Orleans, but the story illustrates one of Mrs. Chopin's most characteristic literary touches—that of surprising the reader with a climax that is a veritable spiritual illumination. I know of no one, not even the writer whom she most suggests, Maupassant, who is so clever at this. It seems a pity to have to point it out—it is so subtly put. Chicot, the Neg Creol, has supported his old mistress during many years of poverty until her death, all the time keeping rigidly the secret of his miserable existence while boasting of the social grandeur of her family—the Boisdures. One might naturally suppose his faithfulness to end with death, but that was not Chicot's idea. "[']Look, Chicot![']" cried Matteo's wife, "[']Yonda go the fune'al. Mus' a be that a Boisdure woman we talken 'bout yes'aday.' But Chicot paid no heed. What was to him the funeral of a woman who had died in St. Philip street? He did not even turn his head in the direction of the moving procession. He went on scaling his red-snapper." Wonderful insight into the heart of woman is shown in the story of

"Athenaise," and the fact that Mrs. Chopin has not hesitated to use one of nature's hidden secrets for its motive, proves alike the freedom of her spirit and her sureness of herself. "A Respectable Woman" is full of psychological suggestion and of subtle, elusive meanings. It will probably tell different things to different people.

"At Cheniere Caminada" flashes a light into a human soul, revealing things that are seldom uncovered except by our contemned [sic] friends the decadents.

Here for motive is one of those passions that prompted Schopenhauer to speak of love as a "malevolent demon" and has given D'Annunzio the material for much of his subtlest human analysis. Mrs. Chopin, however, does not analyze—she grasps, suggests and passes on, leaving the story itself to present her case.

Deliciously wholesome is her humor, and in considering both the woman and the writer, I am reminded of that famous definition of the heroine in George Meredith's "Egoist," where he speaks of her as a "rogue in porcelain." Our "rogue in porcelain"—physically reminding one of Dresden—flashes many a witty thing, but none more roguishly than this, right into the face of Philistia. "But for all his 'advanced' opinions Gourvernail was a liberal-minded fellow; a man or woman lost nothing of his respect by being married." Now what may she mean by that? inquires your matter-of-fact person—but the "rogue" will never tell you.

To sum up in brief the qualities of Mrs. Chopin, the writer: She is an instructive psychologist and absolute mistress of art form. Her art is sincere, delicate and full of the human quality, without which art cannot be, for, according to Swedenborg, art is love. She is modern, universal and untrammeled by convention. She will do greater things than she has done, just as her second book, "A Night in Acadie," is greater than her first[,] "Bayou Folk." In the latter the grace and delicacy of her art is paramount; in the former an intellectual and spiritual quality is added that keeps one brooding long after the spell of charm has passed.

[From "More Novels"]

Kate Chopin tells a story like a poet, and reproduces the spirit of a landscape like a painter. Her stories are to the bayous of Louisiana what Mary Wilkins's are to New England, with a difference, to be sure, as the Cape jessamine is different from the cinnamon rose, but like in seizing the heart of her people and showing the traits that come from their surroundings; like, too, in giving without a wasted word the history of main crises in their lives. That Cape jessamine is sometimes a thought too heavy is perhaps inevitable in the heated South. But enough there is of artistic in the best sense to hold the reader from cover to cover, transported for the time to a region of fierce passions, medieval chivalry, combined with rags and bad grammar, a soft, sliding Creole accent, and the tragedies and comedies that loom with special meaning in a sparsely settled country.

Reprinted from *The Nation* 66 (9 June 1898): 447.

MRS. CHOPIN'S "NIGHT IN ACADIE"

"J.L.G." [JEANNETTE L. GILDER]

"A Night in Acadie" is the title-tale of a collection of short stories by Kate Chopin who, in "Bayou Folk," has already made us familiar with the simple, childlike southern people who are the subjects of her brief romances. "Athénaïse," the longest of the stories, is written with much delicacy and understanding of both man and woman, and is only marred by one or two slight and unnecessary coarsenesses. "Regret" is a charming story of an unmarried woman who is horrified at the descent of a family of young children on her loneliness, and is doubly lonely when they are gone. It would be as true of any kind-hearted, lonely old maid, no matter what dialect she spoke. "A Dresden Lady in Dixie" is a touching account of devotion and self-sacrifice on the part of an old negro; so is "Nég Créol"; and "Odalie Misses Mass" shows that the devotion was sometimes on the other side. All the stories are worth reading. The author is sympathetic and tender, and shows a knowledge of the human heart, young as well as old, as "Polydore" and "Mamouche" prove. She is never very exciting or dramatic; there is even a slight feeling after reading about six of the stories, that one has read something very like the seventh before; but to anyone who wants to be quietly and soothingly interested for an hour, they are to be recommended. A breath of warm summer air, the hum of insects and the scent of flowers seem to hover round the reader, and the pleasant, low-toned 'Cadian patois lingers in his ear. (Way & Williams.)

Reprinted from *The Critic* 29 (16 April 1898): 266.

[Review of *A Night in Acadie*]

"A Night in Acadie" contains twenty-one stories, or sketches, many of which have already appeared in print in eastern periodicals. The principal ones are entitled "Athenaise," "After the Winter," "Polydore," "At Cheniere Caminada," "Mamouche," "A Sentimental Soul," etc. In originality and interest, as well as in the quality and variety of material, these stories show no falling off from the standard set in Mrs. Chopin's previous book. In this, as elsewhere, she deals with the Creoles of southern Louisiana, traversing much the same field as that so successfully worked by Mr. [George Washington] Cable. Mrs. Chopin, however, has a keener insight into the character of the Creole than Mr. Cable, because she loves, as well as understands, them. She has much of Mr. Cable's literary ability, and more than his sympathy for the rude courage and self-abnegation of the Creole fisherfolk.

Reprinted from the *New Orleans Daily Picayune*, 26 December 1897, 9.

The Awakening

[FROM "RECENT NOVELS"]

"The Awakening" is the sad story of a Southern lady who wanted to do what she wanted to. From wanting to, she did, with disastrous consequences; but as she swims out to sea in the end, it is to be hoped that her example may lie for ever undredged. It is with high expectation that we open the volume, remembering the author's agreeable short stories, and with real disappointment that we close it. The recording reviewer drops a tear over one more clever author gone wrong. Mrs. Chopin's accustomed fine workmanship is here, the hinted effects, the well-expended epithet, the pellucid style; and, so far as construction goes, the writer shows herself as competent to write a novel as a sketch. The tint and air of Creole New Orleans and the Louisiana seacoast are conveyed to the reader with subtle skill, and among the secondary characters are several that are lifelike. But we cannot see that literature or the criticism of life is helped by the detailed history of the manifold and contemporary love affairs of a wife and mother. Had she lived by Prof. William James's advice to do one thing a day one does not want to do (in Creole society, two would perhaps be better), flirted less and looked after her children more, or even assisted at more *accouchements*—her *chef d'oeuvre* in self-denial—we need not have been put to the unpleasantness of reading about her and the temptations she trumped up for herself.

Reprinted from *The Nation* 69 (3 August 1899): 96.

[From "Books of the Week"]

Miss Kate Chopin is another clever woman, but she has put her cleverness to a very bad use in writing "The Awakening" (5). The purport of the story can hardly be described in language fit for publication. We are fain to believe that Miss Chopin did not herself realise what she was doing when she wrote it. With a bald realism that fairly out Zolas Zola, she describes the result upon a married woman, who lives amiably with her husband without caring for him, of a slowly growing admiration for another man. He is too honourable to speak and goes away; but her life is spoiled already, and she falls with a merely animal instinct into the arms of the first man she meets. The worst of such stories is that they will come into the hands of youth, leading them to dwell on things that only matured persons can understand, and promoting unholy imaginations and unclean desires. It is nauseating to remember that those who object to the bluntness of our older writers will excuse and justify the gilded dirt of these later days.

Reprinted from the *Providence Sunday Journal*, 4 June 1899, 15.

[FROM "THE NEWEST BOOKS"]

C[HARLES] L. DEYO

There may be many opinions touching other aspects of Mrs. Chopin's novel "The Awakening," but all must concede its flawless art. The delicacy of touch[,] of rare skill in construction, the subtle understanding of motive, the searching vision into the recesses of the heart—these are known to readers of "Bayou Folk" and "A Night in Acadie." But in this new work power appears, power born of confidence. There is no uncertainty in the lines, so surely and firmly drawn. Complete mastery is apparent on every page. Nothing is wanting to make a complete artistic whole. In delicious English, quick with life, never a word too much, simple and pure, the story proceeds with classic severity through a labyrinth of doubt and temptation and dumb despair.

It is not a tragedy, for it lacks the high motive of tragedy. The woman, not quite brave enough, declines to a lower plane and does not commit a sin ennobled by love. But it is terribly tragic. Compassion, not pity, is excited, for pity is for those who sin, and Edna Pontellier only offended—weakly, passively, vainly offended.

"The Awakening" is not for the young person; not because the young person would be harmed by reading it, but because the young person wouldn't understand it, and everybody knows that the young person's understanding should be scrupulously respected. It is for seasoned souls, for those who have lived, who have ripened under the gracious or ungracious sun of experience and learned that realities do not show themselves on the outside of things where they can be seen and heard, weighed, measured and valued like the sugar of commerce, but treasured within the heart, hidden away, never to be known perhaps save when exposed by temptation or called out by occasions of great pith and moment. No, the book is not for the young person, nor, indeed, for the old person who has no relish for unpleasant truths. For such there is much that is very improper in it, not to say positively unseemly. A fact, no matter how essential, which we have all agreed shall not be acknowledged, is as good as no fact at all. And it is disturbing—even indeli-

Reprinted from the *St. Louis Post-Dispatch,* 20 May 1899, 4.

cate—to mention it as something which, perhaps, does play an important part in the life behind the mask.

It is the life and not the mask that is the subject of the story. One day Edna Pontellier, whose husband has vaguely held her dear as a bit of decorative furniture, a valuable piece of personal property, suddenly becomes aware she is a human being. It was her husband's misfortune that he did not make this interesting discovery himself, but he had his brokerage business to think about and brokers deal in stocks, not hearts. It was Mrs. Pontellier's misfortune that another man revealed her to herself, and when the knowledge came it produced profound dissatisfaction, as often happens when love is born in a cage not of its own building. In the beginning she had no thought of wrongdoing, but resentment was hot and made her sullen. Robert Lebrun, whose heart was ensnared before he realized it, went away to Mexico to make money, which was quite the proper thing to do. It would have been the right thing had he gone before it was too late, for then he might have been only a shadowy dream in Edna's life, instead of a consuming reality. This made the poor woman still more discontented. She took to all sorts of foolish fancies to divert her mind. Her children did not help her, for she was not a mother woman and didn't feel that loving babies was the whole duty of a woman. She loved them, but said that while she was willing to die for them she couldn't give up anything essential for them. This sounded clever because it was paradoxical, but she didn't quite know what it meant. She dabbled with brush and canvas. Mademoiselle Reisz told her that to be an artist one must be courageous, to dare and defy. But, unhappily, Mrs. Pontellier was not courageous. So she was not an artist. Mademoiselle Reisz, who was a witch, and knew Robert and Edna better than they knew themselves, did not add, what was really in her mind, that to be a great sinner a woman must be courageous, for great sinners are those who sin for a pure, howbeit unlawful, motive. Edna was not courageous. So she was not a great sinner, but by and by she became a poor, helpless offender, which is the way of such persons— not good enough for heaven, not wicked enough for hell.

Mrs. Pontellier was prepared by unlawful love for unholy passion. Her husband was extinct so far as she was concerned, and the man she loved was beyond her power. She had no anchor and no harbor was in sight. She was a derelict in a moral ocean, whose chart she had never studied, and one of the pirates who cruise in that sea made her his prize. Robert might have saved her from ignoble temptation by supplying a motive for a robust sin, but he was in Mexico and the thought of him only deepened her discontent. The moment came and with it the man. There is always a man for the moment, sometimes two or three. So thought Mrs. Pontellier, and she grew dull with despair. Passion without love was not to her liking and she feared the future. If she had been a courageous woman she would have put away passion and waited for love, but she was not courageous. She let sensation occupy a vacant life, knowing the while that it only made it emptier and more hopeless.

So because she could not forget her womanhood, and to save the remnants of it, she swam out into the sunkissed gulf and did not come back.

It is sad and mad and bad, but it is all consummate art. The theme is difficult, but it is handled with a cunning craft. The work is more than unusual. It is unique. The integrity of its art is that of well-knit individuality at one with itself, with nothing superfluous to weaken the impression of a perfect whole.

[FROM "100 BOOKS FOR SUMMER"]

Would it have been better had Mrs. Kate Chopin's heroine slept on forever and never had an awakening? Does that sudden condition of change from sleep to consciousness bring with it happiness? Not always, and particularly poignant is the woman's awakening, as Mrs. Chopin tells it. The author has a clever way of managing a difficult subject, and wisely tempers the emotional elements found in the situation. Such is the cleverness in the handling of the story that you feel pity for the most unfortunate of her sex.

Reprinted from the *New York Times Saturday Review of Books and Art,* 24 June 1899, 408.

"The Awakening," by Kate Chopin, is a feeble reflection of [Paul Charles Joseph] Bourget, theme and manner of treatment both suggesting the French novelist. We very much doubt the possibility of a woman of "solid old Presbyterian Kentucky stock" being at all like Mrs. Edna Pontellier who has a long list of lesser loves, and one absorbing passion, but gives herself only to the man for whom she did not feel the least affection. If the author had secured our sympathy for this unpleasant person it would not have been a small victory, but we are well satisfied when Mrs. Pontellier deliberately swims out to her death in the waters of the gulf.

Reprinted from *Public Opinion* 26 (22 June 1899): 794.

BIOGRAPHICAL SKETCH (1894)

◆

KATE CHOPIN

WILLIAM SCHUYLER

Mrs. Kate Chopin, the author of "Bayou Folk," was born in St. Louis in the early 'fifties and, as can be readily calculated, is not the "young person" that many of her reviewers are bent on thinking her to be. This wrong impression of theirs regarding her, while it is in some respects flattering, is one which Mrs. Chopin seems anxious to correct. Her father was Thomas O'Flaherty, a native of Galloway, Ireland, and for many years a prominent merchant in St. Louis. Her mother was the daughter of Wilson Faris, a Kentuckian, and Athénaïse Charleville, a descendant of a Huguenot family which had settled in "Old Kaskaskia" in the early part of the eighteenth century. The predominance of Celtic and the presence of so much French blood in Mrs. Chopin's ancestry may account for the delicate and sensuous touch and the love of art for art's sake which characterize all her work, and which are qualities foreign to most Teutonic productions.

Her first childish impressions were gathered just before and during the war and in the latter days of slavery. Her father's house was full of negro servants, and the soft creole French and patois and the quaint darkey dialect were more familiar to the growing child than any other form of speech. She also knew the faithful love of her negro "mammy," and saw the devotion of which the well-treated slaves were capable during the hard times of the war, when the men of the family were either dead or fighting in the ranks of the "lost cause."

Mrs. Chopin's girlish friends remember well her gifts as a teller of marvellous stories, most of them the impromptu flashings of childish imagination; and her favorite resort was a step-ladder in the attic, where, wrapped in a big shawl in the winter, or in airy dishabille in the dog days, she would pore over the stacks of poetry and fiction which were stored there—the shelves of the library being reserved for solid and pretentious cyclopaedias and Roman Catholic religious works. She was not distinguished as a scholar during her rather irregular attendance at the convent school, as she preferred to read Walter Scott and Edmund Spenser to doing any sums or parsing stupid sen-

From *The Writer* 7 (August 1894): 115–17. Reprinted by permission of *The Writer.*

tences, and only during the last two years of her school life did she ever do any serious work. Her schoolmates say that her essays and poetic exercises were thought to be quite remarkable, not only by the scholars, but even by the sisters; and, perhaps, had Mrs. Chopin's environment been different, her genius might have developed twenty years sooner than it did.

But many things occurred to turn her from literary ambition. At seventeen she left school and plunged into the whirl of fashionable life, for two years being one of the acknowledged belles of St. Louis, a favorite not only for her beauty, but also for her amiability of character and her cleverness. She was already fast acquiring that knowledge of human nature which her stories show, though she was then turning it to other than artistic triumphs. She married Mr. Oscar Chopin, a wealthy cotton factor of New Orleans, a distant connection of hers, the Charlevilles having hosts of "cousins" in the Pelican state.

After spending some time in Europe with her husband, she passed the next ten years of her life in New Orleans, engrossed in the manifold duties which overpower a society woman and the conscientious mother of a large and growing family; for six children were born during that period. Toward the close of the decade, her husband gave up his business and removed to Natchitoches Parish, among the bayous of the Red River, to manage several plantations belonging to himself and his relatives. However, his life as a planter was short. He died in 1882, in the midst of the cotton harvest.

It was then that Mrs. Chopin, having rejected all offers of assistance from kindly relatives, undertook the management of her plantations and developed much ability as a businesswoman. She had to carry on correspondence with the cotton factors in New Orleans, make written contracts, necessitating many personal interviews with the poorer creoles, the Acadians, and the "free mulattoes," who raised the crop "on shares," see that the plantation store was well stocked, and sometimes even, in emergencies, keep shop herself. It was hard work, but in doing it she had the opportunity of closely observing all those oddities of Southern character which give so much life and variety to her pages.

In the midst of all her labors she still found time to keep up her reading, which she had never abandoned, but the subjects which now attracted her were almost entirely scientific, the departments of Biology and Anthropology having a special interest for her. The works of Darwin, Huxley, and Spencer were her daily companions; for the study of the human species, both general and particular, has always been her constant delight.

After a few years, when Mrs. Chopin had not only straightened out her affairs, but had put her plantations in a flourishing condition, she returned to her old home, and has ever since made St. Louis her residence.

Having led such a busy life on the plantation, she had learned how to economize her time, and all her social and household duties here, together with her reading, were not sufficient to occupy her mind. Then, urged by the advice of an intimate friend, who had been struck with the literary quality of some of her letters, she began to write, very diffidently at first and only for her friend's perusal, essays, poems, and stories. Finally, she dared to send her productions to the magazines. With the exception of one beautiful little poem, they were promptly returned. Mrs. Chopin contends that they were properly treated, having been, as she says, "crude and unformed." She did not, as an unappreciated genius, abuse the editors, but began to study to better her style. In order to aid her self-criticism she sold and even gave away her productions to local periodicals, and holds that she learned much from seeing her work in "cold type." She wrote a long novel, "At Fault," which was printed in St. Louis in 1890. In this somewhat imperfect work may be seen the germs of all she has done since. The story has some faults of construction, but the character drawing is excellent, and in the case of the young creole, "Grégoire Santien," faultless. During the following year she wrote a great number of short stories and sketches, which she sent about to different magazines, and the most of them were not returned as before. The *Youth's Companion, Harper's Young People,* and *Wide Awake* took all her children's stories, and the *Century Magazine* accepted "A No Account Creole," the longest tale in "Bayou Folk." This story appeared last January, after having been kept for about three years, and was the means of making Mrs. Chopin's name better known to the general public. In the mean time, other periodicals had accepted and published her work, which now numbers some sixty stories, and Houghton & Mifflin accepted the collection of twenty-three tales known as "Bayou Folk."

Mrs. Chopin has also written a second novel, which a few favored friends have been permitted to read, and which, in the estimation of some, is her very strongest work. It is to be hoped that it will soon see the light.

She is particularly favored in not being obliged to depend upon her writing for her livelihood. There is, consequently, no trace of hack writing in any of her work. When the theme of a story occurs to her she writes it out immediately, often at one sitting, then, after a little, copies it out carefully, seldom making corrections. She never retouches after that.

Personally, Mrs. Chopin is a most interesting and attractive woman. She has a charming face, with regular features and very expressive brown eyes, which show to great advantage beneath the beautiful hair, prematurely gray, which she arranges in a very becoming fashion. Her manner is exceedingly quiet, and one realizes only afterward how many good and witty things she has said in the course of the conversation.

While not pretending to be a student, she still keeps well informed of the leading movements of the age, and in literature she decidedly leans to the French school. She reads with pleasure Molière, Alphonse Daudet, and especially De Maupassant. Zola, in her opinion, while colossal in his bigness, takes life too clumsily and seriously, which is the fault she also finds with Ibsen. Americans, in their artistic insight and treatment, are, she thinks, well up with the French; and, with the advantage which they enjoy of a wider and more variegated field for observation, would, perhaps, surpass them, were it not that the limitations imposed upon their art by their environment hamper a full and spontaneous expression. Mrs. Chopin has little to say of the English workers. She treats rather condescendingly a certain class of contemporary English women writers, whose novels are now the vogue. She calls them a lot of clever women gone wrong, and thinks that a well-directed course of scientific study might help to make clearer their vision; might, anyhow, bring them a little closer to Nature, with whom at present they seem to have not even a bowing acquaintance. She has great respect for Mrs. Humphry Ward's achievements; but Mrs. Ward is, *au fond,* a reformer, and such tendency in a novelist she considers a crime against good taste—only the genius of a Dickens or a Thackeray can excuse it.

From time to time Mrs. Chopin returns to Natchitoches to look after her business affairs, and also to refresh her recollections of that land of creoles and 'Cadians. The people of Natchitoches always receive her enthusiastically, since they thoroughly endorse her artistic presentation of their locality and its population; for Mrs. Chopin is not, like most prophets, without honor in her own country.

CRITICISM BEFORE 1969

◆

[FROM *THEIR DAY IN COURT*]

PERCIVAL POLLARD

Another lady who proved to us that dear Thackeray's scruples no longer worried her sex was Kate Chopin. The book I have in mind was called "The Awakening." Like many others that may be named in these pages of mine, it is doubtless utterly forgotten; but it would be illogical for me to proclaim that we had a deal to thank the ladies for, if I had not the documents at hand to prove it.

Again this seemed a subject for the physician, not the novelist. So skillfully and so hardily does the book reveal the growth of animalism in a woman, that we feel as if we were attending a medical lecture. In the old days,—when men, mere men such as Balzac or Flaubert or Gautier, attempted this sort of dissection,—we were wont to sigh, and think what brutes they must be to suppose women made of this poor clay. Surely it was only the males who harbored thoughts fit only for the smoking-room; surely—but, Pouff! Kate Chopin dispelled those dreams; even had they really been possible with Amelie Rives, and "What Dreams May Come," already in circulation.

"The Awakening" asked us to believe that a young woman who had been several years married, and had borne children, had never, in all that time, been properly "awake." It would be an arresting question for students of sleep-walking; but one must not venture down that by-path now. Her name was *Edna Pontellier*. She was married to a man who had Creole blood in him; yet the marrying, and the having children, and all the rest of it, had left her still slumbrous, still as innocent of her physical self, as the young girl who graduates in the early summer would have us believe she is. She was almost at the age that Balzac held so dangerous—almost she was the Woman of Thirty—yet she had not properly tasted the apple of knowledge. She had to wait until she met a young man who was not her husband, was destined to tarry until she was under the influence of a Southern moonlight and the whispers of the Gulf and many other passionate things, before there began in her

Their Day in Court (New York: Neale Publishing, 1909), 40–45; reprint, Johnson Reprint Corporation, 1969. Every effort has been made to locate all persons having any rights or interests in the material published here. If some acknowledgments have not been made, their omission is unintentional and is regretted.

the first faint flushings of desire. So, at any rate, Kate Chopin asked us to believe.

The cynic was forced to observe that simply because a young woman showed interest in a man who was not her husband, especially at a fashionable watering-place, in a month when the blood was hottest, there was no need to argue the aforesaid fair female had lain coldly dormant all her life. There are women in the world quite as versatile as the butterfly, and a sprouting of the physical today need not mean that yesterday was all spiritual.

However, taking Kate Chopin's word for it that *Edna* had been asleep, her awakening was a most champagne-like performance. After she met *Robert Lebrun* the awakening stirred in her, to use a rough simile, after the manner of ferment in new wine. *Robert* would, I fancy, at any Northern summer resort have been sure of a lynching; for, after a trifling encounter with him, *Edna* became utterly unmanageable. She neglected her house; she tried to paint—always a bad sign, that, when women want to paint, or act, or sing, or write!—and the while she painted there was "a subtle current of desire passing through her body, weakening her hold upon the brushes and making her eyes burn."

Does that not explain to you certain pictures you have seen? Now you know how the artist came to paint them just like that.

All this, mind you, with *Robert* merely a reminiscence. If the mere memory of him made her weak, what must the touch of him have done? Fancy shrinks at so volcanic a scene. Ah, these sudden awakenings of women, of women who prefer the dead husband to the quick, of women who accept the croupier's caresses while waiting for hubby to come up for the week-end, and of women who have been in a trance, though married! Especially the awakenings of women like *Edna!*

We were asked to believe that *Edna* was devoid of coquetry; that she did not know the cheap delights of promiscuous conquests; though sometimes on the street glances from strange eyes lingered in her memory, disturbing her. Well, then those are the women to look out for—those women so easily disturbed by the unfamiliar eye. Those women do not seem to care, once they are awake, so much for the individual as for what he represents. Consider *Edna.* It was *Robert* who awoke her. But, when he went away, it was another who continued the arousal. Do you think *Edna* cared whether it was *Robert* or *Arobin!* Not a bit. *Arobin*'s kiss upon her hand acted on her like a narcotic, causing her to sleep "a languorous sleep, interwoven with vanishing dreams." You see, she was something of a quick-change sleep-artist: first she slept; a look at *Robert* awakened her; *Arobin's* kiss sent her off into dreamland again; a versatile somnambulist, this. Yet she must have been embarrassing; you could never have known just when you had her in a trance or out of it.

How wonderful, how magical those Creole kisses of *Arobin*'s must have been, if one of them, upon the hand, could send *Edna* to sleep! What might another sort of kiss have done? One shivers thinking of it; one has uncanny visions of a beautiful young woman all ablaze with passion as with a robe of fire. *Arobin,* however, had no such fears. He continued gaily to awake *Edna*— or to send her to sleep; our author was never clear which was which!—and it was not long before he was allowed to talk to her in a way that pleased her, "appealing to the animalism that stirred impatiently within her." One wonders what he said! It was not long before a kiss was permitted *Arobin.* "She clasped his head, holding his lips to hers. It was the first kiss of her life to which her nature had really responded. It was a flaming torch that kindled desire."

Ah, these married women, who have never, by some strange chance, had the flaming torch applied, how they do flash out when the right moment comes! This heroine, after that first flaming torch, went to her finish with lightning speed. She took a walk with *Arobin,* and paused, mentally, to notice "the black line of his leg moving in and out so close to her against the yellow shimmer of her gown." She let the young man sit down beside her, let him caress her, and they did not "say good-night until she had become supple to his gentle seductive entreaties."

To think of Kate Chopin, who once contented herself with mild yarns about genteel Creole life—pages almost clean enough to put into the Sunday school library, abreast of Geo. W. Cable's stories—blowing us a hot blast like that! Well, San Francisco, and Paris, and London, and New York had furnished Women Who Did; why not New Orleans?

"The black line of his leg moving in and out. . . ." Why, even that Japo-German apostle of plaquet-prose, Sadakichi Hartmann, did not surpass this when he wrote in his "Lady of the Yellow Jonquils": "She drew her leg, that was nearest to me, with a weavy graceful motion to her body. . . ."

It may seem indelicate, in view of where we left *Edna,* to return to her at once; we must let some little time elapse. Imagine, then, that time elapsed, and *Robert* returned. He did not know that *Arobin* had been taking a hand in *Edna*'s awakening. *Robert* had gone away, it seems, because he scrupled to love *Edna,* she being married. But *Edna* had no scruples left; she hastened to intimate to *Robert* that she loved him, that her husband meant nothing to her. Never, by any chance, did she mention *Arobin.* But, dear me, *Arobin* to a woman like that, had been merely an incident; he merely happened to hold the torch. Now, what in the world do you suppose that *Robert* did? Went away—pouff!—like that! Went away, saying he loved *Edna* too well to— well, to partake of the fire the other youth had lit. Think of it! *Edna* finally awake—completely, fiercely awake—and the man she had waked up for goes away!

Of course, she went and drowned herself. She realised that you can only put out fire with water, if all other chemical engines go away. She realised that the awakening was too great; that she was too aflame; that it was now merely Man, not *Robert* or *Arobin,* that she desired. So she took an infinite dip in the passionate Gulf.

Ah, what a hiss, what a fiery splash, there must have been in those warm waters of the South! But—what a pity that poor *Pontellier, Edna*'s husband, never knew that his wife was in a trance all their wedded days, and that he was away at the moment of her awakening! For, other men failing, there are, after all, some things that a husband is useful for, in spite of books like "The Awakening," and that other story of a disillusioned female polygamist, "Hermia Suydam." About the latter story I shall say nothing, since I prefer, later in my book, to consider its author, Gertrude Atherton, in her period of riper judgment and finer art. "Hermia Suydam" was an early indiscretion; it had not even as excuse such finished art as Edgar Saltus put into "Tristram Varick" and "Mr. Incoul"; it may have attracted attention, have aroused discussion; but as a bit of workmanship Mrs. Atherton must often, in later years, have wished that she had never written it. The most you can say for it is that it was a first—no, second—offense.

There was no such excuse for Kate Chopin. She was already distinguished for charming *contes* of Creole life. "The Awakening" was a deliberate case of pandering to what seemed the taste of that moment.

While it is the ladies for whom we have so far made way, you are by no means to suppose that we are not to leave them alone if our attention seem to distress them. They had much to say in that period of letters I am trying to ramble in; but they by no means committed all the crimes, or gathered all the laurels. They did not even have to themselves the field of eroticism; there were D'Annunzios and Le Galliennes and Saltuses who kept pace with them there. But there was undeniably a time, beginning with Mona Caird's inquiry: Is Marriage a Failure? when the ladies seemed to dominate the scene. They achieved, at any rate, this: they showed what women could write, and women read, in their efforts to attain those ambitions so loudly acclaimed by our newspapers: the best selling novels.

Stories by Kate Chopin

Joseph J. Reilly

Optimists like to believe that, in the long run, justice is accomplished in literary history, the unworthy dislodged, the truly great seated among their peers, the neglected called to their place in the sun. Among those last must be numbered that writer of mixed French and Irish stock, Kate Chopin, whose work includes two striking volumes of short stories, "Bayou Folk" (1894) and "A Night in Acadie" (1897). What Hamlin Garland did for the Middle West, Mary Wilkins Freeman for New England, Thomas Nelson Page for the middle South, and Miss [Mary Noailles] Murfree for the Tennessee mountain folk, Mrs. Chopin did for the dwellers along the sluggish marshy streams that meander among the sugar plantations of upstate Louisiana. Leaving New Orleans to Grace King and the pre-war days to G. W. Cable, she sought her material without distinction of class, and her people's knowledge of ante-bellum opulence was largely a tradition.

Mrs. Chopin, like H. C. Bunner, was a student of Maupassant. Her Celtic blood and romantic spirit rejected his icy cynicism and her human sympathy kept her point of view from the rigorous impersonality of his. But her innate talent for story-telling was enriched by studying his virtues and making them her own. Her beginnings are direct, almost laconic: her first sentence starts the reader off like a shot from a pistol; her endings are infallibly "right"; her descriptions[,] whether of things, nature or people, are done with a few sharp strokes; her characterizations are never blurred: her people are not names but three-dimensional and quick with life. And, finally, she mastered the secret of economy in words.

The important thing with Mrs. Chopin as with Maupassant is character rather than situation and, particularly, the response of men—and even more of women—to the passion of love. Maupassant's interest is in the blasé, the unsophisticated, when confronted by the ingenuous and unspoiled, while Mrs. Chopin's is in young men and women at the dawn of romantic passion. There are no elopements as in [Hamlin] Garland, no roués suddenly moved to a change of heart by pity or innocence as in [Bret] Harte, no parade of

From *The Commonweal* 25 (26 March 1937): 606–7. Copyright © *Commonweal;* reprinted by permission of *The Commonweal.*

bleak lives as in Mrs. Freeman, or of worn-out elderly ones, however pathetic or gracious, as in Grace King. The elderly are not excluded but youth is almost always at their side, softening their decline with tenderness, profiting by their experience, or implying the onward flow of life and its unquenchable hopes.

The young men and girls of Kate Chopin's tales are unspoiled. They have not toyed with their emotions until they become their victims nor are they afraid of the promptings of their hearts. They are not unduly introspective; they have no need to be, for their instincts, like homing birds, fly straight and true, even though they sometimes make pretense of fluttering away. Hence these girls are capable of simple and supreme loyalty which triumphs over everything but contempt and abuse. For them love is the great, the crucial and transfiguring experience, the door swinging open to whatever earthly paradise there be, glorified by the abiding satisfactions of the heart.

Mrs. Chopin touches passion with a deft hand. In the case of young women, she is sensitively aware of its revelations, its hesitancies, its fears, while she senses how deeply the young men are troubled by its bitter-sweet torment and bewildered by its divine illogic, and always she treats these things with a certainty and convincingness which owe as much to reverence as to art. Thus 'Polyte, young plantation storekeeper, half in love with Azèlie with the red curved lips, the "dark, wide, innocent, questioning eyes, and black hair plastered smooth back from the forehead and temples," discovers her one night stealing from his supplies. Shocked, he lets her go. "He sat for a long time motionless. Then, overcome by some powerful feeling that was at work within him, he buried his face in his hands and wept, his whole body shaken by the violence of his sobs. . . . After that 'Polyte loved Azèlie desperately. The very action which should have revolted him had seemed, on the contrary, to inflame him with love."

Of course Mrs. Chopin does not confine herself to this sole *motif* nor, when treating it, is she concerned with a single formula. Love dawns and its loyalties find expression in infinite ways; in recounting them she sometimes hints at twists of thought whose subtleties she, like Maupassant, leaves the reader to divine. Thus it is with 'Polyte, instanced above; thus it is with Madame Delile who, on the brink of eloping with the charming M. Sépincourt, learns of her husband's death in battle and at a stroke dismisses Sépincourt from her life and dedicates her youth and beauty to hallowing the memory of the dead.

These subtleties sometimes take another direction as with the middle-aged Mamzelle Fleurette, a sentimental soul strongly attracted to Lacodie, the perky little locksmith who comes to her shop each evening to buy a paper. She checks the feeling rigorously but when he dies and his widow remarries she feels that Lacodie has been forfeited to her and exultingly takes charge of his grave and hangs his picture in her room. Chicot, a half-starved, dull-witted old Negro, is faithful as a dog to an impoverished, worn-out old woman because she bears the adored family name of Boisduré. She dies: his loyalty experiences a curious recoil, abandoning her and centering itself in the large, vague glory of the name she bore. The withered form "was doubtless that of some Boisduré of *les Attakapas;* it was none of his." Tony Bocage, a giant boatman, smitten by Claire Duvigne, a city belle, is hired to take her for a pleasure row and on returning "is stirred by a terrible, an overmastering regret that he had not clasped her in his arms when they were out there alone, and sprung with her into the sea." He resolves not to miss a second chance. So Maupassant might have written, without elaborating on Tony's thoughts or curiously delving into his mind, content with a statement at once laconic and authoritative. But Tony's story in Mrs. Chopin's hands takes another turn into a new—and convincing—subtlety, fashioned to her own pattern, for she was a student of Maupassant's art, not of his psychology. When you finish the tale and learn of Tony's final contentment[,] your memory will recall certain poems of Browning, especially "Evelyn Hope" in which death does not quench but kindle the lovers' faith.

Maternal instinct provides the theme for some of the finest stories. We have it in Mme. Carambeau, long at feud with her son for marrying an American girl, in Mamzelle Aurélie, self-centered and middle-aged, who, on sending back home four children she has mothered for a fortnight, "let her head fall down upon her bended arm and began to cry. Not softly, as women often do. She cried like a man, with sobs that seemed to tear her very soul." Most notably this theme appears in the tale of Athenaïse who, scarcely out of school and married to the widower Cazeau, resents his having married her and hides away from him in a city *pension.* Passion, beauty, and exquisite understanding conspire with unerring characterizations and an ending poignantly tender and exquisitely right to make this story a masterpiece.

Only one of her tales outranks it, a tragedy miniature in proportions, overwhelming in effect, told in a bare 2,000 words, every one significant from the crisp opening sentence to the final closing one which matches O. Henry's "Furnished Room" in the suddenness of its surprise and in the irony and pathos of its devastating revelation. It is called "Désirée's Baby" and is one of the world's great short stories. All Mrs. Chopin's gifts are here in their perfection: directness of approach, sureness of touch, the swift strokes which give the setting and introduce and realize the characters, the amazing economy of words which even she never equaled and Maupassant never surpassed. In a sentence or two she probes the psychology of Désirée and her husband to the quick, after first opening the way by what seem to the unwary scarcely more than casual phrases. The sense of impending tragedy comes early (as it must in so brief a thing) with perfect naturalness and in the turn given a sentence by two words. It is deepened by the picture of Désirée's house where friends visit her and her baby: "The roof came down steep and black like a cowl, reaching out beyond the wide galleries that encircled the yellow stuccoed house. Big, solemn oaks grew close to it, and their thick-leaved, far-reaching branches shadowed it like a pall." As one reads, recollections of other short story masters arise, with whose power and skill in evoking the spirit of tragedy this perfect tale takes its place, Poe, Hawthorne and Thomas Hardy.

From Kate Chopin's two volumes of short stories a modest book containing a dozen tales could be made, which would be an enriching addition to our all-too-few masterpieces. She is incomparably the greatest American short story writer of her sex. Her work deserves wider appreciation. May it soon have proper recognition!

A Forgotten Novel: Kate Chopin's *The Awakening*

Kenneth Eble

When Kate Chopin's novel *The Awakening* was published in 1899, it made its mark on American letters principally in the reactions it provoked among shocked newspaper reviewers. In St. Louis, Mrs. Chopin's native city, the book was taken from circulation at the Mercantile Library, and though by this time she had established herself as one of the city's most talented writers, she was now denied membership in the Fine Arts Club. The St. Louis *Republic* said the novel was, like most of Mrs. Chopin's work, "too strong drink for moral babes and should be labeled 'poison.' " The *Nation* granted its "fine workmanship and pellucid style," but went on, "We cannot see that literature or the criticism of life is helped by the detailed history of the manifold and contemporary love affairs of a wife and mother."

After Mrs. Chopin's death in 1904, a story passed from the *Library of Southern Literature* through F. L. Pattee's *American Literature since 1870* and into the *Dictionary of American Biography* that Kate Chopin's brief writing career came to an abrupt end in her bitter disappointment over the reception of *The Awakening*. The story is false—her manuscript collection shows that she wrote six stories after 1900, three of which were published. But the implications are probably accurate. There is little doubt of the squeamishness of American literary taste in 1900, nor is there much doubt that Kate Chopin was deeply hurt by the attacks on the novel as well as on her own motives and morals. The stories she wrote thereafter lack distinction, and though *The Awakening* was reprinted by Duffield and Company in 1906, it is likely that the author's innocent disregard for contemporary moral delicacies ordained that it should be quickly forgotten.

Today, Kate (O'Flaherty) Chopin is chiefly remembered as a regional writer whose short stories of the Louisiana Creoles are usually compared with the work of George Washington Cable and Grace King. Her writing career is unusual for its brevity: it began in 1889 and ended with her death in 1904. She did not publish until she was thirty-nine, although it is apparent that in

First appeared in *Western Humanities Review* 10, no. 3 (Summer 1956): 261–69. Reprinted by permission of *Western Humanities Review* and James Eble, Executor of the Kenneth and Peggy Eble estate.

the preceding years she read widely and took some pride in her writing as well as in her discriminating tastes in music, art and literature. Given other circumstances, she might have developed into a writer early in her life. As it was, the talent she possessed was quite simply submerged as the result of an early and happy marriage and the raising of a sizable family.

She was born in St. Louis in 1851, educated in a convent school, moved to New Orleans when she married Oscar Chopin in 1870, and there became the mother of six children in the next ten years. She returned to St. Louis after her husband died in 1882, but her life in New Orleans and in Natchitoches Parish, where she lived for two years immediately before her husband's death, gave her most of her fictional material. Her husband's estate was small, and the O'Flaherty family estate had dwindled by the time of her mother's death in 1885. Left alone with a family to support, she may have turned seriously to writing because of a feeling of necessity. From 1889 until her death, her stories and miscellaneous writings appeared in *Vogue, Youth's Companion, Atlantic Monthly, Century, Saturday Evening Post,* and many lesser publications. Her books, in addition to *The Awakening,* are *At Fault* (1890), a novel, and two collections of stories and sketches, *Bayou Folk* (1894) and *A Night in Acadie* (1897).

Her present literary rank is probably somewhere between Octave Thanet (Alice French) and Sarah Orne Jewett. In the fifty years after her death, she has provoked two articles and a doctoral dissertation on her life and work.[1] Her own books are long out of print, and *The Awakening* is particularly hard to find. Their disappearance is not unusual; it is inevitable that much of a minor writer's work will be lost. What is unfortunate is that *The Awakening,* certainly Mrs. Chopin's best work, has been neglected almost from its publication.

The claim of the book upon the reader's attention is simple. It is a first-rate novel. The justification for urging its importance is that we have few enough novels of its stature. One could add that it is advanced in theme and technique over the novels of its day, and that it anticipates in many respects the modern novel. It could be claimed that it adds to American fiction an example of what Gide called the *roman pur,* a kind of novel not characteristic of American writing. One could offer the book as evidence that the regional writer can go beyond the limitations of regional material. But these matters aside, what recommends the novel is its general excellence.

It is surprising that the book has not been picked up today by reprint houses long on lurid covers and short on new talent. The nature of its theme, which had much to do with its adverse reception in 1899, would offer little offense today. In a way, the novel is an American *Bovary,* though such a designation is not precisely accurate. Its central character is similar: the married woman who seeks love outside a stuffy, middle-class marriage. It is similar too in the definitive way it portrays the mind of a woman trapped in marriage and seeking fulfillment of what she vaguely recognizes as her essential nature. The husband, Léonce Pontellier, is a businessman whose nature and preoccupations are not far different from those of Charles Bovary. There is a Léon Dupuis in Robert Lebrun, a Rodolphe Boulanger in Alcée Arobin. And too, like *Madame Bovary,* the novel handles its material superbly well. Kate Chopin herself was probably more than any other American writer of her time under French influence. Her background was French-Irish; she married a Creole; she read and spoke French and knew contemporary French literature well; she associated both in St. Louis and Louisiana with families of French ancestry and disposition. But despite the similarities and the possible influences, the novel, chiefly because of the independent character of its heroine, Edna Pontellier, and because of the intensity of the focus upon her, is not simply a good but derivative work. It has a manner and matter of its own.

Quite frankly, the book is about sex. Not only is it about sex, but the very texture of the writing is sensuous, if not sensual, from the first to the last. Even as late as 1932, Chopin's biographer, Daniel Rankin, seemed somewhat shocked by it. He paid his respects to the artistic excellence of the book, but he was troubled by "that insistent query—*cui bono?*" He called the novel "exotic in setting, morbid in theme, erotic in motivation." One questions the accuracy of these terms, and even more the moral disapproval implied in their usage. One regrets that Mr. Rankin did not emphasize that the book was amazingly honest, perceptive and moving.

The Awakening is a study of Edna Pontellier, a story, as the *Nation* criticized it, "of a Southern lady who wanted to do what she wanted to. From wanting to, she did, with disastrous consequences." Such a succinct statement, blunt but accurate so far as it goes, may suggest that a detailed retelling of the story would convey little of the actual character of the novel. It is, of course, one of those novels a person simply must read to gain any real impression of its excellence. But the compactness of the work in narrative, characterization, setting, symbols and images gives meaning to such an imprecise and overworked expression. Some idea of the style may be conveyed by quoting the opening paragraphs:

> A green and yellow parrot, which hung in a cage outside the door, kept repeating over and over "*Allez vous-en! Allez vous-en! Sapristi!* That's all right."
>
> He could speak a little Spanish, and also a language which nobody understood, unless it was the mockingbird that hung on the other side of the door, whistling his fluty notes out upon the breeze with maddening persistence.
>
> Mr. Pontellier, unable to read his newspaper with any degree of comfort, arose with an expression and an exclamation of disgust. He walked down the gallery and across the narrow "bridges" which connected the Lebrun cottages one with the other. He had been seated before the door of the main house. The parrot and the mockingbird were the property of Madame Lebrun and they had the right to make all the noise they wished. Mr. Pontellier had the privilege of quitting their society when they ceased to be entertaining.

This is Mr. Pontellier. He is a businessman, husband and father, not given to romance, not given to much of anything outside his business. When he comes to Grand Isle, the summer place of the Creoles in the story, he is anxious to get back to his cotton brokerage in Carondelet Street, New Orleans, and he passes his time on Grand Isle at the hotel smoking his cigars and playing cards. When he is on the beach at all, he is not a participant, but a watcher.

> He fixed his gaze upon a white sunshade that was advancing at snail's pace from the beach. He could see it plainly between the gaunt trunk of the water-oaks and across the strip of yellow camomile. The gulf looked far away, melting hazily into the blue of the horizon. The sunshade continued to approach slowly. Beneath its pink-lined shelter were their faces, Mrs. Pontellier and young Robert Lebrun.

It is apparent that a triangle has been formed, and going into the details of the subsequent events in a summary fashion would likely destroy the art by which such a sequence becomes significant. Suffice to say that Robert Lebrun is the young man who first awakens, or rather, is present at the awakening of Edna Pontellier into passion, a passion which Mr. Pontellier neither understands nor appreciates. Slowly Edna and Robert fall in love, but once again, the expression is too trite. Edna grows into an awareness of a woman's physical nature, and Robert is actually but a party of the second part. The reader's attention is never allowed to stray from Edna. At the climax of their relationship, young Lebrun recognizes what must follow and goes away. During his absence, Mrs. Pontellier becomes idly amused by a roué, Arobin, and, becoming more than amused, more than tolerates his advances. When Robert returns he finds that Edna is willing to declare her love and accept the consequences of her passion. But Robert, abiding by the traditional romantic code which separates true love from physical passion, refuses the offered consummation. When he leaves Mrs. Pontellier, she turns once again to the scene of her awakening, the sand and sea of Grand Isle:

> The water of the Gulf stretched out before her, gleaming with the million lights of the sun. The voice of the sea is seductive, never ceasing, whispering, clamoring, murmuring, inviting the soul to wander in abysses of solitude. All along the white beach, up and down, there was no living thing in sight. A bird with a broken wing was beating the air above, reeling, fluttering, circling disabled down, down to the water.
>
> Edna had found her old bathing suit still hanging, faded, upon its accustomed peg.
>
> She put it on, left her clothing in the bath-house. But when she was there beside the sea, absolutely alone, she cast the unpleasant, pricking garments from her, and for the first time in her life she stood naked in the open air at the mercy of the sun, the breeze that beat upon her, and the waves that invited her.
>
> How strange and awful it seemed to stand naked under the sky! How delicious! She felt like some newborn creature, opening its eye in a familiar world that it had never known.

The foamy wavelets curled up to her white feet, and coiled like serpents about her ankles. She walked out. The water was chill, but she walked on. The water was deep, but she lifted her white body and reached out with a long, sweeping stroke. The touch of the sea is sensuous, enfolding the body in its soft close embrace. . . .

She looked into the distance, and the old terror flamed up for an instant, then sank again. Edna heard her father's voice and her sister Margaret's. She heard the barking of an old dog that was chained to the sycamore tree. The spurs of the cavalry officer clanged as he walked across the porch. There was the hum of bees, and the musty odor of pinks filled the air.

Here is the story, its beginning a mature woman's awakening to physical love, its end her walking into the sea. The extracts convey something of the author's style, but much less of the movement of the characters and of human desire against the sensuous background of sea and sand. Looking at the novel analytically, one can say that it excels chiefly in its characterizations and its structure, the use of images and symbols to unify that structure, and the character of Edna Pontellier.

Kate Chopin, almost from her first story, had the ability to capture character, to put the right word in the mouth, to impart the exact gesture, to select the characteristic action. An illustration of her deftness in handling even minor characters is her treatment of Edna's father. When he leaves the Pontellier's after a short visit, Edna is glad to be rid of him and "his padded shoulders, his Bible reading, his 'toddies,' and ponderous oaths." A moment later, it is a side of Edna's nature which is revealed. She felt a sense of relief at her father's absence; "she read Emerson until she grew sleepy."

Characterization was always Mrs. Chopin's talent. Structure was not. Those who knew her working habits say that she seldom revised, and she herself mentions that she did not like reworking her stories. Though her reputation rests upon her short narratives, her collected stories give abundant evidence of the sketch, the outlines of stories which remain unformed. And when she did attempt a tightly organized story, she often turned to Maupassant and was as likely as not to effect a contrived symmetry. Her early novel *At Fault* suffers most from her inability to control her material. In *The Awakening* she is in complete command of structure. She seems to have grasped instinctively the use of the unifying symbol—here the sea, sky and sand—and with it the power of individual images to bind the story together.

The sea, the sand, the sun and sky of the Gulf Coast become almost a presence themselves in the novel. Much of the sensuousness of the book comes from the way the reader is never allowed to stray far from the water's edge. A refrain beginning "The voice of the sea is seductive, never ceasing, clamoring, murmuring, . . ." is used throughout the novel. It appears first at the beginning of Edna Pontellier's awakening, and it appears at the end as the introduction to the long final scene, previously quoted. Looking closely at the final form of this refrain, one can notice the care with which Mrs. Chopin composed this theme and variation. In the initial statement, the sentence does not end with "solitude," but goes on, as it should, "to lose itself in mazes of inward contemplation." Nor is the image of the bird with the broken wing in the earlier passage; rather there is a prefiguring of the final tragedy: "The voice of the sea speaks to the soul. The touch of the sea is sensuous, enfolding the body in its soft close embrace." The way scene, mood, action and character are fused reminds one not so much of literature as of an impressionist painting, of a Renoir with much of the sweetness missing. Only Stephen Crane, among her American contemporaries, had an equal sensitivity to light and shadow, color and texture, had the painter's eye matched with the writer's perception of character and incident.

The best example of Mrs. Chopin's use of a visual image which is also highly symbolic is the lady in black and the two nameless lovers. They are seen as touches of paint upon the canvas and as indistinct yet evocative figures which accompany Mrs. Pontellier and Robert Lebrun during the course of their intimacy. They appear first early in the novel. "The lady in black was reading her morning devotions on the porch of a neighboring bath house. Two young lovers were exchanging their heart's yearning beneath the children's tent which they had found unoccupied." Throughout the course of Edna's awakening, these figures appear and reappear, the lovers entering the pension, leaning toward each other as the water-oaks bent from the sea, the lady in black, creeping behind them. They accompany Edna and Robert when they first go to the Chênière, "the lovers, shoulder to shoulder, creeping, the lady in black, gaining steadily upon them." When Robert departs for Mexico, the picture changes. Lady and lovers depart together, and Edna finds herself back from the sea and shore, and set among her human acquaintances, her husband; her father; Mme. [*sic*] Reisz, the musician, "a homely woman with a small wizened face and body, and eyes that glowed"; Alcée Arobin; Mme. Ragtinolle; and others. One brief scene from this milieu will further illustrate Mrs. Chopin's conscious or unconscious symbolism.

The climax of Edna's relationship with Arobin is the dinner which is to celebrate her last night in her and her husband's house. Edna is ready to move to a small place around the corner where she can escape (though she does not phrase it this way) the feeling that she is one more of Léonce Pontellier's possessions. At the dinner Victor Lebrun, Robert's brother, begins singing, "Ah! si tu savais!" a song which brings back all her memories of Robert. She sets her glass so blindly down that she shatters it against the carafe. "The wine spilled over Arobin's legs and some of it trickled down upon Mrs. Highcamp's black gauze gown." After the other guests have gone, Edna and Arobin walk to the new house. Mrs. Chopin writes of Edna, "She looked down, noticing the black line of his leg moving in and out so close to her against the yellow shimmer of her gown." The chapter concludes:

His hand had strayed to her beautiful shoulders, and he could feel the response of her flesh to his touch. He seated himself beside her and kissed her lightly upon the shoulder.

"I thought you were going away," she said, in an uneven voice.

"I am, after I have said good night."

"Good night," she murmured.

He did not answer, except to continue to caress her. He did not say good night until she had become supple to his gentle, seductive entreaties.

It is not surprising that the sensuous quality of the book, both from the incidents of the novel and the symbolic implications, would have offended contemporary reviewers. What convinced many critics of the indecency of the book, however, was not simply the sensuous scenes, but rather that the author obviously sympathized with Mrs. Pontellier. More than that, the readers probably found that she aroused their own sympathies.

It is a letter from an English reader which states most clearly, in a matter-of-fact way, the importance of Edna Pontellier. The letter was to Kate Chopin from Lady Janet Scammon Young, and included a more interesting analysis of the novel by Dr. Dunrobin Thomson, a London physician whom Lady Janet said a great editor had called "the soundest critic since Matthew Arnold." "That which makes *The Awakening* legitimate," Dr. Thomson wrote, "is that the author deals with the commonest of human experiences. You fancy *Edna's* case exceptional? Trust an old doctor—most common." He goes on to speak of the "abominable prudishness" masquerading as "modesty or virtue," which makes the woman who marries a victim. For passion is regarded as disgraceful and the self-respecting female assumes she does not possess passion. "In so far as normally constituted womanhood *must* take account of something *sexual*," he points out, "it is called love." But marital love and passion may not be one. The wise husband, Dr. Thomson advises, seeing within his wife the "mysterious affinity" between a married woman and a man who stirs her passions, will help her see the distinction between her heart and her love, which wifely loyalty owes to the husband, and her body, which yearns for awakening. But more than clinically analyzing the discrepancy between Victorian morals and woman's nature, Dr. Thomson testifies that Mrs. Chopin has not been false or sensational to no purpose. He does not feel that she has corrupted, nor does he regard the warring within Edna's self as insignificant.

Greek tragedy—to remove ourselves from Victorian morals—knew well *eros* was not the kind of *love* which can be easily prettified and sentimentalized. Phaedra's struggle with elemental passion in the *Hippolytus* is not generally regarded as being either morally offensive or insignificant. Mrs. Pontellier, too, has the power, the dignity, the self-possession of a tragic heroine. She is not an Emma Bovary, deluded by ideas of "romance," nor is she the sensuous but guilt-ridden woman of the sensational novel. We can find only partial reason for her affair in the kind of romantic desire to escape a middle-class existence which animates Emma Bovary. Edna Pontellier is neither deluded nor deludes. She is woman, the physical woman who, despite her Kentucky Presbyterian upbringing and a comfortable marriage, must struggle with the sensual appeal of physical ripeness itself, with passion of which she is only dimly aware. Her struggle is not melodramatic, nor is it artificial, nor vapid. It is objective, real and moving. And when she walks into the sea, it does not leave a reader with the sense of sin punished, but rather with the sense evoked by Edwin Arlington Robinson's *Eros Turannos*:

> . . . for they
>   That with a god have striven
> Not hearing much of what we say,
>   Take what the god has given;
> Though like waves breaking it may be,
> Or like a changed familiar tree,
> Or like a stairway to the sea
>   Where down the blind are driven.

How wrong to call Edna, as Daniel Rankin does, "a selfish, capricious" woman. Rather, Edna's struggle, the struggle with *eros* itself, is farthest removed from capriciousness. It is her self-awareness, and her awakening into a greater degree of self-awareness than those around her can comprehend, which gives her story dignity and significance.

Our advocacy of the novel is not meant to obscure its faults. It is not perfect art, but in total effect it provokes few dissatisfactions. A sophisticated modern reader might find something of the derivative about it. Kate Chopin read widely, and a list of novelists she found interesting would include Flaubert, Tolstoy, Turgenev, D'Annunzio, Bourget, Goncourt and Zola. It is doubtful, however, that there was any direct borrowing, and *The Awakening* exists, as do most good novels, as a product of the author's literary, real, and imagined life.

How Mrs. Chopin managed to create in ten years the substantial body of work she achieved is no less a mystery than the excellence of *The Awakening* itself. But, having added to American literature a novel uncommon in its kind as in its excellence, she deserves not to be forgotten. *The Awakening* deserves to be restored and to be given its place among novels worthy of preservation.

Notes

1.   Daniel S. Rankin, *Kate Chopin and Her Creole Stories* (Philadelphia, 1932).

CRITICISM AFTER 1969

◆

THE AWAKENING: A POLITICAL ROMANCE

LAWRENCE THORNTON

I

It is obvious by now that *The Awakening* echoes characters and events in *Madame Bovary,* but even though she is deeply indebted to Flaubert, Chopin goes beyond merely imitating Emma and the problems Flaubert imagined for his heroine. While Edna Pontellier and Emma are both narcissists, Edna becomes aware of political crises related to her position within Creole society that sharply distinguish her from Emma, who responds to French provincial society only as a mirror of her romantic fantasies.

These differences become immediately apparent through a comparison of two important passages. Twelve pages into *The Awakening* we encounter the well-known evocation of the sea that becomes a central motif in the novel:

> The voice of the sea is seductive; never ceasing, whispering, clamoring, murmuring, inviting the soul to wander for a spell in abysses of solitude; to lose itself in mazes of inward contemplation.
> The voice of the sea speaks to the soul. The touch of the sea is sensuous, enfolding the body in its soft, close embrace.[1]

These sentences are reminiscent of the exchange of platitudes between Léon Dupuis and Emma Bovary, which moves from shared clichés about reading to Léon's avowal of great passion for sunsets and the seashore:

> "Oh, I love, the sea!" said Monsieur Léon.
> "And doesn't it seem to you," continued Madame Bovary, "that the mind travels more freely on this limitless expanse, of which the contemplation elevates the soul, gives ideas of the infinite, the ideal?"[2]

The sea symbolizes imagination in both passages, but there is a considerable difference between Emma's superficial response to received ideas, and Edna's

From *American Literature* 52 (March 1980): 50–66. Copyright Duke University Press, 1980. Reprinted with permission.

romantic but serious exploration of her own soul. Emma's navieté is nowhere more evident than in this confession to Léon that the sea is a catalyst to the "ideal" world of sentimental romanticism. In *The Awakening,* however, the emphasis falls on the seductive, isolating effects of "inward contemplation." Whereas Flaubert is interested in exposing the dry-rot of romanticism, Chopin is concerned with a woman whose susceptibility to romantic codes ultimately gives way to at least a partial understanding of the lie that animates her visions. Edna's knowledge of the deliquescent nature of romantic ideals also informs her view of personal freedom, and thus takes her story in another direction than Emma's.

That direction leads directly to an irresolvable conflict between Edna's vision of herself as an independent woman and the social forces of Creole Louisiana near the end of the nineteenth century. Throughout *The Awakening,* Chopin shows how Edna is deceived both by her private vision and by the society she discovers during the summer on Grand Isle. The hopes she begins to entertain about a new life spring from a congeries of sentimental ideals galvanized by Robert Lebrun, a "Blagueur" (p. 12) who devotes himself to a different woman each summer. Edna's friend, Adele Ratignolle, sees the danger Robert poses to someone as impressionable as Edna and asks him to "let Mrs. Pontellier alone" (p. 20), which he declines to do, even after Adele tells him that "She is not one of us; she is not like us. She might make the unfortunate blunder of taking you seriously" (p. 21). The deception Adele recognizes in Robert mirrors the deception of Creole society which seems to accord women greater latitude than it is willing to grant. That women could smoke cigarettes, listen to men tell risqué stories, and read French novels soon appears as only a veneer covering a solidly conventional society that titillated itself with flourishes of libertinism.[3] For despite the apparent standing within the Creole world (a standing, it should be noted, gained solely through marriage), women are presented as an oppressed class. Edna's gradual understanding of her oppression becomes part of the conceptual framework of her overall rebellion, so that along with my analysis of the consequences of romantic imagination, I want to show how Chopin shapes her materials through detailed social description and social interpretation.

Because of the social conventions that prescribe behavior in her world, Edna has nowhere to go, succumbing to the promises of romanticism while living in a society that will not tolerate the terms she sets for her own freedom. Although she manages by sheer force of will to free herself from the oppressive marriage with Léonce, Edna does not experience freedom; instead, she finds herself trapped by her romantic visions and by what Léonce calls *les convenances.* If *The Awakening* were only another examination of narcissism and the romantic predilections of a bourgeois woman, it would simply repeat the material Flaubert renders in his great novel. Chopin is not Flaubert, but within the range of her talent she treats questions about romanticism, narcissism, and women's independence that are essentially political and thus considerably different from those raised in *Madame Bovary*. Moreover, we care about Edna Pontellier in ways that we cannot care about Emma Bovary because Edna's intimations of an autonomous life force us to consider the problems of freedom and oppression within society, while Emma's whole life revolves around sentimental fatuities. If Edna at times seems predictable and even tiresome, these characteristics are countered by Chopin's subtle rendering of the process of "inward contemplation" that leads Edna to an understanding of an insurmountable social dilemma which can only be escaped in death.

II

For roughly the first half of the novel Chopin subordinates the political implications of Edna's predicament to the solitude and tentative self-exploration that begins to occupy her heroine during the summer idyl on Grand Isle. In the opening scenes Edna's undefined sense of longing is symbolized by the voice of the sea, which encourages the soul "to lose itself in mazes of inward contemplation," so that the relationships between Edna's isolation, her romantic sensibility, and the social significance of her situation do not emerge with any clarity until the guests at Madame Lebrun's establishment gather for an evening of entertainment. Even then, there is no specific statement to link the motifs together; what Chopin gives us instead is the motif of music, which indirectly leads to images of flight and escape. As Mademoiselle Reisz begins to play the piano, Edna recalls the pleasure she derives from listening to her friend, Adele, when she practices. One piece Adele plays Edna calls "Solitude": "When she heard it there came before her imagination the figure of a man standing beside a desolate rock on the seashore. He was naked. His attitude was one of hopeless resignation as he looked toward a distant bird winging its flight away from him" (pp. 26–27). The image of the bird does not assume its full significance as a unifying symbol for another sixty pages when Edna remembers a comment of Mademoiselle Reisz's as she and Alcée sit before the fire in the "pigeon house": "when I left today," she tells him, "she put her arms around me and felt my shoulder blades, to see if my wings were strong, she said. 'The bird that would soar above the level plain of tradition and prejudice must have strong wings. It is a sad spectacle to see the weaklings bruised, exhausted, fluttering back to earth'" (p. 82). As the reader knows, escape from the Labyrinth of self or tradition demands a cunning Edna does not possess. This failure is made explicit on the final page of the novel when she returns to *Chênière Caminada*: "A bird with a broken wing was beating the air above, reeling, fluttering, circling disabled down, down to the water" (p. 113). Trapped in romantic longings whose objects are always vague and shifting in her mind's eye, and in a culture whose codes of duty and responsibility make escape impossible for even the most reluctant of "mother-women" (p. 10), Edna's fate is clearly foreshadowed in the imagery of defeated flight Chopin weaves into *The Awakening.*

At this point, we need to ask why, in a novel addressing woman's fate in society, Chopin chose a male figure to symbolize her heroine's solitude. The reason stems from Chopin's having realized that, on an unconscious level, Edna can only imagine a man in a position suggesting freedom and escape. His failure represents Edna's projection of herself onto the imagined figure. This view is consonant with the rest of the novel where we see that only men are free to act as they like and to go where they want: Robert to Mexico, Léonce to New York, Alcée from bed to bed. Whether it is Grand Isle, *Chênière Caminada,* or New Orleans, men escape, women remain. The New Woman Edna feels emerging from her "fictitious self" (p. 57) demands the prerogatives of men, but in making these demands she can only be destroyed by over-reaching in society that has no place for her.

But there are other reasons beyond the fact that there was little hope for independent women in New Orleans at the turn of the century that must be considered in an account of Edna's failure. Simply put, she cannot see beyond the romantic prison of imagination. To illustrate her myopia, Chopin introduces Mademoiselle Reisz, whose clarity of mind offers a striking contrast to the essentially abstract nature of Edna's quest. Through music she discovers a kindred spirit in Edna, whose vision of the naked man occurs shortly before the musician plays a Chopin Impromptu that arouses Edna's passions and brings her to tears. "Mademoiselle Reisz perceived her agitation. . . . She patted her . . . upon the shoulder as she said: 'You are the only one worth playing for. Those others? Bah!' " (p. 27). She realizes that for her young friend music is the correlative of passion just as it is for her, but once their relationship develops Mademoiselle Reisz discovers that Edna's sensitivity does not encompass the discipline or the clarity of vision requisite to either the artist or the rebel. This is made clear one afternoon when Edna explains that she is becoming an artist. The older woman responds harshly, saying that "You have pretensions, Madame . . . to succeed, the artist must possess the courageous soul . . . that dares and defies" (p. 63).

Once they have begun to meet in New Orleans, the musician's misgivings about Edna's ability to find her way in a new romantic world are expressed in another kind of music. Edna demands to see a letter Robert has written to Mademoiselle Reisz, hoping that she will find some mention of herself. That she is overwhelmed by Robert and misled by their relationship troubles the older woman, whose sense of impending disaster leads her to weave fragments of Wagner's Liebestod into the Chopin piece she has been playing. This double theme of romantic life and death becomes part of the atmosphere of the city, floating "out upon the night, over the housetops, the crescent of the river, losing itself in the silence of the upper air" (p. 64). Mademoiselle Reisz's music symbolizes the antithetical modes of romance represented by Chopin and Wagner, and her evocation of Tristan and Isolde becomes an important part of *The Awakening*'s imagery of destruction.

Mademoiselle Reisz functions as the only example of a free, independent woman whose hardiness Edna must emulate if she is to succeed and soar above "tradition and prejudice." There is no question that the older woman provides Edna with a more viable model than Adele Ratignolle, who is, after all, trapped without even knowing it. Mademoiselle Reisz's apartment becomes a refuge for Edna, and the pianist comes closer than anyone else to making contact and supplying advice that could be helpful as Edna tries to find a place for her new self in the world. Nevertheless, her role in the novel is problematic, for she is an imperfect model whose positive qualities are balanced by abrasiveness and egocentrism. Chopin calls attention to the musician's idiosyncrasies when she introduces her into the story. Robert has gone to ask her to play for his mother's guests and finds her in one of the cottages: "She was dragging a chair in and out of her room, and at intervals objecting to the crying of a baby, which a nurse in the adjoining cottage was endeavoring to put to sleep. She was a disagreeable little woman, no longer young, who had quarreled with almost every one, owing to a temper which was self-assertive and a disposition to trample upon the rights of others" (p. 26). Later, at Edna's dinner party, "Mademoiselle had only disagreeable things to say of the symphony concerts, and insulting remarks to make of all the musicians of New Orleans, singly and collectively" (p. 87). While Edna instinctively rebels against the larger social dictates of Creole society, those social graces that express less overwhelming *convenances* are still important to her, so that her amusement at her friend's disdain of conventions does not mean that she intends to imitate her. More subtly, Mademoiselle Reisz fails as a model because at this point Edna's passions, unlike her friend's, cannot be sublimated to music, but need physical expression. Like all her friends, Mademoiselle Reisz is eventually left behind as Edna increasingly dissociates herself from society and moves further into the mazes of solitude.

The musical motif in *The Awakening* provides specific dramatic referents to Edna's emotional states, but her imaginative life belongs to the realm of fantasy. Following her swim in the Gulf, Edna wants to think about her double experience of freedom and the "vision of death" (p. 29) that came to her in the water. Robert suddenly appears and Edna finds herself explaining how she has been overwhelmed by powerful experiences she does not understand: "There must be spirits abroad to-night," she muses, half-seriously. Picking up the cue, Robert invents a Gulf spirit who has searched for "one mortal worthy to hold him company, worthy of being exalted for a few hours into the realms of the semi-celestials" (p. 30). Robert does not understand Edna's experiences, nor does he particularly care to; his interests are in the direction of establishing himself in Edna's imaginative life. Whether by intention or pure chance, his words do enter her consciousness so that the Gulf spirit becomes a symbolic presence for Edna on Grand Isle and later in New Orleans.

In fact, the next section of the novel is given over to an elaboration of the fantastic. In the course of exposing the structure of fiction devoted to the unreal, Tzvetan Todorov cites the following comment by Olga Riemann: "The hero [of a fantastic tale] continually and distinctly feels the contradiction between two worlds, that of the real and that of the fantastic, and is himself amazed by the extraordinary phenomena which surround him."[4] What Edna experiences during the next few days approximates this situation very closely, for Robert's invention of the Gulf spirit and Edna's vigil before the sea that night lead to an awareness of a "contradiction between two worlds," particularly when she wakes up the next morning:

> She slept but a few hours. They were troubled and feverish hours, disturbed with dreams that were intangible, that eluded her, leaving only an impression upon her half-awakened sense of something unattainable. The air was invigorating and steadied somewhat her faculties. However, she was not seeking refreshment or help from any source, either external or from within. She was blindly following whatever impulse moved her, as if she had placed herself in alien hands for direction, and freed her soul of responsibility. (p. 33)

Like a princess in a fairy-tale, Edna awakens to an enchanted world where the old rules of reality no longer seem valid.

The immediate result of her new perspective is to propose taking a boat trip to *Chênière Caminada* with Robert, and from the moment of their departure to the island the day contains experiences suggesting that reality has been altered. For example, as they sail toward the island, "Edna felt as if she was being borne away from some anchorage which held her fast, whose chains had been loosening—had snapped the night before when the mystic spirit was abroad, leaving her free to drift whithersoever she chose to set her sails" (p. 35). Soon after they reach the island Edna takes a nap. When she awakens, she tells Robert that "The whole island seems changed. A new race of beings must have sprung up . . ." (p. 38). Later that afternoon she and Robert listen to one of Madame Antonie's stories about the Baratarian pirates. As she speaks, "Edna could hear the whispering voices of dead men and the clink of muffled gold" (p. 39). The fantasy continues during the return trip to Grand Isle, for Edna believes that "misty spirit forms were prowling in the shadows and among the reeds, and upon the water were phantom ships, speeding to cover" (pp. 39–40). Edna recreates the atmosphere of these imaginary encounters at the dinner party she gives for her father when she tells the story "of a woman who paddled away with her lover one night in a pirogue and never came back. They were lost amid the Baratarian Islands, and no one ever heard of them or found trace of them from that day to this" (p. 70). It should be clear that the day Edna and Robert spend on *Chênière Caminada* is filled with examples of "extraordinary phenomena."

The fantastic is implied in Chopin's early evocation of the sea, just as it is in Edna's visions of the unbinding of chains, pirate ships, and the lovers who disappear somewhere in the Baratarian Islands, freed forever from the mundane world of responsibility. Taken together, these events establish the atmosphere of Edna's mind, the mood of her thought. In this regard, it is important to see that *The Awakening* does not force the reader "to hesitate between a natural and a supernatural explanation of the events described";[5] only Edna hesitates between the fanastic and the real. The reader becomes increasingly aware of the ironic presentation of events, as well as the distance opening between Edna and reality.

Edna cannot actualize the self that increasingly absorbs her attention because that imagined self has no substance. Even when she is most deeply immersed in her newly discovered world, none of her visions of her self, or of a future, achieve clarity. In this respect, there is a distinction between Edna and Emma Bovary that should be explored. Emma constructs extremely detailed imaginary worlds for herself and Léon, Rodolphe, and Lagardy from the raw materials of sentimental literature, images of Parisian social life, and the drama that unfolds before her on the stage of the Rouen Opera House. But her world begins and ends in that matrix of images, which to her are "pictures of the world." While Robert, in the guise of demon lover, appears in several of Edna's visions, she does not create detailed alternatives to the dreary life she has shared with Léonce. The reason should be clear enough: Edna's awakening corresponds with the attentions she receives from Robert who reifies the "realms of romance" anesthetized by Léonce, but her ultimate desire is for freedom to do as she likes, not, like Emma's, to find the man of her dreams. Thus, the journey into the Baratarian Islands she imagines with a demon lover is less important than her perception that she is "free to drift whithersoever she chose to set her sails."

III

The motifs of music and fantasy that I have discussed so far shape *The Awakening*'s themes of marriage, sexuality, and liberation. For the moment, I want to consider these themes separately in the order I have just mentioned, since that order corresponds to the direction of Edna's growth. Later, I will discuss them as a synthesis, a single perspective on the conditions of Edna's life, and by extension, that of women in Creole society.

All of these themes are announced in the first scene of the novel. Edna and Robert have just returned from a walk on the beach when Léonce remarks on Edna's tan, looking at her as "at a valuable piece of personal property which has suffered some damage" (p. 4). At the same time, Edna surveys her hand "critically," remembers her rings given over to Léonce for safe-keeping, and takes them back. The conflict between freedom and oppression, the problem of narcissism, and Edna's retreat from and return to the symbols of marriage are neatly set out in three sentences. But there is more here, for marriage already appears to be inimicable with Edna's solipsistic character. From this muted beginning, marriage becomes the great fact of the novel, inescapable and monolithic, repeatedly described as oppressive, the source of ennui, and the means by which women are brought to suffer the pain of childbirth, the "torture" of nature as Edna perceives it while watching over Adele Ratignolle's *accouchement*.

We encounter a complex manifestation of Edna's feelings about marriage later that night after Léonce has returned from billiards at Klein's Hotel. She and Léonce have had a disagreement about the care of the children, and Edna begins to cry, overcome by vague feelings that cancel any memory of her husband's former "kindness": "An indescribable oppression, which seemed to generate in some unfamiliar part of her consciousness, filled her whole being with a vague anguish. It was like a shadow, like a mist passing across her soul's summer day. It was strange and unfamiliar; it was a mood" (p. 8). This unspecified malaise is an inseparable part of marriage, producing a mood like a "shadow," or a "mist," phenomena that can obscure the outline of things, perhaps even obscure the self. These images soon become part of *The Awakening*'s symbolic design, for by suggesting that marriage obscures the essential self, they establish quite early one of Chopin's central political concerns. They allow us to see how Edna is oppressed by the facts of marriage and by her temperament in much the same way that the scene at the Banneville grove, where the wind coaxes a murmuring sound from the trees, symbolized Emma's ennui and disillusionment over her marriage to Charles.

The suggestion of obscurity and isolation that emerges from Edna's reverie reappears when Chopin writes that "Mrs. Pontellier was not a mother-woman . . . [one] who idolized their children, worshipped their husbands, and esteemed it a holy privilege to efface themselves as individuals and grow wings as ministering angels" (p. 10). Adele Ratignolle is the type of such selfless creatures: "There are no words to describe her save the old ones that have served so often to picture the bygone heroine of romance and the fair lady of our dreams" (p. 10). What does Chopin mean to suggest by saying that there are no words to describe such women? Primarily, I would argue, that this epigone of the "mother-woman" is an anachronism, even though the beaches at Grand Isle are covered with them and they exemplify society's vision of woman's function. By saying that there are only the old words to describe Adele, Chopin subtly links her to the received ideas of woman's role in society. The "mother-woman" is a fiction. The old words have created a woman who fulfills "our" expectation, and these words, associated with romance and dream, have created the self-image in which women like Adele bask. The point is that the essential self of both kinds of women is obscured, first by the institution of marriage, which separates the inner and outer selves, and second by the myths of womanhood that equate effacement of self, even the adjuring of self, with ideal and natural behavior. Thus both the romantic woman and the woman who mirrors the romantic clichés of a society's myths are blighted by the very terms of marriage.

But one of the novel's most interesting themes becomes apparent when we realize that despite her rebelliousness, the associations Edna brings to marriage as a young woman can never be fully escaped. This is the case despite Léonce's lack of anything like the vigor of her youthful romantic fantasies that culminated in her infatuation with a "great tragedian" whose picture she kept and sometimes kissed. In fact, her entrapment is partly the result of the blandness she experiences with Léonce:

> Her marriage to Léonce Pontellier was purely an accident, in this respect resembling many other marriages which masquerade as decrees of Fate. It was in the midst of her secret great passion that she met him. He fell in love, as men are in the habit of doing, and pressed his suit with an earnestness and an ardor which left nothing to be desired. He pleased her, his absolute devotion flattered her. She fancied there was a sympathy of thought and taste between them, in which fantasy she was mistaken. (p. 19)

Edna then comes to see her marriage, with its initial vague resemblance to her adolescent longings, as a step into the "world of reality," the act of a mature woman who will leave behind forever the "realm of romance and dreams." It is not long before she finds herself forced to confront realities that are clearly antithetical to her modest expectations: "She grew fond of her husband, realizing with some unaccountable satisfaction that no trace of passion or excessive and fictitious warmth colored her affection, thereby threatening its dissolution" (pp. 19–20). So marriage for Edna devolves to fondness, and the absence of passionate emotion seems to guarantee stability.

The stultifying effects of the relationship with Léonce—the price Edna and all other wives pay for stability—are quickly developed. When she visits Adele in New Orleans, "the little glimpse of domestic harmony which had been offered her, gave her no regret, no longing. It was not a condition of life which fitted her, and she could see in it but an appalling and hopeless ennui" (p. 56). In response to Léonce's entreaties for her to attend her sister's wedding, she says that "a wedding is one of the most lamentable spectacles on earth" (p. 6). Later, her awareness of having become a possession increasingly grates against Edna's sense of her individuality, and she gives her opinion of men who treat her as an object near the end of the novel during a conversation with Robert. "You have been a very, very foolish boy," she says,

> wasting your time dreaming of impossible things when you speak of Mr. Pontellier setting me free! I am no longer one of Mr. Pontellier's possessions to dispose of or not. I give myself where I choose. If he were to say, 'Here, Robert, take her and be happy; she is yours,' I should laugh at you both. (pp. 106–07)

Earlier, when Edna first began to express her independence by ignoring the custom of her Tuesday at homes, Léonce responded by saying, "I should think you'd understand by this time that people don't do such things; we've got to observe *les convenances*" (p. 51). Léonce's comment cuts to the heart of what Edna rebels against; for her, marriage has come to seem like only one more convention within the myriad social forms that have become oppressive to her. Although she feels that marriage is "not a condition of life which fitted her," that she is no longer a possession, the facts of her life argue against her interpretation of it. Margaret Culley stresses Edna's delight in her independence as an element of the novel's tragedy. Referring to her comment about no longer being a possession of any man's, Culley says that "We glimpse the ecstasy of the discovery of the power of the self and the refusal to abjure it."[6] But there is a considerable distance between what Edna says and does that makes Culley's assessment more optimistic than the situation warrants. Surely the "delight [Edna] takes in her solitary self"[7] measures the distance between her imagination and reality in a painfully ironic way. Regardless of what she thinks, the shadow cast on Edna's soul by the convention of marriage and society cannot be escaped. Her decision to take her own life acknowledges the impossibility of returning to marriage, or of finding satisfaction in her solitude. It is the logical culmination of despair engendered by the loss of stability and her awareness of never being able to find a substitute for it in her affair with Alcée, or anyone else.

IV

Edna is deceived by the promises of sex just as she is misled by the conventions of marriage, but even though she delights in the adulterous pleasures discovered with Alcée, *The Awakening* is not an erotic novel. Larzar Ziff sees the true significance of her sexuality when he writes that Edna "was an American woman, raised in the Protestant mistrust of the senses and in the detestation of sexual desire as the root of evil. As a result, the hidden act came for her to be equivalent to the hidden and true self, once her nature awakened in the open surroundings of Creole Louisiana."[8] Ziff's observation alludes to the "shadow" Jung characterized as "a moral problem that challenges the whole ego personality, for no one can become conscious of the shadow without considerable moral effort. To become conscious of it involves recognizing the dark aspects of the personality as present and real. This act is the essential condition for any kind of self-knowledge."[9] Ironically, Edna's discovery of the "dark aspects" of her "true self" leads to increased self-knowledge that isolates her from human contact, rather than providing a means by which she could experience emotional and physical gratification.

Such reflexiveness is clearly illustrated in the affair with Arobin. Edna has agreed to go to the races with Alcée and Mrs. Highcamp and later, when he takes her home, we are told that she "wanted something to happen—something, anything; she did not know what" (p. 75). Like Rodolphe when he first meets Emma, Alcée senses an easy conquest. All he has to do is fulfill her expectations:

> His manner invited easy confidence. . . . They laughed and talked; and before it was time to go he was telling her how different life might have been if he had known her years before. With ingenuous frankness he spoke of what a wicked, ill-disciplined boy he had been, and impulsively drew up his cuff to exhibit on his wrist the scar of a saber cut which he had received in a duel outside of Paris when he was nineteen. (p. 76)

This apocryphal story of Alcée's past as a hero out of the pages of Dumas provides the opportunity for an even bolder gesture: "He stood close to her, and the effrontery of his eyes repelled the old, vanishing self in her, yet drew all her awakening sensuousness" (p. 76). Here Alcée's melodramatic persona appeals to Edna for the same reason she was drawn to the cavalry officer and the tragedian—he embodies the "realm of romance" left behind with her marriage and reawakened by Robert.

What follows is as inevitable as Rodolphe's success with Emma, for what Edna wants is an opportunity to express the "animalism" that strived impatiently within her (p. 78). A mutual seduction follows "the first kiss of her life to which her nature had really responded" (p. 83). However, despite this expression of freedom which was clearly inevitable, when Arobin leaves later that night "there was an overwhelming feeling of irresponsibility. There was the shock of the unexpected and the unaccustomed." There was also something more important:

> Above all, there was understanding. She felt as if a mist had been lifted from her eyes, enabling her to look upon and comprehend the significance of life, that monster made up of beauty and brutality. But among the conflicting sensations which assailed her, there was neither shame nor remorse. (p. 83)

The mist "lifted from her eyes" is the same mist Chopin refers to in the passage dealing with the "vague anguish" Edna discovers in marriage. What Edna understands here is that she has been liberated from the kind of life for which she is "not suited," from marriage and from the shadow marriage cast on her sexuality. At the same time, this scene reveals another important aspect of her character. Edna always greets each new experience hyperbolically and she is constantly duped by fresh promises. Her conviction that she can now "comprehend the significance of life" is only another example, since her understanding fades with the waning of her enthusiasm about her passional self. She has learned nothing that could help her escape from the solitude steadily encroaching on her inner life.

The affair with Alcée becomes part of an emerging pattern of longing and restlessness which recalls the shadows and mists of her earlier sense of oppression. At the farewell party she gives to her old life on Esplanade Street such unfocused yearning is obvious:

> . . . as she sat there amid her guests, she felt the old ennui overtaking her; the hopelessness which so often assailed her, which came upon her like an obsession, like something extraneous, independent of volition. It was something which announced itself; a chill breath that seemed to issue from some vast cavern wherein discords wailed. There came over her the acute longing which always summoned into her spiritual vision the presence of the beloved one, overpowering her at once with a sense of the unattainable. (p. 88)

The sense of ennui returns us to the bedroom of her cottage on Grand Isle where she wept without knowing why, and felt a "vague anguish" whose source was inexplicable. The only substantial difference between the passage above and Edna's earlier encounters with hopelessness is the vision of the "beloved one" who is obviously "unattainable." Clearly, her vision has been enlarged while the conditions of her life remain as they were on the night the novel opens.

Thus, every detail in *The Awakening* contributes to a growing impression that Edna's beginning is her end. Ten pages into the novel Chopin writes that "Mrs. Pontellier was beginning to realize her position in the universe as a human being, and to recognize her relations as an individual to the world within and about her" (pp. 14–15). Yet, a sentence later, in a paragraph introducing the first reference to the sensuous voice of the sea, the narrator warns that "The beginning of things, of a world especially, is necessarily vague, tangled, chaotic, and exceedingly disturbing. How few of us ever emerge from such beginnings! How many souls perish in the tumult!" The voice of the sea, as well as the Gulf spirit, holds out to Edna a promise that cannot be fulfilled. When the voice is heard once again on the last page it echoes the earlier promise of the sea, but concludes on the word "solitude," and the invitation to Edna's soul to "lose itself in mazes of inward contemplation" is replaced by the image of the "bird with the broken wing." Moreover, between these images of the sea framing the novel we see other motifs and themes also turning away from the promises they held out for Edna [at] their beginnings: the positive suggestiveness of Chopin's *Impromptu* is transposed to Wagner's evocation of the dying Isolde; the fantastic worlds of *Chênière Caminada* and Grand Isle become the house on Esplanade Street; the sexual passion with Alcée deliquesces into loneliness; and the promise of Robert's attention on Grand Isle turns into his farewell letter.

It is Robert's letter that finally shatters Edna's illusions of escape. After sitting up all night thinking about it, her dilemma finally becomes clear:

She had said over and over to herself: 'To-day it is Arobin; tomorrow it will be some one else. It makes no difference to me, it doesn't matter about Léonce Pontellier—but Raoul and Etienne!' . . . There was no human being whom she wanted near her except Robert; and she even realized that the day would come when he, too, and the thought of him would melt out of her existence, leaving her alone. The children appeared before her like antagonists who had overcome her; who had overpowered and sought to drag her into the soul's slavery for the rest of her days. But she knew a way to elude them. (p. 113)

Edna now understands that Alcée, Robert, and her own sexual awakening belong to a metaphor for the unattainable. Her life has no direction, her world no form, and the emptiness she has come to feel is Chopin's comment on the "realms of romance."

But this is not the end. Edna's void is suddenly filled with a vision of her children, which not only takes her back to her beginning, but also becomes the sign of her "soul's slavery." Regardless of her casual attention to them, and her attempts to break away from marriage, they have always been there. Once, Edna said to Adele Ratignolle that "I would give up the unessential; I would give my money, I would give my life for my children; but I wouldn't give myself" (p. 48). That was when their antagonism was veiled. During her vigil, Edna has come to realize that it is Raoul and Etienne, not Léonce, who bind her to the ennui of a life that does not fit her. And so it is a double vision Edna experiences; she understands the mendacity of her "spiritual vision" and also that the "soul's slavery" her children would drag her back to is too great a price to pay now that she has tasted freedom, however confusedly. The agony she feels has a moral basis because she realizes that continuing to live as she must in a world circumscribed by *les convenances* could only destroy her children, and that realization adds considerably to her stature.

Defeated by the lies of romance and the facts of *les convenances*, Edna's return to the seashore at *Chênière Caminada* is accompanied not by thoughts of Robert or Alcée, but by the overwhelming presence of Léonce, Raoul, and Etienne. As she swims out to sea, her mind is filled with sounds from her youth which are dominated by the clang of the cavalry officer's spurs. We are left to meditate on that sound as Edna dies with intimations of a world that vanished as she reached out to grasp it.

Notes

 1. Kate Chopin, *The Awakening,* ed. Margaret Culley (New York: Norton, 1976), p. 15. Hereafter cited in the text.
 2. Gustave Flaubert, *Madame Bovary,* ed. Paul De Man (New York: Norton, 1965), p. 58.
 3. In *The American 1890s: Life and Times of a Lost Generation* (New York: Viking Press, 1966), Larzar Ziff makes the following comments about Creole Society: "The Community

about which she wrote was one in which respectable women took wine with their dinner and brandy after it, smoked cigarettes, played Chopin sonatas, and listened to men tell risqué stories. It was, in short, far more French than American. . . . [T]hese were for Mrs. Chopin the conditions of civility, and, since they were so French, a magazine public accustomed to accepting naughtiness from that quarter and taking pleasure in it on those terms raised no protest. But for Mrs. Chopin they were only outward signs of a culture that was hers and had its inner effects in the moral make-up of her characters" (p. 297). For a more general examination of the social contexts of fiction than I can explore in this space, see Michel Zeraffa, *Roman et Société* (Presses Universitaires de France), Georg Lukács, *The Historical Novel* (London: Merlin Press, 1962), and Ian Watt, *The Rise of the Novel* (Berkeley: Univ. of Calif. Press, 1965).

4. Tzvetan Todorov, *The Fantastic: A Structural Approach to a Literary Genre,* tr. Richard Howard (Cleveland: The Press of Case Western Reserve Univ., 1973), p. 26.

5. Todorov, p. 33.

6. Margaret Culley, "Edna Pontellier: 'A Solitary Soul,' " in *The Awakening* (New York: Norton, 1976), p. 228.

7. Culley, p. 228.

8. Ziff, p. 304.

9. C. G. Jung, *Psyche and Symbol,* ed. Violet S. de Laszlo (New York: Doubleday Anchor Books, 1958), p. 7.

KATE CHOPIN'S QUARREL WITH DARWIN
BEFORE *THE AWAKENING*

BERT BENDER

I

In the hundred years since Kate Chopin began to publish her stories, she has been praised for her achievements as a local colorist, reviled for her shocking portrayal of woman's consciousness, forgotten, rediscovered, and—in a crescendo of critical acclaim over the last quarter century—celebrated as the pre-eminent feminist in American fiction. But she has never received the credit she deserves as a writer who constantly addressed the most profoundly disturbing of all the questions that troubled Western thought during her time. Although her biographers and critics have long known that she read the new natural history, few have imagined that she took it seriously. In fact, her ten years' work was a prolonged and progressively troubled meditation on the meaning of humanity after the successive shocks of *The Origin of Species* (1859), *The Descent of Man and Selection in Relation to Sex* (1871), and *The Expression of Emotions in Man and Animals* (1872).[1]

She accepted but quarreled with Darwin, as Melville had quarreled with God, or Faulkner with the South. If Melville was tormented with the presence of evil and the impenetrable mystery of life, his commitment to the Biblical reality is apparent in the apocalyptic end of *Moby-Dick* and his expression of hope at the end of *Clarel;* and if Faulkner could detail the many sicknesses of the Southern spirit, his defense of the South is absolute. Similarly Kate Chopin chafed at Darwin's views on women, even as she revered him. She recognized him as the towering new authority on the reality of life and paid him the tribute of questioning him in a detailed study of his work. She never doubted his first revolutionary theory in *The Origin of Species* that mankind had derived from lower animal forms through the agency of natural selection.

From the *Journal of American Studies* 26 (1992): 185–204. © Cambridge University Press, 1992. Reprinted with the permission of Cambridge University Press and the author. Also available in Bender's *The Descent of Love: Darwin and the Theory of Sexual Selection in American Fiction, 1871–1926* (Philadelphia: University of Pennsylvania Press, 1996).

But, although she accepted in general the theory of sexual selection that he had presented at length in *The Descent of Man,* she rebelled against her mentor, drawing on the authority of her own self-knowledge as a woman. With increasing intensity throughout her career, she questioned his interpretation of the female role in sexual selection—especially his views on the inferiority of women and, most emphatically, his theory of the female's modesty, her passivity in the sex drama as a creature without desire.

Darwin's theory of sexual selection is deceptively simple: whereas, in natural selection, certain individuals maintain an advantage over others in the general struggle for existence; in sexual selection, "certain individuals" possess the advantage "over other individuals of the same sex and species, in exclusive relation to reproduction."[2] But the actual workings of sexual selection are highly complex and required many pages of explanation and speculation. Darwin knew that his theory of sexual selection illuminated "the whole process of that most important function, the reproduction of the species" and that it was therefore vital to his general theory of evolution (*Descent,* I, 13); and Chopin immediately saw from her writer's point of view that sexual selection was profoundly illuminating in her work with the age-old and all-important courtship plot. Her stories and novels contain many scenes that dramatize several of Darwin's points about sexual selection in *The Descent of Man*—for example, "the law of battle [among males] for the possession of the female"; the particularly human evolutionary development in sexual selection whereby the males had "gained the power of selection" by having so long held the females in an "abject state of bondage"; the male's physical and mental superiority to the female; and the male's aggressive passion and the female's corresponding passive and modest role in sexual relations.[3]

In her initial response to *The Descent of Man* she was as optimistic as Darwin had been at the end of that book in remarking on the "hope" his theory of evolution offered humankind "for a still higher destiny in the distant future" (2:405). She began her extended meditation on *The Descent of Man* by celebrating the animal innocence of human sexuality. For this view of sex was as liberating for the American woman of the 80s and 90s as it was threatening to the foundations of a genteel society. Chopin saw the new natural history as a resounding defense of Walt Whitman's songs of the "body electric" or "the procreant urge of the world." But midway in her career she created a character who wondered how "love, the unsolved mystery" could count in the "face of . . . self-assertion, . . . the strongest impulse"—self-assertion, the underlying principle of natural and sexual selection.[4] Finally, in *The Awakening* Edna Pontellier asserts the reality of her natural desire. But then she awakens to "the significance of life, that monster, made up of beauty and brutality" and realizes that "it was not love which had held this cup of life to her lips" (967). By this time in her extended meditation on sexual selection Chopin had read *The Descent of Man* with intense scrutiny, and her references to it had become more explicit as in Edna's sexual arousal through the power of music, her argument with Mademoiselle Reisz about why a woman "selects" a man, or in her being compared with female pigeons that select mates they desire.[5] Long having accepted the theories of natural and sexual selection, in general, Chopin now argued mainly that the female plays a far more active and passionate role in the "sexual struggle" than Darwin had suggested. But her meditation on these matters ended in her doubt that "love" could claim a meaningful place in human courtship.[6] The natural history of "love" leads to Edna's "outspoken revolt against the ways of Nature" (995) and to her conclusion that life without "love" is too bitter to bear. Thus, for Edna and the other despondent characters Chopin created late in her career, there is no song of the self like that which Whitman had sung for "Modern Man"—no song especially "of physiology" or of the "Female equally with the Male" in "Life Immense . . . under the laws divine" ("One's-Self I Sing").

II

Chopin first worked with the ideas of sexual selection in an artless and amateurish way in *At Fault,* which she wrote between 1889 and 1890. Her optimistic approach to human courtship and sexuality here is intended to console her troubled characters and her readers about the fact "That you [i.e. her 'friend' the reader] should be driven by earthly needs to drag the pinioned spirit of your days through rut and mire" (858). The problem in *At Fault* is that the would-be lovers (Hosmer and Thérèse) are naturally attracted, but they are temporarily driven apart by the codes of civilization. When they first touch, Thérèse's "warm, moist palm . . . acted like a charged electric battery turning its subtle force upon his sensitive nerves" (762). But these innocent bodies electric are separated when Thérèse learns that Hosmer is divorced and when she demands that he return to and care for his former wife, a desperate alcoholic. Nature eventually intervenes, however—powerfully, benevolently, and unbelievably—when the unfortunate alcoholic wife is swept away by a storm-swollen river. In this first awkward novel, then, love—the swollen river—sweeps the characters toward a happy ending, when Thérèse realizes that she had been "at fault in following what seemed the only right"; together now in their natural love, she and Hosmer are better prepared to endure the "struggle of life" (872).

In order to make sure that her readers did not confuse the happy ending of *At Fault* with those in the "unwholesome intellectual sweets" produced by the "prolific female writers" of her day, Chopin included a voice of wisdom and reality in a minor character named Homeyer (798). With his belief in "the rights to existence" and "natural adjustment," he advises Hosmer to marry Thérèse despite the unfortunate ex-wife (777, 792). And Homeyer's forceful advocacy of "natural adjustment" is reinforced in the novel's happy ending with the words of another marginal character, a "highly gifted" woman who studies "Natural History," collects "specimens" out West, and lives by the credo, "a true knowledge of life as it is" is impossible "without studying certain fundamental truths" (875).

At Fault is interesting not only for what it reveals of Kate Chopin's initial optimism regarding Darwinian natural history; it also reveals the basis of her racial conservatism (which has troubled many of her interpreters) and the first stages of her quarrel with Darwin. The many people of color in Chopin's fiction—blacks, mulattoes, quadroons, and Indians of mixed blood—contribute a great deal to her authentic local color. But her view of racial matters has been either overlooked or misunderstood.[7] Readers of today might well wish that she would have avoided such images as this one, for example, which she thought would amuse anyone "with the slightest sense of humor": an "intensely black" boy squats near a fire, the "firelight [revealing] his elfish and ape like body much too small to fill out [his] tattered" garment (796). But in such images and the following one of "little darkies," we can begin to explain—if not accept—Chopin's views on race. These black children stand "gaping in wide-mouthed admiration at a sight that stirred within their breasts such remnant of savage instinct as past generations had left there in dormant survival" (755).

The theory of racial evolution projected in such images is inseparable from the theory of sexual selection as presented in *The Descent of Man*. The link between these two aspects of evolution is evident in the organization of that book, the two parts of which ("The Descent or Origin of Man" and "Sexual Selection") are linked by Darwin's conclusion to Chapter VII ("On the Races of Man"), that "it can . . . be shown that the difference between the races of man, as in colour, hairyness, form of features, etc., are of the nature which it might have been expected would have been acted on by sexual selection" (I:250). It would be a mistake to label either Darwin or Kate Chopin a racist, but it is undeniable that *The Descent of Man* was mistakenly thought to justify much of the most overt racism that raged far into the twentieth century. Darwin (and, presumably, Chopin) thought that "slavery" was "a great sin" (I:94). But his explanation that "it was not so regarded until quite recently, even by the most civilized nations"; and his (and Chopin's) extensive remarks on "savages" express a benign but condescending view of the darker races that leads all too easily to racist conclusions.[8]

Unlike Darwin, however, Chopin also romanticizes her racial types. Like the old black man Morico in *At Fault,* for example, these simple, natural characters often possess a strength that derives not from the slaves' knowledge of suffering and injustice, as in Uncle Tom, but from their primordial wisdom of Nature's way. So endowed, such characters can sometimes instruct the too civilized whites. Sylvie, in "Athénaïse" (1895), for example, "a portly quadroon of fifty" with "broad coarse features" and "wide nostrils" has "a dignity . . . in the presence of white people" (440). Because she is so "very wise," she can "inquire closely into the nature and character of Athénaïse's malaise," diagnosing it as pregnancy (451). After their interview, Athénaïse begins to breathe unevenly; her bosom is "ruffled" and she feels a "wave of ecstasy," the "first purely sensuous tremor of her life." Now aware that she is "heir to some magnificent inheritance"—motherhood and her "passionate nature," Athénaïse rushes to reunite with her husband, in whose "keeping" she now responds as a natural woman by "yielding her whole body against him" (451–54).

Athénaïse's true nature is of course as Darwin would have it in *The Descent of Man,* where the inferior female submits to the dominant male. And the imagery of racial and sexual domination in "Athénaïse" coheres according to the logic of *The Descent of Man.* Once in the story, Cazeau is disturbed by his recollection of the slave he had helped capture in his youth and, by association, the thought that, as Athénaïse's husband, he is her master. Yet finally he will "keep" Athénaïse, just as she, now contentedly kept, will apparently accept her place as mistress in the Darwinian hierarchy of sex and race. As Cazeau had instructed her when she had rebelled by giving the household keys to "Félicité's keeping": "negro servants [should not] carry the keys, when there [is] a mistress at the head of the household."

The best we can say about Chopin's view of the racial question is that she suggests that civilization had brought an end to slavery, but not that racial domination (as she understood it according to Darwinian thought) had ended or would end in the foreseeable future. Toward the end of her career Chopin would imagine white women who were somewhat freer than Athénaïse, but there is no evidence that she envisioned a similar kind of freedom for people of color.

The implications of sexual and racial dominance are far-reaching in Chopin's fiction, and one cannot follow her closely without considering at least some of them. An excellent discussion of these related matters as they were understood by mainstream Darwinians during Chopin's career is available in Cynthia Eagle Russett's *Sexual Science: The Victorian Construction of Womanhood.* Disentangling "the dismal history of sexual science," she explains how Darwin's ideas about the physical and mental inferiority of women and "savages" developed into a "science" that was taken to be a veritable religion. Certain that they had discovered "the ground rules of the universe," "scientists became the prophets of an updated Calvinism, ordaining some—the white, the civilized, the European, the male—to evolutionary maturity, and others—the dark-skinned, the primitive, the female—to perpetual infancy. The cosmos itself disdained equality."[9]

Russett's moving discussions of the abuses of this science—from the ways brains were measured and psychological tests were administered in order to demonstrate the inferiority of women or blacks, to theories about male variability and female conservatism in evolution (which credited the male with originating evolutionary development or progress)—demonstrate that it was a "masculine power play" (206). But we are also indebted to her for her larger understanding of the "dismal science" and variations of it that intoxicated so many of our writers in so many fields during those years. Darwinian evolution provided the "new ground rules of the universe" and tempted many thinkers including Darwin to feel that, with the keystone in place, each added observation (or even speculation) rendered the new temple of science an ever more glorious erection. Most importantly, as Russett explains, the upheaval in Western thought had created a widespread insecurity whose consequences seem almost inevitable: "If human beings could no longer lay claim to being a separate creation just a little less exalted than the angels, then a human hierarchy of excellence was needed to buffer Victorian gentlemen from a too-threatening intimacy with the brutes" (14). The new science—whose basic theories Chopin heartily accepted—was "an intellectual monument, etched in fear, of the painful transition to the modern world view" (206).

But if Kate Chopin accepted the theories of natural and sexual selection in general, taking them as the new laws of life, she also quarreled with Darwin and with the Victorian gentlemen of science Russett has described. She even included a comic portrait of one such gentleman scientist in *At Fault*. Her "Mr. Worthington regarded women as being of peculiar and unsuitable conformation to the various conditions of life amid which they were placed; with strong moral proclivities, for the most part subservient to a weak and inadequate mentality." Accepting women for "their usefulness as propagators of the species," he would not "remodel" but only "study" them (782). Similarly, he gathers information "in his eager short-sighted way, of psychological interest concerning the negro race" (844). Chopin's assessment of this man— and, paradoxically, her commitment to the Darwinian reality—are evident in her ironic remark that, having fathered "but one child," Worthington had done "less than his fair share" in propagating the race. She clearly denigrates his effete myopia as a scientist in favor of the character Homeyer's passionate advocacy of "natural adjustment" and Mrs. Griesmann's (the naturalist's) promise of "a true knowledge of life as it is" (875).

A true daughter of Darwin who will conduct her field work in Natural History out West, Mrs. Griesmann can help us grasp the paradox of Chopin's quarrel with Darwin and distinguish if from that of her feminist contemporary, Charlotte Perkins Gilman. Gilman's *Women and Economics* (1898) is a study in social evolution that, like Chopin's fiction, assumes the basic theories of natural and sexual selection in the evolution of male "belligerence and dominance" and female "modesty and timidity."[10] But as evolutionists Gilman and Chopin differ profoundly, for Gilman rests her case on the word of Darwin only to refute the idea that his laws were immutable in the face of enlightened social action. She sought to correct the "unnatural" and "morbid" emphasis on "sex-distinction" that had evolved among humans (29–30).

Chopin could not share Gilman's "sublime evolutionary faith that human institutions" could effect real change (Russett 153). She was "not interested in the woman's suffrage movement," as her son reported;[11] and in "Miss McEnders" (1892) she portrayed the comic ignorance of a "Woman's Reform Club" member who delivers a paper titled "The Dignity of Labor." Chopin depicts Georgie McEnders as only a miniature Henry George, Georgie's ideal. And her portrait of Georgie McEnders reflects the profound difference between herself and Gilman. In her views of women (though not of race), Chopin was a far more conservative Darwinian than Gilman. Although Chopin quarreled with Darwin by imagining new species of women, so to speak, unknown in *The Descent of Man,* she held that new forms might emerge only from the individual's struggle, not from social reform. Her constant interest in the solitary individual is always founded in the new biological reality of the individual's struggle to survive through natural and sexual selection.

Thus, when one of Chopin's first new women, Thérèse in *At Fault,* recognizes her "fault" of self-sacrifice for "what [had] seemed the only right," she is free to enter the "struggle of life" and attain a new identity. She finds a happy marriage (a "royal love") with Hosmer that is conspicuously free from the prospects of motherhood (i.e., the female's essential function as propagator of the species); and she has the strength to chide Hosmer for his "absurd . . . nonsense" regarding the "division of labor." The division of labor he had instituted at the mill will enable him to spend more time at home with Thérèse, but he draws her criticism when he assures her that he won't "help with the plantation," for that would rob her of *her* "occupation" (874). For Gilman, this biological principle (that Darwin had found in economic theory) of the division of labor was no laughing matter; as a social program it promised to free women to work outside the home (Gilman 245).

III

Immediately after *At Fault,* Kate Chopin continued in the direction indicated by Mrs. Griesmann by writing a series of stories—her own fieldwork in Natural History—that focus explicitly on essential principles of *The Descent of Man.* In these stories she began to quarrel with Darwin on certain points, but she accepted the idea of sexual selection and construed its workings as optimistically as possible. In "A No-Account Creole" (1888, revised 1891), she addressed the first principle of sexual selection, "the law of battle" for the male's possession of the female. Here she arranged for the dominant male to give up his natural right to possess the female, because he learns from his rival that "the way to love a woman is to think first of her happiness" (101). Thus, Placide overcomes "the brute passion that drives the beast to slay when he sees the object of his own desire laid hold of by another" (100). In creating this outcome and in her choice of names for these characters (Placide and Euphrasïe), Chopin suggests that the male force is potentially benevolent and receptive to female desire. This view of Natural History accepts the Darwinian reality but feminizes it in a way that is as reassuring as that provided by the "glasses" Mrs. Griesmann recommended in *At Fault*—because "they are so restful" (875).

In other stories she wrote at this time, Chopin imagined other new women who were developing towards the full self-assertion they would eventually claim in her later stories by fully regaining the power of selection. As Darwin had explained, man "in the savage state . . . gained the power of selection" by holding women in bondage (2:371); and although he wrote that "the civilized nations" were vastly improved in this regard (women now have "free or almost free choice" [2:356]), Chopin still felt the bind. Nor was she comfortable with Darwin's theory that civilized women selected for "social position and wealth" or for aesthetic purposes (2:356). (The "aesthetic capacity" of female pheasants was the most "wonderful" fact he knew "in natural history," for he saw it as the means "by which our own taste is gradually improved" [2:401].)

After first merely resisting Darwin's analysis of civilized women's motives in selecting, she eventually created natural women who select with complete freedom in accordance with their desires. Liza in "The Going Away of Liza" (1891) is an early version of this kind of liberated woman. Leaving her dominating husband because she "craves to taste the joys of existence," she is compared with a "singular animal . . . seldom seen by the eye of civilized man"; and her enraged husband seems to act according to the law of battle when he strikes a man who reports that another man had seen Liza (113–14). But when "the wind literally [drives] the woman" back into the home on a Christmas eve, "a hungry and hunted thing," the forgiving husband kneels before her in pity. The situation is much more promising for Marianne in the fable, "The Maid of Saint Phillippe" (1891). This young woman looks "like a handsome boy" and roams the woods "stag-like" as she provides for her aging father until his death. She had been completely devoted to her "father's will," but now she rejects a captain's proposal, scorns the thought of "slaves and motherhood," turns her back on an expectant clergyman, and walks freely with her "gun across her shoulder" into "the rising sun" (120–23).

Chopin's general approach in the stories of this period, then, is to allow her women a degree of self-assertion, upsetting as it was to the traditional males, but finally to project a happy readjustment for humankind within the province of a gentler but no less masculine order. This vision of life coheres most clearly—if unbelievably—in "Love on the Bon-Dieu" (1891), an Easter story in which nature, the Darwinian Bon-Dieu, arouses a young man's love. In this courtship, a frail young woman lacking in "wholesomeness and plentiful nourishment," is revived at last by Azenor when "he pressed his lips upon hers . . . till hers were soft and pliant from the healthy moisture of his own"

(153, 163). She had been too modest and he too hesitant to claim her, but knowing at last that "she belonged to him," he carries her to his home "through the forest, surefooted as a panther" (162).

Chopin created several men like Azenor who are potentially brutal, but who err most when they hesitate to claim their women. Her versions of the too-hesitant male are visible throughout her career, from Hosmer (*At Fault*)—through Azenor in this story, the shy fisherman Tonie in "At Chênière Caminada" (1893), Bruno in "A Harbinger" (1891), Telèsphore in "A Night in Acadie" (1896), and "the boy" who is frightened by his developing sexuality into becoming Brother Ludovic in "A Vocation and a Voice" (1896)—to Edna Pontellier's frightened lover, Robert, in *The Awakening*. With the exception of Robert, all these hesitant men are eventually aroused to claim their natural place of dominance.[12] And it is worth noting that much of Kate Chopin's quarrel with Darwin is clearly expressed in her ambivalence toward these men. She can assert the woman's equality as a sexual being most easily in the presence of a gentle or hesitant male, yet she will affirm the essential order of *The Descent of Man,* with all the power it bestows upon the male. And here again the relationship between her Darwinian views and her racial conservatism is clear. As there are many hesitant but finally dominant males in her fiction, far more than merely brutal ones, so there are many black people or people of mixed color who are contented in their places and few if any who express racial discontent.

In "The Bênitous' Slave" (1892), for example, Old Uncle Oswald isn't happy until he can more or less enslave himself again by finding the descendants of his former master: "I b'longs to de Bênitous," he says "contentedly" (190). And in two other stories the link between sexual and racial domination is more explicit: little Aurélia in "A Little Free-Mulatto" (1892) finds her "paradise" only when her father moves her to "L'Isle des Mulâtres"; and Loka (in "Loka," 1892), "a half-breed Indian" is without a place in life until she is finally taken in by a benevolent white male who sees that "she's *vrai sauvage.*" He simultaneously soothes his wife, "resting his hand gently upon [her] head," and expresses his sympathy for Loka: "we got to remember she ent like you an' me, po' thing: she's one Injun," her (218).

Between 1892 and 1894 there is a significant development in Chopin's meditation on the female role in sexual selection: a number of her women find ways—not of going away, as Liza had—but of claiming their places at the center of the biological arena by selecting their own mates. In the first of these stories, "At The Cadian Ball" (1892), when two men (Bobinôt and Alcée Laballière) compete for Calixta at the ball, the wealthier, more civilized, and more aggressive Alcée easily controls the struggle: "his lips brush her ear," and her senses "reel." But at this juncture, the dominant civilized *woman* appears and beckons to Alcée, who follows her away "without a word" (226). Earlier, Clarise had rejected Alcée's passionate advances; but now, with her aroused passion heightened by jealousy, she prevails over Calixta as easily as

Alcée had prevailed over the too-timid Bobinôt. Again, in this rendition of the courtship drama, Chopin apparently quarrels with Darwin, this time with his sense that jealousy is primarily a masculine quality, deriving from the male's passion and possessiveness. Accordingly, in Darwin's view, the male's jealousy has contributed greatly in human evolution by overcoming the "utter licentiousness" that prevailed among (mostly the female) savages: "jealousy [leads] to the inculcation of female virtue" (1:96). And now when Bobinôt and Calixta are alone together, she selects him: "You been sayin' all along you want to marry me, Bobinôt. Well, if you want, yet, I don't care" (226). In these courtships, then, both women exert the power to select in sexual selection, the superior or more civilized woman controlling the whole drama. And this reversal of the normal scenario in *The Descent of Man* leaves both males feeling as though "the face of the Universe was changed" (227).

In another story from these years Chopin creates a woman, 'Tite Reine (in "In Sabine," 1893), whose regal authority is written in her name. Her "will had been the law in her father's household," but now she is unhappily married to "a big good-looking brute," Bud Aiken. Early in the story Chopin suggests that she is working with Darwin's idea about man's having gained the power of selection by holding woman in bondage, for 'Tite Reine is now certainly in bondage to Aiken. He abuses her even more than he does his hired black man. When a visitor arrives at their place, the black man corrects the visitor's mistaken conclusion that he (the black man) has to chop Aiken's wood: "his wife got it to do," along with everything else, it appears, including picking the cotton (325). But 'Tite Reine gains control of her situation by awakening the sleeping visitor that night and convincing him to help her get away. The next day the two conspire to overcome Aiken with food and drink and then leave him in a stupor.

Chopin obviously enjoys the comic disruption of the male domain in these stories, and the anger underlying her comedy is most apparent in her fable, "Juanita" (1894). With her mythic proportions (she is "five-feet-ten, and more than two hundred pounds of substantial flesh"), Juanita controls her own destiny as does no other woman in all of Chopin's stories. Despite her size, Juanita possesses a "fresh and sensuous beauty" that "attract[s] admirers, young and old" (367). Her freedom to select from her many lovers is absolute, and she exhibits no trace of female modesty nor any of the hesitancy that afflicts so many male selectors in Chopin's courtships. But she confounds expectations in her community and refutes Darwin's theory about modern woman's selecting for wealth or social position when she turns away a prosperous businessman, a wealthy farmer, and a Texas millionaire. Instead, she marries and has a baby by "a very poor and shabby . . . one-legged man": "Juanita . . . turned her back upon the whole race of masculine bipeds, and lavish[ed] the wealth of her undivided affections upon the one-legged man" (368). She mounts her man upon a pony and leads him into the woods, "puny, helpless, but apparently content with his fate."

The satiric anger in her portrait of the puny one-legged man is directed not so much at males in general as at the sexual science of Victorian gentlemen. And it would seem that Darwin himself is largely responsible for the masculine misrepresentation of sexual selection, from Chopin's point of view. For, while he acknowledges the bondage of women in pre-civilized cultures, he also underplays *that* struggle between the two sexes in his general definition of sexual selection, whereby the struggle is primarily between members of the same sex. And as she scorns the books of sexual science in "Juanita," reversing the accepted roles in sexual selection, in the companion piece to "Juanita," "The Night Came Slowly" (1894), she scorns "a man . . . with his 'Bible Class' " (366). Here the jaded narrator complains, "I want neither books nor men; they make me suffer" (366).

It is important to recognize that her anger with both the Biblical and scientific descriptions of womanhood is most strident at this point in her career when she had begun to create a female who posed the greatest possible threat to Victorian religion and science by claiming full equality with the male as a passionate participant in the sexual reality. It is one thing for woman to select and select even with impunity as long as she is the goddess of civilization; but it was quite another thing for woman to claim the reality of sexual desire as a motive in selection. Nothing posed so horrible a threat to the central ideal of sexual science and Victorian morality—motherhood—as the beast of desire.

Even the mythic "Juanita" is incapable of actual desire. If she carries her man into the woods so that "they may love each other away from all prying eyes," she does so with a degree of modesty befitting her motherhood. But Chopin ends her fable with a gesture that indicates her real point: "I never expected Juanita to be more respectable than a squirrel" (368). And if we turn to her other story from this period, "A Respectable Woman" (1894), we can see one of Chopin's earliest efforts to create an Edna Pontellier. Mrs. Baroda (the "respectable woman") finds exactly the kind of man the narrator of "The Night Came Slowly" had imagined—not a "Bible Class" man, but one who can "talk to me like the night—the Summer night. Like the stars of the caressing wind" (366). Mrs. Baroda meets her man when Gouvernail (her husband's close friend) visits the Barodas. Gentle, sensitive, and "lovable," he sits with her under a live oak and murmurs the erotic lines from "Song of Myself":

> Night of south winds—night of the large few stars!
> Still nodding night—

Chopin does not reveal whether, before he ended this "apostrophe to the night," Gouvernail had murmured the more daring lines from this section (21) of "Song of Myself": "mad naked summer night," and "Smile, [earth], for your lover comes." She writes that his only "desire [is] to be permitted to exist" and to have an occasional "whiff of genuine life," but he certainly arouses Mrs. Baroda to life: "She wanted to reach out her hand in the darkness and touch him with the sensitive tips of her fingers upon the face or the lips. She wanted to draw close to him and whisper [something] against his cheek . . ." (355). But, conscious of being "a respectable woman," she draws "away from him" and later complains to her husband that his friend "tires" her. Within a year, though, Mrs. Baroda asks her husband to invite Gouvernail for another visit; she has "overcome everything!" (335–36).

Here once again Chopin intensified her quarrel with Darwin regarding sexual selection. With little of the modesty that Darwin attributed to civilized women, Mrs. Baroda selects Gouvernail ("I shall be very nice to him," she says), and both her motive of desire and her situation as a married woman preclude the workings of sexual selection as Darwin had described them. Chopin did not at this stage in her development dare to depict a mother's desire (Mrs. Baroda is not a mother) as she finally would in Edna Pontellier; but she does make it clear that Mrs. Baroda's desire is independent of the drive in sexual selection to propagate the species. In Darwin's theory, civilization had evolved largely because woman's modesty curbs the male's eagerness to couple; and in this theory of the sexual reality, the male's eagerness or lust is not only biologically innocent or red-blooded, but necessary. "In order that [the males] should become efficient seekers," Darwin concluded, "they would have to be endowed with strong passions. The acquirement of such passions would naturally follow from the more eager males leaving a larger number of offspring" (1:274). The woman's role is of course different.

IV

Between 1894 and 1897 (when, in June, she began *The Awakening*), Chopin continued to develop her own feminist variations on Darwin's theme of sexual selection. She created a number of characters, both male and female, who awaken happily to the undeniable reality of their sexual natures—Athénaïse (in "Athénaïse," 1895), for example, whose innocent knowledge of her sexual being "comes to her as the song to the bird, the perfume and color to the flower" (433). She is like "Eve after losing her ignorance," but her guiltless carnal knowledge derives explicitly from Chopin's understanding of sexual selection as Darwin had described it among birds and flowers as well as humankind. Thus, by her own "choice," Athénaïse yields herself to "Cazeau's keeping." And during these years Chopin created a number of foolish women who have the power to select but who select unwisely or comically. One, in "The Kiss" (1894), selects not for passion but for wealth; and another, in "Fedora" (1895), waits too long to select. Until age thirty she had found all men wanting according to her ideal, but now having found a suitable male (she "had to look up into his face"), "she selected him when occasion permitted." (This is Chopin's first use of the word "select" in its sexual sense; she will later use it with more explicit reference to *The Descent of Man* in chapter 26 of *The Awakening*.) But apparently Fedora cannot have the lover she has selected too late. And Chopin is unwilling to relieve Fedora's frustration: Fedora can only assume the male posture of dominance in relation to her would-be lover's little sister. Driving a carriage with whip and rein in hand, she "bends down" and presses "a long, penetrating kiss upon [the astonished girl's] mouth" (469).

There is however a darker accompaniment to woman's desire in Chopin's stories at this time, her growing sense that love might be nothing more than sexual desire and that it is inconstant. Mrs. Mallard considered these possibilities as she responded to the apparent death of her husband in "The Story of an Hour" (1894): "she had loved him—sometimes," and now she realized that "love, the unsolved mystery" is nothing in the face of "self-assertion, . . . the strongest impulse" (353). And in two stories the following year (1895, "Two Summers and Two Souls" and "The Unexpected"), Chopin asserts that the fact of sexual desire discloses "the singular delusion that love is eternal" (457). In the first of these, the unnamed he and she (the "Two Souls"), part after a summer which had been for him "a re-creation of light and life, and soul and senses." But for all his "passion," he fails to act with the appropriate masculine power, saying only "that he loved her," and she cannot respond. She hesitates because she had "thought love meant something different—powerful, overwhelming." Her "senses" are "unawakened." A year later, however, she is "able to feel" his absence, and, even though she is still confused about the meaning of love, writes to him that she loves him and that she thinks she could not live without him. He is shocked by the letter; for, although he "had loved her and . . . suffered" at first, now, like Mrs. Mallard after the "death" of her husband, he can "wake in the morning without the oppression" of remembering his former lover. He can think of her with "unstirred pulses" that signal not only his "indifference" but his "revolt." Yet "he simply went to her, . . . unflinchingly," as to a "business obligation that he knew would leave him bankrupt" (457).

In this story, then, the "rush of existence" or the beating of one's pulses and the waves of passion proceed at the inexorable pace of real time in natural history, as measured by sexual selection: for this reason the ideal of "eternal" love is a "singular delusion" (455–57). And as the rush of passion in this man's life left "love" receding from both souls' grasp, in the other story, "The Unexpected" (1895), passion promises to carry Dorothea not toward "love," but only away from "Death." In this story, both the man and the woman suffer passionately when they are forced to part, but when the man ("an almost perfect specimen") loses his "youthful health, strength and manly beauty," Dorothea undergoes a "devilish transformation." She recoils from him and feels a "shriveling" within herself that she took to be her "heart" but which was actually "only her love." In this story, too, "a clock on the mantle striking the hour" signals the real time of "love" or passion (as in "The Story of an Hour"), and Dorothea is repelled by her dying lover's insistence that they marry so that she can have his fortune, "all I possess," as he says. In "swiftest flight" she speeds through the countryside on her bicycle, "her pulses beating in unison with [the] sensuous throb" of nature; and at last she confides to the leaves, the crawling insects and sky, "Never! . . . not for all his thousands!" (458–61). Dorothea's revolt is an act of sexual selection, but not as Darwin would have it. Scarcely in his image of the modest, civilized woman who selects for wealth or social position, Dorothea asserts her freedom to be a sensuous animal and, paradoxically, a solitary soul in a treacherous time.

In exploring the reality of desire and the inconstancy of love in her stories of 1894 and 1895, Chopin had turned her attention away from the first principle of sexual selection, "the law of battle," but she returned to it in the last stories she wrote before *The Awakening*. And now she responded to it in a different way, without her former optimism or tendency to celebrate the power of sex. She could not deny the Darwinian view of belligerent males and submissive females, but she had also concluded that women and men are both possessed by passion and self-assertion, and that *both* "men and women believe they have a right to impose a private will upon a fellow creature" (353). Thus, with this darker view of life, she presented the courtship of Telèsphore and Zaïda in "A Night in Acadie" (1896). Darwin certainly has his way in this primeval setting where people come to the ball "flying, crawling ahead of the darkness that was creeping out of the far wood" (490). And eventually the rival males must meet in battle: "The brute instinct that drives men at each other's throat was awake and stirring" (497). By the end of the story a natural order prevails, bringing with it the promise of health and psychological well-being for both the male and female. Telèsphore had broken his watch in battle, but now he has learned to tell "the time by the sun, or by instinct, like an animal"; and Zaïda, whose "will . . . had been overmastering and aggressive," now sits "submissively." She is "like a little child [who] followed whither he led in all confidence" (499). Chopin will allow that there is a kind of dark serenity to this ending as the couple make their way "through the woods"; "how dark it was and how still" (499). But she will not call it love. Zaïda is free of an illusion that "had carried her love with it," and she doesn't realize that "love had been part of the illusion" (498).

But if "A Night in Acadie" projects a much darker view of the courtship drama than did Chopin's stories of the early 90s, two of her last "love" stories before she began *The Awakening* are almost surreal. When the woman in "Suzette" (1897) learns that the man she had once "loved . . . desperately" has died in an accident, one probably brought on by his desperation to have her, she feels nothing. *That* love had become a great "weariness" to her. She (a later version of Mrs. Mallard) cannot pause to mourn this death, for she awaits the approach of her new lover, a cowboy, and hears "the distant tramp of an advancing herd of cattle." She stands in "resplendent" expectation, ready to feel "the penetration of his glance." But another "unruly beast," one of the cowboys, attracts his attention. He is indifferent to her and dashes away on his horse in a "single impulse" with the "quickened movement of the herd" (559).

Even the dismal irony of this tale—of love trampled by the unruly beast of passion—is less troubling than the surreal "vision" of "the depths of human despair" that Chopin created two months later in "An Egyptian Cigarette." And this dream or vision projects in miniature Edna Pontellier's despair during the last days of her life. "An Egyptian Cigarette" begins, as do so many of Chopin's last stories, with lovers separated, the woman suffering in a desolate desert landscape because "He will never come back." She says that she had "laughed at the oracles and scoffed at the stars when they told that after the rapture of life I would open my arms inviting death, and the waters would envelop me"; yet in the end, she reaches the river and, like Edna Pontellier in *The Awakening,* enters the water to know "the sweet rapture of rest!" (572).

The narrator tells how she had taken Bardja, her lover, as her one "god"; she "decked [her]self with lilies and wove flowers into a garland and held him close in the frail, sweet fetters." But her desire to hold him close is precisely the force that drives him away on his camel, laughing and "showing his gleaming white teeth." He had left her before, in flaming "fierce anger," but had always returned. Now his indifference seems final because he is "tired of fetters, and kisses, and you." This deadly imposition of "a private will," male or female, "upon a fellow creature" had haunted Mrs. Mallard, as it will finally torment Robert and Edna in *The Awakening.* Just as Robert's "senses" will leave him with only the longing "to *hold* . . . and keep" Edna; so will Edna's "senses" allow her to imagine "no greater bliss on earth than *possession* of the beloved one" (my emphasis, 993, 996). And when Bardja responds to his lover's will by riding away, smiling and showing "his cruel white teeth," Chopin projects an image of the new biological reality of individuals caught in nature's war, not only as creatures struggling to survive through natural selection, but as creatures in the conflict of sexual selection. In her despair, the narrator hears "the wings of a bird flapping above [her] head, flying low, in circles"; a much darker version of this image will appear in Edna's final awakening, when "a bird with a broken wing" beats "the air above" and circles "disabled down, down to the water" (999). The narrator of "An Egyptian Cigarette" hopes to raise her head and "see the evening star," but she cannot find the star of love; nor will Edna, finally, when she realizes "that the day would come when he [Robert], too, and the thought of him would melt out of her existence" (999).

But we can only wonder at what Chopin might have suggested in her conclusion to the narrator's vision in "An Egyptian Cigarette." Having immersed herself in the waters of the Nile, she feels "the sweet rapture of rest," hears "music in the Temple," and finds that Bardja has returned; she asks him, "let us go into the King's garden and look at the blue lily." Perhaps the blue lily (in this context, the lily-of-the-nile) is the object of her meditation because of its bisexual flowers. Like many other writers in her time— Harold Frederic and Charlotte Perkins Gilman, for example—Chopin contemplated Darwin's analysis of the "conditions of life" that might provide no "motive for the separation of the sexes"; such conditions as presently pertain in the case of monoecious plants or hermaphroditic animals. As Darwin had explained, the sexes were not originally separated in either plant or animal life, as evidenced by such phenomena as the human male's rudimentary breasts. Adjusting to "changed conditions of life," some kinds of plants, for example, had evolved a division of sexual labor in the production of "pollen and seeds" whereby each individual could protect its "vital powers . . . [in] the struggle for life to which all organisms are subjected."[13]

In "An Egyptian Cigarette" Kate Chopin briefly indulged her fantasy that a return to the garden of life as explained in *The Origin of Species* might open the way to a different evolutionary pathway—one that would avoid the sexual strife her lovers had known. But, always in search of "a true knowledge of life as it is," she immediately abandoned this fantasy for her masterful analysis of Edna Pontellier's sexual reality. To make her point she began the story of Edna's awakening by introducing her with an image that captures her in her present evolutionary state—"advancing at snail's pace from the beach."

Notes

1. In 1894 William Schuyler wrote that in the middle 80s, "the subjects which attracted her the most were almost entirely scientific, the departments of Biology and Anthropology having special interest for her. The works of Darwin, Huxley, and Spencer were her daily companions; for the study of the human species . . . has always been her constant delight" (in Per Seyersted, ed., *A Kate Chopin Miscellany* [Natchitoches, Louisiana: Northwestern State University Press, 1979], 117). Of all of Chopin's critics, Per Seyersted has done the most with her interest in Darwin, but even he has never examined the question at length. See for example his *Kate Chopin* (Baton Rouge: Louisiana State University Press, 1969), 90. And Chopin's interest in Darwin has been increasingly ignored by more recent scholars. To judge from the latest (and certainly the fullest and most informative) biography, one might conclude that Chopin never read *The Descent of Man* much less that it influenced her portrayal of womanhood. Yet this biographer, who has "been working on Kate Chopin's literary career longer than she did," began her work on Chopin in order to answer the "gnawing" questions, "How *had* Kate Chopin known all that in 1899. What impelled her to write such pointed observations about women and men?" (Emily Toth, *Kate Chopin* [New York: Morrow, 1990], 9).

2. Charles Darwin, *The Descent of Man and Selection in Relation to Sex,* 2 vols. as 1 (Princeton: Princeton University Press, 1981), 1:256. Unless otherwise noted, further references to *The Descent* are from this edition (the first, 1871) and this text, and are cited parenthetically by volume and page.

3. Darwin discusses "the law of battle" at many points in *The Descent;* for Darwin's comments on the human male's having gained the power of selection, see *The Descent,* II, 371

(according to his analysis, among most animals, particularly birds, the females select the victorious or the more attractive males, e.g., those with more elegant plumage); and for his comments on the male's superiority, see, for example, his remark that "man is more powerful in body and mind than woman" (*The Descent*, II, 371).

4. *The Complete Works of Kate Chopin*, ed., Per Seyersted, 2 vols. (Baton Rouge: Louisiana State University Press, 1969), 353. Subsequent references to Chopin's fiction will be to this text, cited parenthetically by page (pages are numbered consecutively why in the two volumes).

5. Readers familiar with Arthur Schopenhauer's chapter, "The Metaphysics of the Love of the Sexes," in *The World as Will and Idea* (first available in the U.S.A. in translation in 1888) will note many ways in which Schopenhauer's critique of "the sexual impulse we call love" anticipated *The Descent of Man*. That Chopin also read Schopenhauer is nowhere more evident than in Ch. 38 of *The Awakening*, when Dr. Mandelet and Edna discuss Nature's "decoy to secure mothers for the race" (Schopenhauer had written of the "illusion" whereby a lover becomes the "dupe of the will of the species"; and Edna feels that it is better to have awakened "than to remain a dupe to illusion all one's life"). It would seem that for Chopin, as for Maupassant and Nietzsche, for example, Darwin both verified Schopenhauer's speculations and in a sense rendered them irrelevant. As David Asher saw on the eve of *The Descent*'s appearance, "what Schopenhauer called 'the *metaphysics* of sexual love,' he might, had he been acquainted with Darwin's theory, have designated by the opposite name," his speculations now having been "proved to be well grounded and to have a thoroughly *physical*, or quite natural basis" ("Schopenhauer and Darwinism," *The Journal of Anthropology*, 3 [1871], 329).

6. For an analysis of these scenes and of Chopin's response to Darwin in *The Awakening*, see Bert Bender, "The Teeth of Desire: *The Awakening* and *The Descent of Man*," *American Literature*, 63 (1991), 459–73. The first of these scenes, the musical performance in Ch. 9, serves as a prelude to Edna's developing desire for Robert, and in it Chopin clearly follows Darwin's analysis of the "wonderful power" of music, the means by which our "half-human ancestors aroused each other's ardent passions" (*Descent*, II, 537). Chopin's description of Edna's response to the music—the "keen tremor" that runs down her "spinal column" and her passionate tears—parallels Darwin's description of such responses to music in *The Expression of Emotions in Man and Animals*. In the second scene (Ch. 26), one of several in which Chopin uses the word "select" in clear reference to Darwin's sexual selection, Edna tells Mlle. Reisz that women do not "select" lovers because of their "presidential possibilities" or wealth (as Darwin would have it); had Mlle. Reisz ever "been in love," she might have known why Edna is drawn to Robert—because, "happy to be alive," she likes his "hair," "lips," "nose," etc. And in a third, more indirect reference to Darwin, Chopin dwells on Edna's decision to move out of her husband's home into her own "pigeon house." Here, apparently, her strategy is to out-Darwin Darwin, undercutting his presentation of civilized women by recalling his own rather extensive remarks about female pigeons. Darwin found it remarkable that female pigeons will often reject the males chosen for them by breeders. If imprisoned with a male she doesn't "fancy," the female will sulk, starve herself, or drive him away; and some are so "profligate" that they "prefer almost any stranger to their own mate[s]" (*Descent*, II, 119).

7. The best discussion of Chopin's racial views is Helen Taylor's *Gender, Race and Region in the Writings of Grace King, Ruth McEnery Stuart, and Kate Chopin* (Baton Rouge: Louisiana State University Press, 1989). But Taylor's discussion of the "unconsciously racist elements" in Chopin's work does not examine the relationship between these elements and Darwinian thought.

8. Darwin added this explanation to the second edition of *The Descent* in 1874: *The Descent of Man and Selection in Relation to Sex*, 2nd edn. (New York: Wheeler, n.d.), 119.

9. Cynthia Eagle Russett, *Sexual Science: The Victorian Construction of Womanhood* (Cambridge: Harvard University Press, 1989), 5, 203; further references to Russett are cited parenthetically.

10. Charlotte Perkins Gilman, *Women and Economics: A Study of the Economic Relation Between Men and Women as a Factor in Social Evolution* (New York: Harper and Row, 1966), 41. Also see Gilman's synopsis of the evolution of sex, p. 29. Subsequent references to this text are cited parenthetically by page.

11. *A Kate Chopin Miscellany*, 167.

12. For a different understanding of Chopin's view of men, one that does not consider her close reading of Darwin, see Joyce C. Dyer's "Kate Chopin's Sleeping Bruties" and her "Gouvernail, Kate Chopin's Sensitive Bachelor"; both essays are collected in Harold Bloom, ed., *Kate Chopin* (New York: Chelsea House, 1987).

13. Charles Darwin, *The Different Forms of Flowers on Plants of the Same Species* (London: Murray, 1877), 334. In *The Damnation of Theron Ware* (1896), Dr. Ledsmar studies monoecious and dioecious plants (i.e. those with male and female flowers on the same plant, and those with male and female flowers on separate plants, respectively) in order "to test the probabilities for or against Darwin's theory that hermaphroditism in plants is a late by-product of these earlier forms" (Harold Frederic, *The Damnation of Theron Ware* [Cambridge: Belknap, 1960], 228); and in *Women and Economics*, Gilman discusses "the evolution of the processes of reproduction," whereby "it was ascertained by nature's slow but sure experiments that the establishment of two sexes in separate organisms, and their differentiation, was to the advantage of the species" (p. 29).

THE TEETH OF DESIRE:
THE AWAKENING AND THE DESCENT OF MAN

BERT BENDER

Kate Chopin's fiction is an extended and darkening meditation on the meaning of human life and love in the light of Darwinian thought. Like many other serious writers of her time, she was struck by *The Descent of Man and Selection in Relation to Sex* (1871). But she read Darwin more closely than did most of her contemporaries, and much more closely than her many interpreters have realized.[1] She did not find Darwin's "main conclusion . . . distasteful" (as he "regret[ted] to think" many readers would).[2] Rather, in his main idea (that "man is descended from some lowly-organised form") and especially in his theory of sexual selection she found scientific support for the celebration of life that she knew and loved in Whitman's song of the "body electric." As she first viewed it, the theory of sexual selection offered a profoundly liberating sense of animal innocence in the realm of human courtship, especially for the Victorian woman.

In her first optimistic, if artless, presentation of the courtship drama, she created a heroine in *At Fault* (1890) who finally recognizes her "fault" of self-sacrifice for "what [had] seemed the only right."[3] Because of her commitment to conventional morality, she had denied the natural "electric" attraction she had felt for a divorced man (II, 762). But Chopin's announced purpose in the novel is to console the reader who she imagines is "driven by earthly needs to drag the pinioned spirit of your days through rut and mire" (II, 858). Thus she arranges for nature to intervene and provide a happy ending: the former wife drowns in a flood-swollen river, clearing the way for the lovers' "natural adjustment" to their predicament (II, 792). Chopin ended *At Fault* by bringing in a "highly gifted" new woman named Mrs. Griesmann to articulate the sense of reality that would support this first novel's happy ending. Mrs. Griesmann is a robust student of "Natural History" who collects "specimens"

From *American Literature* 63 (September 1991): 459–73. Copyright Duke University Press, 1991. Reprinted with permission. Also available in Bender's *The Descent of Love: Darwin and the Theory of Sexual Selection in American Fiction, 1871–1926* (Philadelphia: University of Pennsylvania Press, 1996).

out west and promises that by "studying certain fundamental truths," we can attain a "restful" view "of life as it is" (II, 875).

Mrs. Griesmann also indicates the direction Chopin would take in her subsequent stories, and had she allowed us a closer view of Mrs. Griesmann, we might have seen her with a copy of *The Descent of Man;* for all of Chopin's courtship plots during the next ten years are studies in natural history according to the logic of sexual selection—the primary mechanism in "the whole process of that most important function, the reproduction of the species" (*Descent,* I, 13). Apparently rather simple in its general outlines, sexual selection "depends," as Darwin explains,

> on the success of certain individuals over others of the same sex in relation to the propagation of the species; whilst natural selection depends on the success of both sexes, at all ages, in relation to the general conditions of life. The sexual struggle is of two kinds; in the one it is between the individuals of the same sex, generally the male sex, in order to drive away or kill their rivals, the females remaining passive; whilst in the other, the struggle is likewise between the individuals of the same sex, in order to excite or charm those of the opposite sex, generally the females, which no longer remain passive, but select the more agreeable partners. (II, 398)

Despite the apparent simplicity of sexual selection, however, it took Darwin many pages to explain how it is actually "an extremely complex affair" (I, 296). And as Chopin pursued her own studies in the natural history of sex, she read *The Descent of Man* more and more closely until her references to it became most extensive and explicit in *The Awakening.* But her response to Darwin is complicated in this way: although she accepted his basic premises that evolution proceeds through the agencies of natural selection and sexual selection, she quarreled with his analysis of the female's role in sexual selection. And—throughout the 1890s—as she continued her meditations on sexual selection and its implications for the meaning of love, her initial optimism developed into ambivalence and finally into a sense of despair that Darwin had not expressed in *The Descent of Man.*

Many of her stories dramatize the "law of battle" that dictates "a struggle between the males for the possession of the female," but she also resisted its corollaries concerning the female's passive and modest role in sexual relations and the male's physical and mental superiority to the female.[4] Chopin's women often manage in various ways to deny Darwin's definitions of the female's inferiority. And Chopin was particularly interested in Darwin's interpretation of the evolutionary development among "savage" human beings, whereby the male had "gained the power of selection" by having kept the female in an "abject state of bondage."[5] Although Darwin wrote that "the civilized nations" were vastly improved in this regard (women now having "free or almost free choice" [II, 356]), Chopin still felt the bind. And—

increasingly throughout the middle and late nineties—her women characters not only reclaim the power to select, but select for their own reasons. Eventually, especially in the case of Edna Pontellier in *The Awakening,* Chopin's women select on the basis of their own sexual desires rather than for the reasons Darwin attributed to civilized women, who "are largely influenced by the social position and wealth of the men" (II, 356).

Chopin's ambivalence toward the idea of sexual selection is apparent in two stories she wrote in 1894, five years after she had completed *At Fault* and four years before she began *The Awakening.* On one hand, Mrs. Baroda (in "A Respectable Woman") recognizes the sexual desire she feels for her husband's visiting friend and is at first repulsed by these feelings. She is a "respectable woman." But Mrs. Baroda will soon become one of the most daring women in American fiction during these years. For when she asks her husband to invite their friend for another visit, declaring that "I have overcome everything!" and promising that "this time I shall be very nice to him," it is clear that she is now determined to select the lover she desires. In creating this woman who not only threatens the institution of marriage but whose motive in sexual selection (her desire) is independent of the drive to propagate the species, Chopin modified Darwin's theory of sexual selection in a way that would have offended his Victorian sensibility. But Chopin did not at this stage in her development dare to depict a mother's desire (as she would in Edna Pontellier).

In Darwin's theory, civilization had evolved largely because woman's modesty curbs the male's eagerness to couple; and in this theory of the sexual reality, the male's eagerness is not only biologically innocent or red-blooded, but necessary. "In order that [the males] should become efficient seekers," Darwin concluded, "they would have to be endowed with strong passions. The acquirement of such passions would naturally follow from the more eager males leaving a larger number of offspring" (I, 274). The woman's role is of course different. As Ruth Bernard Yeazell has recently explained, in Darwin's description of "Nature's courtship," "females are at once less lustful and more discriminating" than males: "Like a respectable Victorian novel, *The Descent of Man, and Selection in Relation to Sex* implicitly defers the representation of sex in order to focus on the story of selection."[6] As Yeazell remarks, the "satisfying conclusion" to Darwin's story preserves the ideals of motherhood and the modest woman who knows nothing of appetite or sexual desire (p. 37). Clearly, Chopin had freed the "respectable" Mrs. Baroda from the restrictive definitions of womanhood provided by both *The Descent of Man* and the respectable Victorian novel.

In "The Story of an Hour," on the other hand, Mrs. Mallard feels the ecstasy of being liberated from what seems an agreeable marriage after the apparent accidental death of her husband. But then she comes to question the meaning of love. At first she realizes that there would no longer be a "powerful will bending hers in that blind persistence with which men *and* women believe they have a right to impose a private will upon a fellow-creature" (my emphasis). Then, thinking that "she had loved him—sometimes," she won-ders, "what could love, the unsolved mystery, count for in the face of this pos-session of self-assertion which she suddenly recognized as the strongest impulse of her being!" A few years later, Edna Pontellier's conflict will develop from feelings like these in Mrs. Baroda and Mrs. Mallard. Like Mrs. Baroda, Edna will be determined to select the lover she desires; and like Mrs. Baroda, her desire will develop to the accompaniment of an explicitly Whit-manesque celebration of sexual innocence.[7] But also, after she has acted in response to her desire, Edna will realize that "it was not love which had held this cup of life to her lips" (chap. 28). She will become depressed by what had only puzzled Mrs. Mallard: the meaninglessness of love in natural history. Realizing by 1897 that love has no claim to constancy, that it beats in self-assertion to the evolutionary time of sexual selection, Chopin had come to feel that the human spirit had been denied its place not only in a Christian uni-verse but also in the more limited sphere of human courtship and love.

Chopin's darkening response to *The Descent of Man* is reflected in her translations of Maupassant. In "A Divorce Case," for example, a young man with "a noble and exalted soul" falls "in love." But his love turns to despair, his "dream" to "miserable dust," when he becomes obsessed with the inescapable "bestial instinct" to "couple": "Two beasts, two dogs, two wolves, two foxes, roaming the woods, encounter each other. One is male, the other female," and they couple because the "bestial instinct . . . forces them to con-tinue the race." He realizes that "all beasts are the same, without knowing why. . . . We also."[8] And in "It," another of Maupassant's maddened narra-tors confesses that he cannot stop himself from marrying repeatedly, even though he considers "legal mating a folly." He is "incapable of confining [his] love to one woman" and marries again and again only "in order not to be alone!" (p. 189).

The solitude of Maupassant's characters—like that of Chopin's "solitary soul," Edna Pontellier—follows their shattering realizations that human sexu-ality as presented in *The Descent of Man* denies the myth of constant love. This is not to suggest that Chopin merely rewrote Maupassant; rather, that writ-ing from the female point of view, she addressed the same troubling question that she saw in Darwin and Maupassant. When Edna finally realizes "that the day would come when [Robert], too, and the thought of him would melt out of her existence, leaving her alone," she enters the "abysses of solitude" (chap. 39); and Maupassant's narrator in "Solitude" (again, as translated by Chopin), feels that he is "sinking . . . into some boundless subterranean depths." Sexual intercourse merely intensifies his solitude, for then he is momentarily "deceived . . . with the illusion that [he is] not alone"; "the rapturous union which must, it would seem, blend two souls into one being" ends in "hideous solitude" (pp. 196–97).

Edna Pontellier is a "solitary soul" in this modern sense. We cannot appreciate Chopin's understanding of life if we imagine Edna as the goddess of love reincarnated. For the sea with which Edna is repeatedly associated and in which she dies is millions of years older than that which had given birth to Venus in classic mythology: Edna is a post-Darwinian woman-animal who had evolved from the sea in a world without gods. Nor can we justly evaluate Chopin's work if we fail to see that beyond her unquestionable exploration of the female "self and society"—an exploration which has been so profoundly resonant in the feminist movement of the last quarter century—she explored the larger question of the female (and male) self in *life*.[9]

As a meditation on the Darwinian reality of Edna's life, *The Awakening* begins and ends with the essential fact of motherhood. Edna is of course a mother, but she cannot be like the "mother-women" she sees at Grand Isle, whose "wings as ministering angels" identify them as "the bygone heroine[s] of romance" (chap. 4). By the end of the novel Dr. Mandelet will refer to this "illusion" of angelic love as "Nature['s] . . . decoy to secure mothers for the race," but this cannot console Edna (chap. 38). Attending the birth of her friend's child, she had seen this "little new life" as merely another in the grotesque "multitude of souls that come and go"; thus she revolts "against the ways of nature" and finally sees her own children as "antagonists" (chaps. 37 and 39).

Twenty-eight years old at the beginning of the novel, Edna was ready to become a woman like the one Chopin knew in Whitman's "Song of Myself"—whose "Twenty-eight years of womanly life and all so lonesome" end in the vision of her bathing with the twenty-eight young men (section 11). In her twenty-eighth year, Edna, too, will discover the watery, erotic innocence that Whitman had dreamt for his woman. She will soon be ready to love "young men," to let her hand "descend tremblingly from their temples and ribs" (section 11). And she will know "the first-felt throbbings of desire" on August twenty-eighth, after her midnight swim with Robert (chap. 10). Chopin's emphasis on Edna's twenty-eight years is only one of her many references to Whitman; but Chopin's critics have never grasped the relevance of these references in *The Awakening*. Harold Bloom, for example, has recently concluded that "Chopin's representation of Edna's psychic self-gratification is not essentially altered from Whitman's solitary bliss"; Emerson is her "literary grandfather."[10] But Chopin could scarcely indicate her rejection of Emersonian thought more emphatically than she does in noting that Edna cannot read Emerson without growing "sleepy" (chap. 24). Edna awakens to a new reality. True, she begins her career as a conventional Victorian woman and then awakens in her twenty-eighth year to the joy of Whitman's transcendental eroticism. But as Chopin frees Edna to satisfy her desire for a lover, she will cause her to awaken more fully (in the pivotal twenty-eighth chapter of her story) to realize that desire had not brought her "love." And in the ritual celebration of her twenty-ninth birthday, Edna will know the strife and struggle for self-assertion that Darwin had uncovered in *The Descent of Man:* she will confront the "graven image of Desire" in the face of Victor, with his smile and gleaming "white teeth"—Victor, Robert's brother and antagonist in sexual competition first for Mariequita and now for Edna.[11]

In tracing the story of Edna's development from her twenty-eighth to her twenty-ninth year, Chopin begins where she must—"by the shore," as Whitman did in section 11 of "Song of Myself." But her logic in choosing this setting is not to affirm but to revise Whitman's view of the self in life. Beginning where she knew that life itself had begun according to *On the Origin of Species,* Chopin first presents Edna "advancing at snail's pace from the beach" with Robert. We will last see these creatures of evolution together in chapter 36, which opens in a scarcely Edenic "garden" (where they have met as though "destined to see [each other] only by accident") and which ends in Edna's "pigeon house." Here Chopin will describe the lovers' relationship with explicit references to *The Descent of Man.*

Chopin's first pointed reference to the role of sexual selection in Edna's life occurs in chapter 9. She has already responded to "the seductive odor of the sea," but now she will know the "wonderful power" of music as Darwin described it in both *The Descent of Man* and *The Expression of Emotions in Man and Animals.* Edna's response to Mademoiselle Reisz's piano performance of a piece by Frédéric Chopin is clearly based on a passage from Darwin, the point of which is that music was originally the means by which our "half-human ancestors aroused each other's ardent passions" (*Descent,* II, 337).

Edna had responded to music before, but never as she will during this performance. Before, music had sometimes evoked in her a picture of "solitude" that is again a measure of Chopin's passage beyond Whitman's mid-nineteenth-century view of life. She had imagined "the figure of a man standing beside a desolate rock on the seashore. He was naked. His attitude was one of hopeless resignation as he looked toward a distant bird winging its flight away from him" (chap. 9). Even in this echo from "Out of the Cradle Endlessly Rocking," the "hopeless resignation" of Chopin's man presents a considerably darker view of life and solitude than that projected by Whitman. Still, in this image of a "distant bird winging its flight away," there is a suggestion of the consoling thought which Whitman had imagined in the surviving he-bird's song, or in the solitary thrush's in "When Lilacs Last in the Dooryard Bloom'd." But this image had come to Whitman's "awaken[ed]" imagination in "Out of the Cradle" (in 1859), and when Edna fully awakens to Chopin's view of the Darwinian reality by the end of the novel, the bird will reappear as the image of the spirit defeated—"with a broken wing . . . beating the air above, reeling, fluttering, circling disabled down, down to the water" (chap. 39).

The musical performance on August twenty-eighth is crucial in propelling Edna toward her final bleak awakening, for here her response to the music is as Darwin explained in *The Expression of Emotions:* music can cause a person to "tremble," to feel "the thrill or slight shiver which runs down the backbone and limbs," or to experience "a slight suffusion of tears" that resembles "weeping" caused by other emotions.[12] Thus, during this musical performance in *The Awakening*, "the very first chords which Mademoiselle Reisz struck upon the piano sent a keen tremor down Mrs. Pontellier's spinal column." And because "her being was tempered to take an impress of the abiding truth," she finds that "the very passions themselves were aroused within her soul, swaying it, lashing it, as the waves daily beat upon her splendid body. She trembled, she was choking, and the tears blinded her" (chap. 9). The musical performance moves others, too: "What passion!" one exclaims— "It shakes a man!" Immediately following the performance the group decides to take a midnight swim; and now, like a joyful child taking her first steps, Edna realizes that she can swim. Feeling that "some power of significant import had been given her to control the workings of her body and her soul," she wants to "swim far out, where no woman had swum before" (chap. 10). Later, alone with Robert, she tells him of the "thousand emotions" that had swept through her as a result of Mademoiselle Reisz's playing, and before they part she is "pregnant with the first-felt throbbings of desire."

Chopin indicates at once that Edna's developing desire will eventually lead her into the "abysses of solitude." When she enters the water on this night, she gathers "in an impression of space and solitude" from "the vast expanse of water"; and in her solitary swim she realizes that she might perish "out there alone." Moreover, the simultaneous development of her desire and her sense of solitude will eventually lead her to a clearer understanding of her "position in the universe" as an animal and therefore as a creature empowered to participate fully in the sexual reality as a self-conscious selector (chap. 6). Her development toward claiming the power to select is gradual, but she takes a first crucial step immediately after her swim by refusing to yield to Mr. Pontellier's "desire." And a few days later she awakens more fully to her animal nature after fleeing from an oppressive church service to Madame Antoine's seaside home. Here, awakened from a nap, "very hungry," she "bit a piece" from a loaf of brown bread, "tearing it with her strong, white teeth" (chap. 13).

In his remarks on the canine tooth in human beings, Darwin notes that it "no longer serves man as a special weapon for tearing his enemies or prey." But he sharpens his main point here by adding: "He who rejects with scorn the belief that the shape of his own canines, and their occasional great development in other men, are due to our early forefathers having been provided with these formidable weapons, will probably reveal, by sneering, the line of his descent. For though he no longer intends, nor has the power to use these teeth as weapons, he will unconsciously retract his 'snarling muscles'. . . ."[13] Clearly, Edna's strong teeth indicate her kinship with our "half-human ancestors" in *The Descent of Man*, for she tells Robert that the "whole island seems changed" now: "a new race of beings must have sprung up, leaving only you and me as past relics" (chap. 13).

But now Chopin will force the awakening Edna to endure the frustrations of civilized life, first by having to contend with Robert's sudden departure and the jealousy she feels when Robert writes only to others; and then when she suffers more consciously from the restrictions in her marriage. She rebels against her husband's and society's covenants, refuses to be one of his "valued . . . possessions," and stamps on her wedding ring (chap. 17). And when she obstinately withdraws her normal "tacit submissiveness" in her marriage (chap. 19), she takes another of her crucial steps toward claiming her place in the arena of sexual selection. Before she selects a lover, she rejects her husband's sexual advances, leaving him "nervously" to explain to Dr. Mandelet that her "notion . . . concerning the eternal rights of women" means that "we meet in the morning at the breakfast table" (chap. 22).

Dr. Mandelet counsels Mr. Pontellier to be patient with Edna, for "woman . . . is a very peculiar and delicate organism." But it would seem that even the doctor does not understand the "new set of sensations" Edna experiences in response to her father's visit (chaps. 22, 23). That is, he knows "the inner life" of his "fellow creatures" better than most men; and, seeing the subtle change in Edna after her father's visit ("palpitant with the forces of life . . . she reminded him of some beautiful, sleek animal waking up in the sun"), he guesses that she has taken Arobin as her lover (chap. 23). But he does not theorize, as Chopin does, on how the "laws of inheritance" (as Darwin understood them before Mendel) might have enabled Edna to acquire some of her father's masculine authority and passion. Her father has the essential male qualities that are "accumulated by sexual selection"—"ardour in love" and "courage" (*Descent,* I, 296). An aging Confederate colonel, he still has the power to arouse Madame Ratignolle at a *soirée musicale* (here again Chopin indicates her understanding of the sexual meaning of music): she "coquetted with him in the most captivating and naïve manner," and she invites him to dinner with her on "any day . . . he might select" (chap. 23). The Colonel plays an essential role in Chopin's effort to validate Edna's developing power to select, and in this scene at the *soirée musicale* "her fancy selected" one or two men.

This is perhaps the most intricate part of Chopin's quarrel with Darwin, for in referring to his theory on the laws of inheritance, she exploits a possibility that he allows the female but does not himself develop: to do so would have contradicted his image of the modest woman with "powers of perception" and "taste" (*Descent,* I, 296). In this way, Chopin used Darwin's own theory in order to modify his definition of the sexual reality among humans: building on his "hypothesis of pangenesis," whereby "gemmules . . . are transmitted to the offspring of both sexes," she suggests that Edna is an example of how "both sexes" can be "modified in the same manner" (I, 280, 299). Chopin's point seems clear when she has the Colonel imagine that "he had bequeathed to all of his daughters the germs of a masterful capability" (chap. 23). And, in arranging for Edna's lover, Arobin, to toast the Colonel for having "invented" Edna (chap. 30), Chopin underscores the irony of her quarrel with Darwin. After the Colonel's visit, Edna will attend the horse races; and there, her "blood" and "brain" inflamed, she talks "like her father," causing nearby people to turn "their heads" and Arobin to feel her magnetic force (chap. 25). Later that evening, when Arobin is moved by an impulse to show her the scar on his wrist which he had received—according to Darwin's law of battle for possession of the female—"from a saber cut . . . in a duel . . . when he was nineteen," Edna is agitated and sickened; but Arobin "drew all her awakening sensuousness" (chap. 23). Within days, she will respond to his effrontery not with a "crimson" blush of modesty, as Darwin might have imagined,[14] but with pleasure because it "appeal[ed] to the animalism that stirred impatiently within her" (chap. 26).

By now Edna has awakened enough to her own sexual reality to articulate the main point in Chopin's quarrel with Darwin. In a discussion with Mademoiselle Reisz about the meaning of love, Edna exhibits a wisdom that Chopin will not grant Mademoiselle Reisz, whose "avoidance of the water" is not only amusing (some of the bathers imagined that "it was on account of her false hair") but indicative of her essential sexlessness (chap. 16). Accusing Mademoiselle Reisz of either lying or having "never been in love," Edna proclaims, "do you suppose a woman knows why she loves? Does she select? Does she say to herself: 'Go to! Here is a distinguished statesman with presidential possibilities. I shall proceed to fall in love with him . . . [or with] this financier?' " She admits that she loves Robert when she "ought not to," but Chopin's "ought" refers more to Darwin's theory about why civilized women select (modestly and discriminately, for wealth, etc.) than to the more obvious social prohibition against extramarital love. Edna loves Robert for the same reason that Whitman's imagined woman let her hand descend "tremblingly from [the young men's] temples": "Because his hair is brown and grows away from his temples, because he opens and shuts his eyes," because she likes his "nose," "two lips," and "square chin"—in short, because she is "happy to be alive" (chap. 26).

In her next meeting with Arobin, then, Edna's "nature" responds fully and for the first time to a kiss—"a flaming torch that kindled [her] desire" (chap. 27). And she will awaken next morning—in the pivotal twenty-eighth chapter—to her post-Whitmanian sense of the "significance of life, that monster made up of beauty and brutality." Comprehending life in this new way—"as if a mist had been lifted from her eyes"—she feels neither shame nor remorse, only "regret" that "it was not the kiss of love which had inflamed her, because it was not love which had held this cup of life to her lips" (chap. 28).

But far from denying this regrettable reality, Edna enters bravely and immediately into her new sexual independence by moving out of the family home into her own "pigeon house." In creating Edna's pigeon house, Chopin refers to Darwin's theories of sexual selection as explicitly as she had in her earlier references to the law of battle, the role of music in sexual selection, the relevance of our canine teeth, or the laws of inheritance. Scarcely a merely eccentric name for Edna's new dwelling after the *coup d'état,* "pigeon house" is an emphatic reference to the triumphant female pigeons Darwin describes in *The Descent of Man*—creatures who, like Edna, "occasionally feel a strong antipathy towards certain males [and preference *for* certain other males] without any assignable cause" (II, 118). Quoting a French study, Darwin tells how, when a female pigeon experiences an antipathy for a male, nothing can cause her to submit to him—neither the male's flaming desire nor any inducements a breeder might give her. She constantly refuses his caresses, even if confined with him for a year, sulking in a corner of her "prison," and coming out only to eat or drink; and if he forces his affections, she will repel him in a rage.[15] "On the other hand," Darwin notes, some females will desert their mates if they take "a strong fancy" for another; and some are even so "profligate" that they "prefer almost any stranger to their own mate" (II, 119).

Edna's birthday party is a ritual celebration of her entry into the modern sexual reality that Whitman's woman could not have known when he created her in 1855. Edna "selected [her guests] with discrimination," and Victor, "a graven image of Desire," is among them. When she tries to stop him from singing Robert's love song ("*Ah! si tu savais!*"), placing her hand over his mouth, "the touch of his lips was like a pleasing sting" (chap. 30). Thus, when Robert returns unexpectedly, she will quickly see that the love she had imagined is now impossibly complicated with all the strife even pigeons know in the arena of sexual selection. Robert is jealous of Arobin; she is jealous of the Mexican woman who gave Robert his embroidered tobacco pouch. And when she sleeps with Arobin again—to satisfy "her nature's requirements"— she enters into the hopelessness that will lead her back to the sea (chap. 35). After her accidental meeting with Robert (in a garden), they return to her "pigeon house" and define their irreconcilable differences as would-be lovers: he explains that he had left her because she belonged to Mr. Pontellier and that it was impossible to imagine him setting Edna "free." For Edna, of course, this would be absurdly "impossible," for she is "no longer one of Mr. Pontellier's possessions. . . . I give myself where I choose" (chap. 36). Although Robert is shocked by Edna's assertion of her absolute liberation, his only impulse at last is still "to hold her and keep her." Then—even after Edna revolts against nature when she helps her friend give birth, and even after she hears Dr. Mandelet's explanation about nature's "decoy" for securing "mothers for the race"—she returns to Robert, imagining "no greater bliss on earth than possession of the beloved one" (chap. 38). Even now she, too, would impose her "private will upon a fellow creature" and call it love, as Mrs. Mallard had imagined. And she will follow the illusion of love, nature's decoy, until she returns to her empty "pigeon house" and finds Robert's note.

Edna is now fully awake to her new reality: "Today it is Arobin," she tells herself, and "tomorrow it will be someone else" (chap. 39). Her desire (like the passion she had felt at the musical performance that night when she was twenty-eight) will rise and fall, "lashing" her soul "as the waves daily beat upon her splendid body" (chap. 9). She knows that the sense of her absolute isolation as a solitary soul will descend inevitably when she forgets even Robert. She will find no peace until she feels the "soft, close embrace" of the sea, her true element. And in this despair she sees her children as "antagonists," for *they* are nature's cause in natural and sexual selection—the force within herself by which love's wing was broken.

Notes

1. In his 1894 portrait of Chopin. William Schuyler reported that "the subjects which . . . attracted her were almost entirely scientific, the departments of Biology and Anthropology having a special interest for her. The works of Darwin, Huxley, and Spencer were her daily companions; for the study of the human species . . . has always been her constant delight" (in *A Kate Chopin Miscellany,* ed. Per Seyersted [Natchitoches, La.: Northwestern State Univ. Press, 1979], p. 117). But no critic to date has looked closely at Chopin's response to Darwin. Per Seyersted provided the most reliable insight in his general but undeveloped remark that she "wanted . . . nothing less than to describe post-Darwinian man with the openness of the modern French writers" (*Kate Chopin* [Baton Rouge: Louisiana State Univ. Press, 1969], p. 96). See also Seyersted's "Introduction" to *The Storm and Other Stories by Kate Chopin with The Awakening* (Old Westbury, N.Y.: Feminist Press, 1974), p. 15; and his remarks on Edna's realization "that sex is largely independent of our volition" in his edition of *The Complete Works of Kate Chopin,* 2 vols. (Baton Rouge: Louisiana State Univ. Press, 1969), I, 28. Two other critics have written on naturalism in *The Awakening,* but without examining Darwin's presence in that book: Jerome Klinkowitz, in his chapter, "Kate Chopin's Awakening to Naturalism," *The Practice of Fiction in America: Writers from Hawthorne to the Present* (Ames: Iowa State Univ. Press, 1980); and Nancy Walker, in "Feminist or Naturalist: The Social Context of Kate Chopin's *The Awakening,*" *Southern Quarterly,* 17, No. 2 (1979), 95–103.

2. *The Descent of Man and Selection in Relation to Sex,* 2 vols. in 1 (1871: rpt. Princeton: Princeton Univ. Press, 1981), II, 404. Unless otherwise noted, further references to *The Descent* are from this edition and this text, and are cited parenthetically by volume and page.

3. *The Complete Works of Kate Chopin,* II, 872. Subsequent references to *At Fault* will be to this text, cited parenthetically by page. In subsequent references to *The Awakening,* however—because there are now so many reliable editions of that book—I cite chapter numbers only. Also, since the two stories I discuss here ("A Respectable Woman," and "The Story of an Hour") are so short and so widely collected, I have not cited page numbers.

4. *The Descent of Man,* I, 259; for Darwin's understanding of the female's inferiority, see, for example, his remark that "man is more powerful in body and mind than woman" (II, 371). Cynthia Eagle Russett's *Sexual Science: The Victorian Construction of Womanhood* (Cambridge: Harvard Univ. Press, 1989) is an indispensable guide to the implications of Darwinian thought for the Victorian woman.

5. *The Descent of Man,* II, 371. Among most animals (birds, especially), in Darwin's analysis, the female selects the victorious male or the most attractive one—i.e., the most colorful or highly ornamented one.

6. "Nature's Courtship Plot in Darwin and Ellis," *Yale Journal of Criticism,* 2 (1989), 36–37.

7. Sitting under a live oak alone with Mrs. Baroda, the Barodas' friend, Gouvernail, murmurs these lines from "Song of Myself": "Night of south winds–night of the large few

stars!/Still nodding night"; these lines are contained in Whitman's sentence, "Press close bare bosom'd night . . . mad naked summer night," in section 21, which ends, "O unspeakable passionate love."

8. Thomas Bonner, Jr., *The Kate Chopin Companion, with Chopin's Translations from French Fiction* (New York: Greenwood, 1988), pp. 179, 181. Further references to Chopin's translations of Maupassant are cited parenthetically by page from this text.

9. The distinctions I suggest here in my remarks about Aphrodite and the "self and society" refer to two of the very best essays on *The Awakening*—Sandra M. Gilbert's "The Second Coming of Aphrodite: Kate Chopin's Fantasy of Desire," *Kenyon Review,* 5 (1983), 42–56; and Nina Baym's "Introduction" to *The Awakening and Selected Stories* (New York: Random House, 1981), p. xxxiv.

10. *Kate Chopin,* ed. Harold Bloom (New York: Chelsea House, 1987), pp. 3, 2, 1.

11. Chap. 30; in chap. 16 Edna hears that Robert had once "thrashed" Victor for thinking "he had some sort of claim upon" Mariequita. In chap. 39 Mariequita senses that Victor is "in love with Mrs. Pontellier"; and Victor, jealous of one of Mariequita's lovers, threatens "to hammer his head into a jelly."

12. *The Expression of Emotions in Man and Animals* (1872; rpt. New York: Appleton, 1924), p. 217.

13. *The Descent of Man and Selection in Relation to Sex,* 2nd ed. (New York: Wheeler, n.d.), pp. 40–41. In the second edition, Darwin added this new chap. 2; and Chopin's apparent reference to it is one of several suggestions in her work that her text was the second edition.

14. See, for example, Darwin's discussion of blushing in *The Expression of Emotions* (p. 334). Many of Chopin's characters blush or flush in ways that indicate their animal emotions.

15. The quoted passage (from Boitard and Corbié, "Les Pigeons" [1824]) reads: "Quand une femelle éprouve de l'antipathie pour un mâle avec lequel on veut l'accoupler, malgré tous les feux de l'amour, malgré l'alpiste et le chènevis dont on la nourrit pour augmenter son ardeur, malgré un emprisonnement de six mois et même d'un an, elle refuse constamment ses caresses; les avances empressées, les agaceries, les tournoiemens, les tendres roucoulemens, rien ne peut lui plaire ni l'émouvoir; gonflée, boudeuse, blottie dans un coin de sa prison, elle n'en sort que pour boire et manger, ou pour repousser avec une espèce de rage des caresses devenues trop pressantes" (II, 118–119).

THE BOY'S QUEST IN KATE CHOPIN'S
"A VOCATION AND A VOICE"

PEGGY SKAGGS

That Kate Chopin's *The Awakening* is concerned primarily with a woman's search for her own identity has been clearly established by critics of the last decade,[1] and feminists have rejoiced to find a nineteenth-century novelist with so much insight into the problems twentieth-century women still face in establishing themselves as discrete individuals apart from their roles as wives and mothers.[2] But as a matter of fact, Chopin was concerned far more with the identity problems of all human beings than with the peculiar difficulties society foists upon women, a fact that becomes apparent upon examination of other interesting characters she created, many of whom are male.

For example, "A Vocation and a Voice," selected by Chopin to be the title story for her third volume of collected short stories, features a male protagonist whose search for himself parallels in several ways Edna's quest in *The Awakening*. And, although Edna's famous search for identity is made difficult by the fact that she is a woman in a society dominated by men, the boy's search in the little known "A Vocation and a Voice" is no easier. Indeed, his masculinity creates its own problems, even as Edna's femininity does. In both cases, the characters are forced to recognize and deal with the biological, emotional, and social realities of being female or male, as the case may be.

Chopin views the question of human identity for everyone as a quest growing out of three often contradictory human drives—the drives for a sense of belonging, for love relationships with others, and for selfhood.[3] The protagonist in "A Vocation and a Voice," called only "the boy" until almost the end of a rather long story, is in the beginning virtually homeless, loveless, and "selfless." The story is essentially that of his search for his own identity.

The boy has been sent by Mrs. Donnelly, with whose family he lives as "an alien member" in "The Patch," to deliver a message to her mother in a distant part of the city. He discovers that he has taken a wrong streetcar and, having expected to get his return fare from the lady he was to visit, he begins

From *American Literature* 51 (May 1979): 270–76. Copyright Duke University Press, 1979. Reprinted by permission.

to make his way on foot back toward "The Patch." But his progress is slow, because "With him was a conviction that it would make no difference to any one whether he got back to 'The Patch' or not." Having "a vague sense of being unessential which always dwelt with him,"[4] the boy is happy enough to go along with a gypsy couple he encounters. He enjoys camping out, with the accompanying contact with nature, and contributes his share to the group's welfare by helping to set up and break camp and by doing various chores.

By calling him only "the boy," Kate Chopin emphasizes that he *is* only a boy. "He was rather tall, though he had spoken with the high, treble voice of a girl" (II, 520) and "The young girls did not attract him more than the boys or the little children" (II, 522), the reader is informed. Further, his nameless-ness emphasizes the universality of the experiences he undergoes—the loss of innocence and the accompanying search for place, love, and self.

Suzima, the female member of the nomadic couple he joins, is "robust and young—twenty or thereabouts—and comely, in a certain rude, vigorous fashion" (II, 523). When the boy happens along, she is trying to beat out a grass fire while cursing her absent husband, who seems to get drunk when-ever it is time to break camp. She says, " 'I guess he's drunk down there—him and his mules! He thinks more of them mules than he does of me and the whole world put together' " (II, 525).

Gutro, Suzima's husband, is "a short, broad-girted man, leading his sleek bay mules—splended looking animals—and talking to them as he came along. . . . his hair, as well as his beard, was long, curly and greasy; . . . he wore a slouch hat over a knotted red handkerchief and small golden hoops in his ears" (II, 525). He is often called simply "the Beast."

The boy finds a place, of sorts, in this makeshift family as they meander southward. "The days were a gorgeous, golden processional, good and warm with sunshine, and languorous" (II, 526). They stop for a month in a run-down cabin near a village, where the boy renews the close contact he had enjoyed with the Catholic Church while he lived in "The Patch." When Suz-ima and Gutro decide to move on, the village priest tries to get the boy to stay. But the boy refuses:

" 'I got to go,' he murmured. . . . Yes, he wanted to lead an upright, clean existence before God and man. . . . He liked the village, the people, the life which he had led there. Above all he liked the man whose kindly spirit had been moved to speak and act in his behalf. But the stars were beginning to shine and he thought of the still nights in the forest. A savage instinct stirred within him and revolted against the will of this man who was seeking to detain him" (II, 536).

Suzima often sings as the three walk along the road. "The boy thought he had never heard anything more beautiful than the full, free notes that came from her throat, filling the vast, woody temple with melody. It was always the same stately refrain from some remembered opera that she sang as she walked" (II, 527). In fact, "the one stately refrain" (II, 533) grows so familiar to the boy that he sometimes hears it in his dreams. This idyllic existence continues until one day when the boy happens upon Suzima bathing naked in a little stream. "He saw her as one sees an object in a flash from a dark sky—sharply, vividly. Her image, against the background of tender green, ate into his brain and into his flesh with the fixedness and intensity of white-hot iron." After this event, the woman is at first "less kind" (II, 539) to him, but they soon become lovers.

The effect upon the boy's sense of identity is immediate: "A few days had wrought great changes with the boy. That which he had known before he now comprehended, and with comprehension sympathy awoke. He seemed to have been brought in touch with the universe of men and all things that live. He cared more than ever for the creeping and crawling things, for the beautiful voiceless life that met him at every turn . . . that silently unfolded the mysterious, inevitable existence" (II, 541). Thus, the boy—who began the story without place, love, or self-knowledge—now feels that he has found all three.

In *The Awakening,* Edna is described as having married Léonce Pontellier in an effort to fill two of the three identity-related needs—the needs for a sense of belonging and for love: "As the devoted wife of a man who worshiped her, she felt she would take her place with a certain dignity in the world of reality" (II, 898). And for six years, she was not noticeably troubled by that third need, the need for selfhood. But as the fateful summer progresses and her sense of herself as a discrete human entity begins to unfold, the third need becomes the dominant one. Furthermore, as her selfhood grows stronger, her natural sensuousness is released, leading inevitably to her sexual awakening, an experience which is described in terms remarkably similar to those describing the boy's response, quoted above. In both cases, discovering their own sexual nature leads the characters into self-understanding that far transcends the physical experience. Edna's initial adulterous experience with Alcée Arobin, "the first kiss of her life to which her nature had really responded," is followed by "multitudinous emotions." But "Above all, there was understanding. She felt as if a mist had been lifted from her eyes, enabling her to look upon and comprehend the significance of life, that monster made up of beauty and brutality" (II, 967).

The one element present in Edna's discovery but lacking in the boy's is the consciousness of brutality as a part of experience, but this knowledge is not long in coming to him, also. His love for Suzima and his new sense of selfhood soon make his former place as "the boy" in this household impossible. The crisis occurs one day when Gutro is drunk and Suzima defiant. "Suddenly, the man, in a rage, turned to strike her with a halter that he held uplifted, but, quicker than he, the boy was ready with a pointed hunting knife that he seized from the ground" (II, 542). The boy, thus, not only loses his "place" and the love relationship with Suzima; he is also forced to realize that his new self-knowledge is only partial: "He had always supposed that he could live in the world a blameless life. . . . He had never dreamed of a devil lurking unknown to him, in his blood, that would some day blind him, disable his will and direct his hands to deeds of violence. . . . He felt as if he had encountered some hideous being with whom he was not acquainted and who had said to him: 'I am yourself' " (II, 542). This new concept of himself he finds unbearable, and he immediately enters a monastery, the "Refuge" (II, 544), to escape facing it.

The boy thus acquires, at last, a name—Brother Ludovic—and a new identity, albeit only a partial one: "He often felt that he had been born anew, the day whereupon he had entered the gate of this holy refuge. That hideous, evil spectre of himself lurking outside, ready at any moment to claim him should he venture within its reach, was, for a long time, a menace to him. But he had come to dread it no longer, secure in the promise of peace which his present life held out to him" (II, 543–544). And so, he comes to feel secure in his new "place" and in his knowledge of himself.

Brother Ludovic has a great dream, to build a solid stone wall around the "Refuge." He works feverishly at this task that will take a lifetime to complete. "He liked to picture himself an old man, grown feeble with age, living upon this peaceful summit all enclosed by the solid stone wall built with the strength of his youth and manhood" (II, 544). But one day he learns that this self-image, too, is inadequate. He is working industriously on his wall, when

> Suddenly Brother Ludovic stopped, lifting his head with the mute quivering attention of some animal in the forest, startled at the scent of approaching danger. . . . The air was hot and heavy. . . . He could hear soft splashing at the pool. An image that had once been branded into his soul . . . unfolded before his vision with the poignancy of life.
>
> . . . .
>
> He was conscious of nothing in the world but the voice that was calling him and the cry of his own being that responded. Brother Ludovic bounded down from the wall and followed the voice of the woman. (II, 545–546)

Again, at this climactic point, "A Vocation and a Voice" is strikingly like *The Awakening.* The hypnotic song that draws Brother Ludovic from his "Refuge" is paralleled by the magnetic song of the sea described at two crucial points in *The Awakening,* first when Edna learns to swim alone and again when she walks into the sea for the last time: "The voice of the sea is seductive, never ceasing, whispering, clamoring, murmuring, inviting. . . . The touch of the sea is sensuous, enfolding the body in its soft, close embrace" (II, 893 and 999–1000). Thus, Brother Ludovic and Edna both reveal that having a secure "place," even a "Refuge," is not enough in life; that one's sexual nature is a powerful part of the self, whether masculine or feminine, which will not be denied by rock walls or by social conventions; and that one may never be able to learn all there is to know about the person who dwells within himself or herself.

Although the point of view in "A Vocation and a Voice" is as distinctly masculine as that in *The Awakening* is feminine, the boy's conflicting needs, like Edna's, are universal, transcending sexual limitations. Kate Chopin was concerned with *human* identity. We continue to do her less than justice when we try to make her a spokeswoman for only the female half of the human family.

Notes

1. See Per Seyersted, *Kate Chopin: A Critical Biography* (Baton Rouge, La., 1969) and Peggy Skaggs, "Three Tragic Figures in Kate Chopin's *The Awakening*," *Louisiana Studies,* VIII (Winter, 1974), 345–364.

2. Feminists have, in fact, been predominant among Chopin critics during the past decade. The *Kate Chopin Newsletter,* for example, has been renamed *Regionalism and the Female Imagination* in keeping with its emphasis on feminism. Its editor, Emily Toth, states clearly the feminist view of Chopin's work in "Kate Chopin's *The Awakening* as Feminist Criticism," *Louisiana Studies,* XV (Fall, 1976), 241–251, calling that novel "both a synthesis and crowning achievement of feminist consciousness at the turn of the century" (p. 243). Among other essays developing the feminist perspective are Gladys W. Milliner's "The Tragic Imperative: *The Awakening* and *The Bell Jar,*" *Mary Wollston{e}craft Newsletter,* II (Dec., 1973), 21–27; Clement Eaton's "Breaking a Path for the Liberation of Women in the South," *Georgia Review,* XXVIII (Summer, 1974), 187–199; and Joyce Ruddel Ladenson's "Paths to Suicide: Rebellion Against Victorian Womanhood in Kate Chopin's *The Awakening*," *Intellect,* CIV (July–Aug., 1975), 52–55.

Reminders that Chopin's work transcends mere feminist advocacy, however, have not been altogether absent. See especially Donald A. Ringe, "Romantic Imagery in Kate Chopin's *The Awakening*," *American Literature,* XLIII (Jan., 1972), 580–588.

3. See David J. DeLevita, *The Concept of Identity* (Paris, 1965), p. 193, for a psychologist's definition of identity that closely parallels Chopin's ideas.

4. *The Complete Works of Kate Chopin,* ed. Per Seyersted, 2 vols. (Baton Rouge, La., 1969), II, 521. All subsequent references are to this edition.

THE RESTIVE BRUTE: THE SYMBOLIC PRESENTATION OF REPRESSION AND SUBLIMATION IN KATE CHOPIN'S "FEDORA"

JOYCE [COYNE] DYER

Though brief, "Fedora" is one of Kate Chopin's most vivid and startling explorations of inner life. Chopin's method of characterization in "Fedora" lets us know the protagonist well in only three pages, only seventeen paragraphs. Although Chopin does tell us something about Fedora's buried life through direct narration (Fedora, Chopin observes, was experiencing "a swift, fierce encounter betwixt thought and feeling"[1]), she relies primarily on dramatizing Fedora's emotional confusion through symbolic action. The technique is ideal. It enhances and supplements our understanding of Fedora's psyche in a way that neither authorial analysis nor interior monologue might. For example, it best permits Chopin to capture both the "swiftness" and the "fierceness" of Fedora's struggle: extensive explanations by the author would slow down the narrative's tempo and necessarily lessen the suddenness of Fedora's experience; direct commentary would not be able to present the brutal intensity of Fedora's passion in a way acceptable to the moral sensibilities of her publishers or to the artistic sensibility of Chopin herself. With its use, Chopin can also gain character accuracy: Fedora, to remain believable as a bewildered, overwhelmingly repressed woman, must not be able to articulate her confusion through interior monologue. Chopin's technique helps to make Fedora one of the most astonishing fictional figures of the late nineteenth century and her story one of Chopin's most careful.

Before Fedora is violently awakened by Young Malthers' good looks and manliness, she leads a quiet, well-ordered life governed by rationality and good sense. Fedora has long assumed that she is superior in years and wisdom to her younger brothers and sisters and their friends. She enjoys taking care of them while her mother is away because of the authority the occasion permits her. She looks after the health of the young people and plans games and entertainment for their warm afternoons. And Fedora does not seem to need social contact other than that such "mothering" provides. She certainly does

From *Studies in Short Fiction* 18 (Summer 1981): 261–65. Copyright 1981 by Newberry College. Reprinted by permission of the Editor.

not need men. She has long ago formed a theory about men that now guides her dealings with them: men, quite simply, are not worth the time. She has measured them and found them lacking. Fedora's appearance reflects both her attitude of superiority and her coldness: "Fedora was tall and slim, and carried her head loftily, and wore eye-glasses and a severe expression" (p. 467). Fedora is thirty. Some of the youngsters imagine that she must be at least a hundred years old.

But although Chopin spends a careful paragraph telling us what Fedora is like before she confronts Young Malthers, the author hurries to recall the incident that begins to disrupt the neat patterns Fedora has established for herself. One day Fedora begins to answer a question asked by Young Malthers—a "boy" who is twenty-three but Fedora remembers as a lad of fifteen—and realizes that she, tall and superior, is looking *up* at him. He has matured. Suddenly, Fedora realizes "he was a man—in voice, in attitude, in bearing, in every sense—a man" (p. 468). He begins to exist for her in a way her other acquaintances never have. She memorizes the details of his countenance: the eyes are blue and troubled, the face brown and smooth, the lips strong, firm and clean. "She kept thinking of his face, and every trick of it after he passed on" (p. 468), notes Chopin.

After this encounter, Chopin offers a brief, purposely vague narrative comment about the new sensations Fedora feels after the meeting with Young Malthers. "There was uneasiness, restlessness, expectation when he was not there within sight or sound. There was redoubled uneasiness when he was by—there was inward revolt, astonishment, rapture, self-contumely; a swift, fierce encounter betwixt thought and feeling" (p. 468). Chopin does not return to this technique, however. She withdraws as active commentator. She lets Fedora's actions symbolically dramatize her character's tumultuous inner world.

We begin to see the desperate and pathetic nature of Fedora's conflict as we watch her fondle Young Malthers' clothes. Driven by impulse, she frequently passes by the hall pegs to see if perhaps his hat is hanging upon one. If it is, she eagerly touches it. On one occasion, she discovers a discarded coat of his hanging there as well. She approaches the coat, at first pretending to straighten its folds and pleats. But after she carefully determines that no one is watching, Fedora buries her face in the folds for one rapturous moment. Fedora's need for human contact is so great that even a man's hat and coat offer pleasure. Indeed, we can fully appreciate the pleasure his discarded clothing brings Fedora only after we understand that Fedora's fear of social disapproval and of her own impulses at this time (before the arrival of the sister) will prohibit any contact closer than this. For Fedora, contact with Young Malthers' clothing must substitute for direct sexual contact.

At the same time Fedora feels driven to touch Young Malthers' garments, she develops an urgent and "unaccountable" desire to pick up his sister at the local train station. Fedora, of course, "could hardly explain to her own satisfaction why she wanted to go herself to the station for Young Malthers' sister" (p. 468). But as we follow her there and back, we begin to understand her motives.

Standing at the train station, Fedora responds to the setting in a way that further clarifies our understanding of her confusion. This scene psychologically illuminates the central scene with Miss Malthers that follows. The station is located in a very sensuous nook at the foot of a tree-studded hill. The scene is lovely, inviting to the reader. Nature and natural impulse seem good and right.

> It was in a pretty nook, green and fragrant, set down at the foot of a wooded hill. Off in a clearing there was a field of yellow grain, upon which the sinking sunlight fell in slanting, broken beams. Far down the track there were some men at work, and the even ring of their hammers was the only sound that broke upon the stillness.

Fedora at first responds as it seems right that she should: "Fedora loved it all—sky and woods and sunlight; sounds and smells" (p. 468). Her emotions overpower her for a moment. But she refuses to relax for long. Her reason returns, weakens her emotion, and reinstates rigid control. As we watch her, we observe, with regret and sympathy, that "her bearing—elegant, composed, reserved—betrayed nothing emotional as she tramped the narrow platform" (p. 468).

However, not until Fedora drives Miss Malthers home from the station do we fully realize how severely Fedora's repression and prudent rationality have damaged her emotional and sexual health. Fedora is not at all interested in Miss Malthers' personal traits. Although poor Miss Malthers does not realize it, Fedora is interested only in Miss Malthers' resemblances to her brother. Fedora is strangely, oddly touched and moved by the likenesses between brother and sister: "there was the coloring; there were the blue, earnest eyes; there, above all, was the firm, full curve of the lips; the same setting of the white, even teeth. There was the subtle play of feature, the elusive trick of expression, which she had thought peculiar and individual in the one, presenting themselves as family traits" (p. 469).

Through Fedora's actions that follow, we begin to understand that she senses—probably half-consciously—that the sister who reminds Fedora so much of Young Malthers himself can somehow provide a socially acceptable release for Fedora's passions. She begins to assert herself as a mother figure. In an "elderly fashion," in a hundred-years-old tone, she makes her only speech in the entire story: "You know, dear child . . . I want you to feel completely at home with us. . . . Come to me freely and without reserve—with all your wants; with any complaint. I feel that I shall be quite fond of you" (p. 469). And then, sensing she has established the "proper" relationship, Fedora does a "proper" thing with improper enthusiasm and zest: she encircles Miss

Malthers' shoulders, bends over, and presses "a long, penetrating kiss upon her mouth" (p. 469). The kiss, startling, unexpected, and erotic, demonstrates the very unhealthy nature of both Fedora's emotional life and the social code by which she lives.[2]

Fedora's treatment of her horse throughout this scene continues to suggest that her reason will direct her actions and make them increasingly perverse. Fedora takes great care to control her horse with her whip. Symbolically, she tries to overpower her wildness (represented by the horse's wildness) with her reason (represented by the ability of the whip to control the horse). Fedora drives to the station by herself because she thinks no young person can manage her horse; no young person, in other words, can discipline the passion she feels. "The brute is restive," she explains, "and shouldn't be trusted to the handling of the young people" (p. 467). Significantly, Fedora always clutches a whip or reins in her hand when she rides or prepares to ride. She walks along the station platform "whip in hand" (p. 468). After Fedora meets Miss Malthers at the station, the author cleverly mentions that Fedora drives "handling whip and rein with accomplished skill" (p. 469). And when Fedora leans over to kiss Miss Malthers, she is sure to gather the reins tightly in one hand.

Chopin ends her story with a technically brilliant sentence that, yet another time, shows Fedora resolutely holding the reins. After the kiss that leaves Miss Malthers astonished and not at all pleased, "Fedora, with seemingly unruffled composure, gathered the reins, and for the rest of the way stared steadily ahead of her between the horses' ears" (p. 469). Fedora will continue to repress and discipline her sexual passion, to hold a whip and reins in her hand. In very private moments, she may try to caress the clothing of Young Malthers (or other men) and to press desperate kisses on the mouths of acceptable surrogates, but in public she will forever stare steadily ahead—"unruffled."

As we watch Fedora, we see a perverse, pathetic, desperate woman, a woman who, like Sardou's Fédora of 1882, experiences the severe turmoil of contending emotions, a woman who is capable of strong feeling but will never experience full emotional release or sexual satisfaction. Although Seyersted does not even index "Fedora" in his biography of Chopin,[3] and James E. Rocks refers to the story in only a perfunctory way,[4] this 1897 piece is one of Chopin's finest symbolic studies of repression and sublimation: its title character most certainly deserves to be mentioned in the same breath with Mildred Orme ("A Shameful Affair"), the storekeeper ("Vagabonds"), and Mrs. Baroda ("A Respectable Woman").

Notes

1.   *The Complete Works of Kate Chopin,* ed. Per Seyersted (Baton Rouge: Louisiana State University Press, 1969), I, 468; hereafter cited parenthetically.

2.   The gesture is, admittedly, ambiguous. In Robert Arner's dissertation, he calls "Fedora" "a tale with strong overtones of sexual decadence manifested in the reticent lesbianism of Fedora" ("Music from a Farther Room: A Study of the Fiction of Kate Chopin," Diss. The Pennsylvania State University 1970). And, indeed, there are suggestions of Fedora's Sapphic tendencies in addition to the kiss: her clothes fetish might make some readers wonder if what she truly desires is to become male and assume a man's sexual role; Fedora's obsession with her whip hints at the sexual dominance conventionally attributed to the male in a heterosexual relationship; even her unusual name itself, a word that commonly refers to a man's soft, felt hat, might be meant to provide some indication of her male proclivities. However, as I've attempted to show, there seems to be perhaps even more substantial evidence to suggest that Fedora is transferring her emotion for Young Malthers to Miss Malthers—an inappropriate displacement, certainly, but, nevertheless, a transference Fedora, in all her rigidity and repression, can find socially acceptable. Chopin works hard and carefully to stress Fedora's intense attraction to Young Malthers' masculinity—his voice, his attitude, his bearing, his face and form. And she works with equal intensity to help us understand that it is Miss Malthers' physical similarity to Young Malthers that attracts Fedora, not the girl herself.

3.   *Kate Chopin: A Critical Biography* (Baton Rouge, Louisiana: Louisiana State University Press, 1969).

4.   "Kate Chopin's Ironic Vision," *Revue de Louisiane,* 1 (1972), 116.

Pride and Prejudice: Kate Chopin's "Désirée's Baby"

Robert D. Arner

In a recent article on Kate Chopin's fiction, George Arms confessed bewilderment "at the appearance of 'Désirée's Baby' in so many anthologies, even while admitting its elegance as a well-made tale in the manner of Maupassant." He compared the story to Mark Twain's *Pudd'nhead Wilson* as a work which raises "the question of identity in a racial context" and preferred Twain on the grounds that "his novel makes a complex and pragmatic inquiry not present in Mrs. Chopin's story."[1] Nor is Arms alone in the opinion that "Désirée's Baby" is, for one reason or another, flawed and superficial. Carlos Baker objects to the ending of the tale as "a trick . . . which satisfies the reader's sense of justice while disappointing him with a contrived conclusion,"[2] and Per Seyersted, the most thorough and most sympathetic of Mrs Chopin's critics to date, agrees; the conclusion, he says, is "somewhat contrived," though he quickly adds that it possesses a "bitter, piercing quality" that Maupassant himself could not have surpassed.[3] With respect to Arms's comments, it might be observed that to fault a story of several pages for not dealing with issues in as much depth or from as many perspectives as a novel of more than a hundred pages is at best questionable critical procedure; it is to demand of one genre what we normally expect of another. But even were the validity of Arms's comparison admitted—and I do not wish to suggest that interesting and illuminating similarities of theme do not exist between "Désirée's Baby" and *Pudd'nhead Wilson*—I feel that he has seriously misjudged the complexity of Kate Chopin's tale. In the same way, it seems to me that the claim that Mrs. Chopin betrays the reader's confidence as, for instance, O. Henry so frequently does by attempting to force on him a conclusion she has not prepared for rests on a too hasty reading of the story. In spite of Mrs. Chopin's announced distrust of striving for literary effect and artistic unity—what she termed the "polishing up process"[4]—"Désirée's Baby" gives evidence of a careful craftsmanship that goes well beyond formal elegance and fuses theme, structure, and imagery into one of the most successful of her works.

From *Mississippi Quarterly* 25, no. 2 (Spring 1972):131–40. Reprinted by permission of *Mississippi Quarterly.*

"Désirée's Baby" is the story of a foundling adopted by the Valmondés, at the entrance to whose plantation she is found as a baby. The Valmondés name her Désirée, and when she grows to womanhood she is wooed and wed by a neighbor's son, Armand Aubigny, a descendant of one of the oldest and proudest families in Louisiana. Local rumor has it that Armand treats his slaves cruelly and inhumanely. Désirée bears him a son, but when the boy exhibits Negroid traits Armand spurns both wife and child. His explanation is simple and characteristic: " 'It means that the child is not white,' " he tells Désirée; " 'it means that you are not white.' "[5] In despair Désirée writes to her mother to find out if the accusation is true. Madame Valmondé's brief reply speaks volumes in its careful omissions: " 'My own Désirée. Come home to Valmondé; back to your mother who loves you. Come with your child.' " Instead Désirée takes the baby and disappears into the tangled wilderness around the bayou. Some weeks later, as Armand is systematically attempting to purify his house from all traces of Désirée and the baby, he comes upon the fragment of a letter lodged in a drawer that, ironically, used to contain Désirée's love letters to him. This letter, however, was written by his mother, whom he has never seen that he remembers, to his father, and its final words are also the last words in the story: " 'But, above all, night and day, I thank the good God for having so arranged our lives that our dear Armand will never know that his mother, who adores him, belongs to the race that is cursed with the brand of slavery.' "

Far more is at stake in this ending than the simple discovery that the parent who has driven his wife and child to exile and death on the suspicion that his wife had Negro blood is himself the tainted and guilty party. That indeed might satisfy our sense of justice, but Kate Chopin has more to say on the issues of race and slavery. For one thing, the story makes a point made by a number of other Southern writers both before and after Mrs. Chopin: that there is no absolute distinction between white and black, but rather an imaginary line drawn by white men and crossed at their own choosing. Because the line is so indelibly fixed in the white man's mind, however, acts of renunciation are difficult to perform and no single act is sufficient to redeem the South from the curse of its racial caste system. Thus, though Armand's father marries a woman technically a Negress, the fact remains a secret until the end of the story and no positive results are produced by the marriage. On the other hand, the sins of the fathers are repeatedly visited upon the children, for Armand inherits not only his father's slaves but also a set of rigid social codes prescribing his attitude toward the Negro and re-establishing the relationship between white and black as one between master and slave, possessor and the possessed. Trusting in the absoluteness of this relationship, Armand condemns his wife and child to exile and, as things turn out, to death. But the racial code is proved to be a fiction at the end, as Armand's own mixed parentage establishes, and the victimizer ends up the victim of his own inflexible inhumanity. Of the two discoveries Armand makes at the conclusion of the story, that he is part Negro and that the idea of white racial purity is a myth, the second is the harder to live with, since it deprives him of all semblance of justification for his treatment of Désirée and the baby. He learns, in fact, that his relationship to his father is precisely the same as the one he imagined existed between his son and himself. It is this profound irony of sacrificer become the sacrifice, a reversal of racial identity, that underlies the story and determines—in fact, almost necessitates—the ironic reversal at the end. Form is wed inseparably to theme, and both originate in the realities of the Southern social system.

The antidote to the poison of racial abstraction that destroys Désirée, the baby, and Armand is love, a deeply personal relationship which denies the dehumanizing and impersonal categorization of people into racial groups. The possibility that love may offer individual salvation from the evils of racial definition is suggested first of all by Armand's father's marriage to a Negress and, second, by Madame Valmondé's open acceptance of Désirée and her child even after she believes that the girl is part black. Love demands that people be seen as individuals, not as members of a social caste or as extensions of one's own ego. But the story makes clear that Armand does not really love Désirée; he thinks of her as a possession, a rich prize to display to his friends and to flatter his vanity, and when he thinks that she is black the value of the prize entirely disappears. In the antebellum South anyone can own a black girl, however beautiful she may be. Armand sees his marriage to Désirée solely in terms of what he brings to the union, and it is strongly hinted that one factor influencing his decision to marry her is that, knowing she is adopted, he thinks of himself as indisputably her superior in rank and breeding. She will not be in a position to question his authority but must submit to his judgement in all matters, which in fact she does. This motivation is perhaps hidden from Armand, but the violence and destructiveness of his passion for Désirée is revealed to the reader in a group of key similes. He falls in love with her, Mrs. Chopin writes, "as if struck by a pistol shot." And a few lines further on, she expands on the same theme: "The passion that awoke in him that day, when he saw her at the gate, swept along like an avalanche, or like a prairie fire, or like anything that drives headlong over all obstacles." When Armand is reminded by Monsieur Valmondé that Désirée is nameless and of obscure origin, he dismisses the objections impatiently: "What did it matter about a name when he could give her one of the oldest and proudest in Louisiana?" These passages not only serve to define Armand's willful and headstrong character, but also suggest the role of *hubris* in the story, since Armand's passionate intensity and his pride in possession make him a willing agent of his own destruction. The Southern racial caste system has already begun to victimize Armand by accentuating the flaws in his personality which, but for the circumstances of his being born a master in a slaveholding society, might have remained dormant. As it is, a pride nurtured by artificial racial distinctions ultimately destroys Armand's chances for happiness and personal salvation. Character and environment unite to produce one part of the tragic denouement of the tale.

The several racial themes of "Désirée's Baby" are reinforced by two major patterns of images which, circulating throughout the story, unobtrusively contribute both unity and density of meaning. The first of these is the contrast between light and shadow, whiteness and blackness. Armand is associated with darkness from the outset. His estate is a place of terror and his house inspires fear: "The roof came down steep and black like a cowl, reaching out beyond the wide galleries that encircled the yellow stuccoed house. Big, solemn oaks grew close to it, and their thick-leaved, far-reaching branches shadowed it like a pall." The house, in other words, functions as a symbolic projection onto the landscape of Armand's personality. Armand himself is described, with more than a hint of irony in the first adjective, as having a "dark handsome face." In contrast, Désirée is surrounded by images of whiteness. Recovering from labor, she lies "in her soft white muslins and laces, upon a couch." She stands next to Armand "like a stone image: silent, white, motionless" after she has given him her mother's letter and is awaiting his reaction. On the day she walks into the wilderness around the bayou, she wears "a thin white garment"; her hair radiates a "golden gleam" in spite of its brown color. The reader who has paid attention to these details has little reason to object that the ending of the story comes as a surprise; it has been carefully and deliberately foreshadowed throughout.

A third important color in the story is yellow. Armand's plantation house is yellow and, in view of the association between his personality and the atmosphere surrounding the house, this fact acquires significance. Zandrine, Désirée's nurse during her convalescence, is also yellow. On a racial scale of values, so are La Blanche, a pale Negress mentioned several times in the story, and her son, the boy against whose color Désirée compares her son's color when she first suspects that her baby may be part Negro. So, of course, is Désirée's baby—and so is Armand. In fact, all the Negroes mentioned by name in the story are "yellow" rather than pure black. That so much yellow color is associated with the Aubigny estate, both with its buildings and more important, with its slaves, is another means of foreshadowing the revelation of Armand's true racial identity. But it is also a subtle indictment of the white man's double standards and a measure of his racial guilt: black women may be concubines, but not wives. (The story, it might be noted along these same lines, contains the tantalizingly ambiguous remark that Armand heard his son crying "as far away as La Blanche's cabin.") Mrs. Chopin's arrangement of characters along a spectrum ranging from white to black as a means of underscoring, somewhat paradoxically, the theme that no real or final distinction based on color can be made between slave and master calls to mind a similar technique employed by Gertrude Stein in "Melanctha," though Miss Stein is of course working toward different ends. And it suggests a link between Mrs. Chopin's short story art and the art of the impressionists (we know that she was at least passingly familiar with their work and interested in it[6]): truth is revealed in shifting modulations and tones of color.

The second major figurative pattern in "Désirée's Baby" has to do with the opposition between God or Providence and Satan. It is closely related to the contrast between the kingdom of light and the kingdom of darkness. As early as the third paragraph we are introduced to the idea that Désirée's fate has in some way been pre-ordained by God. Madame Valmondé, speculating on Désirée's origins, comes to the comforting conclusion that "she had been sent by a beneficent Providence to be the child of her [Madame Valmondé's] affection, seeing she was without child of the flesh." Later, this idea of Providential interference in the affairs of men is echoed ironically in Madame Aubigny's belief that God has so arranged things that Armand will never know his mother was a Negress. It transpires that God had other plans all along, however. Through no fault of her own, Désirée brings grief, not happiness, to Madame Valmondé, and she is the agent who, indirectly to be sure, brings Armand to a recognition of his mixed parentage. Thus the ironic reversal at the end of the story is counterpointed by a reversal and a defeat of each mother's expectations. By associating Désirée with Providential design in this poetic and oblique way, Kate Chopin seems to be indicating that God, and not the author, is the ironist who has spun this plot. Not only Armand's character and the social structure of the slaveholding South have a hand in forcing him to confront the reality of the shadow within, but also Providence itself seems to have taken an interest in the arrangements.

Armand himself dimly senses the connection between Désirée and Divinity. In a moment of self-pity, he imagines "that Almighty God had dealt cruelly and unjustly with him; and felt, somehow, that he was paying Him back when he stabbed thus into his wife's soul." By insulting and injuring Désirée, Armand believes that he hurts and insults God as well; he casts both of them out of his house. In this context, Mrs. Chopin's apparently insignificant comment, "the very spirit of Satan seemed suddenly to have taken hold of him," takes on a new dimension of meaning. Armand makes a most excellent earthly representative of Satan. His treatment of his wife is an act of defiance against both God and man (not, of course, against man in Armand's artificial social environment, but as a denial of the human power of love). He shares with Satan the sin of pride: racial and aristocratic pride specifically, but also a pride in his own power to rebel against God. The connection between Armand and Satan is subtly made not only in the sentence already cited, but also in Mrs. Chopin's careful arrangement of characters and her use of fire symbolism in the final scene: "In the centre of the smoothly swept backyard was a great bonfire. Armand Aubigny sat in the wide hallway that commanded a view of the spectacle; and it was he who dealt out to the half dozen negroes the material which kept this fire ablaze." Armand presides over the holocaust, intended to be a ritual of purification from guilt but really a ritual that re-affirms the impossibility of escaping the consequences of the slave system, enthroned in state like the very Prince of Darkness himself.

As Armand's character is defined both by his actions and by the images clustered around him, so is Désirée's. She is called the "idol of Valmondé," a metaphor which strengthens her associations with Divinity and Providence. Her face is "suffused with a glow that was happiness itself," as if joy were an indwelling vital principle, in contrast to Armand's face, which is frequently "disfigured by frowns." And her appearance when she walks into the thickets surrounding the bayou as a sacrifice to Southern racial codes lacks only the halo for complete beatification:

> It was an October afternoon; the sun was just sinking. Out in the still fields the negroes were picking cotton.
>> Désirée had not changed the thin white garment nor the slippers which she wore. Her hair was uncovered and the sun's rays brought a golden gleam from its brown meshes.

If the pattern of character and conflict built around this second set of images seems somehow familiar to us, it is probably because we have seen it, or something very like it, before. It represents another of the apparently endless variations on a theme made popular in Western romance literature by Samuel Richardson's *Clarissa,* a book which one critic has identified as the prototype of all subsequent stories of sentimental love.[7] Mythopoeic in its power, *Clarissa* is the story of a young virginal maiden who is lustily and lustfully pursued through hundreds of pages by the villain, Lovelace, who, when he cannot seduce her, resorts to rape. Dishonored—she suspects that some dark part of her had acquiesced to the deed—Clarissa wastes away and dies. Lovelace is killed in a duel shortly thereafter, and on this note of villainy deservedly punished the novel closes. Throughout, Lovelace is associated with darkness and evil; he is driven by deep and unsearchable urges to seek Clarissa's ruin and his own destruction. Only marriage to Clarissa could have saved him from his evil inner nature, but Richardson, with fidelity to reality and an awareness of the irreconcilable differences between the characters he has created, forbids *Love*lace that salvation.

Richardson's novel is far more complicated than this brief summary suggests and his psychological insights surpass those of Mrs. Chopin in this tale, but in spite of these and other differences "Désirée's Baby" owes much to the popularized Richardsonian tradition. In the "dark handsome face" of Armand Aubigny we can still dimly trace the features of Lovelace. Both men are aristocrats and both are excessively proud of their nobility, though Armand shares none of Lovelace's pride in intellectual attainments or his nearly godless faith in the power of reason. Both men possess enormous sexual energy, but while Lovelace's is directed toward seducing Clarissa, Armand's finds an outlet in the sadistic mistreatment of his slaves; the sexual pursuit central to

Clarissa is reduced in "Désirée's Baby" to a few veiled innuendos concerning the master's relationship with his slaves. Armand's darkness is associated with sensuality and aggressiveness, in contrast to Désirée's whiteness, which represents purity and, in spite of her marriage, inviolability and gentleness. Désirée is unmistakably Kate Chopin's version of the Pure Maiden, the Saviour Woman; she suffers at the hands of a villain to whom, for all his villainy, she is powerfully attracted. Her suffering and her death, however, seem unimportant in the end. The reader has little doubt that she will be rewarded in heaven (whence she came?), that Armand will be punished. Désirée is the superego, to put the case in Freudian terms, to Armand's id. For a brief while she acts as the civilizing and humanizing consciousness for his primitive and animalistic unconscious. She provides him with a socially accepted and sanctified outlet for his brutal passions, a sexual surrogate, as it were, for his will to dominate. During this brief period of marital felicity, significantly, Armand stops mistreating his slaves. But when he discovers, or thinks he discovers, that Désirée is tainted with the blackness that confirms in his mind her essential similarity to his inner sensual and aggressive self, she loses her efficacy for him as a means to grace. Marriage to her was not salvation but, in both racial and psychological terms, surrender to the self within and therefore damnation. Predictably, Armand reverts to his old ways; if anything, he is more cruel to his slaves than formerly, linking them to his "betrayal" by a woman but unaware that they are projections, literally and symbolically, of the darkness that lurks within him.

Combining as it does racial themes with a transmuted seduction theme—what we might term the *Uncle Tom's Cabin* tradition and the *Clarissa* tradition—"Désirée's Baby" turns out to be a surprisingly rich and complex story, one of the best of its kind in American literature. Its richness is the more remarkable and its integration of elements the more noteworthy because Kate Chopin seldom reworked her stories, preferring, as she said, "the integrity of crudities to artificialities"[8]—truth instead of beauty. But the excellence of this tale invites speculation as to how many of Mrs. Chopin's other stories would prove equally rewarding if given a close reading. Above all, the story testifies eloquently to the truth of Fred Lewis Pattee's assertion that Mrs. Chopin "must be rated as a genius, taut, vibrant, intense of soul. . . . Without models, without study or short-story art, without revision, and usually at a sitting, she produced what often are masterpieces before which one can only wonder and conjecture."[9]

Notes

1. George Arms, "Kate Chopin's *The Awakening* in the Perspective of Her Literary Career," *Essays on American Literature in Honor of Jay B. Hubbell,* ed. Clarence Gohdes (Durham, N. C., 1967), p. 222.

2. Carlos Baker, "Delineation of Life and Character," *LHUS,* ed. Robert Spiller, *et al,* rev. 3rd ed. (New York, 1963), p. 859.

3. Per Seyersted, *Kate Chopin: A Critical Biography* (Oslo and Baton Rouge, 1969), p. 94.

4. Kate Chopin, "On Certain Brisk, Bright Days," *The Complete Works of Kate Chopin,* ed. Per Seyersted (Oslo and Baton Rouge, 1969), II, 722.

5. "Désirée's Baby," *Complete Works,* I, 243. Further references are to this edition and will not be identified by page number in text.

6. In her review of Emile Zola's *Lourdes* Kate Chopin mentions impressionism, and in her comments on Hamlin Garland's *Crumbling Idols* she speaks with some authority on the subject of the new style in painting. See also Kenneth Eble's comment (Introduction to *The Awakening,* New York, 1964, p. xi) that "only Stephen Crane, among her American contemporaries, had an equal sensitivity to light and shadow, color and texture, had the painter's eye matched with the writer's perception of character and incident."

7. Leslie Fiedler, *Love and Death in the American Novel,* rev. ed. (New York, 1966), pp. 62–73.

8. "On Certain Brisk, Bright Days," *Complete Works,* II, 722.

9. Fred Lewis Pattee, *The Development of the American Short Story: An Historical Survey* (London and New York, 1923), pp. 325, 327.

NARRATIVE STANCE IN KATE CHOPIN'S *THE AWAKENING*

RUTH SULLIVAN AND STEWART SMITH

Since its revival by Kenneth Eble in 1964, Kate Chopin's *The Awakening* (1899) has received prodigal praise for the courage of its theme, its fluid and unassuming style, and the vividness of its portrait of French Creole society. It has also been commended because it presents without moral censure or implied lesson the story of a woman's growing awareness of and wish to express her own sensuality, an awareness and wish that first lead to infidelity and then to suicide. *The Awakening* is unusual among pieces of fine American fiction because it deals with men and women engaged in adult emotional relationships. "Our great novelists," writes Leslie Fiedler,

> though experts on ambiguity and assault, on loneliness and terror, tend to avoid treating the passionate encounter of a man and woman, which we expect at the center of a novel. Indeed, they rather shy away from presenting in their fictions the presence of any full-fledged, mature women giving us instead monsters of virtue or bitchery, symbols of the rejection or fear of sexuality.[1]

The novel with which *The Awakening* is most consistently compared and to which it bears striking resemblances is Flaubert's *Madame Bovary*. It is a "first rate novel, and we have few of its stature," Kenneth Eble says about *The Awakening;*[2] Edmund Wilson calls it "a quite uninhibited and beautifully written [book], which anticipates D. H. Lawrence in its treatment of infidelity;"[3] and Carlos Baker says it is a novel with "intensity, courage, vigor, and independence."[4] "Mrs. Kate Chopin's *The Awakening*," says Robert Cantwell, "seems to me to be the first novel of its sort written by an American, and to rank among the world's masterpieces of short fiction."[5]

The Awakening also receives special attention and praise from those interested in fiction by and about women, for it has been read as a novel about a woman's emancipation from a stuffy, middle-class marriage with its domestic routines and rigid standards prescribing how to be a good wife and mother. Edna is admired for her courage in acting upon her artistic and sexual

From *Studies in American Fiction* 1 (Spring 1973): 62–75. Reprinted by permission of *Studies in American Fiction* and Northeastern University.

impulses and even in committing suicide as a free act of self-assertion and refusal to return to her domestic trap. And it is said to be a novel about the necessity of being free to choose one's own destiny. Further, one reads almost everywhere in criticism of the novel that Kate Chopin both sympathized with her heroine and on the whole presented her story "objectively." "Kate Chopin sympathized with Edna, but she did not pity her. She rendered her story with a detachment akin to Flaubert's."[6] "The author obviously sympathized with Mrs. Pontellier."[7] The novel manifests a "serene amoralism."[8] One also finds assumed or explicit the conviction that Kate Chopin the woman is inextricably identified with her work; the novel presents "essentially . . . the author's way of looking at life."[9]

These statements of theme and assumptions about the point of view of the novel are inaccurate. Edna never really becomes a free woman because she confuses impulsive action with liberation and because she never understands herself or her own wishes and goals. And, to speak about Kate Chopin *the woman*'s sympathy toward her characters and identification with her own creation is to discuss biography, whereas to speak of the attitudes, values, and ideas Kate Chopin *the author* brings to bear on her fiction is to discuss literature. The author chose to use a complex narrative stance in which Edna is presented alternately as an unusual woman with significant problems admirably dealt with and as a narcissistic, thoughtless woman, almost wantonly self-destructive. These views singly or in concert are not impartial; they are not "objective," "amoral," or "detached."

Of course the author does use an objective point of view sometimes in this novel as, for instance, in presenting Léonce Pontellier in Chapters I and III, where he figures prominently. There Chopin refrains (with some exceptions) from giving his thoughts and feelings, though one notices that the details she chooses are subtly critical of the man, who seems irritated about spending Sundays with his family and prefers playing billiards to dining with his wife. But on the whole, the point of view in *The Awakening* is not objective but omniscient and judicial. The author describes the thoughts and feelings of almost every character; for instance, of Alcée Arobin: "But she laughed and looked at him with eyes that at once gave him courage to wait and made it torture to wait."[10] More, the narrative perspective is judicial: "Robert talked a good deal about himself. *He was very young, and did not know any better*" (p. 8). Mlle Reisz "*had absolutely no taste in dress,* and wore a batch of rusty black lace with a bunch of artificial violets pinned to the side of her hair" (p. 64. Emphases added).

This judicial voice, so ironic about other characters but serious about Edna, is the perspective many readers of *The Awakening* accept, for they seem not to question on what basis such judgments were formed or to notice that sometimes other evidence in the novel contradicts them. The narrator once describes Mrs. Pontellier thus: "Mrs. Pontellier's eyes were quick and bright. . . . Her eyebrows were a shade darker than her hair. . . . *She was rather handsome than beautiful. Her face was captivating by reason of a certain frankness of expression and a play of features. Her manner was engaging"* (p. 7. Emphasis added). This says less about Edna's appearance than about the narrator's opinion of it, for not enough detail is given to support the statements that Edna is "rather handsome than beautiful" (or even that she is handsome) and that her manner is engaging. The narrator's fondness for Edna is even more striking here:

> *The charm of Edna Pontellier's physique stole insensibly upon you.* The lines of her body were long, clean and symmetrical; it was a body which occasionally fell into splendid poses; there was no suggestion of the trim, stereotyped fashion plate about it. *A casual observer, in passing, might not cast a second glance upon the figure. But with more feeling and discernment he would have recognized the noble beauty of its modelling and the graceful severity of poise and movement, which made Edna Pontellier different from the crowd* (p. 37. Emphasis added).

She is like a queen, the narrator insists:

> There was something in her attitude, in her whole appearance when she leaned her head against the high-backed chair and spread her arms, which suggested the regal woman, the one who rules, who looks on, who stands alone (p. 232).

Occasionally the narrative perspective shifts to show Edna as others see her; for instance, as Dr. Mandelet does, or as Victor Lebrun, his mother, and Mlle Reisz do; but with some exceptions (Mlle Reisz comments on how splendid Edna looks in a bathing suit), these descriptions do not match or support the narrator's. The latter often asserts more than it or anything else in the novel demonstrates.

When the narrative perspective moves into Edna's mental environment, it assumes two kinds of omniscience, one of which is as unsupported by convincing evidence as its descriptions of Edna's appearance are. This perspective is omniscient in that it knows what Edna thinks and feels; it also knows more than Edna herself does: "She did not perceive that she was talking like her father as the sleek geldings ambled in review before them" (p. 193). "That she was seeing with different eyes and making the acquaintance of new conditions in herself that colored and changed her environment, she did not yet suspect" (p. 102). When the narrative perspective goes farther than merely recording Edna's inner environment and makes grand assertions about what kind of awakening Edna is experiencing, it becomes unreliable:

> In short, Mrs. Pontellier was beginning to realize her position in the universe as a human being, and to recognize her relations as an individual to the world within and about her. This may seem like a ponderous weight of wisdom to descend upon the soul of a young woman of twenty-eight—perhaps more wisdom than the Holy Ghost is usually pleased to vouchsafe to any woman.

But the beginning of things, of a world especially, is necessarily vague, tangled, chaotic, and exceedingly disturbing. How few of us ever emerge from such a beginning! How many souls perish in its tumult! (pp. 33–34).

The context of this passage is Edna's vacillation about going swimming with Robert; the implication is that her sensuous self is just beginning to awaken.

The importance in Edna's life of such an awakening is, of course, obvious and the novel is convincing on this matter. However, the language describing the awakening is excessive: "her position in the universe as a human being," "the beginnings . . . of a world." Readers are being asked to believe that a woman's dawning sexual awareness is a cosmic event. More, they are being asked to believe that awareness of sexual need results suddenly in understanding of "life" and "truth": "She felt as if a mist had been lifted from her eyes, enabling her to look upon and comprehend the significance of life . . ." (p. 219). "Perhaps it was the first time her being was tempered to take an impress of the abiding truth" (p. 66). But there is no convincing evidence that Edna understands what is happening to her; certainly none that she understands Truth or Life. In fact, despite the number of times the narrator says that Edna thinks, the reader finds only rare examples of either the thinking or its results.

Edna does not think; she is driven. She acts impulsively; she has fancies, dreams, moods, sensations, and passions; but she rarely has thoughts. Once she says to Alcée, " 'One of these days . . . I'm going to pull myself together for a while and think—try to determine what character of a woman I am; for, candidly, I don't know. By all the codes which I am acquainted with, I am a devilishly wicked specimen of the sex. But some way I can't convince myself that I am. I must think about it' " (p. 216). But she apparently never gets around to it. Her conversation with Dr. Mandelet shortly before her suicide proves this. She is incoherent.

"Perhaps—no, I am not going [abroad]. I'm not going to be forced into doing things. . . . I want to be let alone. Nobody has any right—except children, perhaps—and even then, it seems to me—or it did seem—" She felt that her speech was voicing the incoherency of her thoughts and stopped abruptly. . . . "But I don't want anything but my own way" (p. 291).

Edna is thoughtless, impulsive, and ignorant of the consequences of her acts, a truth she herself dimly grasps when she tells Adèle that when as a child she ran away from her father through the sea of meadow grass, she was "a little *unthinking* child . . . , *just following a misleading impulse without question*" (p. 42). She adds, "sometimes I feel this summer as if I were walking through the green meadow again; *idly, aimlessly, unthinking and unguided*" (p. 43. Emphases added). Her acts confirm this self-evaluation, for once she impulsively swims so far out to sea that she fears drowning; she refuses the help Dr.

Mandelet and Adèle offer her; and she gives up household, marital, and maternal responsibilities, moves out of her husband's house, and commits adultery, all without quite understanding what she is doing. "She was blindly following whatever impulse moved her" (p. 82), "going and coming as it suited her fancy, and, so far as she was able, lending herself to any passing caprice" (p. 146). About moving into the pigeon-house, Mlle Reisz says, " 'Your reason is not yet clear to me.' Neither was it quite clear to Edna herself" (pp. 207–208). She has an affair with Alcée Arobin despite the fact that "Alcée Arobin was absolutely nothing to her" (p. 202), and despite the fact that she thinks she loves Robert. She does not consider where in her tiny house the children might live, nor does she think of how she will work things out with Léonce.

Clearly, Edna's "own way" means refusal to accept social convention and insistence upon both asserting and acting upon her wishes; but all these are often described as capricious, unguided, unthinking, and misleading. Despite the partisan narrative assertion that Edna is "realizing her position in the universe as a human being" and that she is "seeking herself and finding herself" (p. 134), she seems not to know what she is doing, where she is going, or what she wants.[11]

Some alternate view of Edna is being offered by these assertions, a view at variance with the adulous judgments given about Edna's appearance and awakening sensuousness. In the long description of Edna's mental state while she is walking to her death, these two views coexist almost discordantly. The partisan view affirms that "she had done all the thinking which was necessary after Robert went away, when she lay awake upon the sofa till morning" (p. 299); that "she understood now clearly what she had meant long ago when she said to Adèle Ratignolle that she would give up the unessential, but she would never sacrifice herself for her children . . ." (p. 299); and that she would not allow them "to drag her into the soul's slavery for the rest of her days. But she knew a way to elude them" (p. 300). About Robert, "she even realized that the day would come when he, too, and the thought of him would melt out of her existence, leaving her alone" (p. 300).

That Edna "had done all the thinking," "she understood," "she realized," "she knew," asserts the partisan view; but the narrative stance seems to split and to offer simultaneously an alternate view of Edna: "she was not dwelling on any particular train of thought" (p. 299); "she was not thinking of these things as she walked down to the beach" (p. 300). Not only was she not thinking as she walked to her death but her night's thinking produced little self-insight and no rational plan of action. It can hardly be called thinking at all. One conclusion Edna draws about her situation is that she owes no allegiance to her husband and rightly feels no guilt toward him. Earlier she had said to Robert, "I am no longer one of Mr. Pontellier's possessions to dispose of or not. I give myself where I choose" (p. 287). She also concludes that her sexual needs will require a series of men and eventually she will be left alone;

and that by meeting her needs this way she will hurt her children. Her alternatives are to give up her needs ("sacrifice herself for her children") and thus be dragged into "soul's slavery"; or to "elude them [her children]" by committing suicide.

Clearly there are other alternatives, one of the most obvious being to leave her husband and live elsewhere (not around the corner from him) and allow the children to remain with Léonce's mother, who cherishes them. If, then, the children believed her to be dead, both of Edna's aims would be realized: she could live as she chose while at the same time protecting her children from knowing about her sexual career or suffering from the "bad" reputation that would result. Edna does not have to die to "elude" or protect her sons. But then it is obvious that despite what the partisan voice says, Edna acts not by reason but by emotion. Indeed, her self destruction looks like an act of aggression against those children who would drag her into her soul's slavery, and against her husband and Robert as well, both of whom must suffer grief and guilt.

Tuning out the partisan voice and heeding the alternate one discloses other negative qualities in Edna: for instance, that she is actuated by highly colored romantic fantasies.[12] Her dream of great love is of "a woman who paddled away with her lover one night in a pirogue and never came back. They were lost amid the Baratarian Islands, and no one ever heard of them or found trace of them from that day to this" (p. 183). Her young womanhood was dominated by dreams of high romance, too; of the great tragedian whose portrait she kissed, of a sad-eyed cavalry officer with clinking spurs, and of a young gentleman engaged to another, dreams she put aside to marry Léonce but which vigorously revived in her infatuation for Robert. Edna at twenty-nine has never outgrown her adolescent dreams about love.

Some of Edna's qualities are conveyed through images—the bird, for example. When Edna tells Mlle Reisz about the illicit passion for Robert, the pianist says, "The bird that would soar above the level plain of tradition and prejudice must have strong wings. It is a sad spectacle to see the weaklings bruised, exhausted, fluttering back to earth" (p. 217). Now Edna knows she wants to soar like a bird, or, when she learns to swim, "she wanted to swim far out, where no woman had swum before" (p. 71). How ironic that in her suicide swim she sees before her "a bird with a broken wing . . . beating the air above, reeling, fluttering, circling disabled down, down to the water" (pp. 300–301). The implication is that Edna's suicide is far from being the courageous act of a strong and free woman. The author makes other disparaging, indirect comments on that suicide, in one instance by juxtaposing Edna's suicide scene with the one in which Victor amuses and teases Mariequita with a comic rendition of Edna's farewell banquet:

> He exaggerated every detail, making it appear a veritable Lucillean [sic] feast. The flowers were in tubs he said. The champagne was quaffed from huge golden goblets. Venus rising from the foam could have presented no more

entrancing a spectacle than Mrs. Pontellier, blazing with beauty and diamonds at the head of the board, while the other women were all of them youthful houris, possessed of incomparable charms (p. 295).

Mariequita is jealous, believing Victor to be in love with Edna. "She grew sullen and cried a little, threatening to go off and leave him to his fine ladies. There were a dozen men crazy about her at the *Chênière;* and since it was the fashion to be in love with married people, why, she could run away any time she liked to New Orleans with Celina's husband" (p. 296). The scene is a kind of parody on Edna's unrealistic life and on the high romantic coloring she gave it.

The suicide is, of course, foreshadowed when Edna swims so far out into the water that she fears death and again in a passage that suggests criticism as well as praise of Edna, for it reminds one that only a few exceptional people survive the tumult of rebirth: "But the beginning of things, of a world especially, is necessarily vague, tangled, chaotic, and exceedingly disturbing. How few of us ever emerge from such a beginning. How many souls perish in its tumult!" (p. 34). Edna "perishes in its tumult."

Finally, the alternate view of Edna conveys the likelihood that her suicide is not an act of self-knowledge or self-assertion nor a wish to protect her children, but the result of a series of depressions that become suicidal after Robert leaves her. "Despondency had come upon her there in the wakeful night, and never lifted" (p. 300). At least nine times in the novel, Edna's mental state is described as depressed, oppressed, or despondent.[13]

As the second narrative view sometimes communicates through images, it also speaks through other devices (other than Edna's despondency) which lead one to understand Edna somewhat differently from the way the partisan view does. One such device is presentation of facts concerning Edna's family and her current relationships, all of which paint a consistent psychological portrait of the kind of woman who might commit suicide because she was denied love by a man important to her. For instance, Edna's mother died when her daughters were young. Her place was taken by a somewhat dour older sister while Edna continually quarreled with a younger one. Her father was a Colonel in the Confederate army; he carries himself stiffly, wears his coats padded, swears ponderous oaths, and treated Edna's mother so badly (" 'Authority, coercion are what is needed . . . the only way to manage a wife' " [p. 186]) that he put her early into the grave. The family was Presbyterian. Edna remembers "running away from prayers, from the Presbyterian service, read in a spirit of gloom by my father that chills me yet to think of" (p. 42). In such a family, Edna never learned to express her feelings but instead lived an intense fantasy life that, in adolescence, blossomed into dreams about inaccessible men.

This portrait of Edna stresses that she was early left motherless, that remembrance of events connected with her father "chills" her and that she was not close to her sisters. Edna comes from an emotionally impoverished home. The motherlessness, especially, explains much of Edna's adult behavior: her relationship to other women in the novel, for instance, to whom she relates the way a child relates to a mother. The pregnant "mother-woman," Adèle, coddles Edna, encourages her to express her feelings, shows concern about Edna's reputation, and worries about Edna's children. Edna's motherlessness also accounts for the intensity of her need to be loved, a need so urgent that when Robert frustrates it, she kills herself.

In one sense, Edna is frustrated because Robert will not let her love him. However, one might wonder about the nature of a love which seems not to focus on the personality and character of its regard, for to Edna, Robert is featureless: "It was not that she dwelt upon details of their acquaintance, or recalled in any special or peculiar way his personality; it was his being, his existence which dominated her thought . . ." (pp. 139–140). He is more real to her absent, and when he returns, his presence disappoints her. She "loves" a fantasy man[14] rather like the tragedian or sad-eyed cavalry officer, both of whom derived much of their fascination from being inaccessible. The real Robert is a safe and sensible (perhaps weak) man who does not want to ruin Edna's reputation or allow her needs to destroy him. Besides, Edna's passions are displaceable. She believes she loves Robert yet she has an affair with Arobin, who means little to her. Edna appears to be a passionate woman who realizes herself in an extramarital affair, but the facts lead one to conclude the reverse: she cannot love; she is, instead, hungry for it.[15]

The novel dramatizes the irony that the awakening which Edna most desires is to sleep and dream, to merge with a warm body, to be indulged, and to be fed, drives related to her early motherlessness and to a need for compensation. The latent wish to be fed is communicated in the novel through one of its dominant images: food. Almost every significant occurrence in Edna's life is associated with food. Because Mr. Pontellier often sends his wife huge boxes of candies and liqueurs, the women on Grand Isle consider him an excellent husband. Meanwhile, he neglects returning to have dinner with his family and forgets the bonbons he promised his sons. One of the Pontellier's most serious quarrels takes place over dinner and concerns supervision of the cook. Two other marriages are assessed in the novel, one as sterile (the Highcamp's), one as ideal (the Ratignolle's), and in both instances the couples demonstrate the qualities of their marriages over dinner with Edna. Dr. Mandelet's diagnostic visit occurs at dinner and Edna celebrates her farewell to her husband and her old way of life with a spectacular banquet. It is immediately after this banquet that she first commits adultery. Mlle Reisz offers Edna chocolates on Grand Isle and hot chocolate and brandy in New Orleans; all such offerings are somehow connected with the absent Robert. Robert himself is almost always tied to food, from the most trivial kind of association, such as the buns and coffee he and Edna hurriedly take for breakfast the morning of their visit to the *Chênière,* through more important events, such as the announcement about his leaving for Mexico made during dinner at Madame Lebrun's. When Mlle Reisz shows Edna a letter telling of Robert's return, Edna joyfully sends a huge box of candy to her sons. When Robert does return, Edna prevails upon him to stay for dinner; and on the occasion of his avowal of love, Edna had shortly before met him accidentally in a small garden where she was dining. Robert's rejection seems to leave her literally hungry, for the next morning she arrives at Grand Isle and, on her way to her death, says to Victor, "What time will you have dinner? . . . I am very hungry" (p. 298). And once more, "I hope you have fish for dinner" (p. 299).

Edna's motherlessness makes appropriate the abundance of images connecting food with love and its loss; motherlessness also seems to account for the double irony that a woman who wishes to awaken should nevertheless wish so often to sleep and dream,[16] and that one who wants to find herself should be described as happily losing herself: "the voice of the sea is seductive . . . inviting the soul . . . to lose itself in inward contemplation" (p. 34). "As she swam she seemed to be reaching out for the unlimited in which to lose herself" (p. 71). "She discovered many a sunny sleepy corner, fashioned to dream in. And she found it good to dream and to be alone and unmolested" (p. 149). At Madame Antoine's she sleeps refreshingly to a lullaby of murmurs: "the voices were only part of the other drowsy, muffled sounds lulling her senses" (p. 94).

The imagery of food, sleep, dreaming, and self-loss seem to culminate in a latent desire to merge with a warm body. In fact, Chopin makes that need for fusion a refrain in her novel:

> The voice of the sea is seductive: never ceasing, whispering, clamoring, murmuring, inviting the soul to wander for a spell in abysses of solitude: to lose itself in mazes of inward contemplation.
> The voice of the sea speaks to the soul. The touch of the sea is sensuous, enfolding the body in its soft, close embrace (p. 34).

Part of this passage is repeated when Edna commits suicide by allowing herself to sink, naked as a newborn (she casts aside her swim suit and "felt like some new-born creature" [p. 301]), into the "soft, close embrace" of that "sensuous" sea. Earlier, the "voice of the everlasting sea" is described as being like a lullaby: "It broke like a mournful lullaby upon the night" (p. 14). Edna's final act is indeed to lose herself, to surrender like a sleepy child to her mother's song and her warm embrace.[17]

In *The Awakening*, then, Chopin dramatizes two almost contradictory views of her heroine, one of them critical and the other sympathetic and admiring. This narrative technique must affect an interpretation of the theme of the novel and should discourage hasty identifications between Kate Chopin and her work. Readers distort the meaning of the novel if they conclude that the author is identified with, say, the sympathetic part of her narrative stance when actually, of course, the author speaks through both. The effect of such a technique in this novel is to present simultaneously two essentially different and incompatible ideals about how people should conduct their lives. The partisan narrative stance speaks for a romantic vision of life's possibilities; the alternate stance for a realistic understanding and acceptance of human limits.

When it is sympathetic, the narrative perspective regards Edna Pontellier as a woman who seeks more than the "freedom" involved in release from social convention, and more even than finding out who she is so she might affirm that. She wants intensity of experience. It does not matter whether she suffers pain or feels ecstasy as long as she can feel deeply. Edna does not admire or want for herself the domestic harmony of Adèle Ratignolle in her happy wife and motherhood.

> The little glimpse of domestic harmony which had been offered her gave her no regret, no longing. It was not a condition of life which fitted her, and she could see in it but an appalling and hopeless ennui. She was moved by a kind of commiseration for Madam Ratignolle,—a pity for that colorless existence which never lifted its possessor beyond the region of blind contentment, in which no moment of anguish ever visited her soul, in which she would have the taste of life's delirium (p. 145).

Temperance, sanity, and rationality are not for Edna, who wants to explore the unknown and forbidden rather than to accept the safe security of her considerate husband in his comfortable mansion. Edna wants to be free to do, but even more, to feel.

This stance sympathizes with Edna's romantic values. In fact, like a fond parent who not only praises his child's virtues but gilds them, the partisan view claims for Edna not only romantic virtues but others that Edna seems neither to have nor to value. For instance, though Edna does not want to be rational, the sympathetic stance nevertheless claims that her awakening means not only full sensuous awareness but conscious understanding as well.

The alternate part of the narrative perspective displays less sympathy for Edna's journey into the underworld of instinctual impulses and does not seem to understand the need an overly-civilized woman might feel for reckless self-abandon. In effect, this view affirms that while making contact with one's instinctual self is good, such contact must somehow be brought into relationship with the demands of the adult world. Impulsiveness, self-indulgence, refusal to accept responsibility, flagrant unconventionality, society will punish, probably severely. Besides, conscience eventually punishes offenses against unconsciously held moral convictions no matter what indulgence reason may presently grant. Edna may refuse motherhood, reject her husband, and become sexually promiscuous, but eventually her unrecognized guilt will demand terrible retribution. The alternate vision also seems to say that "freedom" can be found not in uninhibited instinctual expression but in reason and in recognition of one's own capacities and limits as well as the limits imposed by the environment. Edna can be free only if she consciously recognizes her need for intensity of experience and wishes to find this through sexual adventure. Then she might find a suitable place in which, and people with whom, to realize these desires. She would not be blindly driven to self-destruction or to acts of aggression against her children and husband.

To some readers, the sympathetic view speaks so movingly that they do not hear the sober realism also richly represented in the novel. *The Awakening* portrays neither the feminist's heroine nor an impulsive, somewhat shallow self-deceiver; it portrays both in unresolved tension. Perhaps, then, this complex narrative technique encourages its readers to project their own fantasies into the novel and to see Edna as they wish to see her. One might say that the realistic narrative view appeals most to the reader's adult self; the partisan, to the child, or to the self that would reach beyond its grasp no matter what the tragic consequences.*

Notes

*This paper was presented at the December 1972 meeting of The Group for Applied Psychoanalysis, Cambridge, Massachusetts. Ruth Sullivan is an Assistant Professor of English at Northeastern University. Stewart Smith is a psychoanalyst in Brookline, Massachusetts.

1.   Leslie Fiedler, *Love and Death in the American Novel* (New York: World Publishing Co., 1962), p. xix.
2.   Kenneth Eble, "Introduction," *The Awakening* by Kate Chopin (New York: Capricorn, 1964), p. vii.
3.   Edmund Wilson, *Patriotic Gore* (New York: Oxford Univ. Press, 1962), p. 590.
4.   Carlos Baker, "Delineation of Life and Character," *Literary History of the United States: History,* 3rd ed. rev., ed. Robert E. Spiller, et al. (New York: Macmillan, 1963), p. 858.
5.   Robert Cantwell, "*The Awakening* by Kate Chopin," *GaR,* 10 (1956), p. 489.
6.   Larzer Ziff, *The American 1890's* (New York: Viking, 1966), p. 304.
7.   Eble, p. xi.
8.   Wilson, p. 592.
9.   George W. Arms, "Kate Chopin's *The Awakening* in the Perspective of her Literary Career," *Essays on American Literature in Honor of Jay B. Hubbell,* ed. by Clarence Gohdes (Durham: Duke Univ. Press, 1967), p. 217.
10.   Kate Chopin, *The Awakening* (New York: Capricorn, 1964), p. 224. Henceforth all page references are to this edition and will appear in parentheses in the text.
11.   George Arms stresses both her aimlessness and her apparent absence of conflict: "On the whole, as she reveals herself, her aimlessness impresses us more than her sense of conflict" (p. 217).
12.   Per Seyersted makes this point in his excellent *Kate Chopin, A Critical Biography* (Baton Rouge: Louisiana State Univ. Press, 1969). He says: "What dominates her imagination during this period is not so much a feminist revolt as the idea of a transcendent passion for Robert of the kind suggested by romantic literature; and not seeking help from any source, external or internal, to check it, she dreams about such a love, lending herself to any impulse as if freed from all responsibility." We have in the novel "many elements . . . of the romantic syn-

drome of the great, overpowering, irresponsible love which was the undoing of Emma Bovary
. . ." (p. 141).

13. The interested reader may check pp. 15, 90, 125, 150, 191, 232, 272, 292, and
300.

14. One might notice that the partisan narrator shares Edna's romanticizing, for its
description of Adèle (as an instance) could have come from any medieval romance and the
description of how Robert acts toward certain married women at Grand Isle makes him like
the courtly lover with his lady.

15. Edna has trouble loving her children, too. She is not a "mother-woman" and feels
Fate had not fitted her for motherhood. She is repeating with her sons the pattern of her own
inadequate mothering.

16. George Arms, too, is impressed by how much Edna sleeps. "Amusingly enough, the
author, quite consciously I am sure, allows Edna to do an inordinate amount of sleeping
throughout the novel, in spite of her underlying vitality. . . . It is almost as if the author were
saying: here is my heroine who at critical points of her progress toward an awakening constantly falls asleep" (p. 219).

17. Lewis Leary hears echoes of Walt Whitman in Chopin's use of the sensuous sea
beckoning her heroine to death: "Echoes of the poetry of Whitman can be recognized in these
recurrent murmurings of the sea, especially his 'Out of the Cradle Endlessly Rocking' in which
the sea whispers the strong and 'delicious' word death." Lewis Leary, "Introduction," Kate
Chopin, *The Awakening and Other Stories* (New York: Holt, Rinehart and Winston, 1970), p.
xiii.

ORIGINAL ESSAYS

◆

ARMAND AUBIGNY, STILL PASSING AFTER ALL THESE YEARS: THE NARRATIVE VOICE AND HISTORICAL CONTEXT OF "DÉSIRÉE'S BABY"

MARGARET D. BAUER

"He that hath ears to hear let him hear"

—Mark 4:9

The last thing to go was a tiny bundle of letters; innocent little scribblings that Désirée had sent to him during the days of their espousal. There was the remnant of one back in the drawer from which he took them. But it was not Désirée's; it was part of an old letter from his mother to his father. He read it. She was thanking God for the blessing of her husband's love:—

"But above all," she wrote, "night and day, I thank the good God for having so arranged our lives that our dear Armand will never know that his mother, who adores him, belongs to the race that is cursed with the brand of slavery."[1]

Although several critics have carefully delineated Kate Chopin's preparation for the ironic twist at the end of her 1892 short story "Désirée's Baby,"[2] they still miss the most important point: that Armand Aubigny has been aware *all along* of his own racial heritage. Furthermore, Chopin throughout the story provides details that point to this awareness—so much so that, for the astute reader, the ending provides not an ironic twist, but a confirmation of ugly racial realities underpinning both the text and southern society at large.

Consider again the ending lines of "Désirée's Baby"—the letter that declares Armand's mother's race. Chopin does not show Armand reacting to the contents of the letter: there is no outburst of pain and remorse for his unjust behavior against his wife and child, which led to their presumable demise, no panicked gasp of fear that others will discover his own heritage, no sigh of relief that his wife can be blamed for his son's obvious African heritage.[3] Rather, he exhibits only calm as he "sat in the wide hallway that commanded a view of the spectacle" of a bonfire made up of the traces of Désirée in his life and "dealt out . . . the material which kept this fire ablaze" (244).

This essay was written specifically for this volume and is published here for the first time by permission of the author.

Seemingly incompatible with such reserve is Armand's passionate nature, as it is revealed throughout the story. For example, he supposedly falls in love "as if struck by a pistol shot. . . . The passion that awoke in him that day . . . swept along like an avalanche, or like a prairie fire, or like anything that drives headlong over all obstacles" (240). And later, when the African traces have begun to show in his son's features, the narrator reports that "the very spirit of Satan seemed suddenly to take hold of him in his dealings with the slaves" (242). How then does one explain the absence of expression upon supposedly learning of his own racial heritage? One might suggest that he is simply in a state of shock; however, such calm might also suggest that he is not at this point just learning about his mother's race. "Désirée's Baby," then, is one of the earliest examples of "passing" literature. Indeed, of those members of this genre discussed by Judith R. Berzon in her chapter on passing literature, only Frank J. Webb's 1857 novel *The Garies and Their Friends* and Rebecca Harding Davis's 1867 novel *Waiting for the Verdict* precede the publication of this story.[4]

That Armand had been passing is suggested by the fact that the narrator does not say this is the first time Armand has seen this letter from his mother to his father, though many critics have made this assumption.[5] The narrator merely says that "[t]here was the remnant of [a letter] back in the drawer from which he took [Désirée's letters]" (244). True, it is possible that Armand has an outburst of pain and remorse just after the point where Chopin ends the story. It is also possible that he has read the letter earlier (though still only since Désirée's departure) and since collected himself upon realizing that he can destroy this evidence and no one will ever know his secret. But if one examines more carefully Armand's actions in consideration of the narrative voice of the story and the history of the free people of color in antebellum Louisiana, as well as in light of a bit of child psychology, another conclusion becomes apparent: Armand has been aware, if not of this letter, at least of his mother's—and hence his own—mixed race for some time before the events surrounding the story's conflict.

This scenario of racial self-awareness sheds new light on Armand's actions from the time he "fell in love" with Désirée. Earlier in the story, the narrator points out "[t]he wonder" of it "that he had not loved her before . . . ha[ving] known her since his father brought him home from Paris, a boy of eight, after his mother died there" (240). So what causes his sudden "love" for Désirée? Perhaps Désirée has only recently made that step from awkward adolescent to beautiful woman, or Armand himself has recently developed from a boy, oblivious to female beauty, to a young man, who can now recognize it in his childhood playmate. But perhaps instead Armand, coming upon Désirée that day, suddenly ("as if . . . shot") sees how he can continue his masquerade as Southern (white) gentleman.[6] His one problem in fulfilling the role of (legitimate, white) heir to his father's plantation had been in producing his own heirs: what if his children were to betray his heritage? Upon seeing Désirée sleeping, however, whose slumber emphasizes her vulnerability, he devises a scheme that would protect him should his racial heritage be revealed in the features of his progeny: he will marry the one person in his community whose heritage is unknown and, therefore, whose parentage will naturally be questioned should their children threaten his position.[7] This reading is supported, first of all, by the revelation at the story's end that the letter confirming his mother's race is in the same drawer as the letters Désirée wrote to him during their engagement, a proximity that suggests a connection. If Armand is aware of the existence of this letter from his mother to his father, his keeping it with Désirée's letters suggests that his courtship of Désirée is part of a plan to overcome the threat of his heritage to his position. More compelling is the narrator's comment upon Armand's abrupt change of nature after joining his life with Désirée's: "Marriage, and later the birth of his son had softened Armand Aubigny's imperious and exacting nature greatly. . . . [His] dark, handsome face had not often been disfigured by frowns since the day he fell in love with her" (242). He could relax, having protected himself against suspicion and exposure. After the birth of their son, Armand speaks the truth, though Désirée does not believe him, when he says he would have been happy with either a boy or a girl—as long as the child looked white, which at first it does. When the child darkens, Armand's feelings for Désirée change at the same pistol-shot speed with which he ostensibly fell in love:—"he no longer loved her" after she brought "unconscious injury . . . upon his home and his name" (244) by apparently not having blood "pure" enough to cover for his "tainted" drop.[8] The callous treatment of his wife upon their baby's "metamorphosis" suggests that he never loved her. Rather, it suggests that Désirée had appealed to him only for having inadvertently offered him a chance to risk having children.

The ease with which the reader can mistakenly assume that Armand truly loved Désirée reflects the fact that the narrator is unreliable: in explaining the absence of "the gentle presence of a mistress" at the Aubigny plantation, L'Abri, the narrator misleadingly contends that Armand's mother remained in France after her marriage because she "loved her own land too well ever to leave it" (241). However, one realizes upon reading the letter that closes the story that such patriotism is not the real, or at least not the entire, reason the former Madame Aubigny never came to L'Abri. Rather, it is apparent that Armand's parents remained in France until his mother's death because of her race. No woman with even a trace of African blood in evidence would be allowed by the slaveholding South to be the mistress of L'Abri, the plantation of a white man. Indeed, their marriage would have been illegal in antebellum Louisiana. Although a surprising number of slaveholding plantations in that state were owned by free people of color, marriages were nevertheless prohibited between these people and whites, according to the Louisiana Civil Codes of 1808 and 1825.[9] H. E. Sterkx quotes from the *Civil Code of the State of Louisiana:* " 'Free [white] persons and slaves are incapable of contracting marriage together; the celebration of such marriages is forbidden, and the marriage is void; there is the same incapacity and the same nullity with respect to marriage contracted by free white persons with free people of color.' "[10] Joe Gray Taylor asserts that "[t]here was *never* a period in Louisiana history when marriages between Whites and Negroes were permissible";[11] therefore, the date during which the story is set (which is not indicated) is irrelevant. Interesting to the context of this story, given Armand's mother's homeland, John W. Blassingame explains that white men who wished to *legally* marry women of color usually went to Cuba or France to do so and there lived lawfully with their wives.[12] Sterkx discusses court cases involving such marriages and documents one case in which "the justices decreed marriages between colored persons and White *contracted in France* or any other place for that matter, as null and void in Louisiana"[13]—which would make Armand an illegitimate child with dubious inheritance rights.

The "unreliable" narrator has misled the reader by excusing the Aubignys' residence in France with what was probably the same reason given to the community by Monsieur Aubigny upon his return with his son. It would not be out of "character," then, for this narrator to mislead the reader regarding Armand's "love" for Désirée. The narrator is merely again reporting what is probably the view of the majority of the community regarding Armand's sudden attraction to Désirée: that it was so strong that even he, a man who valued his name so highly, would marry her in spite of her questionable past.[14] The narrative voice of this story can be equated with the voice of the community to which the Aubignys and Valmondés belong, in the way that Shirley Jackson's narrative voice of "The Lottery" seems to emerge from within the community depicted in that story. The events of "Désirée's Baby" are narrated from an observer's standpoint, giving its readers the sense that we are hearing the story from a citizen of the community. In only one instance in "Désirée's Baby" does the narrator provide the thoughts of a character; after Armand tells Désirée he wants her to leave, we are told, "He *thought* Almighty God had dealt cruelly and unjustly with him; and felt, somehow, that he was paying Him back in kind when he stabbed thus into his wife's soul" (244, emphasis added). Still, even here the narrator is vague (paying God back for what, exactly?), and given the narrative voice throughout the rest of the story, one can assume that the narrator is merely reporting how the community would interpret what was going on inside of Armand's head when he threw his supposedly beloved wife and son out of his house. Therefore, Chopin is not "cheating" by having her narrator provide seemingly misleading theories about Armand's love for Désirée or his mother's love for her country. Rather, she is telling the story from the community's point of view in order to emphasize this society's complicity in the ultimate tragedy. As Peggy Skaggs has noted, "at no time does the truth occur to anyone except Désirée herself, . . . despite the clear physical evidence apparent to anyone who might really look at the two parents."[15] The community is blind to the same evidence—for example, Armand's dark skin in comparison to Désirée's light skin and the fact that his background is also somewhat mysterious in that no one has met his mother—that the reader fails to see until after reading the last lines of the story.

Surprisingly, Skaggs concludes her discussion of "Désirée's Baby" by remarking that "[h]ad the truth been known in time [before Désirée's apparent demise] Armand's pride would still have been wounded, but surely he would not have been destroyed, as Désirée and the baby are."[16] That view depends on one's notion of "destroyed" and to whom Skaggs is referring to when she says, "had the truth been known." Since the baby's appearance is evidence that one of his parents has "black blood," then the community is going to demand to know which one it is. To Armand, who valued so highly his family name and, implicitly, position, public revelation of his "black blood" would be devastating. The social status of free people of color, according to H. E. Sterkx, "was just above the slave level."[17] In discussing the one means of legal marriage between Whites and free people of color—by the white partner taking an "oath that he had negro blood in his veins"—Annie Stahl explains that by thus "acknowledging the existence of such a *stain,* he voluntarily shut himself out of the society of his people forever."[18] From this scenario, one can deduce the complete and irrevocable separation that Armand would have experienced from the class he had belonged to his whole life if he were to declare his own "stain." Even the free men of color who owned plantations in Louisiana did not mingle equally with the white Louisiana aristocracy. "Quasi-citizenship" is what Sterkx calls the situation of the free people of color at that time in Louisiana. They may have "enjoyed a better legal position than any of their counterparts in other states of the South,"[19] but they still could not vote, they endured other restrictions, and "at no time were non-Whites ever deemed wholly equal; they were generally recognized by law as second class citizens."[20] As perhaps best discussed by Laura Foner, Louisiana had three distinct castes, Whites, free people of color, and Blacks: "Although free people of color shared the same class position of many Whites as planters, they were socially excluded from membership in that class and were forced to form a separate and subordinate caste."[21] Chopin's contemporary George Washington Cable criticizes this inequality between different races of free men in his 1880 novel *The Grandissimes.* In particular, the authoritative voice of the novel, Joseph Frowenfeld, comments that the free people of color "'want a great deal more than mere free papers can secure them. Emancipation before the law, though it may be a right which man has no right to withhold, is to them little more than a mockery until they achieve emancipation in the minds and good will of the people . . . mean[ing] the ruling class.' "[22] Foner's illustration of the white view toward this middle class supports the historical accuracy of the caste system depicted in Cable's novel:

although the [Louisiana] government and the ruling whites protected the distinction between a free man of color and a slave, they took equal if not greater care to preserve the distinction between themselves and a free man of color. Free Negroes were forbidden to sit next to whites in theaters or public vehicles. They were subject to reenslavement for certain crimes and required to show deference to their former masters. They were also periodically subjected to other humiliating social distinctions.[23]

Foner concludes that "the color line . . . served to preserve a strict social hierarchy with Whites on top and the free coloreds securely 'in their place,' midway between the ruling Whites and the slaves."[24] Would a man who has lived his life "on top" be willing to step down into his "rightful place"? Ideally, yes, rather than send his beloved wife and child to their deaths or continue to enslave people of his own race. However, clearly Armand has inherited his community's belief in his own superiority because of his position as land (and people) owner. As Foner argues, the separate caste of free people of color "mirrored the values of white society and the planter class. Thus they attacked the racial barriers but not the class subordination of the three-caste system, and aspired to full participation in white society rather than its destruction or transformation."[25] Already having reached this desired state of "full participation in white society," why would Armand willingly give up his position?

That position rests upon Armand's concealment of his own—and his mother's—race. If her African heritage was evident enough that she and her husband did not feel they could fool Monsieur Aubigny's white neighbors in Louisiana, then their son would probably have noticed it.[26] In her book on racial differences and child development, psychoanalyst Marjorie McDonald explains that "[t]he sensory capability to make [the] discovery [of different skin colors] . . . exists well before the end of the first year of life."[27] She contends further that "[f]or the infant who is raised biracially, the awareness of different skin colors inevitably comes during his first year."[28] In his book on prejudice and children, psychologist Kenneth B. Clark cites various studies finding "that racial awareness is present in Negro children as young as three years old. . . . [T]his knowledge develops in stability and clarity from year to year, and by the age of seven it is a part of the knowledge of all Negro children." Clark remarks, too, upon "[o]ther investigators [who] have shown that the same is true of white children."[29] From Clark's reportings, then, one can argue that Armand (officially black, raised white) would have been aware of his mother's race by the time of her death when he was eight years old. A mother of six children, Chopin would have probably realized the age her children were when they became aware of racial differences.[30] Thus her including the detail that he was eight years old when his mother died was the means by which she intended her reader to realize, upon reflection, that Armand must have been aware of his mother's race. If children are usually aware by the age of three or four, making him eight years old provides ample time to dispel any doubts.

After his mother's death, as Armand grew up on his father's plantation in America, he would have become aware of the *significance* to his life of the difference between his parents' skin colors, which he had presumably detected as a young child in France. According to Kenneth Clark,

> Learning about races and racial differences, learning one's own racial identity, learning which race is to be preferred and which rejected—all these are assimilated by the child as part of the total pattern of ideas he acquires about himself and the society in which he lives. . . . Furthermore, as the average child learns to evaluate these differences according to the standards of the society, he is at the same time required to identify himself with one or another group. This identification necessarily involves a knowledge of the status assigned to the group with which he identifies himself, in relation to the status of other groups. The child therefore cannot learn what racial group he belongs to without being involved in a larger pattern of emotions, conflicts, and desires which are part of his growing knowledge of what society thinks about his race.[31]

Armand, of course, is a unique case in that he is raised as white by his father. However, that does not mean that he is not aware of and cooperating with his father's deception. As cited above, the findings of both McDonald and Clark support the contention that children grasp the concept of racial difference at a very young age. Clark even discusses the case of one seven-year-old boy who tried to pass for white by insisting that "[h]is brown skin was the result of a summer at the beach." Clark remarks upon the sad consequences of prejudice when even "a child may try to escape the trap of inferiority by denying the fact of his own race."[32]

As he grew older and, particularly, with the death of his father, Armand acquired a keen understanding of the precarious position he was in as heir to his father's estate. In a worst-case scenario, he could be labeled chattel, as happens to the young would-be heiress in Robert Penn Warren's 1955 novel *Band of Angels* (New York: Random House), were anyone else to discover his secret and he not be able to prove that his mother was a free woman of color.[33] Alternatively, his right to have inherited his father's property might be questioned. As Virginia Domínguez explains, mixed-race children in Louisiana had "no rights of inheritance from either father or mother, or from the family estates of either parent," according to the 1825 Louisiana Civil Code, which was "essentially the same also for the 1808 project of the Code . . . and the Code Napoleon."[34] Although Domínguez adds that "[p]aternal acknowledgement [which, indeed, Armand had] makes an illegitimate child a 'natural child' and enables him to inherit *part* of his father's estate,"[35] a legitimate (white) heir would inherit *all* of his father's estate. Armand's father is dead and could not, therefore, speak up for his son at the time his inheritance would be in question.[36] Besides, Domínguez discusses cases in which "[e]ven the right of white persons voluntarily to acknowledge their colored children, when they have no legitimate white children of their own, has been challenged."[37] Put simply by Domínguez, "The attempted transmission of property from a white man to his colored family . . . went against the very intent of Louisiana law."[38]

Not only would Armand have at some point realized that his rights of inheritance would be in jeopardy should his racial heritage be discovered, but also, growing up in Louisiana, he would probably have witnessed the growing prejudice against free people of color, who were considered by a large faction of Louisiana citizens "to be inferior simply because of their African blood."[39] That such prejudice was present in Armand's community is partly evidenced by Désirée's choice to die rather than return to her parents. Evidently, she would rather be dead than black.[40] According to Eugene D. Genovese, in the 1850s the position of free people of color throughout the South began to deteriorate, and "[t]he [Louisiana] state courts . . . did little or nothing to ease the plight of the free Negroes." Furthermore, he adds, "As a particularly vicious counterpart of these legal and social developments, free Negroes faced the persistent danger of being kidnapped and sold into slavery."[41] Following a discussion of various restrictions placed upon free people of color, Laura Foner quotes from the 1859 *Laws of Louisiana,* which "encourage[d] 'free people of African descent to select their masters and become slaves for life.' "[42] She notes, too, that "vigilante groups began nightly rides to seek out and punish free Negroes."[43] Floyd James Davis also discusses the change in attitude toward free people of color after 1850, which resulted in Louisiana moving from a three- toward a two-caste system in which "all persons had to be classed as either white or black"[44]—i.e., the "one-drop rule." According to H. E. Sterkx, "Only 100 percent White ancestry would permit legal entrance to the White race."[45] Again one can turn to Cable's *The Grandissimes* for a fictional corroboration of this attitude as it is explained to the naive Frowenfeld, a stranger to Louisiana and its customs:

> "[W]hen we say, 'we people,' we *always* mean we white people. The non-mention of color always implies pure white; and whatever is not pure white is to all intents and purposes pure black. When I say the 'whole community,' I mean the whole white portion; when I speak of the 'undivided public sentiment,' I mean the sentiment of the white population." (59, Cable's emphasis)

In Louisiana, as in the rest of the South, as Joel Williamson notes, the mulatto had no place in this two-caste hierarchy, particularly after 1850:

> Increasingly, the South grew furiously intolerant of anything that was not distinctly slave or free, black or white. . . . In the pursuit of an ordered society, the upper South and the lower South came together. The lower South gave up its peculiar sympathy with mulattoes and joined an upper South already in place.

Miscegenation was wrong and mulattoes must be made black, both within slavery and without. There was no middle ground in the organic society, no place for one who was neither white nor black.[46]

In self-preservation, Armand made a place for himself. Critics have repeatedly pointed out the irony of the English translation of the name of the Aubigny plantation, since L'Abri offers no "shelter" for the story's tragic heroine. However, by "passing" for the rightful white heir to and master of this plantation, Armand protects himself from the very extradition that Désirée eventually suffers.

As Chopin does not set her story in a particular year, we cannot assume that it takes place after 1850. However, Sterkx argues that "the ever-present fear of racial equality, which became an obsession of many Whites throughout the ante-bellum period . . . found expression [as early as] when America first took control of Louisiana with the passage of laws designed to impress an inferior social position upon the free colored persons."[47] Alice Dunbar-Nelson also reports that owing to the extensive miscegenation that had resulted in (and here she quotes one observer's wording) " 'perfectly white' " Negroes by the late 1810s, a change in attitude toward free people of color began to be evident as early as that decade: "the tendency seemed to be not to check promiscuous miscegenation but to debase the offspring resulting therefrom."[48] Annie Stahl concurs in her remark that free people of color in Louisiana "gradually lost ground during the reactionary period of the 1820's and 1830's."[49] Sterkx traces, perhaps most specifically, the developing campaign to rid Louisiana of free people of color. Those actions particularly relevant to Armand include an act making "any free persons of color who had arrived after January 1, 1825 . . . subject to deportation" or imprisonment, possibly for life.[50] Sterkx reports that one man who passed for white in order to stay in Louisiana, upon discovery, was arrested, fined, and imprisoned.[51] One wonders, given the extreme prejudice against people of color, what would have been done to a man discovered to have, while passing for white, married the daughter of a respected white family. When these laws attempting to rid the state of free people of color proved ineffective, according to Sterkx, "irate private citizens launched individual campaigns of vilification and hatred against free Negroes" and complained to their legislators about "the weaknesses of Louisiana's laws in comparison with [those] of other Southern states."[52] F. James Davis notes, too, that even before the 1850s "the free mulattoes [of Louisiana] enjoyed more privileges than unmixed blacks, but fewer than those enjoyed by whites." Consequently, he adds, in spite of their freedom and prosperity, "[t]here was considerable passing as white";[53] no wonder, given John Blassingame's description of the free person of color as "severely handicapped" owing to his/her association with slaves. "[H]e suffered many penalties as a result," writes Blassingame, continuing, "An anomaly in Louisiana, the free Negro was neither bound nor free."[54] Blassingame later argues the case for passing: "Since white skin was glorified, since Whites had all of the power and most of the wealth and education, many Negroes accepted the concept of the goodness, purity, and sanctity of whiteness and the degradation of blackness. Consequently, many of them tried and a number succeeded in passing for white."[55] One such passer is Armand. Not only does he succeed in passing throughout that part of his lifetime covered by the story's perimeters, but also he has continued to pass for over a century: readers new to the story continue failing to see Chopin's hints about Armand's race and therefore continue to be surprised by her final disclosure.

An understanding of the tightrope on which Armand's life is balanced would explain the implication in the story that Armand is not a kind slave master. His strict rule at L'Abri is a means by which he not only denies but also punishes his race for the potential of great suffering in his life. Indeed, his behavior toward Blacks is consistent with that of many free people of color. For example, a French traveler through Louisiana from 1801 through 1803, F. M. Perrin Du Lac, expressed his opinion that the free mulattoes in particular were " 'enemies . . . of the blacks whom they despise' " and remarked upon these mulattoes' " '[c]ruel[ty] even to barbarity toward [Blacks].' "[56] Laura Foner quotes from an 1852 issue of the *New Orleans Daily Delta* that the free people of color of antebellum Louisiana " 'regard the slave with more disdain and antagonism than the white man.' "[57] In his writings on his first-hand observations of slavery, Frederick Law Olmsted reports that one slave told him of black plantation—and *slave*—owners,

> They were very bad masters, very hard and cruel—hadn't any feeling. "You might think, master, dat dey would be good to dar own nation; but dey is not. . . . I'd rather be a servant to any man in de world, dan to a brack man. If I was sold to a brack man, I'd drown myself. . . . I wouldn't be sold to a coloured master for anything."[58]

A similar opinion was also expressed by Louisiana Judge Phanor Breazeale: " 'I have found by inquiry from old people that free black owners [of slaves] were as a usual thing much more severe on their slaves than the white owners.' "[59] Finally, historian Annie Stahl comments upon the inherited attitude of free people of color toward slaves: "While the whites were superior to them [free people of color], they in turn were superior to the blacks and objected just as strenuously to associating with them as the whites objected to mingling with free negroes."[60]

Also in answer to this issue of Armand's treatment of his slaves, Emily Toth has suggested that Armand "finds his identity in possession and domination,"[61] but one might say that he "asserts" rather than "finds" his identity as a white man by taking "possession" of and exhibiting his "domination" over his father's slaves. Put simply, Armand treats his slaves harshly in order to hide his connection to them from any suspicious eyes—white or black. This contention is supported by the fact that he refrains from abusing them when his son is first born and apparently looks white, allowing Armand to believe his secret is safe. Then, after the commencement of the "air of mystery among the blacks" and the "unexpected visits from far-off neighbors who could hardly account for their coming," the narrator reports that "the very spirit of Satan seemed suddenly to take hold of [Armand] in his dealings with the slaves" (242).[62] It is as if he is redoubling his efforts to display his hatred for members of the black race to deny any responsibility for the African traces becoming evident in his son's features.[63] These efforts include his treatment of his wife and son, which is neither more nor less cruel than other slavemasters' treatment of their slave mistresses and bastard children in this society. Indeed, Armand himself apparently has had a mistress—the slave La Blanche, mentioned several times in the story, including once when Désirée remarks that Armand had heard their child crying " 'as far away as La Blanche's cabin' " (241)[64]—and also has a bastard child, an observation suggested by the narrator when Désirée notices the resemblance between her son and "[o]ne of La Blanche's little quadroon boys": "She looked from her child to the boy who stood beside him, and back again; over and over" (242). That it is this child in particular who causes Désirée to finally see in her own son that which others had already seen suggests that the two boys have the same father.[65] In light of this notion, Armand's turning Désirée and their son out of his house should be viewed as no more cruel than the fact that this apparent son is a slave. In addition to recognizing this horrible (though common) practice of enslaving one's own child, the reader should also note that the present duty of Armand's eldest son, who is half-naked and shoeless, is to fan his own half-brother, the possessor of "a priceless *layette*" (244). Indeed, if not for the revelation regarding his half-brother's "impure" blood, this boy might have served his brother throughout their lives—that is, if the elder boy were not sold (away from his mother). In the first chapter of his *Narrative,* Frederick Douglass reported that bastard slave children were often sold to avoid the difficult situations that could arise when brother owned brother.

Arguing that Armand's marriage to Désirée was part of a diabolical scheme to have a scapegoat should his children reveal his heritage does not align Armand with the villainous "brute Negro" of much of the early literature about Blacks by white authors, as categorized in Sterling A. Brown's 1933 seminal essay on the subject.[66] However, Armand could be viewed as part of a tradition of mulatto villains in American fiction. Emily Toth suggests that, to prepare her readers for the story's eventual disclosure, Chopin gives Armand "the qualities of the Tragic Octoroon male: he is militant, rebellious, melancholy, at the mercy of his fierce passions."[67] One might add to Toth's list that he is also "[h]aunted by fear of detection," a characteristic of the Tragic Mulatto who is trying to pass for white, according to Judith Berzon's study of this character-type in fiction by both black and white writers.[68] That Armand's mixed blood results in tragedy—the apparent deaths of his wife and child—is also consistent with the Tragic Mulatto/Octoroon–type, as the category name suggests. However, in the more traditional story of the Tragic Mulatto/Octoroon, it is the character with mixed blood who eventually dies, sometimes after spending much of his/her life trying to pass. Furthermore, Armand's character is not, as Brown describes the Tragic Mulatto, "a victim of a divided inheritance." According to Brown, many of the mulatto or octoroon characters created by Chopin's white contemporaries are driven by two internal forces: "from his white blood come his intellectual strivings, his unwillingness to be a slave; from his Negro blood come his baser emotional urges, his indolence, his savagery."[69] Though Armand is unwilling to risk becoming either (at worst) a slave or (at best) a second-class citizen, and though he does act savagely against his slaves and later his wife and son, nowhere in the story does Chopin suggest that his behavior can be accounted for by his "white and Negro blood."[70] Indeed, the reader is not told that Armand has any "Negro blood" until the very end of the story. As Toth points out, Chopin's story shows this particular white author's understanding "that it is not a person's inherited race which determines character, but society's reaction to race."[71] Armand's "diabolical scheme" does not come from African savagery. Rather, it reflects fear of Euro-American (particularly Southern Euro-American) savagery against people with any trace of African blood.[72] As Toth remarks, " 'Désirée's Baby' is about environment, the effect of slavery on men's character. . . . Chopin shows that color caste and economic superiority develop certain unenviable but inevitable qualities in the white masters."[73]

The pattern of Armand's story accurately follows the pattern of passing tales, which do not necessarily end in tragic death, particularly when the protagonist is male. Still, these stories, when the character does not in the end embrace his black heritage but instead makes a decision to continue passing, do end with a sense of the continued isolation of the passer in his or her life. Armand's scheme of marrying a foundling in case of detection through his offspring, and his later rejection of this wife and their child, is clearly in character with the behavior of the conscious passer in stories of this genre. As mentioned, Berzon argues that "[t]he most basic fear of the passer is that he will suddenly be exposed." One way that this might occur, Berzon explains, is through the passer's children: "The 'black-baby myth' also haunts many a passer" who "may fear exposure through the birth of a baby that does not look quite white." When such a child is born to a passing man or woman, according to Berzon, what often happens is that the child is "disowned."[74] Hence, the title of the story, "Désirée's Baby," does not only reflect the catalyst for the story's conflict ("Désirée's *Baby*") but also reflects upon Armand's ultimate crime—rejecting his own child[75] and heritage by placing the blame for his son's countenance solely upon his wife's background ("*Désirée's* Baby").

That Armand is knowingly passing for white helps explain why he kept the incriminating evidence of his heritage—i.e., the letter from his mother to his father declaring her race. In *Autobiography of an Ex-Coloured Man,* another example of passing literature, Johnson's protagonist, like Armand, chooses finally to continue passing (in ironic contrast, he does so in part to "protect" his children[76]). However, to the novel's end he, too, holds on to a paper that reveals his heritage, though not so straightforwardly—it is the manuscript in which he had transcribed the songs of his people. In the last lines of the novel, he remarks upon this manuscript: "when I sometimes open a little box in which I still keep my fast yellowing manuscripts, the only tangible remnants of a vanished dream, a dead ambition, a sacrificed talent, I cannot repress the thought that, after all, I have chosen the lesser part, that I have sold my birthright for a mess of pottage!" (211). In the final view of Armand, too, is the sense that his "practical joke on society," to use Johnson's narrator's words (3), has backfired. He is left standing alone, his last chance to live with the love of a wife and child gone (for, again, how many such foundlings could there be in this community with whom he could risk trying to have a family?). The parallel between this manuscript and Armand's letter becomes poignant in light of the opening declaration by Johnson's protagonist that he is "divulging the great secret of [his] life, the secret which for some years [he] ha[s] guarded far more carefully than any of [his] earthly possessions." Johnson's protagonist provides some insight into possible motivations Armand might have had to keep the incriminating letter for so many years: In "analys[ing] the motives which prompt" him to tell his story at this point in his life, Johnson's character begins, "I feel that I am led by the same impulse which forces the un-found-out criminal to take somebody into his confidence, although he knows that the act is likely, even almost certain, to lead to his undoing" (3).[77] Armand may have kept the letter for the same reason a criminal returns to the scene of the crime, the same reason the narrator of Edgar Allan Poe's "The Cask of Amontillado" (1846) confesses his crime: he has saved it out of a mixture of pride and guilt over what he has gotten away with, which is evidenced by the letter. Perhaps, too, like Poe's narrator of "The Tell-Tale Heart," who ultimately understands the inevitability of his own death—which he had feared for so long—part of Armand wanted to be caught in order to end the suspense over when he will be caught and the fear of what will then become of him. In contrast to Poe's characters, however, Armand may finally have burned the letter, though whether he did is not clear in the story: "The last thing to go [into the fire] was a tiny bundle of letters; innocent little scribblings that Désirée had sent to him during the days of their espousal. There was the remnant of one back in the drawer from which he took them." We are told that "[h]e read it" but not that he burned it (244). In any case, one can be sure that, again, unlike the confessions of Poe's characters, which are addressed to a definite, though vague audience (the "you" whom each narrator addresses), Armand's "confession" is heard only by the reader.

Armand may also have kept the letter because it is a part of his identity and thus validates his existence. One might recall here the rage of Nathaniel

Hawthorne's Pearl upon realizing that Hester has removed the "A" from her breast. The precocious Pearl has intuited that the scarlet letter is connected to her own very existence in the world. Hester's removing the letter, then, can be perceived as a rejection of Pearl in that it denies the act that created the child. Therefore, although Pearl has long understood that the scarlet letter is the source of her isolation, she insists that her mother replace it upon her breast. As Hester's scarlet letter is to Pearl a symbol of the source of her life as well as the source of her isolation, so, too, does Armand's mother's letter hold the secret of his identity, which could ostracize him. Thus, though different kinds of "letters," both are brands that sear deeper than the surface of the characters. Armand may deny part of that identity in his everyday existence, but at the same time he must hold on to it. Like Pearl, he understands that it is central to what makes him who he is. That only a "remnant" of the original letter remains may suggest, in fact, that Armand at some time started to destroy the incriminating evidence and yet could not finally throw out the part of it that was so crucial to his identity.[78] If Armand destroyed the letter in the end, such an action could be viewed as his recognition that his life is essentially over.

"Désirée's Baby" thus may be seen as Chopin's challenge to the postbellum plantation literature that idealized the Old South. Reading the story in its historical context reveals the author's knowledge of the conditions in Louisiana for any person of color, slave or free, and her understanding of how the consequences of slavery, miscegenation, and racism extend to all. Like African-American writers of her day, Chopin had to mask her subversive message regarding these horrors so as not to offend some of her readers. As Charles Chesnutt does in many of his conjure tales, she tells her story in a way that would allow her prejudiced reader, like Chesnutt's recurrent white narrator John, to grasp only the surface meaning. Just as John sees in each conjure story only what Uncle Julius was trying to "con" him out of by telling the tale, the narrow-minded reader, after discovering Armand's racial heritage in the last lines of Chopin's story, would view Armand's behavior as corroboration of his/her opinion of African Americans. "Blood will tell," these readers might respond self-righteously upon finding out that it is Armand whose blood is "tainted." At the same time, a reader inclined to be sympathetic to the plight of people of color in the antebellum South would, like John's wife Annie, see through the story to its lessons on the consequences of slavery. Like Annie, then, this reader might cry out, " 'What a system it was . . . under which such things were possible!' "[79] "Such things" happen in Chopin's story: the son of a white man and a black woman who were deeply in love, because he grows up surrounded by the violent racism of his community, develops into a cold, heartless man who will stop at nothing—neither brutal treatment of his slaves, nor cruel rejection of his wife and son—to hide what he perceives to be his shame. This reading of Chopin's story reveals, too, that for the perceptive, sympathetic reader, "Désirée's Baby" is as much Armand's tragic story as it is for either character referred to in its title. Indeed, the title points—by exclusion, appropriately—to Armand, whose story is carefully hidden by its author from those who would prefer to villainize him rather than face up to their responsibility for his actions: he is not some Satanic anomaly but a product of his racist environment.

One may recall here Jesus's words explaining his method of teaching lessons:

> . . . He that hath ears to hear let him hear . . . but unto them that are without [insight], all these things are done in parables: That seeing they may see, and not perceive; and hearing they may hear, and not understand; lest at any time they should be converted, and their sins should be forgiven them. (Mark 4:9, 11–12)

Like Jesus, Chopin understood that she would have to be careful when dealing with unpopular topics such as slavery, racism, and miscegenation. She appears to have perceived that much of her 1890s audience was not yet ready for an open condemnation of the social system that allowed tragedies to occur such as those suffered by the Aubigny family. That "Désirée's Baby" has not been fully understood reflects why racism still exists: like the people of Armand and Désirée's community, the majority of us remain blind to what goes on right in front of us as long as the social order remains stable. We shake our heads but do not probe, afraid of what we will discover beneath the surface—that the villain is not the one who is black, but instead, our community itself is the villain.

Notes

1.   Kate Chopin, *The Complete Works of Kate Chopin,* ed. Per Seyersted (Baton Rouge: Louisiana State University Press, 1969), 244–45; hereafter cited in the text.

2.   See in particular Robert D. Arner, "Pride and Prejudice: Kate Chopin's 'Désirée's Baby,' " *Mississippi Quarterly* 25 (Spring 1972): 131–40.

3.   Per Seyersted mistakenly writes that "the revelation—after [Armand] had driven [Désirée] to her death—that it was he who was Negroid, *comes as a complete shock to him,* as it does to the reader" (*Kate Chopin: A Critical Biography* [Baton Rouge: Louisiana State University Press, 1969], 122; emphasis added). In truth, Chopin does not show Armand either "shocked" or reacting in any other way.

4.   Judith A. Berzon, *Neither White Nor Black: The Mulatto Character in American Fiction* (New York: New York University Press, 1978).

5.   In summarizing the plot of the story, Per Seyersted again mistakenly writes that "[w]hen burning everything that reminds him of her, [Armand] *finds* an old letter to his father from his mother" (*Kate Chopin,* 94; emphasis added). Other critics have made the same faulty assumption regarding when Armand first sees the letter: Emily Toth says that it is only "[a]fter burning Désirée's effects [that] Armand finds [the] letter" ("Kate Chopin and Literary Convention: 'Désirée's Baby,' " *Southern Studies* 20 [Summer 1981]: 205), a reading she would repeat in her biography of Chopin (*Kate Chopin,* [New York: Morrow, 1990], 215) and with

which Barbara C. Ewell (*Kate Chopin,* Literature and Life Series, [New York: Ungar, 1986], 69) and Ellen Peel ("Semiotic Subversion in Désirée's Baby,' " *American Literature* 62 [June 1990]: 224, 228–29) agree. Even Anna Shannon Elfenbein, the one critic who asks, "Does Armand suspect his racial 'taint' subconsciously" (*Women on the Color Line: Evolving Stereotypes and the Writings of George Washington Cable, Grace King, Kate Chopin* [Charlottesville: University Press of Virginia, 1989], 131; see also note 26), writes that "only later [after Désirée leaves] does Armand discover [his racial heritage] in a letter written by his mother to his father" (126). Richard H. Potter ("Negroes in the Fiction of Kate Chopin," *Louisiana History* 12 [1971]: 49) and Peggy Skaggs (*Kate Chopin,* Twayne's United States Authors Series 485 [Boston: Twayne, 1985], 25) remark similarly. Indeed, I have traced this assumption back to 1966 in Larzer Ziff's brief mention of the story in his *The American 1890s: Life and Times of a Lost Generation* (New York: Viking, 1966), 297. However, in perhaps the first mention of the story in a critical book, Fred Lewis Pattee is more careful in his summation of the events: "Armand, who is clearing the old bureau of all of Désirée's belongings, happens upon an old letter in his mother's handwriting" (*The Development of the American Short Story: An Historical Survey,* [New York: Harper, 1923], 327). "Happens upon," one notes, does not indicate whether or not it is the first time he has seen it. Similarly, Robert Arner, in his aforementioned article on the craftsmanship of the story, is also careful with his wording: "Some weeks later, as Armand is systematically attempting to purify his house from all traces of Désirée and the baby, he *comes upon* the fragment of a letter lodged in a drawer" ("Pride and Prejudice," 132; emphasis added). In a later discussion of the story, however, Arner writes that "Armand discovers [the letter] after he has driven away Désirée and the baby" ("Kate Chopin," *Louisiana Studies* 14 [1975]: 51). Also, in both articles, Arner makes several assumptions that are not narrated specifically in the text regarding "two discoveries" that he contends "Armand makes at the conclusion of the story[:] that he is part Negro and that the idea of white racial purity is a myth" ("Pride and Prejudice," 133; "Kate Chopin," 52, with slightly different wording). The narration does not indicate that Armand makes *any* discoveries: we are not given Armand's thoughts at this point.

6.   Interesting parallels can be seen between Armand's masquerade and Thomas Sutpen's "design" in William Faulkner's *Absalom, Absalom!* (1936). Both authors ultimately condemn the social order more harshly than they do these scheming characters who fail to take into consideration the feelings of the people whom they use towards their ends.

7.   Anna Elfenbein makes a similar contention about Armand's motives, though she suggests that they are not conscious:

> In marrying Désirée, so visibly white, and in fathering a baby also apparently white, at least for three months, Armand may have assuaged his secret subconscious racial fears. A dark-skinned aristocrat[, Armand] may vaguely remember his racially mixed mother (he was eight years old when he left Paris, where his parents lived together).

Elfenbein supports her theory by pointing out that "Armand is the only racially obsessed character in Chopin's story" (*Women on the Color Line,* 126–27).

8.   Many critics also assume that Désirée is definitely "white." As discussed by Ellen Peel, the secrets of Désirée's heritage are never revealed ("Semiotic Subversion," 233). On this subject, in his discussion of the story's fairy tale elements, Jon Erickson shows how the beginning of the story follows the pattern of a fairy tale about a foundling: "It is common in these stories that the heroine should be discovered by a passing [an ironic choice of words in light of the present reading] 'prince' and that the prince should experience . . . the 'shock effect' of beauty"; however, "[t]he question of origin . . . hover[s] in the background" ("Fairytale Features in Kate Chopin's 'Désirée's Baby': A Case Study in Genre Cross-Reference," *Modes of Narrative: Approaches to American, Canadian and British Fiction,* ed. Reingard M. Nischik and Barbara Korte [Wurzburg: Konigshausen, 1990], 59). Erickson explains how the end of

Désirée's narrative—her death—is particularly disappointing to the reader because of the expectations of how such a story should end: "The standard expectation is that the child will turn out to be of interesting [i.e., "good"] parentage" (58). Although he goes on to show how the story's ending—the disclosure about the villain Armand's parentage—satisfies the reader, Erickson, like other critics, does not address the fact that Désirée's heritage is still unknown.

9.   Virginia R. Domínguez, *White by Definition: Social Classification in Creole Louisiana* (New Brunswick: Rutgers University Press, 1986), 25–26.

10.   H. E. Sterkx, *The Free Negro in Ante-Bellum Louisiana* (Rutherford: Fairleigh Dickinson University Press, 1972), 243; Sterkx's bracketed insertion.

11.   Joe Gray Taylor, *Negro Slavery in Louisiana* (Baton Rouge: LA Historical Association, 1963), 232; emphasis added. Annie Lee West Stahl comments that not only were such marriages "forbidden by law," but also they were "condemned by the instinct and sentiment of a majority of the people" ("The Free Negro in Ante-Bellum Louisiana," *Louisiana Historical Quarterly* 25 [1942]: 375).

12.   John W. Blassingame, *Black New Orleans, 1860–1880* (Chicago: University of Chicago Press, 1973), 20.

13.   Sterkx, *Free Negro,* 244; emphasis added.

14.   One might contrast the narrative voice of this story with that of Chopin's *The Awakening.* In this novel, whenever the characters misread Edna's moods, the narrator provides the correct reading of what is going on within the character. For example, after noting that Léonce "could see plainly that [Edna] was not herself," the narrator corrects his assessment: "That is, he could not see that she was becoming herself and daily casting aside that fictitious self which we assume like a garment with which to appear before the world" (939).

15.   Skaggs, *Kate Chopin,* 26. Mary E. Papke notes similarly, "Even though Armand himself has a somewhat shadowy past and an equally dark present, there is never a moment, until the final disclosure, that suspicion falls on anyone but Désirée" (*Verging on the Abyss: The Social Fiction of Kate Chopin and Edith Wharton* [New York: Greenwood, 1990], 54).

16.   Skaggs, *Kate Chopin,* 26.

17.   Sterkx, *Free Negro,* 240.

18.   Stahl, "Free Negro," 309–10; emphasis added.

19.   Sterkx, *Free Negro,* 171.

20.   Sterkx, *Free Negro,* 160.

21.   Laura Foner, "The Free People of Color in Louisiana and St. Domingue: A Comparative Portrait of Two Three-Caste Slave Societies," *Journal of Social History* 3 (? 1970): 420. Stahl comments similarly on the position of the free people of color in Louisiana: "It is true that they possessed many of the civil and legal rights commonly enjoyed by the whites, but they were disqualified from political rights and social equality" ("Free Negro," 304).

22.   George Washington Cable, *The Grandissimes: A Story of Creole Life,* American Century Series, (1880; New York: Hill, 1957), 144; hereafter cited in the text.

23.   Foner, "Free People of Color," 417. John Blassingame also addresses the subject:

On practically all public occasions when Negroes interacted with whites, Negroes had to be in a subordinate position; there had to be a visible demonstration of the white man's superiority. . . . [P]ractically all jails, theaters, Protestant churches, schools, hospitals, and streetcars were rigidly segregated, and restaurants, hotels, and private clubs generally excluded Negroes. (*Black New Orleans,* 16)

24.   Foner, "Free People of Color," 417.

25.   Foner, "Free People of Color," 430. Stahl quotes part of an announcement published in the December 28, 1860 issue of the *New Orleans Daily Delta* by the city's free people of color, which illustrates their support of the caste system:

"The free colored population of Louisiana . . . own slaves, and they are ready to shed their blood for her defense. They have no sympathy for abolitionism; no love for the North, but they have plenty for Louisiana . . . they will fight for her in 1861 as they fought in 1814–'15. All they ask is a chance and they will be worthy sons of Louisiana." ("Free Negro," 323; Stahl's elipses)

Calvin Dill Wilson reports on one free person of color who served in the Confederate army and later, in his old age, applied for a pension from the state of Georgia for doing so, although, as Wilson points out, he must have known "that the success of his cause would, in all probability, have continued slavery." Wilson believes that this example illustrates the fact "[t]hat the free negroes had not always conscience or sentiment against slavery" ("Black Masters: A Side-Light on Slavery," *North American Review* 181 [November 1905]: 690). Also supporting his contention is a letter he received from Judge Phanor Breazeale of Natchitoches, Louisiana who reported that " 'in [his] Parish the colony of "free colored people" have preserved in the forty years since the war absolutely intact their status, and have positively refused to come in contact with the freed slaves, either socially or otherwise' " (690). Wilson argues, too, that one motivating force behind free people of color owning black slaves "was ambition . . . the cold and selfish desire to attain a real or an apparent superiority over other blacks . . . ambition to rise into the class of masters, and to stand, so far as possible, on the same level as white men" (685).

26. Like Anna Elfenbein (see note 5), Roslyn Reso Foy has suggested that "Armand was certainly old enough to remember his mother," though she does not state whether or not this would include noticing his mother's color. She argues, however, that, regarding his recollection of his mother, "circumstances have caused him to suppress the past" ("Chopin's 'Désirée's Baby,' " *Explicator* 49.4 [Summer 1991]: 223). She does not specify what circumstances exactly, but perhaps she is referring to the circumstances of his surroundings—i.e., living in a society that enslaves people of his mother's (and thus his own) race. However, Armand has probably not suppressed his past to the point of having forgotten his racial heritage.

27. Marjorie McDonald, M.D., *Not by the Color of Their Skin: The Impact of Racial Differences on the Child's Development* (International University Press, 1970), 95.

28. McDonald, 104.

29. Kenneth B[ancroft] Clark, *Prejudice and Your Child* (Boston: Beacon, 1955), 19.

30. Chopin does not, however, allow her mother character this insight. In the letter to her husband, Madame Aubigny expresses her relief that " 'Armand will never know' " of her race (245). This does not belie Chopin's awareness and use of this aspect of child psychology. Armand is his mother's first and only child, so she might not have picked up on what would have been repeatedly played out before a mother of six.

31. Clark, *Prejudice,* 23. See also Mary Ellen Goodman, *Race Awareness in Young Children* (Cambridge: Addision-Wesley, 1952).

32. Clark, *Prejudice,* 37. See also Clark's discussion of a "coloring test," during which

15 per cent of the children with medium-brown skin color and 14 per cent of the dark-brown children . . . colored their 'own' figure with either a white or a yellow crayon or with some bizarre color like red or green [though] these same children were quite accurate in their ability to color the leaf, the apple, the orange, and the mouse.

Clark concludes from this experiment, "Their refusal to choose an appropriate color for themselves was an indication of emotional anxiety and conflict in terms of their own skin color." Of those who colored themselves white or yellow he adds, "Because they wanted to be white, they pretended to be" (43).

33. H. E. Sterkx quotes from a Louisiana newspaper a recommendation for the enslavement of free people of color, which, he says, also "found expression in the Immigration statute of March 15, 1859." Part of the recommendation reads, " 'That if any free persons of color shall enter within the limits of the State he shall be sold as a slave at public auction. . . . That all free persons of color who are now in the state in contravention of its laws shall also be sold as slaves for life at public auction' " (*Free Negro,* 115). As will be shown in later references to Sterkx's studies, Armand's presence in Louisiana may have been illegal according to Louisiana laws; thus he was in danger of being sold into slavery.

34. Domínguez, *White by Definition,* 62.

35. Domínguez, 63; emphasis added. According to Sterkx, a black child who

> had been legally acknowledged . . . was qualified to receive [only] one fourth of an estate, provided there were no legitimate [i.e., white] children of the testator. This amount was increased to one-third, provided the surviving relatives were even more remote in kinship . . . [T]he balance of the estate went to any surviving legitimate relations. (*Free Negro,* 179)

Sterkx reports, too, on a proposition introduced at the 1872 Constitution Convention, though not passed, which would have kept free people of color "from acquiring real estate by inheritance or purchase" (172–73). This proposition reflects many people's animosity against black heirs to white estates.

36. Again, Warren's *Band of Angels* (New York: Random House, 1955) can be used as an intertextual tool. Warren's plantation owner's failure to write out manumission papers for his daughter results in her being sold along with the rest of his property after his death.

37. Domínguez, *White by Definition,* 64.

38. Domínguez, 83

39. Sterkx, *Free Negro,* 246. Sterkx quotes from an open letter to the free people of color in one newspaper that expresses the sentiments of the most radical haters of this group:

> "You cannot live in the United States with the white man in peace, you cannot ever hope to approach anything like an equality with him, this idea on your part would be repugnant to the laws of natural reason, nature, and nature's God. We advise you to flee the society of the white man voluntarily before you are compelled to do so by his irrevocable decrees. Take a fair price for your lands and we will [e]nsure you speedy purchasers. . . . [T]his is the kind of population we want—all white citizens and their slaves—no free colored citizens in our midst. Then we may look for the dawn of better society, better government and more general prosperity among us as white citizens." (298–99)

40. I do not mean to argue that Désirée's apparent suicide is committed solely because of her belief that she is black. I agree with those critics who argue that she turns to the swamp instead of her parents also because she has lost her role in life as Armand's wife. For example, Peggy Skaggs remarks upon the irony that "although functioning within the same bigoted tradition that causes [or *seems* to cause] Armand to send her coldly away to perish, Désirée wants only to regain her place as [his] beloved wife. . . . [H]er place and even her name depend upon a man's regarding her as a prized possession" (*Kate Chopin,* 26). Mary Papke adds to this realization regarding Désirée's behavior,

> Her identity is inextricably dependent upon her relationship to Armand as his wife and mother of his child. . . . Schooled too well in the manners and constraints of true womanhood, Désirée herself denies the possibility of life outside

Armand's world and instead chooses a suicidal descent into and not beyond the bayou. (*Verging on the Abyss*, 55)

41. Eugene D. Genovese, *Roll, Jordan, Roll: The World the Slaves Made* (New York: Pantheon-Random, 1972), 399–400.

42. Foner, "Free People of Color," 428. Sterkx explains that such an act was passed "to placate militant White factions demanding restrictive measures" that they had proposed in order "to deprive free colored persons of their already guaranteed rights under the law" (*Free Negro*, 198).

43. Foner, "Free People of Color," 428n.

44. F[loyd] James Davis, *Who is Black?: One Nation's Definition* (University Park: Pennsylvania State University Press, 1991), 41.

45. Sterkx, *Free Negro*, 247.

46. Joel Williamson, *New People: Miscegenation and Mulattoes in the United States* (New York: Free, 1980), 74.

47. Sterkx, *Free Negro*, 240.

48. Alice Dunbar-Nelson, "People of Color in Louisiana, Part II," *Journal of Negro History* 2 (1917): 56.

49. Stahl, "Free Negro," 315.

50. Sterkx, *Free Negro*, 98.

51. Sterkx, *Free Negro*, 108–109.

52. Sterkx, *Free Negro*, 113.

53. Davis, *Who Is Black*, 37.

54. He lists some of these "penalties":

Although his property rights were protected and he had the right to sue and to be sued, the free Negro had no guarantee of justice in Louisiana's courts. He was barred by law from engaging in a public horse race or owning any establishment where liquor was sold; arson and the rape of white women were capital crimes only when Negroes were involved; and the free Negro might be arrested at any time as a runaway slave. (Blassingame, *Black New Orleans*, 14–15)

55. Blassingame, 21.

56. Donald E. Everett, "Free Persons of Color in Colonial Louisiana," *Louisiana History* 7 (? 1966): 38.

57. Foner, "Free People of Color," 429.

58. Frederick Law Olmsted, *The Cotton Kingdom: A Traveller's Observations on Cotton and Slavery in the American Slave States, Based Upon Three Former Volumes of Journeys and Investigations by the Same Author*, ed. Arthur M. Schlesinger, (1861; New York: Knopf, 1953), 262. H. E. Sterkx quotes from a newspaper account describing the " 'lash marks on the breast and iron rings on both legs' " of a fugitive slave belonging to a free man of color (*Free Negro*, 281).

59. Wilson, "Black Masters," 690.

60. Stahl, "Free Negro," 374. Regarding this sense of superiority, Sterkx remarks, "Colored aristocrats dressed, thought, and in many ways acted as haughty as their White counterparts towards the 'lowly,' but they could never hope to cross the color line and become peers of the White ruling class" (*Free Negro*, 283–84).

61. Toth, "Kate Chopin," 206.

62. Upon apparently recognizing the African features in his son, Armand does not immediately confront Désirée with accusations. Although there is "an awful change in [his] manner" (242), he says nothing until she brings up the subject to him. If he truly believed himself to be "innocent," and if he is so disgusted by the evident "blackness" of his wife, why does he wait? On the other hand, if indeed he is aware of his own responsibility for the child's

appearance, then perhaps he is delaying the moment when the whole "game" is over. As mentioned, only with Désirée could he dare to try to have a family without risking his own detection.

63.   Toth, too, remarks upon the fact that Armand "relax[es] his iron grasp on his slaves" after his son's birth and then resumes it with a vengeance after he, according to Toth, "thinks he has discovered mixed blood in Désirée," but she does not explain the reason for these changes in his treatment of his slaves (206). The explanation offered by Richard Potter and apparently accepted by most readers is unsatisfactory: "So powerful is their love that Armand's very character undergoes profound changes as he gradually eases his tyrannical rule of the plantation. The birth of a son only heightens the effect" ("Negroes," 49).

64.   The suggestion that Armand has this mistress is further evidence against his being so much in love with Désirée.

65.   Cynthia Griffin Wolff ("Kate Chopin and the Fiction of Limits: 'Désirée's Baby,' " *Southern Literary Journal* 10.2 [Spring 1978]: 128) and Ellen Peel ("Semiotic Subversion," 226) have also made this suggestion. Anna Elfenbein proposes a provocative theory about La Blanche and her son: "The possibility that she may be Désirée's predecessor [—i.e., also once married to Armand], sent to the slave quarters for having given birth to a mulatto son" (*Women on the Color Line,* 128). However, there is not enough information about La Blanche in the story to support this theory. That the narrator (again, the voice of the people) refers to her child as a quadroon, a term indicating that a person is a quarter black, implies that La Blanche's racial heritage is known. Besides, although the community could allow the aristocratic Armand to declare the race of a foundling, it could not allow him to so besmirch the reputation of just anyone—and what are the chances of there being more than one such foundling in this community? It is much more likely that La Blanche is exactly what she appears to be—Armand's slave mistress. He uses her in much the same way he uses Désirée—to help him carry out his pretense that he is no different from any other plantation owner.

66.   Sterling A. Brown, "Negro Character as Seen by White Authors," *Journal of Negro Education* 2 (April 1933): 179–203.

67.   Toth, "Kate," 207. Surprisingly, in her biography of Kate Chopin, Toth is much harsher with Armand than she had been in her earlier article, calling him "one of the most evil men in [Chopin's] fiction" (*Kate Chopin,* 215).

68.   Berzon, *Neither White Nor Black,* 102.

69.   Brown, "Negro Characters," 194–95.

70.   Richard Potter also calls Armand a Tragic Mulatto and his explanation is similar to my contentions here:

> [H]is tragedy lies not in the presence or absence of the characteristics of either race. Rather, his tragedy lies in his own ignorance and, more significantly, in his own prejudice against the Negro race. So strong is this antipathy that it destroys the things he most loves. So strong is this prejudice that it destroys his capacity to love. ("Negroes," 49)

71.   Toth, "Kate Chopin," 203. Several critics hasten to defend Chopin's revelation that, ultimately, the "evil" character in this story is the one of the pair who *definitely* has an African heritage (Désirée, as has already been suggested, might also be part African)—that is, they feel the need to defend Chopin against charges of racism. Cynthia Wolff, for example, writes, "The lesser existence into which Armand sinks stems not from his Negroid parentage, but from a potential for personal evil that he shares with all fellow creatures" ("Kate Chopin," 129). In a reading quite similar to Toth's, Mary Papke sums up her discussion of the story with:

> Chopin leaves the reader with an awareness of where the fault for [Désirée's tragedy] lies: not merely in the frail hands of powerless individuals but in the

actions of all individuals who support this patriarchal, racist world[,] the social faults of which finally widen into the black abyss that engorges Désirée. (*Verging on the Abyss,* 56)

In contrast to these critics, Barbara Ewell argues that "Chopin's association of black with Satanic evil and the discovery that the cruel villain of the piece *is* Afro-American reveals her continuing ambivalence about race." She adds, however, "Even so, her portrayal of the senseless destruction that arises from unexamined pride and fears comments powerfully on the ironic, wasteful nature of prejudice" (*Kate Chopin,* 71–72). For refutation of Ewell's accusation regarding Chopin's "ambivalence about race," one can again turn to Toth, who rightly points out that in this story, "[w]hite and black are . . . signs of morality, not of race" ("Kate Chopin," 206). Also, as Richard Potter argues

> Few stories have shown more vividly the tragedy inherent in irrational prejudice and hate. Few stories have presented so poignant and devastating an indictment of the entire concept of slavery. . . . [Chopin] sees that slavery, not inherent traits or inferiorities, is responsible for the Negro's problems. . . . [H]er realistic view of Louisiana society will not allow her to shrink from portraying that society corrupted by the institution of slavery. ("Negroes," 49–50)

72. In light of this contention, one can find an interesting comparison between Armand and the protagonist of James Weldon Johnson's 1912 novel *The Autobiography of an Ex-Coloured Man* (New York: Knopf, 1927; hereafter cited in the text), as his character is explained by Judith Berzon. Part of Berzon's response to the view of Edward Margolies that Johnson's protagonist's "weaknesses are shown to stem chiefly from his own character and not essentially from the society that terrifies him" (*Native Sons: A Critical Study of Twentieth-Century Negro American Authors* [Philadelphia: Lippincott, 1968], 26) includes from the novel a statement on American society, "the only civilized, if not the only state on earth, where a human being would be burned alive" (Johnson 188). Berzon implies that the reader should not be so surprised or so critical of the "ex-coloured man's" decision to protect himself against such violence by hiding part of his racial heritage (*Neither White Nor Black,* 156–57). Similarly, readers of "Désirée's Baby" who come to agree with the argument that Armand knows about his heritage should not judge him—a man who lives among slaveowners, some of whom may treat their slaves brutally, all of whom have the power and authority to do so—too harshly for trying to hide his black parentage. Still, it is troubling to see how both characters seem to respond to the cruel treatment of people of their race by, as Robert E. Fleming points out of Johnson's protagonist, "choos[ing] to ally [themselves] with the persecutors rather than the persecuted, to be one of those who can, without shame or remorse, treat other human beings as animals" ("Irony as a Key to Johnson's *The Autobiography of an Ex-Coloured Man,*" *American Literature* 43 [March 1971]: 95).

73. Toth, "Kate Chopin," 205.

74. Berzon, *Neither White Nor Black,* 143–144.

75. Again one might think of Faulkner's Thomas Sutpen, whose "design" was also destroyed by his unwillingness to acknowledge his "black" son.

76. Berzon, *Neither White Nor Black,* 158.

77. Two other motives Johnson's protagonist lists are interesting when this novel is read intertextually with "Désirée's Baby": first, his remark that he "find[s] a sort of savage and diabolical desire to gather up all the little tragedies of [his] life, and turn them into a practical joke on society" (3), which is what Chopin (as well as Armand) does with the ending of her story; and second, his "vague feeling of unsatisfaction, of regret, of almost remorse, from which [he is] seeking relief" (3), which readers seem to expect would be Armand's reaction following the ending of the story. Indeed, I do not mean to suggest that Armand does not ever feel any

regret or remorse regarding his actions toward Désirée. I merely wish to remind the story's readers that these feelings are not expressed in the story and that what *is* in the story suggests that he would not be surprised by the contents of the letter that so shocks the newcomer to "Désirée's Baby." These comparisons between Armand and Johnson's protagonist help to establish a basis for using a 1912 novel to support this reading of a story written in 1892. The similar situations relate the characters' psyches to each other, so that one can understand Armand's unspoken motivations through Johnson's protagonist's explanations of his. The comparison also allows for a more sympathetic reading of Armand than might otherwise result from this paper's assertions about his purposeful actions.

78.   In further support of this contention is the detail Chopin includes regarding Armand "search[ing] among some papers" on a table (243). This action is left ambiguous and may only be a means of getting Armand into Désirée's room for the confrontation regarding their son (one recalls that he had been avoiding his wife). At the same time, Chopin may send Armand in to look for something for a reason: so that, upon rereading the story in light of its ending, the reader might wonder what he was looking for. Perhaps he is making certain that, besides the one letter he feels compelled to save, there are no other incriminating papers that he has overlooked in the past and that Désirée could find and use against him once she realizes their child is "black."

79.   Charles Waddell Chesnutt, *The Conjure Woman* (1899; Ann Arbor: University of Michigan Press, 1969), 60.

"Acting Like Fools": The Ill-Fated Romances of "At the 'Cadian Ball" and "The Storm"

Lawrence I. Berkove

Since its long-delayed publication in 1969, "The Storm" has generally been read as Kate Chopin's protest at the narrow and unnatural morality of turn-of-the-century America. The story's startling last sentence in particular has been taken to be her boldly amoral stand on an adulterous affair between two young and willing participants. This critical position is not hard to understand, considering the revolutionarily frank sensuality of the story's scene of passion. Inasmuch as Chopin's novel *The Awakening,* which was completed in 1898, the same year as "The Storm," is widely regarded as an affirmation of women's sensuality, "The Storm" would seem to be a reinforcement of this position. Chopin was, without doubt, an extraordinarily bold writer, but she was better than bold; she was thoughtful. "The Storm" is even better than its advocates have heretofore realized, for instead of writing merely a daring defiance of established morality, Chopin has even more daringly emplaced a courageous defense of morality, demonstrating an unsuspected mastery of irony to build her case.

"The Storm" is a sequel to "At the 'Cadian Ball" (1892). The earlier story is less spectacular than "The Storm," but despite the six years separating their composition (and probably their narratives), they fit together seamlessly. Both stories share the same setting, the same four protagonists, the same history, and the same theme, i.e., romantic impulsiveness as folly. Society's disapproval of impulsiveness, especially of sexual license, is shown to be sensible as well as moral, for such license is ultimately damaging to the individuals involved as well as to the circle of family and community around them. Chopin steadily projects this position by implication in both stories through her deft construction of character and plot, brilliantly subtle irony, and short but trenchant authorial commentary.

Chopin did not attempt to publish "The Storm" in her lifetime, hence it did not see print until 1969.[1] Per Seyersted described it as "the story [Chopin]

This essay was written specifically for this volume and is published here for the first time by permission of the author.

knew she could never hope to get published."[2] Chopin no doubt felt that its graphic sex scene was inappropriate for its time, but even so, that she wrote the scene proves only that she was ahead of her era in literary experimentation; it does not mean that she approved—or refrained from disapproving—of Alcée and Calixta's adultery. Chopin is too good an author to have been preachy. The personalities she describes are those of human beings, neither of saints nor of devils, and it seems to be her wont to evoke understanding about human motivation first and foremost, and judgment later. But inasmuch as the moral issue of adultery is central to "The Storm," Chopin must have had an opinion on it. In contrast to the prevailing view that she ended the story noncommittally, a careful examination of the text makes clear that Chopin was not at all neutral toward the "natural" adulterous action but was instead critical of it. In Chopin's view, morality is an essential part of humanity, and it is morality, not nature, that ultimately characterizes humans.

This view appears in both stories. Although the earlier story must and can stand by itself—and nothing indicates that Chopin planned, in 1892, to write a sequel to it—the two stories are remarkably congruent in characterization, plot, and theme, and crucial similarities between the earlier and later story suggest that they both came out of the same matrix of authorial values. In both stories, Chopin shows her skepticism of "natural" human inclinations by portraying what happens when people allow sexual impulse to govern them. Even the earlier story depicts, with foreboding overtones, the consequences of impetuousness that drives two ill-fated romances to become unwise marriages.

The four main personalities in "At the 'Cadian Ball" also appear in "The Storm." Although their situations change, their characters do not. They grow older but do not grow up. It is therefore essential to see how their characters are established in "At the 'Cadian Ball."

From the first paragraph of the earlier story, Calixta is described in pejorative terms. She is called "that little Spanish vixen," and the reader is told that "the Spanish that was in her blood" made her different from the rest of the prairie people and was the reason they "forgave her much that they would not have overlooked in their own daughters or sisters." What was different about her was an open sexuality not countenanced by the community. Even her virtuous admirer, Bobinôt, is captivated not by her whole being but rather by her particular physical attributes—tantalizing eyes; flaxen hair; broad, smiling mouth; "tiptilted nose"; and full figure (219).

She also has a rich contralto voice, but ominously, Bobinôt thinks of it as having "cadences in it that must have been taught by Satan" (219). "A breath of scandal" is whispered about her from her trip the previous year to the town of Assumption, and her friend Fronie, in the midst of an argument on the church steps over a lover, calls Calixta a "cocotte," a fast woman (219). This remark, uttered in anger, is not substantiated in the earlier story but is borne out in the sequel, when Calixta indulges her passionate and impulsive temperament.

The man she was linked with at Assumption is Alcée Laballière, a wealthy, young, handsome, upper-class planter. Alcée is also passionate and impulsive; it is natural that Calixta is deeply attracted to him. Alcée is best understood by Bobinôt, who regards him as a rival. Bobinôt knows that Alcée's main interests are card-playing and discussing crops or politics, but he also knows that "a drink or two could put the devil in [Alcée's] head," and that "a gleam from Calixta's eyes, a flash of her ankle, a twirl of her skirts could do the same" (220). Alcée, therefore, is dangerous to Bobinôt not because he is a serious rival for Calixta's hand, but because he and Calixta both have a bit of the devil in them and together could do something on the spur of the moment that would endanger Bobinôt's suit.

Alcée, however, is not seriously interested in Calixta. He is infatuated with Clarisse, his beautiful cousin (225) and the goddaughter of his mother. Clarisse lives in his house, but the distance implied by their relationship as kin frustrates him. Then one day, when "he must have been crazy," he comes in from working in the fields and abruptly "clasped Clarisse by the arms and panted a volley of hot, blistering love-words into her face" (220). This declaration takes her by surprise. Her first reaction to it is a coldly formal reproach, "Monsieur!" (220). Nevertheless, the embrace changes their relationship, and it gets her to thinking.

Until Alcée confesses a passion for her, Clarisse appears not to have felt any for him. There was no courting. As he saw her, she was "[c]old and kind and cruel by turn, and everything that was aggravating" (220). Not until he leaves for the ball, two nights later, does she suddenly become "wild," conclude that she is in love with him, and impulsively go after him. Whether love or some jealous fear of losing him motivates her is unclear. No evidence of a developing, mutual romance between Alcée and Clarisse appears in the story except for one word in her confession of love to him. She tells him that if he didn't come back with her, she "could n't stan' it,—again" (227). The word "again" at first seems surprising, but in context it is a reference to his visit the year before to Assumption, where he and Calixta were linked in scandal. With that word, therefore, Clarisse retroactively establishes herself as a rival of Calixta.

In contrast to these three attractive but impulsive young people is Bobinôt, with whom the story opens. "[B]ig, brown, and good-natured" (219) is our first glimpse of him, a teddy-bear of a man. He is straight, steady, and deeply in love with Calixta, but he is also "dull-looking and clumsy" (223). When she mocks him at the ball, he takes it with characteristic good nature. Such is his love for her that he feels that "[i]t was better to receive even such notice as that from Calixta than none at all" (224). Bobinôt is an innocent in both the negative and positive senses of the word: naïve but also honest and not devious. Things happen to him; he does not cause things to happen.

A storm precipitates the action in "At the 'Cadian Ball." It is a cyclone that devastates the nine hundred acres of rice Alcée had planted and worked so hard over. After Clarisse's rejection, this is the second major setback he received in two days. As he interprets events, "God A'mighty an' a 'oman" have joined forces against him, and he decides to compensate himself with a "li'le fling" at the Cajun ball (222). He had not originally intended to go. Judging from Clarisse's contemptuous reaction, "Nice conduc' for a Laballière" (222), attending the ball was somewhat beneath his station—and he acts on an impulse he does not choose to scrutinize: "he was in a mood for ugly things to-night" (223). Bobinôt also had not intended to go to the ball, but changes his mind when he realizes that Calixta would be there and that Alcée might attend. "Poor Bobinôt" is alone in his perception of the motives of his rival and that trouble was brewing with Alcée (223).

It is natural but not auspicious that Alcée and Calixta find each other at the ball. Neither is in love with the other; Alcée loves Clarisse and both expect that Calixta will eventually marry Bobinôt, although Calixta's response to Alcée's inquiry on this point, "I don't say no, me" (224), is at best unenthusiastic. Both are therefore looking for some excitement to divert them; Alcée is reckless and Calixta demonstrates "abandon" (223). Both are physically attractive, and both had shared a scandalous relationship the year before at Assumption. Both have a bit of the devil in them, and the text notes with unusual asperity, "[t]hey were acting like fools" (224).

When Alcée and Calixta meet they quickly pick up their affair where it had left off the year before. But just as Alcée propositions a willing Calixta with the mock threat that he may drown himself unless they both return to Assumption, Clarisse appears unexpectedly and implores Alcée to go with her. Alcée's mood is broken instantly: "He would have followed [Clarisse's] voice anywhere" (225). The shallowness of his attraction to Calixta is unmistakable when, in his hurry to join Clarisse, she reminds him to bid farewell to Calixta, whom he has already forgotten. He does so with a "Good-night, Calixta" (226) and an offer of a handshake.

Two marriages come out of that evening at the ball. Dumped by Alcée, Calixta proposes to Bobinôt after she indifferently ("I don' care") accepts his offer to walk her home. She is not in love with him. She obviously chooses him in a resentful reaction, and she seals the pact with a "business-like" handclasp (226). She refuses to kiss him, moreover, and the author is surprisingly explicit in her criticism of the whole affair when she describes Calixta's face: it "was almost ugly after the night's dissipation" (226).

Clarisse also essentially proposes to Alcée on their ride home when she confesses her sudden desire for him. The text raises the question of whether Alcée knows what love is when it describes his reaction: "He began to wonder if this meant love. But she had to tell him so, before he believed it. And when she told him, he thought the face of the Universe was changed—just like

Bobinôt" (227). The comparison to Bobinôt—who is deceived in his belief that Calixta loves him—is an ironic one; it means that Alcée is no wiser than Bobinôt in matters of love. In light of this, the rest of the paragraph is also ironic.

> Was it last week the cyclone had well-nigh ruined him? The cyclone seemed like a huge joke, now. It was he, then, who, an hour ago was kissing little Calixta's ear and whispering nonsense into it. Calixta was like a myth, now. The one, only, great reality in the world was Clarisse standing before him, telling him that she loved him (227).

The stream of consciousness of this last passage reveals Alcée's admission of insincerity with Calixta, exposes his fickle nature, and betrays his own susceptibility to romantic nonsense. Like Calixta, he believes what he wants to; now he wants to believe that Clarisse is the true love of his life.[3] The physical cyclone destroyed his rice crop, and now an inner cyclone of his feelings has destroyed his judgment.

Chopin allows herself one last ironic comment in the concluding line of the story: "*le bal est fini*"—i.e., "the ball is over." The ball was a time of romantic illusion. Real life begins when the music stops. For Alcée and Clarisse it will mean a marriage based on sudden gusts of passion; for Bobinôt it will mean a marriage in which his love is not reciprocated; and for Calixta it will mean a marriage of convenience. Her only passion is for passion, and Bobinôt will not supply that. The concluding line therefore ominously recalls the refrain of a popular song of the time: "Many the hopes that have vanished after the ball."[4]

Although her writing career was relatively short, Chopin very early demonstrated a mastery of skillful sparseness. Almost an Emily Dickinson of prose, she wrote stories whose boldness of conception was balanced by a tight style with densely layered ironies. Chopin's unconventionalities of plot or daring frankness are elements to be considered in overall interpretation, but they are not the only elements and may not even be the major elements. Her main concern was to render life intelligently as well as accurately, with the complexity it deserves, and to avoid simplistic reduction of its dilemmas. An underappreciated part of Chopin's extraordinary skill is her ability to subtly undercut bold but morally untenable positions that she has sympathetically represented. This skill is at its peak in "The Storm." "At the 'Cadian Ball" can stand by itself, but it improves when viewed with its sequel. Likewise, "The Storm" stands by itself but benefits from the running start provided by the earlier story.

The care with which Chopin crafted "At the 'Cadian Ball" is evident in the later story, for she is able to pick up the same personalities, situations, and themes, and in the sequel not only use them again, but also reaffirm them. A quick survey of "The Storm" reveals how closely it resembles its predecessor. The four protagonists, although they have grown slightly older, have not changed in character. The sequel also opens with Bobinôt and ends with a glimpse of all the major characters. A storm again drives the main action of both stories. Yet although shorter, "The Storm," is the better story. It is more complex, deeper, and more daring. It is richer, and more accomplished in technique.

Easily the most controversial feature of "The Storm" is its last line, "So the storm passed and every one was happy" (596). Coming as it does after the powerfully sensuous and daringly explicit scene in which Calixta and Alcée enjoy adulterous sex with each other during a tumultuous thunderstorm, the line seems to sanction the act. "Who was hurt?" it seems to say. "If none of the principals object, why should we?" Probably the strongest case to date that supports this position is Emily Toth's. As Toth reads the story, "Kate made the passion a matter of mutual power and desire. . . . Kate's two lovers come together without deception or guilt" (320). Placing the story in the contexts of both Chopin's personal life and oeuvre, Toth observes that "living among freethinking intellectuals who made fun of bourgeois proprieties" had made Chopin much bolder. Whereas the action of "At the 'Cadian Ball" had taken place "mostly at night, at back doors," she says, " 'The Storm' proceeds boldly during the day, in the married woman's own home. . . . [Chopin] had come to feel that there was no shame in sexual desire—only in hypocrisy" (321–22).[5]

It is surprising that Toth has contrasted both stories in terms of surreptitious, "back door" activity at night versus bold activity in the daytime, for neither characterization is correct. That the ball occurs at night and that Alcée leaves for it at night are hardly "back door" actions, and that the adulterous action takes place in the daytime hardly makes it bold. Moreover, living among "freethinking intellectuals" no more causes an author to become liberal than living among conservatives causes a writer to become conservative. These generalizations are misleading.

Much of Toth's interpretation derives from the article "Is Love Divine?" which Chopin wrote for the St. Louis Post-Dispatch. It appeared on 16 January 1898, after she had already written a draft of The Awakening and six months before she wrote "The Storm." Toth quotes a surprising reflection of Chopin's on the subject of predestination: " 'One really never knows the exact, definite thing which excites love for any one person, and one can never truly know whether this love is the result of circumstances or whether it is predestination' " (310). Although authors such as Mark Twain have used predestination in the traditional, religious sense as a theme,[6] many others, such as Henry James, express the notion of fate through the more secular perspective of determinism.[7] If this theme is what Chopin meant by predestination, then it illuminates a good deal of her fiction, including The Awakening and "The Storm."

Toth summarizes a second statement as suggesting that "choice played a very small role in love":

> I am inclined to think that love springs from animal instinct, and therefore is, in a measure, divine. One can never resolve to love this man, this woman or child, and then carry out the resolution unless one feels irresistibly drawn by an indefinable current of magnetism (310).

How Chopin qualifies this comment, far from restricting choice, as predestination does absolutely, actually allows both an author and his or her characters more flexibility. If love is only "in a measure" divine, for example, then it is also partly not divine. Determining the proportions of the emotion, particularly the not-divine portion, would be the kind of challenging literary project that Chopin previously undertook in "Two Portraits" (1895). Furthermore, if love were divinely ordained in total, would God induce someone to love in a way contrary to His commandments? Chopin would surely have recognized this obvious logical trap. However, if love is only a function of animal instinct, a human being need not act on that instinct. Western religion differentiates between love and lust by defining acceptable and unacceptable objects of love and ways of expressing the same powerful drive. Rather than assuming that Chopin's remarks in the *Post-Dispatch* article are clear conclusions on her subject—love—we might better regard them as positions she was exploring and look to "The Storm" for evidence of how she resolved the issues involved. Given the histories and characters of Calixta and Alcée, the way the story's text treats the episode, and Chopin's wariness about adopting simplistic positions, it seems highly unlikely that Chopin seriously meant to categorize their act of sudden and blind passion as divine love, as acceptable love, or as anything worthy of the name of love.

"The Storm" is set in the same place as "At the 'Cadian Ball" but occurs several years later. Bobinôt and Calixta, now married, have a four-year-old son named Bibi. The story opens with a view of Bibi and Bobinôt at the local store. Bibi's presence at the opening is significant because, as a new addition to the four main personalities of the previous story, he symbolizes the marriage and the mutual commitment and trust it should imply. One image of these ideals appears at the end of the first section with the line "Bibi laid his little hand on his father's knee and was not afraid" and another in Bobinôt's purchase of a can of shrimps, "of which Calixta was very fond." These acts, and the earlier description of Bobinôt's habit of conversing "on terms of perfect equality with his little son," show that Bobinôt is a good husband and father. Nevertheless, the mood for the entire story is set by the section's description of storm clouds rolling in with "sinister intention" (592).

The story does not paint Calixta and Alcée as schemers. She and Alcée had not planned to meet, let alone commit adultery. The rainstorm—another cyclone—has caught him on the road, and although he lives nearby and might have ridden on, his wish to escape a drenching in Calixta's home is innocent. He greets her by name and properly asks permission to wait out the storm on her porch, and she properly addresses him as "M'sieur Alcée" when she grants it. Calixta is honestly concerned for Bobinôt as the storm hits, but a lightning strike nearby so unnerves her that Alcée clasps her by the shoulders and "unthinkingly" draws her into his arms. So the adulterous passion begins without premeditation. Alcée suddenly discovers that contact with her body "aroused all the old-time infatuation and desire for her flesh." When she glances up at him, her fear is replaced by a "drowsy gleam that unconsciously betrayed a sensuous desire. He looked down into her eyes and there was nothing for him to do but to gather her lips in a kiss. It reminded him of Assumption" (594). Chopin's text clearly describes their mutual attraction as a spontaneous as well as natural emotion, but it also distinguishes their feelings from love. Calixta is in the grip of a "sensuous desire," and Alcée equally has a "desire for her flesh."[8] The relationship between the two of them is characterized as an "infatuation," literally "foolish behavior."

The story's next paragraph is not so kind to them. We learn what had happened at Assumption that had scandalized the community. The two of them had indulged their passion, kissing until Alcée almost lost control of himself, and "to save her" he resorted "to a desperate flight." This flight reflects honorably upon Alcée at the time, and it also shows that he had choice and could control himself. The remaining lines of the paragraph contrast, unfavorably, the present Alcée to the earlier one.

> If [Calixta] was not an immaculate dove in those days, she was still inviolate; a passionate creature whose very defenselessness had made her defense, against which his honor forbade him to prevail. Now—well, now—her lips seemed in a manner free to be tasted, as well as her round, white throat and her whiter breasts (594).

Alcée's reasoning is faulty. Inasmuch as he introduced the subject of honor, if honor forbade him to prevail against a virgin, it should have been even more forceful in the case of a married woman, to whom the commandment against adultery applied. As we know from his honorable actions in Assumption, it is not that he now had no choice, that he could not stop himself, but that he did not want to.

The description of the act of passion that follows is indeed impressive, and Chopin deserves all the credit she has received for its daring and its "realism," but there is more to it than that. Calixta has already been described as a "passionate creature," but in abandoning herself so utterly to her passions and becoming a mere "creature," she forfeits some of the other desirable qualities of her humanity. Much as Bobinôt saw her in "At the 'Cadian Ball," she is described not as a whole woman but as parts of a woman: as "firm, elastic flesh that was knowing for the first time its birthright," as breasts that "gave themselves up in quivering ecstasy," as a mouth that "was a fountain of delight." Her passion is present in "generous abundance" (595), but nothing else is there—no thought, no hesitation, no moral scruples, no reflection. It is a portrayal that unexpectedly illustrates the Victorian fear that women could not be depended upon to govern themselves, that they were only passionate "creatures," frail vessels when it came to thought or resistance to temptation.

Calixta's subsequent actions also support another Victorian stereotype of women as morally elastic. She laughs as she lies in Alcée's arms; she laughs as he rides away; she laughs at dinner with her husband and son. But she also has begun to lie. In the midst of the sex act, her passion was "without guile or trickery" (595). Yes, she is genuine and honest in her passion, but this condition ends with the departure of her lover. When her husband and son return, she lies. She tells Bobinôt that she was "uneasy" while he was away, and "seemed" to express "nothing but satisfaction" at the safe return of her husband and son. She kisses them with unexpected enthusiasm—Bobinôt expected recriminations—and at dinner they all laughed so loudly that "anyone might have heard them as far away as Laballière's" (596).

The only "anyone" of consequence at Laballière's is Alcée. If he does hear them, this explains why he writes his wife, Clarisse, that night, encouraging her to stay a month longer at Biloxi with the babies. He also lies to her about the real reason, pretending that he is willing to sacrifice himself for their health and pleasure. It is fairly clear that he hopes for a repeat performance with Calixta, and if Calixta intended for her laughter to carry to his house, he indeed had reason to hope.

The consequence of Clarisse's abrupt desire for Alcée in "At the 'Cadian Ball" is spelled out in the sequel by her pleasure at receiving her husband's letter. The visit to Biloxi is described as the first "free" breath of "pleasant liberty" she has enjoyed since her marriage. The marriage itself is summed up in one ironic sentence: "Devoted as she was to her husband, their intimate conjugal life was something which she was more than willing to forego for a while" (596).

Coming as it does just after this sentence, the last sentence of the story, "So the storm passed and every one was happy," must also be read ironically. Reading it "straight" would not only ascribe to Chopin anachronistically liberal attitudes, it would also create a host of problems that she was too good a writer and thinker not to have avoided. The last line intends to depict different kinds of happiness, none of them desirable.[9] Bobinôt and Bibi are happy by virtue of their ignorance. They continue to trust Calixta and to extend her a dedicated love they mistakenly believe is reciprocated. Clarisse, not overly fond of Alcée anymore, is happy in being able to stay away from him for a while longer. She also is happy in her ignorance of her husband's adultery. Surely Chopin cannot be seriously characterizing such deceptions as happiness.

Calixta and Alcée are "happy" because their long suppressed passion for each other has been at last satisfied—at least for the time being. But it is not love. It is only passion, only desire, only an "infatuation." No serious thought has been given to the future. Alcée has given himself another month in which to enjoy Calixta again, but he is already married and has children, and divorce is not a serious possibility. What happens if they are caught, or if she becomes pregnant? Calixta does not even think about the next hour. They are "acting like fools." It is difficult to believe that Chopin considers this precarious state of affairs to be true happiness.

Reading the last line as amoral, matter-of-fact realism also begs some important moral questions that Chopin could not have intelligently ignored. To be specific, if everyone was truly happy at the end of the story, is this story intended to be a "realistic" picture of married life? Is this kind of behavior what makes for a happy marriage, or only what passes for one? Is the story an endorsement of occasional escapades of immorality on the grounds that everyone needs to give in, sometimes, to nature, because in the long run satisfying natural desire is beneficial because it promotes happiness? If such escapades can be excused on these grounds, is happiness the greatest good in life, even greater than morality? To put it a little differently, is Kate Chopin advocating hedonism?

Certainly one of the strongest elements in the story is the relationship it implies between man and nature: a storm comes up, releases pent-up energy, and then passes over. This event is followed by happiness, so why should humans deny their affinity to nature? Kate Chopin would be a less impressive author if she were guilty of such simplistic thinking. Writings by Shakespeare (e.g., *King Lear*) to Stephen Crane (e.g., "The Open Boat"), to Ernest Hemingway (e.g., "The Three-Day Blow") have demonstrated the falseness of the analogy between human beings and natural phenomena. Storms may be personified, but they are not living persons. They do not know the intimacy of love and children; they are ephemeral; they lack memory and consciences; and they do not have to face consequences. When Alcée responds to the storm in "At the 'Cadian Ball," it is to imitate it by seeking a fling and getting "in a mood for ugly things." When the passion between him and Calixta parallels the storm in the sequel, the former pattern is repeated. Imitating nature, they exchange human standards for something mindless and irresponsible. That they can be "happy" afterwards is not particularly a compliment to them.

As with the issue of happiness, the symbolism of nature in these stories is loaded with pitfalls. A recent discussion of *The Awakening* reminds readers that Chopin was sufficiently influenced by current trends in international literature not to have treated nature "as a medium of transcendence in the Romantic sense."[10] The limited applicability of nature to human affairs is also apparent in these two stories if we recognize that natural storms cannot be brought back at will, but that Alcée certainly, and possibly Calixta, are looking forward to a repeat performance. Storms, moreover, are isolated and irregular phenomena, whereas adultery tends to set a pattern. Storms are destructive though transient; human relationships, especially those involving love and family, cannot thrive in storms. These are self-evident considerations that Chopin could not have overlooked.

Finally, the presence of children in "The Storm" reflects one more enormous difference between human nature and physical nature: humans recognize an obligation to their offspring. Bibi is not the only child in the story; Alcée and Clarisse also have babies. If the affair between Alcée and Calixta blows up or is exposed—and such affairs are very hard to conceal in small towns and close-knit communities—the children will be hurt. All of these direct and likely consequences of "following nature" make the amoralistic approach a highly dubious one for Chopin to have followed.

In claiming that Kate Chopin is critical of the adulterous relationship that had its roots in the scandal at Assumption, grew through the recklessness and impulsive self-indulgence of its principals in "At the 'Cadian Ball," and ripened into passionate infatuation in "The Storm," I do not intend to paint Chopin as a narrow Sunday-school moralist. Rather, the care that she has taken with the consistent development of the principal characters in the two stories, and the progression of relationships that begin on the wrong foot in the earlier story and progressively worsen throughout both stories, refute the belief that Chopin abruptly reverses herself in the last sentence of "The Storm" and intends this conclusion to be read literally. The tone of that sentence is ironic, and to miss that tone is also to overlook the careful and extensive preparations for it that constitute the main matter of both stories.

It would be an exaggeration to categorize these stories as moral fiction, but it is also an exaggeration to deny or downplay the moral strands that run through them. They are far from being the only stories in her canon that demonstrate moral concerns about sexual matters; "A Respectable Woman" (1894) and "Athénaïse" (1895) are two others in which such concerns are readily apparent. What makes "The Storm" seem so different are two factors. Intrinsically, it is the most daring and sexually explicit of all her stories. Extrinsically, its rediscovery coincided with a feeling among many that the sexual taboos of the 19th century were outdated. But "The Storm" is also one of Chopin's most accomplished literary creations, and in it her irony, though delicate, is absolutely crucial to its understanding. That Chopin is ultimately critical of Alcée and Calixta's adultery must be recognized not because of any moral predisposition or prejudice on the part of readers, but because the texts of the two stories lead us directly to that conclusion and because the alternative positions are fraught with too many and too obviously insupportable difficulties. It is to her credit that Chopin created convincingly life-like personalities and depicted their careers sympathetically. As a realist, however, and especially as an ironist, she knew that men and women are, classically, led into error by what pleases them. True morality stems from hard thinking as well as great effort of will. These two stories support morality by making readers face up to the consequences of acting foolishly and ignoring it.

Notes

1.　Kate Chopin, *The Complete Works of Kate Chopin,* ed. Per Seyersted, hardcover ed. (Baton Rouge: Louisiana State University Press, 1993), 592–96. Hereafter cited in the text.

2.　Per Seyersted, "Kate Chopin's Wound: Two New Letters," *American Literary Realism 1870–1910* 20 (Fall 1987): 72.

3.　There is a hint, in the line "Calixta was like a myth, now," of an allusion to the myth of Callisto, whose name Calixta bears in a French adaptation. Juno, jealous of her husband's attraction to the beautiful maiden Callisto, turned her into a bear. This allusion is not fully developed in Chopin's story, but it does suggest jealousy on the part of Clarisse and helps explain her power to suddenly destroy Calixta's appeal to Alcée.

4.　"After the Ball" (1892) was the well-known song:

> After the ball is over, after the break of morn—
> After the dancers' leaving; after the stars are gone;
> Many a heart is aching, if you could read them all;
> Many the hopes that have vanished after the ball.
> (Charles K. Harris, "After the Ball," *Favorite Songs of the Nineties* [New York: Dover, 1973], 1–5)

5.　Emily Toth, *Kate Chopin* (New York: William Morrow, 1990). Robert D. Arner anticipated this reading in "Kate Chopin's Realism: 'At the 'Cadian Ball' and 'The Storm,' " *Markham Review* 2 (February 1970): 1–4, one of the earliest interpretations of the story. Subsequent discussions, such as those by Per Seyersted, *Kate Chopin: A Critical Biography* (Baton Rouge: Louisiana State University Press, 1969); Peggy Skaggs, *Kate Chopin* (Boston: Twayne, 1985); and Chung-Eun Ryu, "Nature and Sexuality in the Fiction of Kate Chopin," *Journal of English Language and Literature* 35 (Spring 1989): 131–47, have also generally tended to regard the story as a deliberately amoral celebration of sexuality.

6.　Twain does not openly refer to predestination in his fiction, but the presence of it powerfully shapes his work. For a discussion of its operation, see my essays: "The 'Poor Players' of *Huckleberry Finn*," *Papers of the Michigan Academy of Science, Arts, and Letters* 53 (1968): 291–310; "The Reality of the Dream: Structural and Thematic Unity in *A Connecticut Yankee*," *Mark Twain Journal* 23 (Spring 1984): 8–14; and "Mark Twain's Mind and the Illusion of Freedom," *Journal of Humanities,* special issue (1992): 1–24.

7.　Although I discuss Toth's quotations in her biography, I have also consulted the full text of Chopin's remarks in Emily Toth's subsequent article, "Kate Chopin on Divine Love and Suicide: Two Rediscovered Articles," *American Literature* 63 (March 1991): 115–21. "Predestination" is normally a specific religious term and implies a deity who makes choices for humans.

"Determinism" also describes a situation in which human choice is preempted, but the cause is usually something secular, such as genetics, psychological makeup, sociological conditions, and so on. I see little evidence in these stories of the operation of divinity behind events. Therefore, either what was on her mind when she made this remark did not manifest itself in her fiction, or it has eluded my recognition of it, or else she used "predestination" in a more generic sense to refer to determinism or "fate."

8.　In her biography, Toth writes: "When Kate Chopin came to write about men who kindle desire, and who devote themselves to sexual pleasure, she named them all Alcée, an abbreviated form of Albert Sampité: Al. S——é and Alcée are both pronounced 'Al-say' " (169). The exact nature of the relationship between Chopin and her Clouterville neighbor, Albert Sampité, is still under speculation. Although talk of a romantic affair persisted to recent times, all accounts presented by Toth appear to be either based on rumor or highly inferential, and Toth herself admits that "an affair in the 1880s was not simply a matter of physical consummation" (168). Whatever went on in Chopin's own life, in all her fictional uses of someone named Alcée, that man is associated with desire but not love. Sara deSaussure Davis, in her discussion of Alcée in *The Awakening,* writes that "Chopin tellingly calls Alcée's effect upon Edna '*narcotic,*' something that induces sleep and with prolonged use becomes addictive" ("Chopin's Movement Toward Universal Myth," *Kate Chopin Reconsidered: Beyond the Bayou,* ed. Lynda S. Boren and Sara deSaussure Davis [Baton Rouge: Louisiana State University Press, 1992], 204).

9.   In his biography, Seyersted glimpsed but did not pursue potential difficulties with his claim that the emphasis of the story "is on the momentary joy of the amoral cosmic force" when he qualified it with his preceding recognition that the story's last line "is of course ambiguous. Mrs. Chopin may refuse to sit in judgment on morals, but she covers only one day and one story and does not exclude the possibility of later misery" (166–67).

10.   Dieter Schulz, "Notes Toward a *fin-de-siècle* Reading of Kate Chopin's *The Awakening,*" *American Literary Realism 1870–1910* 25 (Spring 1993): 74.

Kate Chopin's Fascination with Young Men

Linda Wagner-Martin

Hoping to suggest more than a writer's enthusiasm for adolescent male characters, my title purposely misleads. Its double entendre may be useful in drawing the reader's attention to some qualities of Chopin's oeuvre, for throughout her career she imbued her positive characters—men as well as women—with healthy sexual passions. Long before she translated fiction by Maupassant in the mid-1890s,[1] a practice often credited with teaching her how to express the sensuality of some of her later fiction (*The Awakening*, "A Respectable Woman," "The Storm"), she was writing stories of the sexual—in an age that pretended the attraction that led to marriage was more intellectual than physical.

Chopin used the quality of passion to depict women as well as men. However, in most of her early fiction, women with erotic feelings suppress those feelings, and their heroism lies in that repression. The narrative instability of the protagonist Thérèse Lafirme, the young widow in the 1890 novella *At Fault*, lies in that conflict between a socially approved renunciation and her real passion for David Hosmer. Only after she has come to love the taciturn and embittered Hosmer does Thérèse—a dedicated Catholic—discover that he is divorced. Renouncing her feelings, Thérèse urges him to remarry his alcoholic wife, and thus causes a repeat of the trauma that plagued his first decade as a married man. No reader can comfortably accept Thérèse's solution to the dilemma, and Chopin finally salvages a satisfying passion between Hosmer and Thérèse, although at great sacrifice to a believable plotline. There are other willful and spunky women in Chopin's early writing[2]— Euphrasie in "A No-Account Creole;" Fifine, the child who sells her father's violin in "A Very Fine Fiddle;" Lolotte in "A Rude Awakening"—but seldom does Chopin link sexual energy with the kinds of passion to act that she describes early in the 1890s.

Chopin most often makes passion and its sometimes accompanying rebelliousness palatable to the late-Victorian reader in her adolescent male

This essay was written specifically for this volume and is published here for the first time by permission of the author.

characters. Here she has a veritable field day, and also unintentionally offers her reader a glimpse of what her life as a single parent, the mother of five growing boys, must have been like. If Kate Chopin the novice writer knew any psyche intimately, it was that of the headstrong, sexually aware teenage boy. (Her first son was born in 1871[3] and the other four followed quickly. By the time she was writing fiction—in the late 1880s—she had specimens aplenty of male responses to life, and of the problems headlong passion created for not only the men involved, but for their culture.) Her only daughter, Lélia, named for the George Sand heroine, was the last child born.

Chopin's earliest short stories, as well as *At Fault,* are interesting fictions largely because they contain charming young male characters of generous imagination and humane ambition. In fact, a focus on the men—or, more accurately, the boys—in what appear to have been long and short versions of the same story, "A No-Account Creole" (1888) and *At Fault,* forces the reader to recognize that the kernel narrative is of the Santien family, with its three charming sons, Hector, Placide, and Grégoire. Placide is the hero of the short story, and Grégoire one of the leads in the novel.

In a story familiar to Southern history, the grandfather of the Santien tribe, Lucien, carved out the thousand-acre plantation through the efforts of his hundred slaves. Those gone after the Civil War, his son Jules could not save the land, and *his* sons—all but Placide—have also left the place, which is now owned by New Orleans creditors. At the heart of Natchitoches parish, the old Santien place in its disrepair on the Red River contrasts with the thriving Duplan estate on the neighboring Cane River. Euphrasie, the only child of Pierre Manton, the Creole manager of the Santien place, has been reared on the Duplan plantation since the death of her mother; Mme. Duplan is the local angel of the county.

Euphrasie returns to the dilapidated Santien plantation, hoping to save it, and meets the man of her dreams in Wallace Offdean, the New Orleans manager sent to reclaim the property. But Euphrasie has already agreed to marry Placide Santien, who has loved her since she, an infant, was placed in his arms when he was six. The rigidity of the marriage plot in full sail, however, is less the complication in this narrative than the fact that the reader has already been won by Chopin's characterization of the charmingly irresponsible Placide.

Clever with his hands, "a born carpenter,"[4] Santien yet does little to keep his family's estate in repair. Instead he works on his small house in a neighboring town, a house he intends for Euphrasie. Taking "great delight" in his work, the man has also become known for his expert painting of houses, and for his "indifference" to making money. Called "a no-account Creole" by the thriftier people in the parish, Placide might have become anything. Smart enough to go to college, he and his brothers spent their time there in "mutiny and revolt" (85), inciting the whole campus. According to Chopin, Placide was already "such a splendid fellow, such a careless, happy, handsome fellow" that he could have married anyone who knew him (Euphrasie is considered beneath him). After all, "he was a Santien always, with the best blood in the country running in his veins" (84).

So convincing is Chopin's portrayal that the reader is as suspicious of Wallace Offdean (a reaction surely triggered in part by his name) as Placide is. In his frantic dislike of the poised urban businessman, whom he calls "Yankee" to show his loathing, Santien illustrates the ungovernable passion that marks his family, a passion that almost causes Offdean's death. When Placide realizes that Euphrasie has fallen in love with Offdean, however, he breaks the engagement, thereby saving her reputation and freeing her to marry his rival. (In the process of breaking with her, Placide is once more charged with being "no count"; but Euphrasie understands why he acted as he did, and tells her father, " 'Placide has saved me!' " [102].)

In *At Fault,* the youngest Santien, Grégoire, courts the ingenue character, Melicent Hosmer, David's visiting sister. The setting for this narrative stays within Natchitoches parish, but moves to the Lafirmes' 4,000-acre plantation, Place-du-Bois. Thérèse Lafirme, with the help of Uncle Hiram, runs the plantation, which lies next to the Duplans', who appear in this work too. It is Thérèse's joy in her nephew Grégoire, bursting with vitality and ardor, that leads her to warn Melicent not to toy with the Creole. However, in a twist perhaps more suitable to a subplot of a longer work, Grégoire's unrequited love leads to his death after he begins drinking and behaving recklessly (Melicent leaves without even a goodbye). Here, the charm of the young Creole is vouched for by nearly everyone in the novella, from black servants to townspeople to plantation owners. As Aunt Belindy said "between paroxysms of laughter, 'dats a piece, dat Grégor.' " And Uncle Hiram agreed, " 'Dat boy neva did have no car' fur de salvation o' his soul' " (830).

Although *At Fault* was not published commercially (Chopin herself had it printed), it is a less clumsy narrative than many first works. Grégoire's romantic subplot conjoins a villainous financial plot, which employs another young man—this one a stormily passionate but surly youngster named Joçint. Thérèse asks Hosmer, who owns a mill, to hire Joçint, out of affection for the young man's father, but Joçint only makes trouble and finally sets the mill on fire. Trapped by explosive flames, the unarmed Joçint dies when Grégoire discovers—and shoots—him for arson. The town is divided about Grégoire's summary execution for the killing, but Melicent calls his act murder.

Chopin works hard to make Grégoire's broken heart real, to show "a stupor of grief holding him vise-like" (826). The reader believes his suffering—his face "ashen"—and his insulting the family priest, buying liquor, and racing his horse run true to foolishly macho behavior. Using Thérèse as her moral barometer, Chopin has her defend her nephew; and the solemnity and anguish in the community once word comes of Grégoire's rash death proves that the young man was much loved. The author's barbed irony is also unmistakable as she portrays the pretentious Melicent wearing mourning after she hears of the man's death.

In these early works, Chopin's themes may be less stable than her narrative structures. Faced with the handsome Santiens, the reader has difficulty sorting through the tenor of their acts: at what point does irresponsibility become injurious? When does passion demand responsibility? For both story and novel, Chopin chooses titles that suggest guilt. Placide, for all his charm, maintains the label of "no-account Creole." And much of *At Fault* examines the issue of who is responsible for moral failures.

But first, the reader must decide what those moral failures are. Even when Grégoire shoots Joçint, the act of murder is defended by most of the town's powerful citizens. More generally, who is "at fault" in this book about passion? Faced with a chance to love again, the beautiful (and wealthy) Thérèse is also a Catholic, so when she discovers David's divorce, she must turn sharply off the course of their year-long relationship. Rather than love David, she insists that he return to his alcoholic former wife. When he brings Fanny to the Lafirme plantation, Thérèse finds herself in a caretaker role. She then discovers that she cannot repress her feelings for the man she loves. But the reader must decide the reference for the title: obviously, David is originally at fault for marrying beneath him (as the long scenes placing Fanny among her common friends attest). Then he is at fault for courting Thérèse, though he does this with so few words that his behavior is hardly courtship. Then he is at fault for remarrying Fanny and bringing her to the plantation, where she has no friends—and therefore turns to drink.

The gravest fault in society's eyes is Fanny's, because she drinks. Without any explanation of why she drinks (although living with David might depress the strongest of women), and with little description of her background or persona, Chopin's characterization of the young beauty who won David's heart ten years earlier falls flat. But the alcoholic Fanny becomes the perfect foil for the virtuous Mrs. Lafirme, whose life of goodness and renunciation is a model for the community.

Clearly, Chopin herself (even in 1890) does not believe in renunciation, and so she uses Fanny's accidental death as the means of reuniting the lovers. Neighbors may still talk about their marriage, but Thérèse has learned not to care about gossip—she has her man, and nothing else matters. Although Thérèse finally admits that she was, indeed, "at fault" by insisting that David remarry Fanny, the reader sees that admission as ironic. Surely our Lady Bountiful, the woman discussed by everyone in the book as a paragon of giving and virtue, has not made such an inordinate mistake. The reader has too much evidence—and too many literary paradigms—in mind to find her apology convincing. Thérèse, complete with a saintly name, has lived the life women are expected to live, and therefore she has been rewarded. The Catholic church, rather than being some ogre in her consciousness, remains a sanctuary; she has no reason, then, to question the edict that a divorced man is off-limits for her. God will take care of problems, and she is rewarded—albeit through Fanny's death—for her noble stand.

Chopin walks a thin line here, between seeming to agree with conventional morality and yet writing stories of people who are not living conventional lives. Hosmer was a divorced man, showing through his withdrawal that he was no longer an acceptable member of society. Fanny's alcoholism is so objectionable, so reprehensible, particularly in a woman, that it is not even named. *At Fault* is filled with knowing looks, blinks at her trickery to buy liquor, and a rigorous denial that she needed to be watched every minute of every day—all this rather than any substantive attempt to help her quit drinking. And Thérèse could be considered a self-righteous snob, thoroughly insulated from the realities of unpleasant lives (not only Fanny's drinking but her married friends' flirtations with men who are themselves married give the book the flavor of the demimonde). Yet Thérèse and David are the would-be lovers whose liaison is the focus of the narrative. Like Edith Wharton and Ellen Glasgow, other turn-of-the-century women writers, Chopin aimed to tell realistic stories without offending the women who would buy her books; she could not appear to know much about the underbelly of approved society. Careful of their own reputations as middle and upper class women, Chopin, Glasgow, and Wharton had to assume that the values of such women (who led sheltered lives, as prescribed by society) were the values of their readers.

In 1890, Chopin was only beginning to question both literary tropes and cultural ones. She had probably, according to biographer Emily Toth, renounced her love for Albert Sampité—given that he too was married, despite the fact that he was one of the roguish, sensual men she found hard to resist.[5] The passionate attraction she describes so well in all her fiction may have been Chopin's greatest personal temptation, and her use of writing to deflect her energies away from other passionate involvements was probably wise. She was a woman with many talents, many erotic understandings, and already, many children. Unlike the choice Edna is to make a decade later, when she says she will not give up her life for her children, Chopin probably did give up Sampite—and the scandal that would have accompanied their relationship—for those children. Or she might have broken off their relationship because of her own Sacred Heart training or because she was, at heart, a very moral woman. But at any rate, one reason she insisted on publishing *At Fault* was that it made a purposefully ambivalent statement about the roles society forces people to play and a very clear statement about the force of passion, illicit or sanctified, in even mature people's lives.

So while Placide could give up Euphrasie, riding off to some other life and other conquests, Thérèse had much more difficulty giving up David—the difference less gender specific than age determined. How many other eligible men were going to walk into the widow's life? How many other good-looking and sexual people were going to cross her path? More practical than it might appear to be and less patterned on the great marriage novels of the 19th century than it might have been, *At Fault* teases the reader with its cleverly misleading title, and its almost misleading characterization of the "good" Thérèse Lafirme and the "sexual"—read "bad"—David Hosmer.

The comparative woodenness of Hosmer, who at key moments relies on the opinions of a mysterious sidekick named Homeyer, a man who never appears, makes the reader long for the embodiment of urgent male passion in Chopin's younger male characters. Thérèse's relationship with Hosmer, accordingly, seems lifeless, a kind of discourse of abstract dialectic. If passion hardens into silence—or abstraction—as men age, then the impetuous youngsters of other Chopin stories are almost preferable.

Azenor, the "handsome, stalwart" (153) and observant young carpenter in "Love on the Bon-Dieu," falls in love with Lalie, the terribly poor grandchild of Madame Zidora, the parish shrew. Close to Easter, he meets the retiring and fragile girl at the cottage of Père Antoine, a recurring figure in Chopin's Natchitoches stories, as Lalie waits for the parish priest to give her permission to exchange eggs for shoes at the store. Chopin plays the sentimentality, and the religious motif, to the full by focusing on the girl's shabby clothing (she wears the same skirt and josie throughout the story), and on Azenor's understanding of the hypocrisy of material wealth and social place. When he physically rescues Lalie, ill from overwork in the fields, from her grandmother's house, Chopin describes him as "surefooted as a panther" (162). Less erratic than the Santiens, Azenor is decent and compassionate, himself embodying "the spirit of Christ" he looks for elsewhere.

This story fits the theme of many of Chopin's early tales in that it is less a conventional romance than the story of a young man helping others, sometimes strangers, sometimes family. "Bertrand Delmandé, a fine, bright-looking boy of fourteen years,—fifteen, perhaps" (124), is the hero of "A Wizard from Gettysburg." Again, the story rides on the reader's affection for this kind boy, who leads a distraught, injured old man home on his horse so that he may care for him. Ironically, he sits the derelict in his father's chair on the veranda, and as the man recovers his long-lost memory, he turns out to be the father of the Delmandé family, a lost survivor of the battle of Gettysburg. One of Chopin's most clichéd tales, even this holds the reader through the unfeigned goodness of the adolescent boy.

"For Marse Chouchoute" more specifically illustrates the young man motivated only to help his family. In this case, Armand Verchette (nicknamed Chouchoute) becomes postmaster of Cloutierville in order to give his ailing mother the thirty dollars a month salary. Chopin describes Armand as a Santien-like "delightful young fellow; no one could help loving him. His heart was as warm and cheery as his own southern sunbeams. If he was born with an unlucky trick of forgetfulness—or better, thoughtlessness—no one ever felt much like blaming him for it, so much did it seem a part of his happy, careless nature" (105). Headed for disaster in his responsible role delivering the mail, the sixteen-year-old Chouchoute has the good fortune to benefit from the utterly selfless dedication of his young black friend, Wash.

As the story moves from the presentation of yet another of Chopin's lovable young Creoles to the more formally constructed tale, it lapses into the fanciful. In this case, Wash dies attempting to get the mail to the train on time when he discovers that Chouchoute, at a dance in a remote woodlands cabin, has forgotten about it.

That Chopin builds her plot upon the unquestioning sacrifice of the young black boy, giving him characteristics that are superior to Chouchoute's, suggests that readers today may be unnecessarily critical of the roles blacks play in Chopin's fiction.[6] Nearly every one of these early stories has a strong black figure—usually female—who is essential to the development of the protagonist. In *At Fault,* both Thérèse and Fanny seek advice from the wise and generous Marie Louise, the woman who raised Thérèse and now lives, free from work, in her own cabin. In "A No-Account Creole," the woman La Chatte plays a similar role; in "A Rude Awakening," Aunt Minty is central to the household; and in "Love on the Bon-Dieu," Tranquiline is entrusted with the care of Azenor's bride-to-be. The thirty-five-year-old black woman La Folle (Jacqueline) is the virtual protagonist of "Beyond the Bayou," as she leads a reclusive life after being traumatized by the sight of her badly wounded master during the Civil War. Gaunt and lean, La Folle "had more physical strength than most men" (175) and farmed her patch successfully in isolation. The bond between her and the master's beloved son, Cheri, was deep; she had often cared for him in her cabin, and she had memories of him stroking her black hand, resting his head against her knee, and falling asleep in her arms. Coming to hunt on her land, Chéri accidentally shoots himself in the leg, and to save his life, La Folle carries him to the mainland and thereby breaks the psychological bonds that have confined her for years.

Chopin's gallery of male characters in her early fiction also includes a number of small boys. The winsome Chéri in "Beyond the Bayou" has for neighbors the twins "Boulôt and Boulotte," who are several years older. These boys must try to survive in abject poverty because their father, Sylveste Bordon, seldom works at his job on the Duplan estate—he would rather fish. In "A Rude Awakening," Bordon's eldest child and the boys' strong older sister, Lolotte, is driven to rash action (working on the Duplan estate herself, in place of her father) because of the illness of the undernourished youngest brother, the four-year-old Nonomme. Chopin draws the seventeen-year-old's character in a scene that shows her love for the little boy:

> Lolotte's bare brown feet made no sound upon the rough boards as she entered the room where Nonomme lay sick and sleeping. She lifted the coarse mosquito net from about him, sat down in the clumsy chair by the bedside, and began gently to fan the slumbering child. . . . The cabin was dark and quiet. Nonomme was crying softly, because the mosquitoes were biting him. In the room beyond, old Sylveste and the others slept. When Lolotte had quieted the

child, she went outside to get a pail of cool, fresh water at the cistern. Then she
crept into bed beside Nonomme, who slept again. (138)

The author trades more dramatic events for the solemnity of the simple adolescent girl's spending both her waking hours and her sleeping ones to care
for the child whose illness stems from the family's poverty as much as from
infection. When Lolotte acts—stealing her father's horse and heading for the
plantation—the reader understands what motivates her "misbehavior." In
fact, after the long denouement, when Lolotte has been lost for months and
the boys have gone to live with Aunt Minty, and Mme. Duplan has been caring for Nonomme, the Duplans make clear to Sylveste what his responsibilities are as a father. He is made to learn from Lolotte's selfless actions. In the
words of Mme. Duplan, " 'I shall trust these children into your hands once
more, and I want you never to forget again that you are their father—do-you
hear?—that you are a man!' " (144).

In some other of Chopin's early fictions, as here, the capacity for passion-
ate commitment to a child determines much about the adult character. When
David and Fanny Hosmer lose their beautiful three-year-old son, the reader is
led to assume that the life goes out of their marriage (one of the flaws of
Chopin's *At Fault*, however, is that any such direct relation between loss and
Fanny's drinking is not made). Repressing the memory of the child blocks
David from living a full life, and the scene at the end of the book in which he
whispers intimately with Thérèse suggests a childlike, if eroticized, play
between them. In "A Wizard from Gettysburg," the elder Bertrand Del-
mondé comes out of his years-long reverie at the mention that there is no
money to send his child to school. He confuses the younger Bertrand with the
older son, St. Armand (who would have been a small boy before the war)
because he relives his concern for his children. Chopin nails that motivation
into place at the end of the story when the broken man does not, in fact, recognize his wife, but rather asks her for shelter for himself and " 'his two little
children' " (130).

And what does Chopin say, very indirectly and discreetly, about the essential quality—passion—that drives so many of these characters, a few of whom
are female, such as Lolotte and the adolescent Fifine in "A Very Fine Fiddle,"
who are somewhat androgynous, but who otherwise are male? In her review of
Hamlin Garland's "Crumbling Idols," she implies that writers need to include
sexual passion: "Human impulses do not change and can not so long as men
and women continue to stand in the relation to one another which they have
occupied since our knowledge of their existence began" (693). In terms of
familial passion, the single time she commented about her relationship to her
children, she again backed into complimenting them—for their own qualities
and for their importance to her writing. In "On Certain Brisk, Bright Days,"
she described the kinds of questions writers are sometimes asked:

I trust it will not be giving away professional secrets to say that many readers would be surprised, perhaps shocked, at the questions which some newspaper editors will put to a defenseless woman under the guise of flattery.

For instance: "How many children have you?" This form is subtle and greatly to be commended in dealing with women of shy and retiring propensities. A woman's reluctance to speak of her children has not yet been chronicled. I have a good many, but they'd be simply wild if I dragged them into this. I might say something of those who are at a safe distance—the idol of my soul in Kentucky; the light of my eye off in Colorado; the treasure of his mother's heart in Louisiana—but I mistrust the form of their displeasure, with poisoned candy going through the mails. (723)

As Chopin writes with both humor and love about those idolized and treasured children, the reader has the same sense of joy that reading her early fiction brings.

While we rightly valorize Kate Chopin for being a champion of realistic characterization of women, for creating women who recognize—and often act on—physical passion, her earliest fiction reminds us that she began her career drawing loving and yet realistic portraits of a bevy of young men whose youthful charm remains vivid. That she continued to work that vein—particularly in the interplay between Robert and Victor Lebrun in *The Awakening,* as well as that between Etienne and Raoul, Edna's own sons—has sometimes been overlooked. Kate Chopin was a woman writer whose skill in depicting believable, and lovable, boys and young men possibly kept her from being seen as the first man-bashing feminist writer of this century.

Notes

1. Thomas Bonner, Jr., publishes Chopin's translations in his *The Kate Chopin Companion, With Chopin's Translations from French Fiction* (Westport, Conn.: The Greenwood Press, 1988); see also Emily Toth, *Kate Chopin* (New York: William Morrow, 1990) and Richard Fusco, *Maupassant and the American Short Story* (Philadelphia: University of Pennsylvania Press, 1994).

2. The very earliest of her stories are, for me, less interesting variants on the marriage plot. In "Wiser Than a God," Paula renounces her love for George Brainard to become the professional musician her parents (both dead) intended. In "A Point at Issue!," Eleanor Gail marries but insists on a nontraditional relationship—for a while. "Miss Witherwell's Mistake" and "With the Violin" are slight surprise-ending stories, whereas "Mrs. Mobry's Reason" is a chilling gothic tale. I do not discuss these stories in this essay.

3. See Toth's *Kate Chopin* for accounts of the six children's births and childhoods. As Toth notes in her essay "Chopin Thinks Back Through Her Mothers," "Certain parallels between Kate Chopin's life and works are readily apparent" (in *Kate Chopin Reconsidered: Beyond the Bayou,* ed. Lynda S. Boren and Sara deSaussure Davis [Baton Rouge: Louisiana State University Press, 1992], 16).

4. Kate Chopin, *The Complete Works of Kate Chopin,* ed. Per Seyersted, hardcover ed. (Baton Rouge: Louisiana State University Press, 1993), 84; hereafter cited in the text.

5. Toth, *Kate Chopin,* 164–72ff.

6. Judith Fetterley and Marjorie Pryse repeat the commonplace, for example, in their otherwise good introduction to Chopin in *American Women Regionalists, 1850–1910* (New York: W. W. Norton, 1992), 409. Helen Taylor reads only a few of Chopin's works in *Gender, Race, and Region in the Writings of Grace King, Ruth McEnery Stuart, and Kate Chopin* (Baton Rouge: Louisiana State University Press, 1989).

"The House of Sylvie" in Kate Chopin's "Athénaïse"

Heather Kirk Thomas

The imagination that produces work which bears and invites rereadings, which motions to future readings as well as contemporary ones, implies a shareable world and an endlessly flexible language.

Toni Morrison, *Playing in the Dark*.[1]

Per Seyersted, perhaps Kate Chopin's most influential critic, considers her lengthy story "Athénaïse" among her "most important efforts."[2] Written 10–28 April 1895 and published in the fall of 1896 in the *Atlantic Monthly*, the story not only exhibits the Cane River and New Orleans settings that earned Chopin acclaim in *Bayou Folk* (1894) but, more significantly, anticipates the overtly sexual themes of her mature work.[3] For these reasons Helen Taylor, among others, views "Athénaïse" as a precursor to Chopin's 1899 novel *The Awakening,* and both the story and its title character have received sustained critical attention.[4] By contrast, Chopin's characterization of Sylvie, the hard-working, middle-aged, black woman who runs the New Orleans boarding house where Athénaïse briefly resides, has escaped notice. This lapse appears doubly ironic, considering that Chopin's literary practice of effacing women of color has been so recurrently disparaged. To ignore Sylvie's narrative function is also to misread "Athénaïse"'s operative irony, which raises substantial questions about transitional stages in women's lives, including their deficient preparation for marriage, by contrasting a young white woman's marital loss of identity with a mature African-American woman's capable self-sufficiency.

The narrative features Athénaïse Miché Cazeau, a two-months' bride disillusioned in her marriage to the handsome widower Monsieur Cazeau, a conventionally laconic but nonetheless loving Cane River planter. Similar to Janie Crawford's repulsion to her first husband in Zora Neale Hurston's *Their Eyes Were Watching God* (1937), Athénaïse declares that she " 'can't stan' to live with a man; . . . his ugly bare feet—washing them in my tub, befo' my very eyes, ugh!' "[5] Her first petulant flight from Cazeau's Bon Dieu plantation

This essay was written specifically for this volume and is published here for the first time by permission of the author.

merely returns her to her parents' adjacent farm, but eventually she succumbs to her rakish, adored brother Montéclin's proposal that she flee from Cazeau to New Orleans. At this point, he orchestrates her secretive disappearance and secures lodgings at Sylvie's French Quarter boarding house, a locale he also frequents when visiting the city. During her month-long stay at "the house of Sylvie" (440), Athénaïse meets a cosmopolitan Creole journalist, Monsieur Gouvernail, who falls a little in love with her.[6] However, any adulterous liaison is avoided when she discovers her pregnancy, a revelation that returns her "in a wave of ectasy" (451) to her husband where "her lips for the first time respond to the passion of his own" (454). The story's insinuation that maternity fully awakens the young bride's passionate nature constitutes the singular brazen element of its otherwise conventional conclusion. In any case, Montéclin's disgruntled response to his sister's reconciliation with her husband—"he could not help feeling that the affair had taken a very disappointing, an ordinary, a most commonplace turn, after all" (454)—may mirror the reaction of some readers.

Per Seyersted, however, argues that the story's embedded critique of women's marital disempowerment likens Athénaïse "indirectly ... to a slave"; Helen Taylor similarly considers it Chopin's most explicit analogy between "marriage and slavery."[7] In this sense, in Athénaïse's chastened return to her husband's Bon Dieu plantation, we might consider her sold "up river." But Chopin regularly created alternative versions of female emancipation and confinement in her fiction. On the one hand, she experimented with thematic reconfigurations: exploring the ameliorative effects of a surrogate mother's love in "Polydore" (1895), for example, then deconstructing that myth in the later, Faulknerian nuances of "The Godmother" (1899). On the other hand, she commonly utilized parallel female characters or foils within single narratives: for example, in "A Sentimental Soul" and "Regret" (both written in 1894), in "Two Summers and Two Souls" (completed in 1895, immediately after "Athénaïse"), as well as her widely recognized trio—Mademoiselle Reisz, Adèle Ratignolle, and the woman in black—in The Awakening. In "Athénaïse" Chopin follows her customary practice by appointing the proprietor of the "house of Sylvie" as an ironic foil to the title character's personality in that Sylvie, an unmarried, African-American businesswoman, enjoys emotional, economic, and (presumably) sexual emancipation in New Orleans. White, pregnant, and Catholic, Athénaïse is essentially trapped even before she begins her journey.

Stereotyping of racial minorities was a common feature of 19th-century regional writing, and Chopin created her share of "Black Mammies" and fanatically loyal ex-slaves.[8] The majority of her black female characters have no family names, illustrated by "Mandy," "Betsy," and "Suze" in her first novel At Fault (1890), and others receive the honorary title "Aunt," a form of address alleging an affectionate bond with white families.[9] Chopin presumably copies Southern custom in both matters. Completed in 1892 but never published in her lifetime, the sketch "A Little Free-Mulatto" focuses specifically on free black families, but Chopin rarely created full-bodied characterizations of such people. Hence Sylvie's delineation as a woman of color who is also a New Orleans entrepreneur is not only atypical of Chopin's oeuvre but of American literature in general.

Couched in conventional local color language, the introductory description appears, at first glance, to diminish this exceptional woman of color:

> She was a portly quadroon of fifty or there-about, clad in an ample *volante* of the old-fashioned purple calico so much affected by her class. She wore large golden hoop-earrings, and her hair was combed plainly, with every appearance of effort to smooth out the kinks. (440)

But the overall narrative pays Sylvie uncommon homage as a woman of "dignity" whose strong racial features inscribe "the loftiness and command of her bearing" (440). In fact, the text states specifically that Sylvie's manner is supremely respectful, never obsequious, in the presence of her white patrons, notwithstanding she "believed firmly in maintaining the color line, and would not suffer a white person, even a child, to call her 'Madame Sylvie'" (440–41).

Anna Shannon Elfenbein notes that in Chopin's stories with black characters, "Her detached observations reveal both the extent to which oppressed people are shaped by the stereotypes applied to them and the extent to which they may use these stereotypes to dupe their oppressors."[10] The survival of "the house of Sylvie, on Dauphine Street" (440) in the heart of the French Quarter commercial world would normally demand that its proprietor adopt "the mask," Paul Laurence Dunbar's term for the obsequious face Southern racist convention required. Sylvie's position as the head of a business, however, excepts her from the traditional address "Aunt Sylvie." In addition, from "those of her own race"—her employees and others who value her economic achievement—she commands the title "Madame Sylvie," a form of respect she is said to have "exacted religiously" (441). A successful entrepreneur, Sylvie obviously pays lip service to Southern mores but demands deference when and where she can. Chopin's clarification of Sylvie's prerogatives in this matter cannily confronts Southern codes of etiquette as they intersect with issues of race and class. In "Madam's Past History" (1943), Harlem Renaissance poet Langston Hughes makes the same point about a self-employed black woman who extorts respect for a lifetime of work: "My name is Johnson— / Madam Alberta K. / The Madam stands for business. / I'm smart that way. . . . I do cooking, / Day's work, too! / Alberta K. Johnson— / *Madam* to you."[11]

The story's first mention of Sylvie's Dauphine Street townhouse—"a three-story gray brick, standing directly on the banquette, with three broad stone steps leading to the deep front entrance" (440)—associates its proprietor with an inherent air of respectability. In calling a boarding house "the house of Sylvie" Chopin not only contributes a French flavor to this Creole tale but also conveys a sense of economic sovereignty, like the powerful traditions invoked by "the House of Chanel" or "the House of Lords." The residence's public face, fronted by a second-story balcony, overlooks Dauphine Street. In the flagstone courtyard, invisible from the street, "fragrant flowering shrubs and plants" thrive in beds and in "tubs and green boxes," while the guest rooms within are "plain" but "exquisitely clean." To Athénaïse, who did not take well to housekeeping herself, "the whole place smelled of cleanliness" (440). She resolves "to live on indefinitely in this big, cool, clean back room" (442).

Sylvie's reputable "clientèle" hails mainly from "the southern parishes," ladies and gentlemen stopping a few days in New Orleans for business or pleasure. In fact, she "pride[s] herself upon the quality and highly respectable character of her patrons" and also rents out the house's "sanctuary of elegance," its formal front parlor, to "parties of respectable and discreet gentlemen desiring to enjoy a quiet game of cards outside the bosom of their families" (442). Clearly, the respectable gentlemen gather in Sylvie's front parlor because their equally respectable womenfolk discourage or prohibit these masculine pursuits. When they wish to enjoy a convivial evening at cards and smoke in peace, they come to Sylvie's. (The same impulse precipitated Mark Twain's inclusion of an attic billiards room in his Hartford mansion.) Interestingly, in a story about women's loss and gain in marriage, Chopin's irony extends beyond Athénaïse's quandary to critique how women themselves might reinforce the notion of separate spheres.

But Sylvie's racial and material rise has ensued from pleasing both her male and female clients. Installing the discomfited Athénaïse in her new quarters, the owner is irrefutably in charge. She moves "slowly and majestically about the apartment," checking the towels, smoothing the bed linens, and offering fresh water to ensure all is perfection. If the girl requires anything else, she is to " 'call Pousette: she year you plain,—she right down dere in de kitchen' " (441). If less tyrannical a hotelier than Leona Helmsley, Sylvie nevertheless rules with a practiced authority, which includes keeping a sharp eye on the aging, recalcitrant housemaid who occasionally neglects her duties. On one occasion Pousette forgets to bring ice water to Athénaïse's room. When summoned, she begs that no one tell her mistress about her lapse: " 'Vou pas cri conté ça Madame Sylvie?' " (448) Indeed Sylvie's high standards take an equivalent toil on her own leisure, as "almost every moment of her time was occupied in looking after her house." Athénaïse would enjoy a conversation from time to time, but Sylvie refuses because "her deferential attitude towards her lodgers forbade . . . gossipy chats" (449). To engage in gossip would violate her clients' right to privacy and in the long run might affect her income. By contrast, Athénaïse, who sorely requires her own funds, plans daily to locate "some suitable and agreeable employment" (442), but ruling out "two little girls who had promised to take piano lessons at a price . . .

embarrassing to mention" (451), she eventually determines she has no acceptable marketable skills.

A further disparity between Sylvie's and Athénaïse's capabilities concerns their various conceptions of housekeeping, and the narrative's sensual description of a typical meal at Sylvie's reveals another facet of her knowledge and expertise. Normally, Sylvie's guests do not receive board (except for Gouvernail, who takes Sunday breakfast), but she has agreed as a favor to Montéclin to provide for Athénaïse while she is in hiding.[12] Gracious dining here contrasts sharply with Athénaïse's disdain for her former housekeeping duties, which resulted in her peevish rejection of the keys to her husband's pantries, a gesture reflecting a naive hubris more than any enlightened disavowal of woman's work. Sundays Chez Sylvie, the "immaculately set" table near the window is spread with "delicate river-shrimps and crushed ice," "a few *hors d'oeuvres*," "a small golden-brown crusty loaf of French bread," a half-carafe of wine, and "the morning paper." Lamb chops followed by "café au lait" complete the feast (443). Chopin's savory description highlights Sylvie's culinary wisdom and creative touch. She might spend long hours overseeing her business, but when *le bon temps rouler* at Mardi Gras, she would know how to enjoy herself with food and friends. Athénaïse, by comparison, grew up amidst Cajun laughter and dancing, and her Cane River neighbors applaud her mother's "gumbo filé" (428). But until her sojourn with Sylvie, she appears to have disassociated the anticipation, preparation, and delights of the table with herself. She now has the opportunity to study an expert housekeeper, to savor fine food and wine, and to observe sophisticated table settings, a course of silent instruction to which Gouvernail also contributes during their educational excursions and private tête-à-têtes.

Sylvie's secluded garden also figures in Chopin's edification theme, particularly when examined alongside the story's most portentous symbol, the "great solitary oak-tree" (433) standing on Cazeau's plantation. After Athénaïse's first defiant flight to her parents, Cazeau collects and then accompanies her home. But at the finale of their journey when he sights this ancient, massive landmark, he abruptly recalls an incident in his childhood when his father permitted "Black Gabe," an exhausted runaway slave, to rest from the travails of his capture in its dense shade. Cazeau's chilling recollection, considering present developments, makes the oak tree suddenly appear "hideous," just as the locals' conviction "at the time that Black Gabe was a fool, a great idiot indeed, for wanting to run away" from such a "considerate master" (433) taunts him from the past. Per Seyersted interprets Black Gabe as a symbol of the Archangel Gabriel, the messenger of Mary's conception, and the oak tree, as "woman's immutable destiny which makes her the tree of life."[13] Chopin's satire of the elder Cazeau as a "considerate master" from whom a slave would be a fool to escape clearly parallels the son's dilemma. Sylvie's French Quarter garden, however, offers a benevolent contrast to the malevolent oak tree as well as to Seyersted's essentialist conception of woman's nature. In New Orleans, Athénaïse spends long hours in this sylvan retreat, caring for the flowers, admiring the "cape jessamine"'s bouquet (449), and hearkening to "a mockingbird that hung in a cage" and "a disreputable parrot that belonged to the cook next door, and swore hoarsely all day long in bad French" (451). Earlier the narrative suggests that Athénaïse would eventually come to "know her own mind" as instinctively as "the song to the bird, the perfume and color to the flower" (433). Compared with the evil antebellum tree of knowledge dwarfing Cazeau's plantation, Sylvie's lush courtyard seems prelapsarian; more importantly, it supplies the three preconditions mentioned above that will enable Athénaïse to "know her own mind." The brilliantly-colored flowers, their sensual perfume, and the plaintive lament of the caged birds work their magic on Athénaïse. This diminutive Eden arouses her senses and quiescent sexuality, easing her metamorphosis into womanhood prior to her realization that she is expecting a child.

But Sylvie offers Athénaïse more than a garden retreat and the leisure in which to assimilate her experience. Like Mademoiselle Reisz, she also serves as a "very wise" counselor to the "very ignorant" Athénaïse (451), who knows surprisingly little, for a planter's daughter, about human reproduction. Hence when she complains of feeling "not herself" (451), it falls to Sylvie to interpret her symptoms, offer the obvious conclusion, and later just as candidly inform Gouvernail, since "[t]here was no subject known to her which Sylvie hesitated to discuss in detail with any man of suitable years and discretion" (453). Sylvie's diagnosis drastically changes Athénaïse's course of action, but before she departs for Bon Dieu, her landlady presents her with a symbolic farewell gift: an heirloom "set of pattern" (apparently for maternity or infant garments) analogous to the designs Adèle Ratignolle imparts to Edna. Sylvie's generosity expresses a sororal bond transcending race, but the very nature of her gift as well as its ominous, allegorical name portend the young woman's future.[14] Athénaïse accepts Sylvie's patterns "with reverence, fully sensible of the great compliment and favor" (453) but leaves only some castoffs for the housemaid Pousette: "a handkerchief, a petticoat, a pair of stockings with two tiny holes at the toes, some broken prayer-beads, and finally a silver dollar" (452).

Considering Athénaïse's fiscal straits, however, Pousette's compensation might not be as stingy as it seems. The daughter of tenant farmers, Athénaïse undoubtedly had no dowry. She also has no funds in New Orleans except what little her brother borrowed to pay her room and board or what she later acquires from "Harding & Offdean, her husband's merchants," to purchase a layette and presents for her family (452). In 19th-century Louisiana, the Napoleonic Code controlling a husband's estates was still regnant; indeed, after her husband, Oscar, died in 1882, Chopin had to petition the courts for her marital property and guardianship of her six children. Although Athénaïse improved her estate by marrying Cazeau, during her month's stay in the city she very likely realized that the "house of Sylvie" was more monetarily secure than she, a silent partner in the "house of Cazeau." Thus in contrasting an autonomous woman of color with the fiscally dependent Athénaïse, Chopin delivers a dismal truth. The monetary survival of 19th-century, white Louisiana wives in general depended upon their husbands' liberality.

John Carlos Rowe argues that Chopin's writings in general rarely expressed any form of "sisterhood" with "women from other classes, races, and economic conditions."[15] For this reason alone Sylvie's sympathetic characterization is of distinct importance in Chopin's corpus, notwithstanding its extraordinary significance as a rare literary illustration of an entrepreneurial woman of color. Perhaps the earliest prototype is the protagonist of Harriet E. Wilson's rediscovered novel *Our Nig* (1859), the first known to be published by an African-American woman. Disguised as an "Autobiography," the novel relates the story of Alfrado or "Frado," a free woman of color and former servant who supports herself in the North by making straw hats, then by concocting and selling dye "for restoring gray hair to its former color" from a recipe acquired from a benefactor.[16] When poor health forces Frado out of work, she writes and then publishes *Our Nig*. Destitute but disdaining employment as a domestic servant, Frado, a.k.a. Harriet E. Wilson, joined the ranks of 19th-century women who turned to writing to pay their bills. Whereas white women might advance their writing on their own merits, Wilson, like Frederick Douglass and Harriet Jacobs, required a supporting appendix of testimonials affirming the author's character to market her book.

The resilient Celie, who rises above her violent and abusive childhood in Alice Walker's novel *The Color Purple* (1982), remains perhaps our most famous literary entrepreneurial woman of color. Ironically, Celie's successful business grew out of her own physical imperfections. Because her awkward figure palls in comparison with the statuesque Shug Avery, she decides to sew herself loose-fitting pants for camouflage and comfort. Eventually she finds a successful vocation as the designer of "Folkspants, Unlimited," a unisex garment. Celie's flourishing enterprise provides her with creative and meaningful employment, her first earnings, and an ever-increasing circle of customers. As Celie puts it, " 'I got love, I got work, I got money, friends and time.' "[17] She demonstrates that the way to escape Mr. _____, her cruel and neglectful husband, is with "a needle and not a razor" in her hand.[18] One disparity between Walker's and Chopin's portrayals of black entrepreneurial women lies in the authors' emblematic wordplay. Celie's "patterns" for "Folkspants"—both as mode of dress and as business—bring her freedom and security, but "Madame Sylvie" already possesses what Celie newly acquires. It is precisely Sylvie's disruption of 19th-century racial and gender "patterns" that makes her gift to Athénaïse so paradoxical in light of the conventional mold to which the younger woman is expected to conform.

Andrew Delbanco proposes that *The Awakening* is ultimately a "cautionary tale—in much the same way that Frederick Douglass, for example, set out to shock his white audiences by hinting at the barbarism that slavery would eventually unleash in the enslaved."[19] Helen Taylor reads similarly "Athénaïse" as an *exemplum* narrative exhibiting "the problems of self-definition for women, defined and spoken for as they are by men."[20] But "Athénaïse" cautions both sexes about the inevitable conflict between self and other. Although the heroine calls "marriage a trap set for the feet of unwary and unsuspecting girls" (434), portrayal of the husband, who despite his spurs and callouses is not fundamentally at fault for his young wife's unhappiness, is one of its essential ironies. Rather Chopin, like Alice Walker, seems to criticize the institution itself as an uneasy merger in which the spouses infrequently share a substantial conversation, a companionable dinner, an evening at cards, or even a smoke. Chopin's enjoyment of the above activities has been well documented; hence it seems plausible that in presenting both sides of the marital coin she identified as much with the card players who eluded the ladies in Sylvie's front parlor as with the ingenuous bride who braved convention by defecting to Sylvie's second-story rooms.

Charlotte Perkins Gilman's autobiographical story "The Yellow Wallpaper" (1892) works well pedagogically alongside "Athénaïse." However, it is Gilman's evaluation of the cultural symbolism associated with hotel and apartment living that sheds light on the function of "the house of Sylvie" in Chopin's story. In *Women and Economics* (1898), Gilman's analysis of gender and monetary inequalities, she quips that "[t]o man, so far the only fully human being of his age, the bachelor apartment of some sort has been a temporary home for that part of his life wherein he had escaped from one family and not yet entered another."[21] For exactly this reason, Gouvernail has spent three transitional years at Sylvie's "living amid luxurious surroundings and a multitude of books" (443). But Athénaïse, after her education with the Catholic sisters, went from her parents' home directly into her husband's (a route Chopin also took herself). Hence "the house of Sylvie" provides the site of Athénaïse's first taste of freedom, a *locus amoenus* between carefree girlhood and the assumption of marital responsibilities. Like the lighthearted bachelor who declares he will "take mine ease in mine inn,"[22] Athénaïse enjoys a time of reflection at Sylvie's apart from her husband and family, a time to reevaluate herself, her faltering marriage, and her future. Refurbishing her wardrobe with "pure white" and flower-sprigged dresses (442), she even assumes a new identity in this safe house. To assuage her loneliness she putters long hours in the garden, jots down her thoughts in letters, and converses regularly with a sophisticated man of the world. She finds it "diverting" to watch the passersby from the townhouse's private balcony and, above all, savors "the comforting, comfortable sense of not being married!" (444). Clearly, Athénaïse finds more than a room of her own in New Orleans. She experiences, if only symbolically, the first "house of Athénaïse."

At the close of her New Orleanian sabbatical, she feels "pride and satisfaction"—"as if she had fallen heir to some magnificent inheritance"—in her decision to return to Cazeau and the household keys: "No one could have said now that she did not know her own mind" (452). Certainly her idealistic conviction remains to be tested, but the evaluation that the story equates marriage with women's enslavement seems unduly harsh. Schooled by the nuns and spoiled by her family, Athénaïse had little conception of a wife's duties or delights when she wed; consequently, she was doomed to disappoint everyone involved. Cazeau, too, held the unrealistic expectation that their union would resemble "the sun shining out of the clouds . . . like w'at the story-books promise after the wedding" (435). After a month at Sylvie's, however, Athénaïse is better prepared to assume her companionable, conjugal, practical, and maternal responsibilities. No longer an unenlightened girl, she departs a woman, like "Eve after losing her ignorance" (453). What she makes of her marriage and motherhood is now up to her.

In the final analysis, the story is not so much about women's enslavement *in* marriage but about women's preparation *for* marriage. And in Athénaïse's example, Chopin teaches that young women, like young men, would profit from a transitional period for emotional growth and at least some rudimentary sex education before they are wooed and moved, like chattel, from one house to another. As "The Yellow Wallpaper"'s conclusion shockingly reveals, late 19th-century women already possessed the "key" to patriarchal confinement, but they first had to unlock the door themselves. In Chopin's story, Athénaïse's three foils likewise instruct us in disclosing that Sylvie, a working woman of color, proves a more reliable guide and surrogate mother than either Madame Miché, who expects marriage to be "a wonderful and powerful agent in the development and formation of a woman's character" (434), or Sister Marie Angélique, who accuses Athénaïse of "turning deaf ears" to her divine calling to become a nun (431).[23] The story also denounces the Victorian double standard, which expected women to have no sexual desires but to submit passively to their husbands, whereas men like Gouvernail and Montéclin were free to pursue discreet affairs.[24] In "Athénaïse" Chopin affirms that women can enjoy sex and find fulfillment in marriage and motherhood but that their chance for happiness increases in direct proportion to their knowledge of these intimate, familial, and practical roles.

Whatever the author's intentions in "Athénaïse," it contributed significantly toward her literary maturation. She labored uncommonly long over its composition and was undoubtedly delighted when it was accepted by the *Atlantic Monthly,* only her second story to appear there.[25] Some say that her maternal grandmother, Mary Athénaïse Charleville Faris, provided the inspiration for the title character.[26] Another anecdote reports that Oscar's mother, Julia Benoist Chopin, left her "mean and dictatorial" husband for several years in the 1850s but, like Athénaïse, later returned.[27] Whatever the influence of biographical materials upon "Athénaïse," it is unquestionably one of Chopin's best stories. As a prelude to *The Awakening,* Sylvie's characterization anticipates Grand Isle hotelier Madame Lebrun, just as the short story narrative uses the novel's bird imagery, house and clothing iconography, opposing rural and urban settings, character foils, and finally those prophetic paper "patterns."

Earlier in this century, Zora Neale Hurston campaigned that it was of "vast importance" for Americans to read stories about average, everyday people of color who worked "above the servant class" if we were ever "to do away with that feeling of difference which inspires fear and which ever expresses itself in dislike."[28] Needless to say, Madame Sylvie's egalitarian portrayal was creatively and politically ahead of its time. Except in widowhood, Madame Cazeau will presumably never achieve her landlady's options or freedoms. Ultimately, "Athénaïse"'s candor concerning female sexuality as well as its frankness about the impact of all gender relationships upon the achievement of selfhood mark a significant stage in Chopin's growth as a storyteller, an evaluation only enhanced when the story is reconsidered with Sylvie's integral, indeed, crucial characterization in mind.

Notes

1. Toni Morrison, *Playing in the Dark: Whiteness and the Literary Imagination* (New York: Random House, 1993), xii.

2. Per Seyersted, *Kate Chopin: A Critical Biography* (Baton Rouge: Louisiana State University Press, 1969), 114.

3. The story appeared in the August and September issues of the *Atlantic Monthly* as "Athénaïse: A Story of Temperament" and was reprinted in *A Night in Acadie* (1897). See *The Complete Works of Kate Chopin,* ed. Per Seyersted, hardcover ed. (Baton Rouge: Louisiana State University Press, 1993), 426–54, 1025.

4. Helen Taylor, *Gender, Race, and Region in the Writings of Grace King, Ruth McEnery Stuart, and Kate Chopin* (Baton Rouge: Louisiana State University Press, 1989), 179. For discussions of "Athénaïse," see Taylor, 179–82; Per Seyersted, *Kate Chopin,* 112–14, 130–32; Barbara Ewell, *Kate Chopin* (New York: Ungar, 1986), 108–12; Pearl L. Brown, "Kate Chopin's Fiction: Order and Disorder in a Stratified Society," *The University of Mississippi Studies in English* 9 (1991), 128–30; and Emily Toth, "Kate Chopin Thinks Back Through Her Mothers: Three Stories by Kate Chopin," in *Kate Chopin Reconsidered: Beyond the Bayou,* ed. Lynda S. Boren and Sara deSaussure Davis (Baton Rouge: Louisiana State University Press, 1992), 18–21, 24–25; and Toth's biography, *Kate Chopin* (New York: William Morrow, 1990), 274–75.

5. Kate Chopin, "Athénaïse," in *The Complete Works of Kate Chopin,* 431; hereafter cited in the text.

6. Gouvernail also appears in "A Respectable Woman" (1894) as well as *The Awakening.*

7. Per Seyersted, *The Complete Works of Kate Chopin,* 27, and Helen Taylor, *Gender, Race, and Region,* 180.

8. For analyses of Chopin's African-American characterizations, see Barbara C. Ewell, *Kate Chopin,* 68–73; Helen Taylor, *Gender, Race, and Region,* 138–202; Anna Shannon Elfenbein, *Women on the Color Line: Evolving Stereotypes and the Writings of George Washington Cable, Grace King, Kate Chopin* (Charlottesville: University of Virginia Press, 1989), 117–57; and Eunice Manders, "Kate Chopin's 'Wretched Freeman,' " in *Perspectives on Kate Chopin: Proceedings of the Kate Chopin International Conference* [6–8 April, 1989], ed. Grady Ballenger, Karen Cole, Katherine Kearns, and Tom Sarnet (Natchitoches, La.: Northwestern State University Press, 1992), 37–45.

9. Some of Chopin's lengthier characterizations of older women of color are "Old Aunt Peggy" (*Bayou Folk*), "Aunt Dicey" in "A Gentleman of Bayou Teche" (*Bayou Folk*) "Aunt

Pinky" in "Odalie Misses Mass" (1895), "Aunt Tildy" in "Ozeme's Holiday" (1896), "Aunt Halifax" in "Dead Men's Shoes" (1897), "Aunt Lympy's Interference" (1897) and "Aunt Crissy" in "The Gentleman from New Orleans" (completed in 1900 but published first in *The Complete Works of Kate Chopin*). Aunt Belindy in *At Fault* is perhaps the most three-dimensional of the characters.

10. Elfenbein, *Women on the Color Line,* 118.

11. Langston Hughes, "Madam's Past History," in *American Literature,* ed. Emory Elliott, (Englewood Cliffs, NJ: Prentice Hall, 1991), 2:1173–1174.

12. Interestingly, Chopin's "In and Out of Old Natchitoches" (1893), which mentions Athénaïse Miché's approaching marriage, contains a precursor to Sylvie's characterization, a middle-aged white woman who likewise runs a French Quarter boarding house. Unlike Sylvie's hardworking example, however, "Maman Chavan" lounges about in a "white *volante*" (266), drinks sauterne at breakfast, smokes cigarettes, and enjoys a friendship with Hector Santien, a notorious gambler who, like Gouvernail, similarly takes Sunday breakfast at her townhouse.

13. Per Seyersted, *The Complete Works of Kate Chopin,* 27.

14. Sylvie obtained this "set of pattern" from "a foreign lady of distinction whom she had nursed years before at the St. Charles hotel" (453), a vetting that not only testifies to Sylvie's rise in the economic world from her earlier position as a nurse-domestic, but also furnishes added subtlety in its implication that the patterned life of a wife and mother is as yet "foreign" to the expectant bride.

15. John Carlos Rowe, "The Economics of the Body in *The Awakening,*" in Boren and Davis, *Kate Chopin Reconsidered,* 134.

16. Harriet E. Wilson, *Our Nig; or, Sketches from the Life of a Free Black,* ed. Henry Louis Gates, Jr. (New York: Random House, 1983), 137.

17. Alice Walker, *The Color Purple* (New York: Harcourt Brace Jovanovich, 1982), 183.

18. Walker, 125.

19. Andrew Delbanco, "The Half-Life of Edna Pontellier," in *New Essays on "The Awakening,"* ed. Wendy Martin (Cambridge: Cambridge University Press, 1988), 106.

20. Taylor, *Gender, Race, and Region,* 182.

21. Charlotte Perkins Gilman, *Women and Economics: A Study of the Economic Relation Between Men and Women as a Factor in Social Evolution* (Cambridge: The University Press, 1911), 265.

22. Gilman, 265.

23. In an "entrepreneurial workshop" hosted by the Department of Marketing at Loyola College, Baltimore, the participants were asked to consider these questions: "What skills, life experiences does this entrepreneur bring?" and "What skills, experiences must this entrepreneur acquire *before* opening this enterprise?" The first question reveals why the fifty-year-old Sylvie owns a living business. The second highlights the qualities Athénaïse lacks to begin the business of living.

24. Gouvernail, who associates with a liberal crowd, hopes someday to hold Athénaïse with "a lover's arms"; her marriage "made no particle of difference" to him (450). Montéclin takes frequent, solitary trips to New Orleans, and Cazeau, a widower, was married for ten years before his wife's death.

25. "Tante Cat'rinette," published in September 1894, was Chopin's first story in *Atlantic Monthly* (Seyersted, *The Complete Works of Kate Chopin,* 1017).

26. For a biographical account of Mary Athénaïse Charleville Faris (1799–1887), see Emily Toth, "Kate Chopin Thinks Back," in Boren and Davis, *Kate Chopin Reconsidered,* 18–21, 24–25. In *Kate Chopin,* 30, Toth states that "Athénaïse" was "named for Kate's grandmother."

27. Seyersted, *Kate Chopin,* 36.

28. Zora Neale Hurston, "What White Publishers Won't Print," in *I Love Myself When I Am Laughing . . . and Then Again when I Am Looking Mean and Impressive: A Zora Neale Hurston Reader,* ed. Alice Walker (New York: The Feminist Press, 1979), 169, 173.

Her Own Story: The Woman of Letters
in Kate Chopin's Short Fiction

Nancy A. Walker

Readers of Kate Chopin's *The Awakening* have long found intriguing the pas-sage near the end of chapter XXIV in which Edna Pontellier becomes drowsy while reading Ralph Waldo Emerson.[1] In the context of the novel, this moment occurs when Edna is experiencing a rare period of contentment: her husband and children are away; she has just dined alone on a "luscious ten-derloin;"[2] and when she goes to bed, "a sense of restfulness invaded her, such as she had not known before" (956). Images of rest and peace so pervade this section of the novel that we might assume that Edna has found pleasure rather than boredom in the pages of Emerson's essays. Indeed, as she sits in the library, Chopin remarks that Edna "realized that she had neglected her reading, and determined to start anew upon a course of improving studies" (956). Yet by this point in the novel, Edna's character has been so well estab-lished as a mixture of impulse and languor that an attentive reader would be skeptical about Edna adhering faithfully to a "course of study", and in fact Chopin never alludes to this plan again. Some readers, such as Chopin's biog-rapher Emily Toth, view the author as taking a deliberate swipe at Emerson in this passage. Toth detects a "sly cynicism" in the description of Edna grow-ing sleepy over her book, "using Emerson not for wisdom but as a soporific" as a way of conveying Chopin's rejection of Emerson's identification of women with sentiment rather than with intellect or will.[3] This identification is, of course, far from unique to Emerson. The traditional association of women with emotion and intuition rather than reason and intellectual activ-ity prompted the 17th-century poet Anne Bradstreet to express the fear that her critics would charge that a needle would fit her hand better than the pen.

Regardless of whether one sees the reference to Emerson as incidental or as a veiled rejection of some of his ideas, the fact that Edna grows sleepy while reading is part of a pattern in *The Awakening* that shows how Edna's relation-ship to reading, writing, and language is problematic. Early in the novel, she

This essay was written especially for this volume and is published here for the first time by permis-sion of the author.

218

reads with "profound astonishment" a book that is being passed from one to another of the summer visitors at Grand Isle; apparently shocked by its frankness, she reads it "in secret and solitude" (889–90). Edna far prefers romantic fantasies, such as the "legends of the Baratarians and the sea" that Madame Antoine tells on the *Chênière Caminada* (920). Although Robert Lebrun loans Edna books, she would rather be read to and be told stories than read on her own, just as Madame Delisle, in Chopin's stories "A Lady of Bayou St. John" and "La Belle Zoraïde," depends upon Manna-Loulou's story-telling to put her to sleep every night.[4] As the parrot on the opening page of *The Awakening* speaks "a language which nobody understood" (881), so Edna seems at times to be baffled by written discourse. When, for example, Madame Lebrun offers to let Edna read a letter that Robert has written, she examines "the envelope, its size and shape, the post-mark, the handwriting" as though trying to decipher an exotic artifact (928).

Patricia S. Yaeger argues that *The Awakening* embodies a struggle between Edna's inchoate, unarticulated desires and "the objectifying world of [male] discourse she inhabits."[5] I would expand Yaeger's point to suggest that, if we look closely at Chopin's short fiction as well as her novel, we can see a variety of relationships between female characters and the acts of reading and writing that testify to Chopin's acute awareness that a facility with language may be empowering, but that conventional intellectual processes are not the only avenues to knowledge; indeed they may be restrictive. The written-language skills of her women characters range from illiteracy to professional involvement with words, and the degree of ease with which a woman is involved with written discourse sometimes serves as a metaphoric index of her self-esteem and sense of individual agency. 'Tite Reine, in the story "In Sabine," can neither read nor write, and her illiteracy has trapped her in an abusive relationship with her husband, Bud Aiken. " 'If I would know how to read an' write,' " she tells Grégoire, " 'an' had some pencil an' paper, it's long 'go I would wrote to my popa' " (330). The 'Tite Reine whom Grégoire remembers, "whose will had been the law in her father's household" (329), now lives in fear of her husband but has lacked the means to call for help.

At the other extreme from 'Tite Reine is the title character in "Charlie," a young woman whose energy and zest for life are rendered metaphorically by her natural gift for writing poetry. By the standards of her plantation culture, Charlie is a rebellious tomboy who would rather ride her horse than study her lessons in the schoolroom with her six sisters. From her name (a nickname for "Charlotte") to her penchant for long rambles in the woods, Charlie is more conventionally masculine than feminine, which endears her to her widowed father, for whom "she filled the place of that ideal son he had always hoped for and that had never come" (644). In fact, when her father is seriously injured, Charlie returns home from the ladies' seminary to which he had reluctantly sent her to acquire discipline and social graces, and prepares to run the plantation—a job that her sisters' piano and dancing lessons have not fitted them to assume. It is Charlie's skill as a writer that enables her to succeed both at the seminary and on the plantation: in both "feminine" and "masculine" worlds. Her seminary classmates "had small respect for her abilities until one day it fell upon them with the startling bewilderment of lightning from a clear sky that Charlie was a poet" (658). In fact, she wins a competition for written tributes to the woman who had founded the seminary. After her father's accident, it is once again skill at writing that serves as a sign of her ability to oversee the business of the plantation. When her father expects a visit from "Mr. Gus," a neighbor who has been assisting him, Charlie asserts, "I know as much as he, more perhaps when it comes to writing letters" (668).

The writing and reading of letters assumes enormous importance in Chopin's short fiction.[6] To be sure, the mail was a major source of news in an era before the telephone and electronic media, especially in the rural areas in which many of Chopin's stories are set. But the frequency with which letters function as major plot elements—especially as they affect women's lives— suggests that Chopin uses them to represent all written discourse and the power of knowledge that it embodies. In one of Chopin's best-known stories, "Désirée's Baby," a long-hidden letter contains the information that could have saved Désirée's life: that her child's Negro blood came from her husband's family, not her own. The "lie" in "Dr. Chevalier's Lie" is the letter he writes to the family of a young prostitute who has been shot to death, telling them she died of an illness and thus preserving their pride in her for leaving Arkansas for the big city. At the end of "The Storm," following his sexual encounter with Calixta, Alcée Laballière writes a letter to his wife, Clarisse, encouraging her to remain in Biloxi for a while longer; Clarisse reads Alcée's letter with a pleasant sense of release from her "conjugal life" for a while (596). Sometimes the letter itself becomes a sensual object. In "Her Letters," the unnamed woman tears off with her teeth the corner of an envelope with her former lover's name on it, and "tasted it between her lips and upon her tongue like some god-given morsel" (399). This correspondence, which she orders destroyed at her death, is the only evidence that she has been capable of passion.

An examination of three of Chopin's short stories will help to show the range and complexity of the author's exploration of the relationship between women and the written word. In "Athénaïse," published in 1896, she uses reading and writing to delineate the confused young girl's distance from the world of the intellect, which is represented by the journalist Gouvernail. "Miss Witherwell's Mistake" (1891), one of Chopin's most satiric stories, juxtaposes a self-important small-town newspaper columnist with her niece, a young woman who writes her own life script rather than fiction. The third story, "Elizabeth Stock's One Story," was intended as part of Chopin's collection A Vocation and a Voice, which was not published during her lifetime.[7]

Written in 1898, at a time when Chopin was at the height of her professional writing life, "Elizabeth Stock's One Story" demonstrates that Chopin was still aware of—and perhaps to some extent still experienced—cultural barriers to women's participation in the literary process.

The title character of "Athénaïse" is a young Cajun woman who has recently married an older widower for whom she feels little but distaste. Although he is kind to her, she dislikes the physicality of marriage, and regrets that she had not listened to the nuns who told her she had a religious vocation. As she tells her brother Montéclin, " 'W'en I think of a blessed life in the convent, at peace! Oh w'at was I dreaming of!' " (431). Athénaïse has something of the rebellious nature that Chopin was later to develop more fully in the more worldly Edna Pontellier. Both characters act instinctively to remove themselves from unpleasant circumstances; neither woman, as Chopin says of Athénaïse, "accept[s] the inevitable with patient resignation, a talent born in the souls of many women" (433). Both women leave their husbands' houses—Edna moves to the "pigeon house," and Athénaïse runs away from Cazeau, first to her family's home and then to a rooming house in New Orleans. Although the endings of the two narratives are dramatically different—Athénaïse returns eagerly to Cazeau when she learns that she is pregnant, whereas Edna leaves behind all family ties in her final swim in the ocean—in both cases Chopin suggests that intuition may be at least as compelling as reason.

At the beginning of section III of "Athénaïse," Chopin describes her character's relationship to the intellect and nature, respectively:

> People often said that Athénaïse would know her own mind someday, which was equivalent to saying that she was at present unacquainted with it. If she ever came to such knowledge, it would be by no intellectual research, by no subtle analyses or tracing the motives of actions to their source. It would come to her as the song to the bird, the perfume and color to the flower. (433)

Athénaïse is thus allied in an almost Emersonian sense with the natural world. She reacts to pleasure with "frank, open appreciation," and "dissimulation was as foreign to her nature as guile to the breast of a babe" (433).

This straightforward, uncomplicated approach to life is heightened when Athénaïse is removed from her rural environment of horses, dances, and gumbo filé to Sylvie's rooming house in the French Quarter. It is in this rooming house that the journalist Gouvernail lives, so Sylvie has told her, "amid luxurious surroundings and a multitude of books" (443). As a professional writer, Gouvernail represents the world of the printed word, and by extension, reason and the intellect. The first time that he and Athénaïse meet at breakfast, Gouvernail begins a pattern of sharing with her parts of his world, to which she is largely indifferent. On this occasion, he hands her part of the newspaper for which he writes—"the part which contained the

Woman's Page and the social gossip" (443). But even this bow to her supposedly feminine interests fails to capture Athénaïse's attention; instead of reading this section of the newspaper, she muses on the contrast between her expectations of this "literary celebrity" and the youthful Gouvernail.

Chopin next uses the written word as a measure of the distance between the worlds of Athénaïse and Gouvernail when Athénaïse (otherwise inexplicably) asks Gouvernail to address a letter that she has written to her brother. As she dictates the address, "she wondered a little at a man of his supposed erudition stumbling over the spelling of 'Montéclin' and 'Miché' " (445). Her affectional world is so familiar to her that she cannot imagine anyone not being "literate" in its ways. Gouvernail, however, understands more about Athénaïse than the spelling of her brother's name. When, sensing her loneliness, he searches his bookshelves for something to lend her to read, he rejects both philosophy and poetry. "He had not sounded her literary tastes, and strongly suspected she had none; that she would have rejected The Duchess as readily as Mrs. Humphry Ward" (446). When he finally decides on a magazine, she reports that "it had entertained her passably." She is drawn not to the printed text—"a New England story had puzzled her, . . . and a Creole tale had offended her"—but to the illustrations, which had "pleased her greatly," especially a picture of one of Remington's cowboys that reminds her of Montéclin (446).

When, at the climax of the story, Athénaïse is finally initiated into knowledge, it is the knowledge of her own body—a biological rather than an intellectual enlightenment. As Sylvie explains the facts of life to her, Athénaïse realizes that she is carrying Cazeau's child, and "her whole being was steeped in a wave of ecstasy" (451). In Gouvernail's presence, she feels as "embarrassed as Eve after losing her ignorance" (453), but significantly, she does not require his assistance in addressing and mailing a letter announcing her return to her husband. Having acquired the information she needs to make her marriage a source of joy, Athénaïse is no longer barred from written communication; she writes to Cazeau "with a single thought, a spontaneous impulse" (451).

If Athénaïse's new-found facility with language is tied to her entrance into that group of women that Chopin calls in *The Awakening* "mother-women," Miss Witherwell, in "Miss Witherwell's Mistake," is a woman who uses language in the service of the lowest common denominator of public taste: for the Saturday edition of the Boredomville *Battery,* she writes popular romances and domestic advice columns. The object of Chopin's satire in this story is Miss Witherwell's self-importance as a writer for the small-town newspaper. She proofreads her "tale[s] of passion, acted beneath those blue and southern skies" (59), and her articles on "The Wintering of Canaries" and "Security Against the Moth" as meticulously as if they were the most enduring works of literature, removing "those demoniac vagaries, in which the type-setter proverbially delights" (59). As a woman writer, she takes pains to preserve her respectability as a homemaker (albeit a single one), recounting how inspiration has struck while she was washing dishes or lining a trunk and failing to realize that the pieces she writes are as banal and repetitious as these household chores. The fact that she has "a moneyed interest in the *Battery*" (59), Chopin hints, plays no small part in that paper's eagerness to print her effusions.

The ostensible "mistake" of the story's title is Miss Witherwell's asking her niece, Mildred, to go to the newspaper office to proofread one of her weekly articles ("The Use and Abuse of the Corset") while she stays home to nurse a cold. In doing so, she unwittingly places Mildred in proximity with the young man she has been sent to Boredomville to forget—her father having declared him unfit to marry her because he is not wealthy. But Miss Witherwell's real mistake is in being a romantic rather than a realist, and the story becomes part of the late-19th-century debate about literary realism. Mildred, her romance with Roland Wilson rekindled by her visits to the *Battery* office, cleverly seeks her aunt's sanction of their relationship by pretending to write a story and asking Miss Witherwell's advice about its ending. So caught up does Miss Witherwell become in helping Mildred with the plot of her "love story" that she fails to recognize it as Mildred's own tale of being separated from and then surreptitiously reunited with her lover. As Mildred works to plot her own life, her aunt draws on a store of hackneyed plot elements to effect the reconciliation of the "fictional" lovers. When Mildred protests that, as a writer, she is "extremely realistic" and cannot "force situations," Miss Witherwell looks at her "aghast": "The poison of the realistic school has certainly tainted and withered your fancy in the bud, my dear. . . . Marry them, most certainly, or let them die" (65). Having thus obtained her aunt's sanction for her "fictional" ending, Mildred marries Roland Wilson, and at the end of the story Miss Witherwell has grown "older in years, but not in reality," and still writes her "brilliant articles" for the Boredomville *Battery* (66).

The aptly named Miss Witherwell represents the woman writer who clings to outmoded notions of feminine gentility and romance. Chopin's Elizabeth Stock represents women's traditional exclusion from language and literature. In "Elizabeth Stock's One Story," the title character, "an unmarried woman of thirty-eight" (586), has "always felt as if [she] would like to write stories," but whenever she tries to think of a plot, she finds that "some one else had thought about [it] before [her]" (586). Living in the small town of Stonelift—which resembles the Boredomville of "Miss Witherwell's Mistake"—Elizabeth Stock is surrounded by other people's stories. Not only is the town so small that "people were bound to look into each others' lives" (587), but Elizabeth is the town postmistress, daily handling the mail that comes in and out of Stonelift by train. When she attempts to make use, as an author, of these daily dramas, for example writing about "old Si' Shepard that got lost in the woods and never came back," she is discouraged by her Uncle

William, who tells her, "this here ain't no story; everybody knows about old Si' Shepard" (586). Elizabeth had better, Uncle William thinks, "stick to [her] dress making" (586). The only story Elizabeth Stock can tell, then, is her own, and it is the unpublished manuscript of her own story, found by an unnamed and unsympathetic frame narrator, that becomes Chopin's story.

"Elizabeth Stock's One Story" is a paradigmatic story of the woman writer. Written a year before the publication of *The Awakening* and the subsequent accusations that its author was "unwomanly," this short story shows more clearly than any of her other fictions Chopin's keen awareness of the gendered nature of writing. Elizabeth is told by Uncle William to give up the pen in favor of the needle, as Anne Bradstreet had feared being told more than two centuries before, and when she persists in trying to think of a story that hasn't been told before and that "everybody" doesn't already know, she recounts "turning and twisting things in my mind just like I often saw old ladies twisting quilt patches around to compose a design" (587). After she has written her "one story" and is hospitalized in St. Louis with consumption, the narrator tells us, "she relapsed into a silence that remained unbroken till the end" (586). The statement by the condescending (perhaps male?) narrator that Elizabeth was "much given over to scribbling" (586) even recalls Nathaniel Hawthorne's comment about the "d——d mob of scribbling women" earlier in the 19th century,[8] and Chopin's use of the "found manuscript" device recalls Hawthorne's use of it in *The Scarlet Letter.* Chopin's narrator, representing the judgment of the outside world, declares that in the "conglomerate mass" of Elizabeth Stock's "bad prose" and "impossible verse," he has found only "the following pages which bore any semblance to a connected or consecutive narration" (586).

But what is Elizabeth Stock's "one story" about? When Elizabeth finally sits down "quiet and peaceful" on an autumn day, what story does she choose to tell? Ostensibly, she wants to explain "how I lost my position" as postmistress; actually, she tells the story of a proud, independent woman, an aspiring writer, whose sense of responsibility to others brings about both her professional and her physical downfall. She announces herself with dignity: "My name is Elizabeth Stock. I'm thirty-eight years old and unmarried, and not afraid or ashamed to say it" (587). Although she self-effacingly claims to have lost her job "mostly through my own negligence" (587), she actually becomes the tragic heroine of her story, braving an ice storm to take an important postcard to the town's leading citizen. The exposure to the elements causes her to become ill, and someone in Stonelift reports her for reading other people's postcards, although she claims it is "human nature" to "glance at" a postcard, and believes that "if a person had anything very particular and private to tell, they'd put it under a sealed envelope" (587).

As a writer, Elizabeth Stock composes her one story in private and then is silent, her life remaining a "sealed envelope," its contents disclosed only to the dismissive narrator. Yet in addition to setting Elizabeth against a literary tradition of which she cannot be a part, Chopin also suggests that her entire relationship with language is problematic. Most obviously, it is an act of reading—the postcard—that puts her job in jeopardy, and when she receives the letter that dismisses her from the position of postmistress, she resembles Edna Pontellier studying the envelope from Robert—she cannot trust herself to understand what it says and must ask Vince Wallace, her would-be suitor, to interpret it for her. When Elizabeth does read, it is a novel from her local library. She has not been educated to have sophisticated tastes in literature, and when she tries to think of plots for the stories she wants to write, she resembles Miss Witherwell in falling back on the formulas of popular fiction: "I tried to think of a railroad story with a wreck, but couldn't. No more could I make a tale out of a murder, or money getting stolen, or even mistaken identity" (587). For Elizabeth Stock (whose name suggests a storehouse of untold stories), education—and hence literature—is the province of men. The person who takes her job at the post office is a "poetical-natured young fellow" (590), and one of her regrets at losing her job is that she cannot continue to pay for the education of her nephew Danny, who was "full of ambition to study" (591).

As her own career attests, Kate Chopin was not, like Elizabeth Stock, excluded from literary culture; indeed, by the time she wrote this story her short fiction had received national acclaim, and she was soon to publish the novel for which she is best known today. Yet the largely negative reaction to *The Awakening* upon its publication could not have come as a complete surprise to her. However one interprets the message of the novel, Chopin took risks in both the content and style of her story, violating both social and literary conventions.[9] That she was a published author sets her apart from Elizabeth Stock, but her account of that character shows that she understood the exclusionary forces that could silence a woman writer. At the same time, however, characters such as Athénaïse and, to an extent, Edna Pontellier, who are motivated more by instinct than by reason, suggest that Chopin refused to privilege a masculine-identified discourse of intellectual analysis. Instead of being disadvantaged by not belonging to the world of "letters," Chopin posits, women may be freed to discover their own truths in their own ways.

Notes

1.   Donald A. Ringe, in an early article on *The Awakening* ("Romantic Imagery in Kate Chopin's *The Awakening*," *American Literature* 43[January 1972]:580–88), uses the reference to Emerson—along with other evidence in the novel—to support his reading of Edna as a woman going through a process of transcendental self-discovery, a process that culminates in the isolation of extreme individualism. Charles W. Mayer, in "Isabel Archer, Edna Pontellier, and the Romantic Self" (*Research Studies* 47, no. 2[June 1979]:89–97), makes a similar point. Assuming that Edna is reading Emerson's seminal essay *Nature,* which distinguishes between the "Me" and the "Not Me," Mayer suggests that Edna's struggle is with these two poles of exis-

tence, and that, lacking Emerson's faith in a transcendent God, she is vulnerable to "influences that tempt her to give up almost before the struggle has begun" (92). Other critics interpret Edna's sleepy response to Emerson's writing as a rejection of philosophical systems that do not meet her needs. Kenneth Eble posits that such a rejection parallels Edna's negative response to her father's Presbyterianism ("A Forgotten Novel: Kate Chopin's *The Awakening*," *Western Humanities Review* 10[Summer 1956]:261–69). More recently, Virginia M. Kouidis has argued that through Edna's response "Chopin uses Emerson . . . as representative of the system that denies Edna's aspiration," pointing to the "emphatic gender bias of the Emersonian tradition" ("Prison into Prism: Emerson's 'Many-Colored Lenses' and the Woman Writer of Early Modernism," in *The Green American Tradition: Essays and Poems for Sherman Paul,* ed. H. Daniel Peck [Baton Rouge: Louisiana State University Press, 1989], 118).

2. Kate Chopin, *The Complete Works of Kate Chopin,* ed. Per Seyersted, hardcover ed. (Baton Rouge: Louisiana State University Press, 1993), 955; hereafter cited in the text.

3. Emily Toth, *Kate Chopin* (New York: William Morrow, 1990), 53.

4. Apparently being read to aloud was a source of enjoyment for Chopin herself. In her essay "As You Like It," she reports being ordered by a doctor to rest her eyes for a period of time, and notes that "There is something very pleasing and restful in being read to" (*Complete Works,* 709).

5. Patricia S. Yaeger, " 'A Language Which Nobody Understood': Emancipatory Strategies in *The Awakening*," in *Kate Chopin: "The Awakening."* Case Studies in Contemporary Criticism, ed. Nancy A. Walker (Boston: Bedford Books of St. Martin's Press, 1993), 286.

6. Chopin herself was a skilled writer of letters, and one of the factors in her decision to write fiction after the death of Oscar Chopin was the encouragement of friends in St. Louis who had received her letters from Louisiana. See Toth, *Kate Chopin,* 174–75.

7. Although the twenty-three stories in *A Vocation and a Voice* were included in Per Seyersted's 1969 two-volume *Complete Works,* the collection that Chopin envisioned was not published until the Penguin Classics edition of 1991, edited by Toth.

8. Nathaniel Hawthorne, *Letters of Hawthorne to William D. Ticknor, 1851–1864* (Newark: The Carteret Book Club, 1910), 1: 78.

9. For a summary of the kinds of risks Chopin took when she wrote *The Awakening,* see Elaine Showalter's essay "Tradition and the Female Talent: *The Awakening* as a Solitary Book," in Walker, "Case Studies," esp. 177–82.

PICTURE PERFECT: PAINTING IN *THE AWAKENING*

KATHRYN LEE SEIDEL

For the last fifteen years, contemporary literary critics have begun the process of examining the metaphors that writers use to describe the creative process as it applies to women. The publication of Sandra Gilbert and Susan Gubar's analysis of 19th-century fiction, *The Madwoman in the Attic: The Woman Writer and the Literary Imagination* (1979), inaugurated a decade of critical studies in which the female protagonist in fiction is seen as an artist figure who often represents the author herself. In this paradigm, the novel's central character is often silenced by the men who try to define and control her. In *Tomorrow Is Another Day: The Woman Writer in the South, 1859–1936* (1981), Anne Goodwyn Jones examines several novels of the American South written by women. Jones asserts that Southern women writers often create characters whose boldness is a projection of the authors' creative aspirations. More recently, Marianne Hirsch, in *Mother/Daughter Plot: Narrative, Psychoanalysis, Feminism* (1989), describes how the female protagonist with artistic ambitions must differentiate herself from her mother, the voice of patriarchal society, to assert her individual identity. The parallel of the main character's problems to the plight of the woman writer becomes the focus of much of this criticism.

Some authors, however, overtly portray women actively at work as artists—musicians, painters, and so on—who create "folk art," fine arts, and what can be called the art of the everyday. In so doing, these authors have their artist engage in a dialogue with the art world, that elite of critics, patrons, and dealers whose roles are dedicated to the preservation of art as a precious commodity. Art critics, until relatively recently, have been guardians of the European artistic tradition, which emphasizes exclusivity and a formalist evaluation of art.[1] For example, in 1913 Clive Bell wrote, "The representative element in a work of art may or may not be harmful, but it is always irrelevant. For to appreciate a work of art, we must bring with us nothing

This essay was written specifically for this volume and is published here for the first time by permission of the author.

from life, no knowledge of its affairs and ideas, no familiarity with its emotions."[2]

In addition to standard notions of what constitutes art and how it is evaluated, women artists from the recent past to the present face limitations of time, accessibility of materials, and training. Such an artist often must create her art without "models," as Alice Walker writes in *In Search of Our Mothers' Gardens* (1984), and without awareness of the tradition of female creativity. In fiction, the woman artist creates in the midst of these forces, which are often personified in her family, friends, and mentors. These people join with art critics and patrons, speaking with great authority regarding the subjects, intentions, and outcomes of art. They often support the conventional notion that art is exclusive and unique, that its value is determined by its inaccessibility, or as John Berger writes, that it is a commodity to be hung in a museum or private home, not used or made accessible to the populace except as an object of awe.[3] The work of Joanna Russ in her book, *How to Suppress Women's Writing* (1983), can be adapted to summarize the components of the intricate process by which women fiction writers are devalued and suppressed:

—informal prohibitions (including discouragement and the inaccessibility of materials and training) . . . ,
—belittlement of the work in various ways,
—isolation of the work from the tradition to which it belongs . . . ,
—assertions that the work indicates the author's bad character and hence is primarily of scandalous interest,
—and simply ignoring the works, the workers, and the whole tradition.[4]

Who can be an artist, what is defined as art, and who owns art are culturally based questions. In fiction, even when the woman artist is producing conventional forms such as water colors and oil paintings, she faces a variety of impediments from her critics. She must contend with lack of privacy, space, materials, and education, as Virginia Woolf points out in *A Room of One's Own* (1929): the great women writers "live in you and in me, and in many other women writers who are not here tonight, for they are washing up the dishes and putting the children to bed"; women writers must "have five hundred a year . . . and rooms of [their] own."[5] Female artists must determine whether their art will pose a challenge to their family and to their culture's definition of the role of women. They must select an artistic tradition in which to work—be it the convention of the day, an individualized selection, or the communal voice of a selected group.

One writer who raises these concerns is Kate Chopin in *The Awakening*. Writing at the turn of the century, Chopin was well aware of the cultural legacy that favored male-centered painting, yet she was also aware that women painted, primarily to please their families, less frequently to earn their living, and occasionally to please themselves. She knew well that few female artists could leave father, husband, and friends and journey to Paris, then the magnetic pole for female artists who chose to leave the milieus of their origins.[6] The female-centered support of like-minded women artists would not appear until the 20th century. The late 19th century, however, was a time when a woman artist who rejected the paternalistic patterns chose isolation in doing so.

When reading *The Awakening,* one is so struck by Edna Pontellier's overwhelming discovery of her own sexuality that it is easy to overlook her artistic awakening and her attempts to nurture her creative ability. Edna appears to have the economic prerequisites that Woolf defines as essential to the artist: as the wife of a wealthy man she has income, she has servants to cook and provide child care, and she has ample education. She has time, space, and money, and despite the impediments to her development as a painter voiced by her family and friends, she develops nonetheless. The growth of her art is characterized by three distinct stages: her early mimetic work that reinforces the paternalistic values of her culture; her rebellious portraits; and her daring, original drawings that she creates after moving into her own house.

Early in the novel, the narrator reports that Edna is sketching, an activity that "she sometimes dabbled with in an unprofessional way."[7] The narrator's comment appears to belittle Edna's efforts until we read that "she liked the dabbling. She felt in it satisfaction of a kind which no other employment afforded her" (891). Edna's initial motive for creating art is not merely to have a pastime but to engage in a positive, pleasurable endeavor. Moreover, she begins to wish to improve. Selecting Madame Ratignolle as her subject, Edna proceeds to attempt to imitate the great masters by perceiving her as a "sensuous Madonna" (891). Her choice of her close friend as her model, depicted in a conventional pictorial mode, is well within the accepted subjects for a woman painter. Edna's technique shows "natural aptitude" (891), according to the narrator, and this observation is corroborated by Robert, who says, "*elle a de la force*" (891). These two judgments of Edna's early efforts suggest a positive assessment of her abilities.

Adèle Ratignolle, on the other hand, is disappointed that the work does not look like herself; she expected a mimetic, realistic drawing. Is her comment one that indicates Edna's flawed technique, or is Edna attempting a more impressionist sketch? Edna said she wished to capture the Madonna-like essence of Adèle, so Edna's purpose was not photographic realism. When Edna then crumples the sketch, she does not do so because it does not look like Adèle or because Adèle criticized it; her reason is that the sketch does not capture this intangible quality. In the 19th century, European and American painting was challenging the tradition of mimetic realism. The impressionists were already known throughout America, and it is likely that Chopin's intellectual circle was well aware of their work. According to Emily Toth, Chopin was certain to have seen a mural painted by impressionist Mary Cassatt at an exposition in 1893.[8] Moreover, Chopin's friends in the salons of St. Louis knew of the Aesthetes such as Walter Pater and later Oscar Wilde, who urged the doctrine of "art for art's sake" in which a work of art is judged not by its moral stance or its reproduction of reality but by the qualities of beauty that produce a strong response in the viewer.[9] Edna's concept of artistic expression appears closer to that of the Aesthetes and impressionists than the realists.

Not only does Edna's technique bring criticism from Adèle, but she also urges a conventional motive for painting. Adèle's concept of the proper role for the woman artist is expressed in her own pleasant piano accompaniment, which she says is "a means of brightening the home and making it attractive" (904). To her, the role of art for women is domestic decoration. In this Adèle and Léonce Pontellier, Edna's husband, agree absolutely—the Pontellier house is filled with paintings and statues that give him the "genuine pleasure" of having "bought" and possessed them (931). Pontellier becomes angry because Edna's increasing devotion of her time to art removes her from the family and also because her claim to privacy prevents her art from accruing to the inventory of his possessions. Moreover, her physical absence annoys him because he believes Edna must be physically available to him at all times—recall the scene in chapter III in which he awakens Edna in order to chat about his day. Pontellier regards her body as his to command; Edna's desire to paint is an assertion that she wishes to own her own body. Edna wishes to possess her art, not give it to her husband to possess and display, just as she wishes to regard her body as her own.

Emblematic of her increasing concern for her paintings is her enhanced critical attitude toward them. A person who otherwise thinks about herself only vaguely, Edna scrutinizes the "shortcomings and defects" of her art (936). Gathering a number of sketches, she visits Adèle and asks her opinion of them. In this, she seeks the "praise and encouragement" (937) of a woman, a sign of Edna's need to be part of a community of artists who take seriously art produced by women. Edna is also giving Adèle her final test, and her last chance, to be the kind of friend she needs: one who will urge her to study painting seriously. Adèle, however, lacks the ability to see the art as anything other than a decorative commodity to enhance the middle-class home. She selects the Bavarian peasant, perhaps the most sentimental of the lot, and the basket of apples as "worthy of framing and . . . lifelike" (937). Her aesthetics remain mimetic, her tastes saccharine. Moreover, as Doris Davis insightfully indicates, Adèle's vocabulary regarding the art uses the words *worth, value,* and *exhibited,* thus underscoring its monetary aspects.[10] When Adèle shows the two sketches to her husband, Adèle has done what she recommends Edna should be doing—displaying the art for the pleasure of her husband, who is its rightful owner and its only appropriate critic. At this point Edna presents the sketches to Adèle, an act that ends the first phase of Edna's artistic development. Edna is finished with the decorative arts of domesticity, just as she is certainly finished with her current domestic situation. Adèle wants to turn art into a domestic commodity; Edna refuses to do so, just as she rejects being another object of art to be owned by her husband.

Indeed, the second phase of her art begins in the very next chapter when Edna quarrels with Léonce. She spends increasing time in her attic, painting. Her husband perceives her as another madwoman in the attic: "it seems to me the utmost folly . . . to spend in an atelier days which would be better employed contriving for the comfort of her family" (939). Comparing her with Adèle, Pontellier enjoins her to paint for her family, not to be sequestered in the attic. " 'I feel like painting,' " Edna says, to which Pontellier replies, " 'then in God's name paint! But don't let the family go to the devil' " (939). When this argument has no effect on Edna, Pontellier changes the ground of his argument to that of amateur art criticism, telling Edna Adèle is " 'more of a musician than you are a painter' " (939). Unsupported by Léonce, Edna now paints in defiance of his wishes and in spite of his negative assessment of her ability.

In her bright and cheerful atelier, she now works with "great energy and interest" (939), exploring new subjects for her art. She first paints her children, then the "quadroon" maid, then the housemaid whom Edna perceives has a "back and shoulders . . . molded on classic lines," and whose "hair, loosened from its confining cap, became an inspiration" (940). These choices are increasingly bold, a far cry from the ficticious and stereotypical Bavarian peasants she gave to Adèle. Moreover, the loosening of the maid's hair suggests the physical freedom Edna feels as well as her increasing sense of power over her models and materials. Edna's decision to paint an African-American woman is a daring choice of subject. Not displayed as a slave (that is, a possession, as was typical of artistic representations of Blacks) nor as a figure in the background (an artistic convention of paintings such as Titian's *Venus of Urbino* and Rembrandt's *Bathsheba and Her Maid*), this woman addresses the canvas as the sole model. In fact, it would be many years before American and European painters featured such subjects in the foreground.[11]

Not only are her pictures showing new subjects, but she also begins to have a new feeling as she paints. She feels a "current of desire" (940) as she creates; she feels "happy to be alive" (940). Noting Edna's happiness when painting, Cynthia Griffin Woolf comments that Edna's art does not engage her in the world but rather allows her to remain passively frozen in the bliss of orality.[12] The evidence shows, however, that, because of her painting, her connections to others become significant.

Unlike many women artists, Edna has the advantage of having an artistic role model, Mademoiselle Reisz. In contrast to Adèle, for whom music is a pastime to amuse her family, Reisz is an artist whose work is scrutinized by the public; she is a pianist who is respected for her passionate playing. Although she is much in demand among the upper middle class for after-dinner entertainments, Reisz can never play in concert or make much money as a musician, because such public performances were considered unseemly for a woman. Although Reisz knows the limitations of her society upon the woman artist, she encourages Edna to continue to paint. The choice between art and family, however, is one with which Reisz cannot help Edna; Reisz has chosen to be forever single, just as Edna, by default, has already made the opposite choice, since her marriage and children are irreversible. In this society, a woman must choose between these alternatives. When Edna tells Mlle. Reisz that she wants to be a painter, the older woman laughs and says that an artist must "possess a courageous soul ... that dares and defies" (946). This ambiguous statement goads Edna to attempt not only to defy her marriage vows but also to expand her artistic repertoire. Joanna Frueh has pointed out that art created by men is evaluated positively if it is heroic and "defiant."[13] Whitney Chadwick in "Women Artists and the Politics of Representation" argues that conventional art historians have preferred the "masterpiece," an art work whose subject is a male who defines masculinity as dominant, powerful, and potentially violent or whose subject is a female who is subordinated by the gaze of the (male) artist/viewer, who assumes the dominant role.[14] Mademoiselle's advice urges Edna to take this approach to her art. Yet Edna continues to see her art as self-expression and as a way of understanding herself and her close relationships. These motives for art are the values associated with female artists, according to Frueh. Thus, as a role model, Reisz urges a conceptualization of art that ironically repeats the patriarchal patterns Edna is attempting to understand and, later, to elude.

As Edna comes closer to an adulterous relationship with Alcée Arobin, she becomes more experimental with her painting. No longer interested in the safe content for women's art—scenery and portraits of friends—she attempts to sketch her dour Calvinistic father. Chopin gives an original account of the female artist with the male model: under Edna's gaze, her father sits "rigid and unflinching, as he had faced the cannon's mouth in days gone by" (950). The comparison of his facing Edna to facing a cannon reveals that, metaphorically, Edna as an artist has power and control over him, a situation much changed from her meekness with him when she was a child. The fact that he faces the cannon's *mouth* suggests Edna could devour him if she chose, a metaphor for women's power. Moreover, her ability to render her father motionless echoes the myth of the Medusa, whose gaze paralyzes men who see her. By painting her father, Edna gains the ability to define him, to control his image before the world. Perhaps because they are at last on an equal footing, the sessions allow Edna to feel warmly toward her father for the first time in her life, and her art begins a process of healing the rift between them.

When Edna moves out of her husband's mansion into the small home she calls her pigeon house, she appears to have the freedom to paint as she desires. Having obtained "a room of her own," Edna works hard. Laidpore, an art dealer, reports that her work has grown "in form and individuality" (963.) We are not told much about what she paints, only that she is far more satisfied with her efforts than she was before. The narrator reports, "she began to look with her own eyes, to see and to apprehend the deeper undercurrents of life" (978). The one work of art about which we do learn, however, is significant. She chooses another male as her subject, deciding to sketch the head of her lover, Alcée Arobin. She asks him for a photograph so that she might study it when he could not sit for her. This apparently innocuous request leads to an incident that greatly influences her relationship with Robert Lebrun, the man she loves. Robert discovers the photograph, and as in polite Creole society, a wife and mother should not be painting the head of a man who is not her husband or father, the discovery works as a plot device with which Chopin ensures Robert's discovery of Edna's affair with Arobin. The conventions of what women were allowed to paint reveal Edna's indiscretion.

Alcée interrupts Robert and Edna at the very moment Robert has discovered the photograph. Edna asks that Alcée take it back, as a way of rejecting him. Alcée reluctantly agrees. He recognizes the photograph as an icon of his relationship with Edna, and his reluctance to retrieve it indicates his desire to continue the affair and not be superceded by Robert. He leaves, recognizing that he has been rejected and that their affair is at an end.

Edna nonetheless works consistently at her painting. She finds a dealer with whom she negotiates the sale of some studies, and a rumor floats about that she plans to study in Paris. Her work achieves some recognition beyond her domestic circle; it even sells. Edna needs this income, reporting that she is able to pay for the pigeon house entirely herself with her trust and with the income from her art. The monetary motive does not mean that she abandons the motive of self-discovery; on the contrary, that motive appears to have given her art power and passion. The sale of these sketches puzzles critic John Carlos Rowe, who asserts that their sale confirms the opinion that they are of subjects so banal that only her friends stoop to buy them.[15] He forgets Edna's gift of her most conventional sketches to Adèle; her later works of her maid, her father, and Arobin are personal and unconventional signs of her growing mastery of her environment and her art. Rowe states that for the "moderns" such as Stein, James, Woolf, and Eliot, a woman's identity is created by her making art, and that Edna fails the test of modernism in that what she makes is not art. But Edna's later work reveals, to the contrary, that she *does* create art, not banality, and is indeed a would-be modern who defines herself through art. The limitations of the patriarchal gaze can cloud the vision even of those who in other ways are well-respected commentators. Barbara C. Ewell more accurately concludes that Edna cannot fulfill her promise as a painter.[16] Joyce Coyne Dyer agrees, noting that Edna's painting increases in "confidence, originality, and sensuality," but that "she does not succeed in becoming an artist."[17] Edna does create her art as a way of creating herself. Becoming a worker, a producer, not a mere emblem of her husband's wealth as a leisure-class wife, she resists seeing herself as a work of art and thus a commodity. Her art follows the Byronesque conceptualization of the artist as alienated and alone; the contemporary concept of art as enhancing community is not available to Edna, as the community of artists represented by Adèle supports only the conventional, while the community offered by Mlle. Reisz is eccentric and leads to isolation.[18]

Having made this progress, Edna nonetheless commits suicide; her motives for doing so are a complex puzzle. With regard to the relationship of Edna's artistic awakening and the suicide, critics have had little to say. Carole Stone charts the contrast between biologic and artistic creativity, pointing out that Adèle's giving birth reminds Edna of the "torture" of both types of creativity.[19] Had the novel ended prior to the suicide, the image of Edna as a newborn, "naked in the open air" (1000), would accord well with the theme Nancy Walker identifies in contemporary fiction in which "the central character becomes an artist of some sort, the profession serving as both a metaphor for self-creation and the tangible embodiment of dreams and fantasies."[20]

Throughout *The Awakening,* Edna takes positive, aggressive actions to learn her art, even in the face of hostile critics. She improves as an artist, and with her portraits of her father and her lover, achieves an autonomy and control over them and herself, a self-assurance she does not usually have in the other aspects of her life. Ultimately, however, for Edna not artistic expression nor love, friendship, or sex can reconcile her creativity, her personal growth, the expectations of her society, and her own tortured sense of self. When she acts as an artist she feels her strength, but she cannot transfer this knowledge to other aspects of her life.

Edna's inability to find a resolution is less related to her being trapped by 19th-century convention than to what Sandra Gilbert and Susan Gubar identify as the anxiety of 20th-century women writers who oscillate "between their matrilineage and their patrilineage in an arduous process of self definition."[21] Edna certainly must reconcile the stern Calvinism of her father, the patriarchal, proprietary assumptions of her husband, and the biological demands of her own motherhood. Her pseudo-mothers, Adèle and Mlle. Reisz, cannot nurture her, for they also represent female traditions with which Edna is uncomfortable. One is the smothering motherhood of Creole women, utterly devoted to their pregnant bodies and to their offspring. The other is that of the female artist as unnatural outcast, living as a madwoman in the attic, with her bubbling cauldron of hot, sweet chocolate a poor substitute for fulfilling human relationships. Lacking a mother whom she remembers, Edna looks to the two female-centered models offered by her milieu, but neither can assist Edna in what she must do to be able to live and thrive: she must give birth to a new female-centered model of creativity, not one subsumed by biology nor one in which she is transformed by the patriarchy into a work of art.

The image of this new self being born is the description of Edna naked in the open air. The scene alludes to the transcendentalist essential self, alone and at one with nature. But the image also derives its power from the cultural icon of Botticelli's *The Birth of Venus,* which presents the female naked, a woman created out of the foam. Chopin's references to Italian art which include "sensuous madonnas" and "an Italian character study" that Edna sketches end with this allusion to Botticelli's famous painting. As Sandra M. Gilbert has written, Chopin carefully alludes to the Venus archetype.[22] She had anticipated it in a comment offered by Victor, who recalls the night of her splendid dinner; he reflects that "Venus rising from the foam could have presented no more entrancing a spectacle than Mrs. Pontellier, blazing with beauty and diamonds . . ." (997). Seeking an image in Western culture of the naked woman, Chopin chose this well-known icon. Goddess of love, Venus has her own autonomy and establishes her own traditions. As an image of birth, the final scene shows not the birth of an infant but the birth of a fully grown adult. As Venus, joined with the sensuous "embrace" of the sea, Edna completes the imagery of water as a medium for birth and creativity. A creature of the foam, Edna as Venus cannot live on the land; she is a phenomenon, a unique creation, without a like people and without a land she can call home. Grande Isle, as Gilbert and Gubar have proposed, is a woman-centered island, a her-land, but it is a land for sensuous Madonnas, not for Venus. Edna has created herself, and this act precludes any hope of her joining others like herself. Her birth as a new self creates a life that can live for only a few moments before the foam that gave it birth softly annihilates it.

Notes

1. Comment on the art world is found in Tom Wolfe, *The Painted Word* (New York: Farrar, Straus and Giroux, 1975) and in Germaine Greer, *The Obstacle Race* (New York: Farrar, Straus and Giroux, 1979).

2. Clive Bell, *Art* (1913; reprint, New York: Capricorn, 1958), 27.

3. John Berger, *Ways of Seeing* (London: British Broadcasting Corporation and Penguin Books, 1972), 22.

4. Joanna Russ, *How to Suppress Women's Writing* (Austin: University of Texas Press, 1983), 5.

5. Virginia Woolf, *A Room of One's Own* (1929; reprint, New York: Harcourt, Brace, Jovanovich, 1951), 117.

6. Shari Benstock, *Women on the Left Bank, Paris, 1900–1940* (Austin: University of Texas Press, 1986).

7. Kate Chopin, *The Awakening* in *The Complete Works of Kate Chopin,* ed. Per Seyersted, hardcover ed. (Baton Rouge: Louisiana State University Press, 1993), 891; hereafter cited in the text.

8. Emily Toth, *Kate Chopin* (New York: William Morrow), 221.

9. See for example Walter Pater's *The Renaissance* and Oscar Wilde's "Preface" to *The Picture of Dorian Gray.*

10. Doris Davis, "*The Awakening:* The Economics of Tension," in *Perspectives on Kate Chopin,* ed. K. Kearns. (Natchitoches, La.: Northwestern State University Press, 1990), 127–59.

11. See for example an essay by Lorraine O'Grady, "Olympia's Maid: Reclaiming Black Female Subjectivity," in *New Feminist Criticism: Art, Identity, Action,* ed. Joanna Frueh, Cassandra L. Langer, and Arlene Raven. (New York: Icon Editions, 1994), 152–70.

12. Cynthia Griffin Woolf, "Thanatos and Eros: Kate Chopin's *The Awakening,*" *American Quarterly* 25(October 1993):449–71.

13. Joanna Frueh, "The Dangerous Sex: Art, Language and Male Power," *Women Artists News* 10, no. 5–6(September 1985):10.

14. Whitney Chadwick, "Women Artists and the Politics of Representation," in *Feminist Art Criticism: An Anthology,* ed. Arlene Raven, Cassandra Langer, Joanna Frueh. (New York: HarperCollins, 1991), 171.

15. John Carlos Rowe. "The Economics of the Body in Kate Chopin's *The Awakening,*" in *Kate Chopin Reconsidered: Beyond the Bayou,* ed. Lynda S. Boren and Sara deSaussure Davis (Baton Rouge: Louisiana State University Press, 1992), 136.

16. Barbara C. Ewell, *Kate Chopin* (New York: Ungar, 1986), 154.

17. Joyce [Coyne] Dyer. *The Awakening: A Novel of Beginnings* (New York: Twayne, 1993), 93.

18. Reisz may also represent the community of "unnatural" women, the lesbian artist figure, as I have argued in my essay, "Art Is an Unnatural Act: Mademoiselle Reisz in *The Awakening,*" *The Mississippi Quarterly* 46(Spring 1993):199–214.

19. Carole Stone, "The Female Artist in Kate Chopin's *The Awakening:* Birth and Creativity," *Women's Studies* 13(December 1986):23–32.

20. Nancy Walker. *Feminist Alternatives: Irony and Fantasy in the Contemporary Novel by Women* (Jackson, Miss.: University Press of Mississippi, 1990), 134.

21. Sandra Gilbert and Susan Gubar, *The Madwoman in the Attic: The Woman Writer and the Nineteenth-Century Literary Imagination* (New Haven: Yale University Press, 1979), 169.

22. Sandra M. Gilbert, "The Second Coming of Aphrodite: Kate Chopin's Fantasy of Desire," *Kenyon Review* N.S. 5(Summer 1983):3–54.

LAND'S END: *THE AWAKENING*
AND 19TH-CENTURY LITERARY TRADITION

PRISCILLA LEDER

Readers who discover Kate Chopin's 1899 novel *The Awakening*—from the scholars of the 1960s and 1970s who rescued it from obscurity to the undergraduates of the 1990s who encounter it in survey classes—often find it remarkably "modern." In 1962, Edmund Wilson declared it "a very odd book to have been written in America at the end of the nineteenth century."[1] Since Wilson wrote this statement, however, critics have discovered in the novel elements of such 19th-century movements as romanticism, transcendentalism, realism, local color, and naturalism and have compared Chopin to 19th-century writers ranging from Whitman to Dreiser.[2] In a 1988 essay on teaching *The Awakening,* Peggy Skaggs aptly summarized much of this criticism, declaring that "this novel can be viewed as both a product and a climax of 19th-century American literary tendencies."[3] Skaggs's brief concluding remark provides a point of departure for this essay, which will demonstrate how Chopin incorporates elements of the major literary and intellectual movements of her century while consistently demonstrating their limitations. In doing so, she creates a work that is very much of the end of the century— at once part of it and looking beyond. The novel's complex explorations of the intellectual climate of the 1800s parallel Edna Pontellier's search through various sources for meaning in her life. In telling the story of a 19th-century woman who searches for but fails to find a mode of living that allows for full expression of her being, Chopin reveals how the literary modes of her century prove inadequate.

Edna begins her journey by discovering the limitations of domesticity as exemplified by the confining roles of wife and "mother-woman"; Chopin approached her novel from a background of local color and domestic fiction but with a sense of its limitations. Edna learns to appreciate and assert her sexuality, but her own experiences and the ordeal of Adèle Ratignolle's childbirth teach her that sexuality also limits her. Chopin's depiction of Edna's sex-

This essay was written specifically for this volume and is published here for the first time by permission of the author.

ual education evokes literary naturalism, which liberates by acknowledging the power of sexuality but limits by reducing it to an inexorable force, often destructive of women. At the same time, through her seaside musings and her friendship with Robert Lebrun, Edna becomes conscious of a deeper significance within herself and nature. Chopin describes this dawning consciousness in language reminiscent of Emerson; however, as that language reveals, Edna finally cannot sustain Emerson's evanescent doctrine of the infusion of the divine in and through all things. With Edna's failure, Chopin demonstrates the impossibility of the transcendental vision. All of these explorations take place simultaneously and end when Edna swims out to sea to escape the limitations that have thwarted her.

Edna's developing self-awareness begins with an increasing consciousness of what she has previously taken for granted—her social position as an upper-middle-class urban woman and her difference from the members of the Creole culture of her husband. Chopin began *The Awakening* conscious of her own reputation as a writer of realistic fiction and perhaps already dissatisfied with its limitations. During the previous four years she had published two collections of realistic local color fiction, *Bayou Folk* and *A Night in Acadie*. Although both works were generally well received, the reviews often dwelt on the region to the neglect of the writer. According to Emily Toth, the first review of *Bayou Folk*, in the *New York Times* of 1 April 1894, "devoted all but two sentences to pronouncements about Louisiana life and culture—many of them wrong."[4] Though an extreme example, the *Times* review is in many ways typical: Chopin's reviewers often emphasized "charm," "picturesque situations," and "that subtle, alien quality which holds the Creole apart."[5] In doing so, they slighted Chopin's artistry while ostensibly praising it, describing some sketches as "rude cartoons whose very rudeness brings out a more vivid effect," or as "just a brief incident of [*sic*] idea sketched in with a few rapid strokes," as if the stories were tossed off casually, with little effort.[6] In June of 1894, Chopin complained to her diary about the reviews of *Bayou Folk*, remarking upon the "very small number which show anything like a worthy critical faculty."[7] Her comments on local color in her October 1894 review of Hamlin Garland's essay collection *Crumbling Idols* suggest the source of her dissatisfaction with those reviews. Chopin asserted that "social problems, social environments, local color and the rest of it are not *of themselves* motives to insure the survival of a writer who employs them."[8] Given that belief, she must have found critics' emphasis on the local and the picturesque in her own work frustrating.

Works that survived, Chopin believed, expressed some lasting, underlying truth about unchanging "human impulses." Realism and local color, on the other hand, emphasized the particular, what Chopin called the "mutable."[9] In keeping with this emphasis, neither form reflected or created a coherent world view. Rather, they were defined in terms of style and technique. Eric Sundquist points out that "American realism virtually has no school; its most dominating and influential advocate, William Dean Howells, often seems to ride along in a strange vacuum, nearly unheeded in his continual insistence on the proprieties of the everyday, stable characterization, and moral certainty. . . ."[10] As Sundquist implies, Howells emphasizes the limits of the appropriate rather than postulating any underlying philosophy or purpose for the writer.

Chopin began *The Awakening* with a sense of the limitations of realism and local color. In the course of the novel, Edna's painting dramatizes the struggle to transcend those limitations. In one scene, Adèle Ratignolle comments enthusiastically on the realistic qualities of Edna's paintings:

> "Surely, this Bavarian peasant is worthy of framing; and this basket of apples! never have I seen anything more lifelike. One might almost be tempted to reach out a hand and take one."
>
> Edna could not control a feeling which bordered upon complacency at her friend's praise, even realizing, as she did, its true worth.[11]

No doubt Edna feels that Adèle's opinion lacks value because of her lack of expertise. Given Adèle's enthusiasm for the works' verisimilitude, we may also surmise that the "complacency" that tempts Edna is the impulse to be satisfied with the successful depiction of surfaces.

Adèle serves as model as well as critic. In a scene in which Edna exercises her "natural aptitude" for painting, she produces a likeness that disappoints Adèle because it does not resemble her. The painting also fails to satisfy Edna, perhaps because it does not capture the Madonna-like quality that she saw in her friend (891). Chopin thus evokes two standards of judgment often applied to realistic and local color fiction—that it resemble its subject and that it express a "pure" ideal.

As Chopin describes them, Edna's subsequent subjects seem very much defined by the social roles assigned to them. In posing for Edna, the children's quadroon nurse remains "patient as a savage" (939). And Edna's father, a Kentucky colonel reminiscent of Colonel Grangerford in *Huckleberry Finn*, literally constrains himself to maintain his image:

> He resented the intrusion of the children, who gaped with wondering eyes at him, sitting so stiff up there in their mother's bright atelier. When they drew near he motioned them away with an expressive action of the foot, loath to disturb the fixed lines of his countenance, his arms, or his rigid shoulders. (950–51)

Besides Adèle's discredited praise, these descriptions of Edna's subjects are all Chopin reveals of the actual appearance of Edna's paintings. This emphasis upon subject emphasizes verisimilitude; moreover, it invites us to associate Edna's art with the social status of her subjects.

Though the act of painting gratifies her, and her work, according to her teacher, "grows in force and individuality," Edna's art never affords her lasting fulfillment or a reason for living. Unwilling to live for her art, Chopin implies, Edna never becomes a "true" artist. Mademoiselle Reisz, the musician, serves as both judge of and standard for "true" artistry. As judge, she tells Edna that she has "pretensions" in aspiring to become an artist and warns her that "to succeed, the artist must possess . . . the soul that dares and defies" and the wings to "soar above the level plain of tradition and prejudice" (946, 966). On one level, Mlle. Reisz's remarks refer to the artist's life: the artist, especially a woman artist of that time, must be willing to forgo conventional social and economic rewards, as she herself has done. However, taken in the context of Mlle. Reisz's own artistry, "the level plain of tradition and prejudice" also suggests the limitations of artistic convention, which Edna cannot seem to escape any more than she can escape social convention.

Just before Edna hears Mlle. Reisz play for the first time, Chopin tells us that "Edna was what she herself called very fond of music. Musical strains, well rendered, had a way of evoking pictures in her mind" (906). In fact, the playing of the conventional Adèle evokes four rather conventional "pictures," which Chopin describes, including that of a solitary man watching in "hopeless resignation" as a distant bird wings away from him. But when Mlle. Reisz begins to play, Edna waits in vain for "the material pictures which she thought would gather and blaze before her imagination" (906). Instead, she finds that the music conveys emotion directly rather than evoking "pictures." True artists, like Mlle. Reisz and Fréderic Chopin, whose music she plays, go beyond "material pictures" to leave "an impress of abiding truth." Edna (perhaps for the first time, the author tells us) is ready to receive this truth, but her own pictures (i.e., her paintings) never attain the force necessary to convey it.

Through her depiction of Edna's artistic "pretensions," Chopin exposes the limitations of the literary forms that made her reputation but that, she believed, could never confer immortality on an artist because they failed to convey a universal truth. Not surprisingly, she also explores the literary movements of her time—naturalism and transcendentalism—which developed literary forms based on what they considered to be such truths. For naturalists, truth was revealed through the scientific method of detached observation and articulated in the scientific laws that were being discovered through such observations of human behavior.

In *The Practice of Fiction in America,* Jerome Klinkowitz observes that *The Awakening* incorporates elements of all the major American literary movements of the 19th century and concludes that naturalism predominates.

The book stands simply as an advance in American literature, and the areas of its achievement are clearly ones pioneered by naturalism. So many of the devices of the naturalistic novel are operative—influences of heredity and environment, exposure to a new and threatening environment which in turn brings out animal instincts, a frank treatment of those instincts, a descent on the social scale to find more vital life, the presence of an understanding man of science, and a solution like so many other naturalistic novels, where the central figure is at the conclusion swept up into the book's controlling images. . . .[12]

Klinkowitz catalogs major naturalistic devices, but his own discussion of *The Awakening* tends to describe the action rather than demonstrate exactly how those devices drive it. In fact, some of the naturalistic devices Klinkowitz names are figments of his interpretation. Where Chopin does evoke naturalism, she demonstrates its limitations.

Except for Léonce's casual remark that he comes "of tough fiber," Chopin makes no mention of heredity (947). Of course, Edna's gender and, presumably, her sexual drive, is inborn, but strictly naturalistic fiction often attributes very specific behavior to inherited tendencies. For example, Frank Norris's Trina McTeague has "all the instinct of a hardy and penurious mountain race—the instinct which saves . . . for the sake of saving, hoarding without knowing why."[13] In combination with the circumstances of Trina's life, that "instinct" comes to possess her and ultimately helps destroy her. No such specific inherited instinct ever grips Edna.

Although she is not driven by heredity, environment does affect her, and a new environment arouses impulses previously repressed. At the resort on Grand Isle, she responds to the ease and physical stimulation of a beach vacation as well as to the human environment created by the Creoles. Edna feels some confusion and wonder at their relative sexual openness: "their entire absence of prudery," their indulgence in playful flirtation, and their physical expression of affection.[14] In this atmosphere of ease and openness, she begins to feel desire for Robert and to think about her own emotional history—when Adèle strokes her hand, for example, she recalls her youthful tendency toward infatuation. Furthermore, the faintly exotic environment allows for a play of fantasy that evokes new possibilities: after her nap on the *Chênière*, Edna imagines herself awakened to a new world whose only familiar inhabitant is Robert (919); even after her return to New Orleans, she captivates a dinner party with a story "of a woman who paddled away with her lover one night in a pirogue and never came back" (953).

Though it helps to shape her destiny, Edna's new environment is not "threatening," as Klinkowitz asserts, nor does it resemble the "threatening" environments that confront women characters in the novels of the American naturalists who were Chopin's contemporaries. Theodore Dreiser's Carrie Meeber and Hamlin Garland's Rose Dutcher both travel to Chicago to make their ways in the world, and both feel overwhelmed by what they experience. As Rose's train rolls into Chicago, she perceives "Webs of railway tracks spread out dangerously in acres of marvelous intricacy, amid which men moved, sooty, grimy, sullen and sickly. Terrors thickened. . . . The darkness grew, making the tangle and tumult a deadly struggle."[15] The mysterious, complex city threatens the uninitiated newcomer, who reacts with a primitive awe and fear of the unknown. That fear (and the similar feeling that grips Carrie at the beginning of her search for employment) typifies the "instinctive" response that naturalistic novelists so frequently depict.[16]

For Rose and Carrie, Chicago calls up another instinct—that of survival. As they explore the city, each finds herself challenged to aspire to wealth and fame. Carrie, for example, "long[s] for dress and beauty with a whole and fulsome heart."[17] Of course, pretty clothes and fashionable furniture are hardly necessary for survival, yet they mark the fittest like the plumes of an exotic bird. Dreiser presents Carrie's decision to become Drouet's mistress as a victory of "instinct and desire," while showing that she is compelled as much by the security, comfort, and luxury he represents as by sexual desire.[18] Like Carrie, Rose feels challenged by the city. Gazing at the houses on Lake Shore Drive, "She turned and faced them with set teeth and a singular look in her half-closed eyes, and in her heart she said: 'Before I die I'll go where I please in this city. I'll be counted as good as any of you—poor as I am.' "[19] Garland's language pictures Rose as an animal preparing for a fight. The "instincts" Rose and Carrie display, and even Trina's "instinctive" hoarding, are all part of the need to protect the self against threats and to respond to challenges. Unlike the cities that confront these naturalistic protagonists, Edna's new environment invites her to expand and open herself—to drop her defenses rather than muster them.

Beguiled rather than threatened by her environment, Edna rarely experiences the "instinctive" fear and aggression of naturalistic protagonists. (The flashes of terror she feels during her first and last swims out to sea appear and disappear quickly.) However, Chopin does frankly depict the "instinct" that caused some readers to regard her book, like those of her naturalist contemporaries, as shocking. In *Kate Chopin: A Critical Biography*, Per Seyersted compares Chopin's treatment of sex to that of the "American pioneer writers of the 1890's, the group which comprises such authors as Crane, Garland, Norris, and Dreiser."[20] He compares *The Awakening* to *Maggie: A Girl of the Streets, Rose of Dutcher's Coolly, McTeague,* and *Sister Carrie.*

According to Seyersted, "not only does Mrs. Chopin treat sex at least as amorally as any of the other four writers, but she also describes it more openly than they do. Their heroines . . . are all rather sexless compared to Edna."[21] They seem relatively sexless because they experience sex as a force outside themselves rather than as a part of themselves. In their sexual initiations, Maggie and Carrie appear as the objects of male desire, driven by the need for physical and emotional security rather than by their own wants. As noted above, Carrie responds to "the fine invisible passion which was emanating *from Drouet,* the food, the still unusual luxury" (my emphasis).[22] Crane uses Maggie's repeated pleas for reassurance of Pete's love to signify that she has had sex with him, revealing both her need for security and her misgivings about sex.[23] Trina and Rose experience desire, but find it alien and troubling. After turning down a proposal of marriage from a man who attracts her, Rose "felt as if sex were an abomination, and she wished for freedom from love."[24] After McTeague's first kiss, Trina feels that "something had leaped to life in her—something that had hitherto lain dormant, something strong and over-powering. It frightened her now as she thought of it, this second self that had wakened within her. . . ."[25] That "strong and overwhelming" impulse, which mirrors the overwhelming masculine strength that evokes it, lies beyond Trina's control and, when her life begins to deteriorate, comes to control her.

Edna, in contrast, first feels desire, then acts upon that feeling. At the beginning of her first sexual encounter with Alcée Arobin, "They continued silently to look into each other's eyes. When he leaned forward and kissed her, she clasped his head, holding his lips to hers" (967). Stimulated by "the first kiss of her life to which her nature had really responded" (967), Edna, aroused but not overwhelmed, acts to prolong the experience. Later, she initiates sexual contact with Robert. As Seyersted explains, "We witness how Alcée arouses Edna and how she in turn sets Robert on fire with a voluptuous kiss."[26] Thus, although the frank treatment of sex in *The Awakening* resembles, and even exceeds, that of its naturalistic contemporaries, sexual desire is intrinsic to the protagonist rather than being an outside force brought to bear upon her.

Biology shapes destiny for Edna just as for her naturalistic counterparts; however, she experiences its force differently. As Seyersted points out, "Edna has children and the other heroines do not."[27] Moreover, Edna consciously resents the most directly biologic aspect of motherhood—childbirth. Assisting at the birth of Adèle's fourth child, "With an inward agony, with a flaming, outspoken revolt against the ways of Nature, she witnessed the scene of torture" (995). Adèle apparently accepts "the ways of Nature" by undergoing childbirth without anesthetic, but Edna has taken chloroform during her own deliveries and thereby avoided the full consequences of "Nature." Evidently she does not wish fully to experience herself as a biologic instrument, a mechanism for adding to "the great unnumbered multitude of souls that come and go" (994). With Edna's revolt, Chopin goes beyond the limitations of the naturalist's world view, which imagines individuals, especially women, as controlled by nature.

Although she refuses to see herself as merely the instrument for their production, Edna dies for her children as she had declared herself willing to do. When she lies despondent on the night before her suicide, Edna thinks " 'Today it is Arobin; to-morrow it will be some one else. It makes no difference to me, it doesn't matter about Léonce Pontellier—but Raoul and Etienne!' " (999). The first two "its" refer to relationships, both present and potential, that bring sexual gratification, diversion, and a temporary sense of purpose in life, but the rest of the thought focuses on the consequences of those relationships. A middle-class woman simply acting upon her impulses, sexual and otherwise, would eventually cease to be respectable. Such a loss of respectability might not "matter" for Edna or for her husband, but it would harm her children's futures. Thus she contrives a suicide that will appear to be an accidental drowning, leaving her children motherless but respectable. Moreover, when she dies for her children, she does so out of conscious consideration for their futures. In a strictly naturalistic work, a mother's life might gradually, inexorably, be consumed by her children.

The issue of Edna's respectability evokes another naturalistic device that Klinkowitz believes to be present in *The Awakening*—"a descent on the social scale to find more vital life."[28] He asserts that Edna's "social world . . . has begun to collapse. Her close friend Mme. Ratignolle confesses that she can no longer be seen visiting Edna, apologizing, 'Of course, it wouldn't matter if Mr. Arobin had not such a dreadful reputation.' "[29] Though Adèle does warn Edna about Arobin, the "it" refers to his visits to Edna, which Adèle has mentioned in the previous sentence, not to Adèle's own visits. That subject arises a few moments later when Adèle in departing, declares, " 'I shan't be able to come back and see you; it was very, very, imprudent today" (980). She considers the visit "imprudent" not because of Edna's reputation but because of her own advanced pregnancy. She has "dragged herself over [to Edna's], avoiding the too public thoroughfares" (979). She seems concerned both with her health and with the convention that pregnant women should not appear in public. She fails to attend Edna's dinner party because she is "to the last degree *souffrante* and unpresentable," though her husband attends, which he surely would not have done had Edna been disgraced (969–70).

In moving into the small house around the corner, Edna does experience "a feeling of having descended in the social scale, with a corresponding sense of having risen in the spiritual" (977). But her "feeling" results more from a descent on the economic scale, which has moral significance because she is no longer living on her husband's money. As we have seen, when she seriously contemplates a descent on the *social* scale, she decides to kill herself rather than subject her children to the consequences of her descent. Thus her death comes not as the last step in a descent, as do the deaths of Maggie and Trina, but rather as a "revolt" against the forces, both social and biologic, that make for such a descent. Just as Edna sees her suicide as a way of eluding that which would enslave her soul, Chopin creates her suicide as an escape from the grinding, soul-denying denouement of the strictly naturalistic novel.

The night before her suicide, Edna encounters her family physician, Dr. Mandelet, who says, " 'you seem to be in trouble . . . perhaps I might help you. I know I would understand. . . .' " Edna rejects his offer, declaring " 'some way I don't feel moved to speak of the things that trouble me,' " and insisting that " 'I don't want anything but my own way' " (996). Although Edna cannot articulate or comprehend her reluctance to submit her inner self to Dr. Mandelet's scrutiny, she may resent the implication that she is "in trouble," which implies some sort of disorder or failure to conform. She acknowledges instead that "things" trouble *her,* putting herself at the center, implicitly wishing to alter or eliminate those "things" rather than adjusting herself to get "out" of trouble. As Anne Goodwyn Jones puts it, "Dr. Mandelet is part and parcel of the values Edna rejects."[30]

As the "understanding man of science" whose presence Klinkowitz enumerates as a naturalistic device, Mandelet sees Edna in terms of the science of his day, evoking the "laws" that so often operate in naturalistic fiction. When her husband complains to him of Edna's behavior, he inquires, " 'Nothing hereditary? . . . Nothing peculiar about her family antecedents, is there?' " (948). Assured that Edna comes of good stock, he declares: " 'Woman, my dear friend, is a very peculiar and delicate organism— a sensitive and highly organized woman, such as I know Mrs. Pontellier to be, is especially peculiar' " (949). The word "peculiar" reveals both his reliance on categories such as "normal" and "abnormal" and his assumption that women are outside the norm. "Organism" shows his tendency to seek biologic explanations for human behavior. Later, when he observes Edna, "she remind[s] him of some beautiful, sleek animal waking up in the sun," and he speculates that she might be having an affair (952–53). Looking at Edna as a biologic creature allows him to acknowledge her sexuality, just as the naturalistic novelists acknowledged sex as a powerful human motive. On the other hand, it reduces her to a bundle of drives and defines her as "peculiar"—outside the norm. When Chopin has Edna reject his advice and imagine later that "perhaps" he would have understood, she expresses her own mixed reaction to the naturalistic fiction of her day. On the one hand, naturalism acknowledged that women were sexual beings; on the other, it reduced them to the victims of their own and (especially) others' drives.

Thus, while naturalistic fiction expressed a lasting "truth" based on scientific law, Chopin's evocations of naturalism in the novel reveal that she found that truth reductive and its materialist assumptions limiting. For Chopin and for Edna, the transcendentalism of Emerson offered another universal truth—one that could be liberating rather than limiting. The transcendentalists exhorted their readers to live according to their inner selves rather than according to social conventions. "Nothing is at last sacred but the integrity of your own mind," Emerson writes in "Self-Reliance." ". . . the only right is what is after my constitution; the only wrong is what is against it."[31] Insofar as Edna rebels against the strictures of social convention and wants only her "own way," she seems to follow Emerson's dictates. According to Donald A. Ringe, "the author makes abundantly clear that a process is occurring that closely resembles the transcendentalist theory of self-discovery."[32] Chopin tells us that "she was becoming herself and daily casting aside that fictitious self which we assume like a garment with which to appear before the world" (939).

However, in one moment of apparent self-discovery, Edna implicitly rejects transcendentalism: Left alone in her elegant house, she spends the afternoon exploring it, seeing it with fresh eyes and mentally possessing it as her own domain. "Then Edna sat in the library after dinner and read Emerson until she grew sleepy" (956). Virginia M. Koudis summarizes various interpretations of Edna's reaction to Emerson and argues that Chopin comments on Emerson's limitations as well as Edna's.[33] On the one hand, Edna's somnolence reveals her "narrow vision," which cannot encompass Emerson's breadth. On the other, Emerson represents the limitations upon women's freedom through the attitudes his writing reveals: "From his use of the masculine pronoun to his substantive distinction between male and female vision, Emerson shapes and reflects the sexual chauvinism against which women have had to defend and define themselves."[34] Because Chopin never specifies which of Emerson's essays Edna reads, we can't be sure how much of this chauvinism she experiences, but it seems reasonable to assume that, whether or not she is aware of it, Edna feels alienated by it and escapes into sleep.

Personal and anecdotal evidence indicates that Edna is not unique in her response to Emerson. Perhaps she is not only alienated by his attitudes toward women but also lulled by his leisurely, contemplative style. The evanescence of that style reflects the mystery at the heart of its subject. Self, nature, and some sort of universal spirit or supreme being dissolve into one another:

> We learn that the highest is present to the soul of man; that the dread universal essence . . . is that for which all things exist, and that by which they are; that spirit creates; that behind nature, throughout nature, spirit is present; one and not compound it does not act upon us from without, that is, in space and time, but spiritually, or through ourselves.[35]

The reader who demands precise definitions and boundaries might be frustrated by discourse like that of this passage from "Nature," but Edna relaxes into sleep rather than tensing with irritation. She reacts like a trusting infant, perhaps reassured that "spirit is present" like a tender parent. Noting how often Edna sleeps and eats in the course of the novel, Cynthia Griffin Woolf argues that she is fixated at the oral stage of her development—the point at which the infant does not completely differentiate between self and other.[36] Given that assumption, the oneness Emerson celebrates may have a particular appeal for Edna.

For many readers of *The Awakening,* Edna's sense of boundlessness, her failure to differentiate fully herself as an individual, remains a flaw in her character and even a flaw in Chopin's conception of her. Through Edna's tendency to remain undifferentiated, Chopin, like other classic American writers, illustrates the evanescence of transcendentalism, its tendency to distance its adherents from everyday life. In her contemplation of the boundless sea, Edna resembles Melville's transcendentally minded sailor, who imperils himself by meditating from the mast head, who "takes the mystic ocean at his feet for the visible image of that deep, blue, bottomless soul, pervading mankind and nature" and thus risks "drop[ping] through that transparent air into the sum-mer sea, no more to rise for ever."[37] The problem is not so much that Edna's vision is too narrow, as Koudis argues, but that transcendentalism is too broad.

Edna's relationship with Robert Lebrun embodies her confrontation with the transcendental vision. In introducing and describing Robert, Chopin notes that "His eyes gathered in and reflected the light and langour of the summer day" (883). This description recalls the famous passage in Emerson's "Nature": "I become a transparent eyeball; I am nothing; I see all; the currents of the Universal Being circulate through me . . ."[38] The light which Robert both takes in and emanates "circulates" through him, uniting him with the scene at which he gazes. In gazing at him in turn, Edna sees both an example of transcendental interaction between nature and the beholder and a "nature" with which to unite herself. She evidently responds to those possibilities, for her sense of herself expands as a result of her friendship with Robert and of her own perceptual interaction with the "light and langour" of the seacoast at Grande Isle. "In short, Mrs. Pontellier was beginning to realize her position in the universe as a human being, and to recognize her relations as an individual to the world within and about her" (893).

Her discovery of a single world both within and about her begins the transcendental process, but Chopin warns that "the beginning of things, of a world especially, is necessarily vague, tangled, chaotic, and exceedingly disturbing" (893). In the case of Edna's interaction with Robert, the vagueness and confusion lies in her inability to distinguish between Robert himself and the inchoate longing she has focused upon him.

> It was not that she dwelt upon details of their acquaintance, or recalled . . . his personality; it was his being, his existence, which dominated her thought, fading sometimes as if it would melt into the mist of the forgotten, reviving again with an intensity which filled her with an incomprehensible longing. (936)

If, for the transcendentalist, spirit lies "behind and throughout" nature, then nature itself becomes evanescent, a projection of an immaterial spirit, "melting" before the gaze and leaving it to gaze upon nothing. As the story unfolds, Robert withdraws from Edna rather than remain long enough to melt out of her existence. His departure, ostensibly to protect her from disgrace, recalls the patronizing attitudes toward women that characterize Emerson, according to Koudis.[39] Robert, like the doctrines of transcendentalism, ultimately either hardens into a "representative of the system" or melts into an ungraspable vagueness.

In addition to Emerson, Chopin refers to another transcendental writer—Walt Whitman. As Louis Leary has demonstrated, her imagery, especially the key image of the sea, clearly evokes Whitman's.[40] However, she does not use that imagery to demonstrate the limitations of his theory and practice, probably because he is a poet rather than a writer of fiction like herself. Primarily, the Whitmanian imagery of sea, landscape, and birds helps to convey the sensuality and expansiveness of Edna's experience. Compared to Whitman's poems themselves, these images underscore Edna's inability to place herself at the center of her own experience. Whitman's poems often end with a resolution in which the experiences of the poem come to center in the poet. For example, in "Out of the Cradle Endlessly Rocking," which Leary aptly compares to The Awakening, Whitman ends the poem by declaring that the events described therein "awakened" his "own songs," and "with them the key, the word up from the waves"—death.[41] Thus the sea, and the death it evokes, becomes part of Whitman and his songs. Edna's sea, in contrast, invites her to become part of it: "The voice of the sea is seductive, never ceasing, whispering, clamoring, murmuring, inviting the soul to wander in abysses of solitude" (999). Ultimately, she heeds that invitation and loses herself in death.

Edna's suicide has been seen as both a failure and a triumph because Edna fails to create a satisfying new life for herself even as she succeeds in escaping the restrictions of her old life.[42] Just as Edna escapes the confines of both her society and her biology, Chopin rejects the limitations of realism and naturalism. Through Edna's dissolution into the waves, she demonstrates the disturbing evanescence of transcendentalism. Hence Edna's suicide can also be viewed as the conclusion of Chopin's examination of the major literary movements of her century. Like Edna, Chopin escaped the limitations of her era, yet she could not create a new form to contain the scope of her vision, which may help explain why she wrote relatively little after The Awakening. Seen in this way, the suicide appears once more as both failure and triumph— the failure of 19th-century literary forms to do justice to women's experience and the triumph of a work that at once evokes and exceeds those forms, swimming with its heroine toward the 20th century.

Notes

1. Edmund Wilson, Patriotic Gore: Studies in the Literature of the American Civil War (New York: Oxford University Press, 1962), 591. Wilson considers the novel "odd" primarily because of its frank treatment of sex.

2. Many of these discussions are cited in this essay. See also Joyce Coyne Dyer, "Lafcadio Hearn's Chita and Kate Chopin's The Awakening: Two Naturalistic Tales of the Gulf Islands," Southern Studies 23(Winter 1984):412–26, and Emily Toth, "Timely and Timeless: The Treatment of Time in The Awakening and Sister Carrie," Southern Studies 16(Fall 1977):271–76.

3. Peggy Skaggs, "The Awakening's Relationship with American Regionalism, Romanticism, Realism, and Naturalism," in Approaches to Teaching Chopin's "The Awakening," ed. Bernard Koloski (New York: Modern Language Association of America, 1988), 84.

4. Emily Toth, Kate Chopin, paperback ed. (Austin: University of Texas Press, 1993), 225.

5. The excerpts Toth quotes repeatedly emphasize these qualities. See especially pages 225–29 and 298–305. The phrases quoted above appear on pages 226 and 227.

6. Toth, 226, 227 (Toth's notation).

7. Toth, 228–29.

8. Kate Chopin, "*Crumbling Idols* by Hamlin Garland," in *The Complete Works of Kate Chopin,* ed. Per Seyersted, hardcover ed. (Baton Rouge: Louisiana State University Press, 1993), 693.

9. Chopin, "*Crumbling Idols,*" 693.

10. Eric J. Sundquist, ed., *American Realism: New Essays* (Baltimore: Johns Hopkins University Press, 1982), 4.

11. Kate Chopin, *The Awakening,* in Seyersted, *The Complete Works of Kate Chopin,* 937. Hereafter this edition of *The Awakening* is cited in the text.

12. Jerome Klinkowitz, *The Practice of Fiction in America: Writers from Hawthorne to the Present* (Ames: Iowa State University Press, 1980), 39.

13. Frank Norris, *McTeague: A Story of San Francisco.* Edited by Donald Pizer. (New York: W. W. Norton, 1977), 77.

14. Pages 889 and 890 describe Robert's habit of "constitut[ing] himself the devoted attendant of some fair dame or damsel"; page 897 describes Adèle's stroking Edna's hand, which at first confuses, then pleases Edna.

15. Hamlin Garland, *Rose of Dutcher's Coolly* (Chicago: Stone and Kimball, 1895), 182.

16. Theodore Dreiser, *Sister Carrie,* unexpurgated ed. (New York: Viking Penguin, 1981), 17.

17. Dreiser, 23.

18. Dreiser, 73, 78.

19. Garland, 197.

20. Per Seyersted, *Kate Chopin: A Critical Biography* (Baton Rouge: Louisiana State University Press, 1969), 190.

21. Seyersted, *Kate Chopin,* 191.

22. Dreiser, 78.

23. Stephen Crane, *Maggie: A Girl of the Streets,* in *Great Short Works of Stephen Crane,* (New York: Harper and Row, 1965), 158.

24. Garland, 153.

25. Norris, 50.

26. Seyersted, *Kate Chopin,* 191–92.

27. Seyersted, *Kate Chopin,* 192.

28. Klinkowitz, 39.

29. Klinkowitz, 46.

30. Anne Goodwyn Jones, *Tomorrow Is Another Day: The Woman Writer in the South, 1859–1936* (Baton Rouge: Louisiana State University Press, 1981), 163.

31. Ralph Waldo Emerson, "Self-Reliance," in *The Portable Emerson,* ed. Carl Bode and Malcolm Cowley (New York: Viking Penguin, 1946), 141–42. Subsequent citations of Emerson's essays refer to this collection.

32. Donald A. Ringe, "Romantic Imagery in Kate Chopin's *The Awakening,*" *American Literature* 43(January 1972):582.

33. Virginia M. Koudis, "Prison into Prism: Emerson's 'Many-Colored Lenses' and the Woman Writer of Early Modernism," in *The Green American Tradition: Essays and Poems for Sherman Paul,* ed. H. Daniel Peck (Baton Rouge, Louisiana State University Press, 1989), 118. On 116 she summarizes various readings of Edna's sleepiness.

34. Koudis, 118.

35. Emerson, "Nature," 42.

36. Cynthia Griffin Woolf, "Thanatos and Eros," in *The Awakening,* ed. Margo Culley, 2d ed. (New York: W. W. Norton, 1994), 234.

37. Herman Melville, *Moby Dick,* ed. Harrison Hayford and Hershel Parker (New York: W. W. Norton, 1967), 140.

38. Emerson, "Nature," 11.

39. Koudis, 121.

40. Lewis Leary, "Kate Chopin and Walt Whitman," in Culley, *The Awakening,* 217–20.

41. Walt Whitman, "Out of the Cradle Endlessly Rocking" in *Leaves of Grass,* ed. Sculley Bradley and Harold W. Blodgett (New York: W. W. Norton, 1973), 253.

42. Suzanne Wolkenfeld provides a succinct synthesis of critical commentary on Edna's suicide in her essay "Edna's Suicide: The Problem of the One and the Many," in Culley, *The Awakening,* 241–47.

Notes on Contributors of Original Materials

◆

Margaret D. Bauer received her Ph.D. from the University of Tennessee in 1993, with a dissertation on Ellen Gilchrist. Prof. Bauer has written for *Studies in Short Fiction, South Central Review,* and the *Southern Literary Journal.* She has been a visiting professor at Texas A&M University and Wabash College.

Lawrence I. Berkove is Professor of English at the University of Michigan, Dearborn. A noted authority on 19th-century American fiction, Prof. Berkove has written for the *Mark Twain Journal, American Literary Realism,* the *CEA Critic,* and the *Southern Quarterly.* He has edited Joseph Goodman and Rollin Daggett's *The Psychoscope* (1994), *The Fighting Horse of the Stanislaus: Stories and Essays by Dan De Quille* (1990), and Ambrose Bierce's *Skepticism and Dissent: Selected Journalism, 1898–1901* (1986).

Priscilla Leder is Associate Professor of English at Southwest Texas State University in San Marcos, Texas. She has published essays on Kate Chopin, Sarah Orne Jewett, Flannery O'Connor, and Alice Walker and has also taught in California, Oklahoma, and Louisiana.

Alice Hall Petry is Professor and Chair of the Department of English at Southern Illinois University, Edwardsville. A Brown University Ph.D., Prof. Petry has been a Fulbright Scholar in Brazil, a USIA lecturer in Japan, a Senior Postdoctoral Fellow of the American Council of Learned Societies, and a visiting professor at the University of Colorado, Boulder. Her books include *Understanding Anne Tyler* (1990), *A Genius in His Way: The Art of Cable's "Old Creole Days"* (1988), *Fitzgerald's Craft of Short Fiction: The Collected Stories, 1920–1935* (1989), and *Critical Essays on Anne Tyler* (1992).

Kathryn Lee Seidel is Professor of English and Associate Dean of Arts and Sciences at the University of Central Florida, Orlando. She is the author of *The Southern Belle in the American Novel* (1985) and coeditor of *Zora in Florida* (1991). Prof. Seidel's essays on Kate Chopin, Ellen Glasgow, and Toni Morrison appear in such journals as the *Mississippi Quarterly, Tulsa Studies in Literature by Women,* and the *Southern Quarterly.*

Heather Kirk Thomas teaches 19th-century American literature, as well as the writings of women and minorities, at Loyola College in Baltimore. Her essays on Kate Chopin, Herman Melville, and Emily Dickinson appear in *American Literature, American Literary Realism,* and *Studies in American Fiction.* She is coeditor of *Journal Volume 6: 1853* for the Writings of Henry D. Thoreau Edition, forthcoming from Princeton University Press.

Linda Wagner-Martin is Hanes Professor of English and Comparative Literature at the University of North Carolina, Chapel Hill. Her most recent book is *Telling Women's Lives, The New Biography,* and a revisionist biography of Gertrude Stein is forthcoming (both from Rutgers University Press). Prof. Wagner-Martin is coeditor of *The Oxford Companion to Women's Writing in the United States* and its companion anthology, *The Oxford Book of Women's Writing.*

Nancy A. Walker is Professor of English and Director of the Women's Studies Program at Vanderbilt University. She is the author of *A Very Serious Thing: Women's Humor and American Culture* (1988), *Feminist Alternatives: Irony and Fantasy in the Contemporary Novel by Women* (1990), *Fanny Fern* (1992), and *The Disobedient Reader: The Woman Writer and Traditions of Narrative* (forthcoming). She edited the Case Studies in Contemporary Literature edition of Kate Chopin's *The Awakening* for Bedford Books in 1993. Prof. Walker currently serves on the Executive Council of the Modern Language Association.

Index

♦